NATURE'S BEST
REMEDIES

NATURE'S BEST
REMEDIES

Top Medicinal Herbs, Spices, and Foods for Health and Well-Being

NANCY J. HAJESKI

WASHINGTON, D.C.

CONTENTS

FOREWORD
WHY NATURE'S REMEDIES MATTER

There has been tremendous growth in all things "natural" over the past 20 years. No longer relegated to health food stores, organic foods, natural skin care products, nutritional supplements, and herbal remedies have all gone mainstream. Yoga, meditation, and tai chi classes are now widespread and fashionable. More and more people are coming to realize that eating a healthy diet, using natural remedies, and weaving meditation and mind-body medicine into our lives can make us more resilient, and that these lifestyle changes can make us more resistant to disease, allow us to recover more quickly when we do get sick, and help protect our health during periods of prolonged stress or strain.

The Centers for Disease Control and Prevention reports that roughly 1 in 3 adults in the United States now uses a complementary health approach,

Leaves, roots, flowers, and fruit can have healing powers.

supporting my own observation that people today are very interested in natural treatments, a passion that I have shared for the past 40 years. As a physician board certified in integrative medicine, I have partnered with many patients as they sought to improve their health. I have witnessed the dramatic transformation that can happen when people clean up their diet, learn to manage their stress, become more physically active, and nourish their inner spiritual life.

I have also spent much of my career teaching health care professionals how to think more broadly about health. I served as the fellowship director for many years at the University of Arizona's Center for Integrative Medicine, founded by Andrew Weil, M.D. I heard many physicians express frustration at their lack of training in nutrition, dietary supplements, mind-body medicine, and other natural remedies. They wanted more tools to help their patients optimize their health without always having to rely solely on pharmaceutical drugs. The specialty of integrative medicine, which has gained prominence over these past few decades, certainly includes the use of prescription medicines and surgery, but it also embraces other traditional, evidence-based approaches to healing.

Let's take chronic pain. The opioid epidemic is a real and dangerous problem in the United States, and the numbers clearly show why. Pain affects roughly 100 million Americans. That's more than all those with diabetes, heart disease, and cancer combined. So if acupuncture has been shown effective for treating neck and back pain, why not recommend it? If taking turmeric, an herb commonly used in curry, can help with knee arthritis, it seems logical to give it a try. Magnesium has been shown in multiple studies to reduce the number and severity of migraine headaches, a condition that affects almost 37 million

Tieraona Low Dog harvests chamomile in her garden at Medicine Lodge Ranch.

Americans. It's inexpensive and over the counter and both the American Headache Society and the American Academy of Neurology state that it is probably effective and should be considered for those requiring migraine preventive therapy.

There is overwhelming evidence that for many minor problems and stress-related conditions, lifestyle approaches are an effective and safe first choice. These include dietary guidance, strategies for coping with stress and improving sleep, and the judicious use of dietary supplements and herbal remedies for promoting health. I have discussed these subjects at length in the books I have written with National Geographic: *Life Is Your Best Medicine, Healthy at Home, and Fortify Your Life.*

And now I am delighted to recommend *Nature's Best Remedies* by Nancy Hajeski. This rich resource is a wonderful addition to anyone's self-care library. It is filled with practical guidance for managing many common problems, with clear instructions for therapies that can be incorporated easily at home. Whether you are looking for natural approaches for

insomnia, canker sores, headaches, or heartburn, you will find them here, among the beautiful and informative pages of this book. There are chapters for different life stages, such as pregnancy and childbirth; tips for healthy aging; an extensive section on commonly used herbs and spices; and a very nice chapter on using essential oils.

I love the chapter called Nature's Power Pantry, which provides great information on some of the most nutritious foods, with strategies for buying and integrating them into your weekly meal plan. An additional bonus is the last chapter, which focuses on natural pest control and safe household cleaners— such an important topic, and one that is not usually covered in a book on natural remedies.

Are you ready to take charge of your own well-being? Congratulations! In *Nature's Best Remedies,* you will find a great partner to take along the way.

—Tieraona Low Dog, M.D.
Pecos, New Mexico

Introduction
BE AT YOUR BEST
DISCOVER THE BENEFITS OF NATURAL ALTERNATIVES FOR YOUR HEALTH, DIET, AND HOME

We all know there are certain areas of our lives that could use improving—personal hurdles that have to be overcome, career decisions that should be addressed, or family conflicts that need to be resolved. It will come as a relief to know that one area of your life—your health—can be improved and brought into better balance through your initiative alone. It only requires a strong dose of resolve and the means to gain the knowledge that will enable you to make the proper choices.

It's never wise to throw yourself into a major revamp without forethought—just think how chaotic a simple closet clean-out quickly becomes—but sometimes just establishing a few goals can start you on the right road. Suppose you want to boost your general wellness and also address a few health issues. Begin by assessing the ways you've let your health care lag and your nutritional intake slide. Next, familiarize yourself with some of the natural options you can choose to correct these lapses.

It's reassuring when you begin to understand that there are natural remedies to help you treat almost any disease, ailment, or condition known to science. And many of these remedies involve nothing more radical than adjusting the foods you eat. No matter what your health concerns—indigestion, allergies, asthma, arthritis pain, headaches, PMS, infertility, erectile dysfunction, urinary tract infections,

endocrine issues, fatigue, insomnia, anxiety, and depression—they can become more manageable and even disappear once you focus on foods with the specific nutrients, micronutrients, antioxidants, and probiotics that will help you treat illness. And by maintaining wellness and supporting your immune system, you can combat, or even prevent, the onset of serious diseases like type 2 diabetes, cancer, and heart disease.

A World of Options

It's also good know that a healthy diet needn't mean starving yourself or choking down Scandinavian flatbreads or some ancient bean from the rain forest (chocolate doesn't count). Healthy fruits and vegetables and lean meats and seafood, even the more exotic varieties, are now available almost everywhere—you simply need to find the ones that appeal to you and use them to replace the processed, packaged high-fat, high-sugar, low-nutrient foods you have probably been consuming.

(RIGHT) Some of nature's best remedies are healthy, nutrient-packed fruits, like berries.

(OPPOSITE) You can grow many of the ingredients for nature's remedies, including healthy fruits, vegetables, and herbs.

Consider shrimp and other seafood, properly sourced, as healthful alternatives to meat.

Even if you are a picky eater, there are options. Perhaps you avoid most fruits, but might enjoy a fresh banana smoothie made with almond milk. Or you can't yet give up meat, but are perfectly happy eating shrimp and tuna. Or you don't like broccoli, but crave corn on the cob. For every dislike, there is a similar food that you might very well grow to love, or at least like. And in case there are some foods you just can't touch (read: liver), vitamin and mineral supplements, while not as potent as natural micronutrients, can fill in the nutritional gaps.

Plus there are health-building herbs, spices, and condiments that add few calories to dishes but contribute a world of flavors. Some of these can even be grown at home or in your garden. There are also essential oils of plants and herbs that, through the practice of aromatherapy, may act as curatives, anti-inflammatories, stimulants, and relaxants, and which can be used for the practical, if less glamorous, purposes of repelling insects and purifying the air.

New Attitudes, New You

Once you have determined to make certain changes, you will be amazed at how quickly these new attitudes and behaviors become a part of your life. Meals that were once a chore to prepare now become a pleasant task, especially once you realize you are feeling more fit, more alert, more energetic, and more involved in the world around you.

If you are pregnant or planning on becoming pregnant, there are many holistic options—natural childbirth, midwife and doula care, birthing classes, delivery at home or in a family-care center, and breastfeeding—all safe, healthy ways to experience the birthing journey as intimately and as naturally as possible and without having to face a potentially alienating, clinical hospital setting.

Aging, too, is something that can be affirming, even rewarding, if you approach it from a natural perspective—one in which physical, mental, and emotional health are given equal importance. And if you are baby boomer who has not been overly scrupulous about making wise health choices as you've grown older, relax. It's never too late to seek the path of wellness. You will still reap the benefits of eating properly, maintaining cognitive skills, staying involved in your life and the lives of those around you, and keeping fit and active.

Your home also benefits from natural choices. You can eliminate potentially harmful products that contain hazardous toxins and chemicals and replace them with safe, natural substances that have been used as effective cleaners and antimicrobials for centuries.

Ultimately, this book showcases the nutrient-packed power foods you should be eating and the herbs, plants, and essential oils that can help you treat diseases and ailments, as well as maintain a youthful appearance and detoxify your home. It will show you how to take a natural outlook toward the approach of new life . . . or teach you how to maintain good health and expand your social and mental parameters as you age. It is also full of practical tips and suggestions, easy-to-follow recipes, and do-it-yourself projects. By using it as a guide, you can take a hands-on approach to improving your health and well-being and that of your family.

How to Use This Book

This book is presented in two parts: Nature's Cures and Nature's Pharmacopoeia. Nature's Cures focuses on how to employ natural remedies to cure or control common physical ailments and also how to cope with emotional and mental stresses. It then delves into the special issues that come

with each stage of life, from pregnancy, childbirth, and infancy to aging—and how natural remedies can make sure you handle any stage of life with grace and good health. Nature's Pharmacopoeia turns to the elements of nature's remedies—the medicinal herbs and beneficial spices, as well as the healthful fruits, vegetables, grains, and other foods that you can stock in your medicine chest and pantry so that you can maximize your health. It also features sections on essential oils and on natural ways to keep your home clean without harmful chemicals. Throughout, you will find Up Close looks at key topics. And as you proceed, don't forget to review the Lifestyle Reboot Checklist on pages 302-303 to see how well you are progressing in your journey through the world of natural remedies.

KEY ITEMS

- DID YOU KNOW?: *interesting and informative factoids*
- MAKE IT YOURSELF: *featured recipes and projects*
- HEALTH BENEFITS / HEALTHY SOLUTIONS: *major nutritional or health properties*
- RESCUE REMEDY / PANTRY PICK: *short, easy-to-follow recipes and tips for natural wellness*
- SUPPLEMENTAL BOX: *covers tips, related topics, or unusual aspects of the featured topic*

Look no farther than your local supermarket shelves for some of the most versatile ingredients for concocting natural remedies. You can turn inexpensive items like white vinegar, baking soda, lemons, and limes into effective, nontoxic home cleaners, as well as safe internal remedies.

PART I
NATURE'S CURES

CHAPTER 1

REMEDIES FOR COMMON PHYSICAL AILMENTS

Introduction
TREAT ILLNESS NATURE'S WAY
LET THE "MAGIC" OF NATURAL REMEDIES RESTORE HEALTH AND VIGOR

Over time, human beings have discovered that there is at least one natural cure for almost every affliction that besets us, a remedy that incorporates the powerful healing compounds found in herbs and plants. In the not-so-distant past, these beneficial substances—like carotenoids or flavonoids—might have been viewed as magical healing spirits that dwelled within a flower or tree. Today, we know that there are a host of chemical constituents in plants that, magical or not, can destroy bacteria and fungus; fight infection; decrease inflammation; boost the immune system; support digestion, circulation, and respiration; regulate hormone and blood sugar levels; and lower cholesterol. These beneficial compounds can also ease the pain of swollen joints, aching muscles, chronic headaches, and bodily injuries.

The Secret of Nature's Cures

Herbs and plants hold the secrets to treating many common illnesses like colds, flu, and sore throats, and they can speed recovery from respiratory infections. They can help banish nuisance complaints like dandruff, gas, bad breath, bug bites, calluses, or dry skin or hair. But more important, they can also address serious health issues—heart disease, high cholesterol, obesity, cancer, and diabetes. In many cases, medicinal herbs can reduce the deleterious effects of these diseases or conditions, if not prevent them entirely.

Not surprisingly, one of the oldest uses for natural remedies has been solving reproductive problems, including male and female sexual complications, prostate issues for men, and menstrual irregularities or menopausal symptoms for women. Additionally, humans have been intent on finding herbs and plants that would spark intimacy and keep the libido healthy well into old age. Modern partners are still investigating many of these reproductive solutions and time-tested aphrodisiacs.

There are also plenty of natural remedies if you have cosmetic concerns—and who doesn't? If too much sun has left your skin dry or wrinkled or with age spots, there are steps to follow to undo some of the damage and precautions you can take to prevent any further exposure to those harmful UV rays. If your hair or nails are in need of some first aid, herbal treatments will restore the attractive appearance of your hands and add a gleaming shine to your hair.

If unfamiliarity makes you hesitant to try natural remedies for a health problem, speak to the proprietor of a health food store. He or she can guide you toward one product or several choices that address your specific needs. You will learn that some herbal solutions work alongside, or augment, conventional prescription medicines. You may find that you prefer to take a tablet or capsule supplement rather than mix up a powder. Or you might want to go straight to essential oils, where the "essence" of the plant's power resides. Best of all, once you have become a convert, you will find you can prepare a number of these herbal remedies at home.

(LEFT) Many plants can be used to make herbal remedies.

(OPPOSITE PAGE) An elderflower infusion. Both flowers and berries of elder have a long history as herbal treatments.

A tea made from ginger, honey, and lemon can soothe the symptoms of nasal and sinus congestion.

RESPIRATORY REMEDIES

FIGHT OFF SEASONAL OR ENVIRONMENTAL AILMENTS

Colds and other upper-respiratory issues have doubtless plagued *Homo sapiens* since we first walked upright. It's not surprising that the earliest cultures concocted herbal treatments for these persistent nose-and-throat ailments. The search for an actual cure, however, is still ongoing. In spite of all the modern medicines that address the symptoms of colds and other ailments of the upper-respiratory tract, such as sinusitis and laryngitis, many people still rely on time-tested traditional remedies.

The common cold is caused by a virus, or to be specific, more than 200 viruses. With so many strains to contend with, the creation of a vaccine is unlikely.

> ### DID YOU KNOW?
>
> • *In the early 1600s, the "doctrine of signatures" posited that plants that looked like certain organs could treat those body parts. Lungwort (Pulmonaria officinalis), with flowers that resemble lung tissue, became a popular herbal remedy for cough, colds, and bronchitis.*

The virus lodges in the mucous membranes of the throat, forcing the healthy cells to replicate more virus cells. The numerous cold symptoms we suffer are actually attempts by the body's immune system to rid itself of these microinvaders.

Healthy Solutions

Some traditional treatments, such as rubbing camphor ice on the sufferer's chest, have only a placebo effect: you believe it works, so you feel better. But other herbal remedies do have a genuine effect on the sniffling, sneezing, watering eyes, raspy throat, and fatigue of a bad cold. The following herbal treatments are effective against colds and will also work to ease some seasonal allergies.

ELDERBERRY A simple syrup of phytonutrient-rich elderberries can reduce inflammation and relieve congestion. Make sure to use black elderberry (*Sambucus nigra*) because other members of the elderberry family can be toxic.

RESCUE REMEDY: *Simmer ½ cup of dried elderberries with 3 cups of water for 30 minutes. Strain into a bowl and, when cooled, add 1 cup of honey. Mix well, and then store in a mason jar in the refrigerator; it will keep for three months. Taking 1 tablespoon daily can stave off illness; for colds, take 1 tablespoon every four hours.*

GARLIC A clove of crushed garlic in a glass of warm water hardly sounds inviting, but when combined with the juice of one lemon and a teaspoon of honey, this simple drink, taken three times a day, will put your cold on hold. Garlic (*Allium sativum*) is known for its immune-boosting properties, and for centuries it has been the popular go-to herb when a cold strikes.

GINGER A hot tea made from ginger (*Zingiber officinale*) is just the thing to ease a scratchy throat. It also lessens the swelling in the mucous membranes, allowing the mucous to flow out instead of creating pressure in nasal passages and sinus cavities. A compound called gingerol initiates this release of congestion. The spicy tang of the tea also loosens phlegm. Any hot tea is beneficial for a cold because it furnishes needed fluids and provides steamy vapors to ease breathing, but ginger tea is a notch above the others.

RESCUE REMEDY: *Pour 4 cups of boiling water over 6 to 8 tablespoons of grated ginger root in a glass jar. Add a pinch of cinnamon, a squirt of lemon juice, and 1 teaspoon of honey. Cover jar, steep for 40 minutes, and then strain and drink. Store remainder in the refrigerator for up to a day.*

HERBAL SYRUP This blended herbal syrup contains marshmallow root (*Althea officinalis*) and licorice root (*Glycyrrhiza glabra*). Both are rich in the mucilage that quiets a deep cough and eases a sore

---

FLUSHING WITH A NETI POT

Practitioners of yoga first incorporated the neti pot into their health routines, but the popularity of this small, kettle-shaped pot, designed to irrigate inflamed or infected sinus cavities, soon spread beyond the ashram. You simply add boiled water that has cooled to a comfortable temperature to a mix of minerals in the pot, and pour it into one nostril until the water begins to seep out the other nostril. It is not nearly as uncomfortable as it sounds, and it results in the release of painful sinus pressure.

---

throat by coating its delicate mucous membranes. Another plus is that most kids will swallow it. Take one or two tablespoons three times a day to quell a cough, ease congestion, or soothe a sore throat.

RESCUE REMEDY: *Combine 1 tablespoon each of licorice root, marshmallow root, ground cinnamon, and chopped ginger. Simmer the mixture in a pan with 4 cups of water and 1 cup of honey for 10 minutes. Cool the syrup, and then keep it in the refrigerator in a labeled glass jar; it will keep three to four weeks.*

MULLEIN A common wildflower that grows along roadsides and in open fields, mullein (*Verbascum thapsus*) features small yellow flowers and downy leaves that grow on a tall stalk. Dried mullein makes an outstanding expectorant, thinning out phlegm so it can be coughed up.

RESCUE REMEDY: *In a mug combine 1 or 2 tablespoons dried mullein leaves or flowers or 4 to 6 tablespoons of fresh flowers and/or leaves with 2 or 3 teaspoons of dried thyme (another fine expectorant) or 5 teaspoons fresh thyme. Pour 1½ cups of boiling water over the herbs. Stir, strain, and add honey or lemon to taste. Drink twice or thrice daily for congestion.*

Mullein flowers

THE CIRCULATORY SYSTEM

IMPROVE HEART HEALTH WITH REDUCED STRESS AND HERBAL SOLUTIONS

The heart and its network of blood vessels, known as the circulatory system or the cardiovascular system, circulates the approximately five liters of blood found in the average human. Driven by a hard-working muscular organ, this system is responsible for transporting oxygen, nutrients, hormones, and cellular waste products throughout the body. Deoxygenated blood travels from the right side of the heart to the lungs during pulmonary circulation, and highly oxygenated blood travels from the left side of the heart to the rest of the body during systemic circulation. The three main types of blood vessels are the thick, muscular, elastic arteries, which carry blood away from the heart;

> ### DID YOU KNOW?
>
> * Even though the heart is only the size of a closed fist, it is capable of sending five liters of blood coursing through our veins and arteries every minute, even while the body is at rest. When working at its maximum capacity, the heart can pump an astounding 20 to 25 liters per minute. Is it any wonder we cherish this small, remarkable engine?

the thin-walled veins, which are the large vessels that return blood to the heart; and the capillaries, the thinnest blood vessels, which are found in almost all body tissue.

This vital system is prone to many serious ailments, including heart disease, blood diseases, and circulatory issues, as well as hardening of the arteries, high cholesterol, high or low blood pressure, stroke, blood clots, or bleeding in the brain. Coronary heart disease is the number one killer of adults in the United States, and stroke is the fifth leading cause of death. On the plus side, for many centuries, practitioners of natural medicine have focused on strengthening the heart and reversing circulatory problems, often with surprisingly encouraging results.

Healthy Solutions

Since the dawn of recorded history, most people lived active lives—they farmed, performed manual labor, served in the military, or produced goods by hand—and they ate a diet that was high in fiber and low in fat and protein. That culture was almost the opposite of how we live today, with high-fat, low-fiber diets combined with largely sedentary lifestyles—lifestyles that take a toll on our cardiovascular health. Yet there are plenty of natural options you can choose to help reverse circulatory system damage or even stop it from occurring.

FIND STRESS BUSTERS Studies repeatedly show a link between chronic emotional stress and increased risk for life-threatening diseases related to the heart. Although the busiest among us claim that they simply can't get away from stress—on the job or at home—the answer is to take real control and

An extract or essential oil of motherwort, a perennial mint, is used to make a natural heart tonic. A staple of traditional herbal medicine, motherwort also goes by the names heartwort, throw-wort, lion's ear, and lion's tail.

prioritize your goals. Put the desire for a long, healthy life ahead of job advancement or having the ideal "picture-perfect" home and family. Be realistic. Be accepting of limitations. Then find a relaxing hobby and take up yoga or meditation.

Hawthorn berries and leaves

STAY IN MOTION Regular exercise—even walking for 20 minutes three times weekly—can strengthen your heart, help maintain your weight, and oxygenate your blood. Ideally, a regimented exercise routine should include stretching, strength training, long-distance cardio, high-intensity interval training, and integrative core movement. If you are uncertain of where to begin, join a gym and enlist the aid of a trainer. It won't be long before you are creating your own heart-healthy workout routines.

VENERABLE HERBAL HELPERS There are a number of time-tested herbal medicines that can help boost heart function.

- Since the time of the ancient Egyptians, garlic has proved to be an effective treatment for high and low blood pressure, elevated cholesterol, and coronary heart disease. Take two cloves a day or a daily garlic supplement.
- An extract of motherwort (*Leonurus cardiaca*), a perennial mint, has been used for millennia as a heart tonic, promoting circulation, lowering cholesterol, and regulating blood pressure.
- In both Eastern and Western cultures, hawthorn (genus *Crataegus*) has been used to treat chest pain, congestive heart failure, and irregular heartbeat, with results confirmed by modern studies. Doses range from 160 to 900 mg daily.

RESCUE REMEDY: *The active compounds in hawthorn are found in its leaves, flowers, and berries, but the tea is made from the berries. To prepare, mix 1 tablespoon of dried berries in 2 cups of boiling water. Let the berries steep for 10 to 15 minutes. Do not use this tea if you are on any medication to lower blood pressure. Hibiscus tea, called sour tea in the Middle East and red sorrel in English-speaking countries, is also an effective herbal treatment for high blood pressure.*

VALUABLE SUPPLEMENTS Certain vitamins and minerals that are necessary for you to maintain optimal heart health are available as supplements.

- Magnesium helps maintain a steady heartbeat and normal blood pressure. Check with your doctor for the proper dosage.
- Omega-3 fatty acid works to balance blood lipids, like cholesterol and triglycerides. Eat two servings of fish weekly, or take 1,000 mg daily.
- Vitamin D deficiency is associated with cardiovascular risk, so make sure you are getting at least 400 to 800 IU of D3 daily.
- In studies, CoEnzyme Q 10—CoQ10—was shown to increase the performance of the heart muscle and slightly reduce blood pressure. Take 100 to 200 mg daily.

IS ASPIRIN RIGHT FOR ME?

The popular painkiller aspirin has another significant health benefit—it reduces the clumping action of platelets and makes it difficult for your body to form blood clots, especially in men. If you have a family history of cardiovascular disease or have suffered a heart attack or stroke yourself, ask your doctor if you should begin aspirin therapy—taking an 81 mg baby aspirin daily. The low risk of internal bleeding is outweighed by the health benefits in most cases.

RELIEF FOR JOINT PAIN

EASE THE PAIN OF SPRAINS, STRAINS, TENDINITIS, AND BURSITIS

Joints are the articulations, or points, where two or more bones meet. Their support structures include tendons, ligaments, muscles, and cartilage, which form capsules, or strengthening bands, around the joints. Joints are found in, among other places, the shoulder, elbow, wrist, hip, knee, ankle, and the spinal vertebrae. Types of joints range from simple immovable joints, like those found in the plates of the skull, to complex ball-and-socket joints, like the hip. Because our major joints need to move to be effective—flex limbs toward the body or extend limbs away from the body—they are vulnerable to injuries from falls, roughhousing, auto accidents, and sports.

Sprains, the stretching or tearing of the ligaments surrounding a joint, are often the result of a sudden misstep or tumble. Strains involve stretching or twisting the tendons or muscles; they can be acute but are often caused by repetitive tasks, like working on an assembly line. Tendinitis is a painful inflammation or irritation of the tendons that connect muscles to bones; bursitis is the inflammation of the fluid-filled sacs that ease friction in certain joints. If a joint injury is severely painful or you suspect a fracture, see your doctor immediately.

> ### DID YOU KNOW?
>
> • *Frankincense, the biblical gift to the infant Jesus, is an aromatic resin that comes from* Boswellia, *a flowering plant native to Africa and Asia. Its gum resin or extract acts against inflammation by shrinking inflamed tissue and disabling the white blood cells that cause swelling.* Boswellia *supplements are found in health food stores.*

Healthy Solutions

Humans have been seeking treatment for body aches and joint pain since the first cave dweller tripped over a log and sprained an ankle. Happily, nature provides a bounty of solutions.

EPSOM SALTS These white grains are the mineral compound magnesium sulfate. Epsom salts are a traditional remedy for pain.

> RESCUE REMEDY: *To make a wrist or ankle soak, place ½ cup of Epsom salts in a large bowl of warm water, and immerse the limb until the mixture cools. Or place 2 cups of salts in a warm bath, and immerse your whole body for 15 minutes. For a soothing fragrance, add herbs, like lavender or thyme, or rose petals to the salts.*

MAGNESIUM Our bodies rely on this mineral for more than 300 biomechanical responses, yet we do not produce it. As a treatment for pain—especially arthritis discomfort—it relaxes muscles and nerve endings by relieving stiffness. Add magnesium to your diet with supplements or by eating legumes, nuts, and plenty of dark leafy greens.

MASSAGE Increasing circulation to an afflicted area can be accomplished by massaging it with hand-warmed oils. Extra virgin olive oil is not only soothing, it also contains a compound called oleocanthal that inhibits the inflammatory enzymes

Soaking sore joints in a warm Epsom salts bath has long been a remedy for tight muscles and achy, stiff joints.

COX-1 and COX-2—similar to the effect of aspirin. The active ingredient in horse chestnut (*Aesculus hippocastanum*) is called aescin and is said to reduce tenderness and swelling. Massage 2 percent aescin gel over the injured area every two to three hours.

> RESCUE REMEDY: *To make a rejuvenating massage oil, combine 5 to 10 drops of eucalyptus and peppermint oil (both contain analgesic properties) with 1 or 2 tablespoons of a carrier oil like olive, grapeseed, or almond. Place the mixture in a small dark glass bottle, and keep in your medicine cabinet to rub on achy spots or injured joints.*

White willow bark tea

ARNICA For centuries, the anti-inflammatory herb *Arnica montana* has been the go-to treatment for aches, pains, swelling, bruising, and injuries. An arnica gel, cream, or ointment applied topically to the affected area—providing there is no broken skin—will soon ease both pain and swelling.

CAPSAICIN The heat found in hot peppers (genus *Capsicum*) comes from a component called capsaicin. Capsaicin has the ability to inhibit a neurotransmitter called substance P, which sends pain signals to our brains. By blocking the signal, it reduces discomfort. A body rub that contains capsaicin is effective against the pain of injured tissue as well as for joints swollen and throbbing from arthritis flare-ups.

> **FOLLOW THE PRICE PROTOCOL**
>
> As soon as possible after you injure a joint, follow this formula to prevent additional damage to the area.
>
> P = Protect the joint immediately with a support or brace and limit movement.
>
> R = Rest the joint and avoid activities that might worsen the pain.
>
> I = Ice the joint for 15 to 20 minutes two or three times daily.
>
> C = Compress the joint with an elastic wrap to reduce swelling.
>
> E = Elevate the joint above heart level.

> RESCUE REMEDY: *Make your own hot rub using 3 tablespoons of cayenne powder, 1 cup of oil (olive, grapeseed, or almond), and a ½ cup grated beeswax. Mix the cayenne with the oil, and warm the mixture in a double boiler over medium heat for 5 minutes. Gradually stir in the beeswax until it has thoroughly melted. Chill the mixture for 10 minutes, whisk it, chill another 15 minutes, and then whisk it again. Place in a lidded glass jar, and store in the refrigerator for no more than 10 days.*

WHITE WILLOW BARK This species of willow (*Salix alba*) is an ancient anti-inflammatory pain reliever that dates back to the days of Hippocrates in the fifth century B.C. Around 1830, scientists discovered that white willow owes its effectiveness to an active ingredient called salicin, which the body converts to salicylic acid, a substance similar to the active ingredient in aspirin.

> RESCUE REMEDY: *To make a pain-combating tea, combine 2 teaspoons of powdered or chipped white willow bark with 1 cup of boiling water, and steep for 30 minutes, then strain. It will be somewhat bitter, so add honey and lemon to taste; drink twice daily.*

SUPPLEMENTS Bromelain, an enzyme found in pineapples, is believed to reduce the inflammation and swelling of joint injuries. It can increase the effect of antibiotics, however. The mineral zinc may also help wounded tissues heal more quickly.

LONG-TERM JOINT HEALTH

RELIEVE THE DISCOMFORT OF OSTEOARTHRITIS AND RHEUMATISM

As we age, our joints are prone to a number of diseases that can worsen over time. The most common is osteoarthritis, also called osteoarthrosis or degenerative joint disease (DJD), which afflicts roughly 27 million Americans over the age of 25. DJD is progressive, as daily wear and tear erodes the cartilage in our joints. Cartilage is the hard tissue that covers—and buffers—the ends of our bones, allowing them to meet and move freely. When this layer is worn down, the result is joint and bone pain. The most common targets of DJD are the spine, neck, hips, knees, and hands, notably the end of the fingers and the thumbs. Symptoms may include pain that comes and goes; stiffness; trouble moving or performing daily tasks like dressing; inflammation; and enlarged, achy fingers with bone spurs (osteophytes) on the knuckles. Depression, insomnia, and weight changes can also occur. In addition to aging, other causes might be excess weight, injuries, repetitive motion tasks, or certain genetic defects.

> **DID YOU KNOW?**
>
> • *SAM-e is a molecule that helps to create strong joints. It does this by delivering sulfur to your cartilage, thus providing pain relief similar to that of aspirin or ibuprofen. Because it is not found in any foods, you must take SAM-e as a supplement; look for products containing butanedisulfonate in your health food store.*

Rheumatoid arthritis (RA) is the second most common form of arthritis. Because it results from the immune system attacking the healthy tissues of the joints, it is classified as an autoimmune disease. Like DJD, it can lead to pain, swelling, and eventual joint malformation. It may also cause fatigue, lowered immunity, fever, and changes to skin, lungs, eyes, or blood vessels.

Healthy Solutions

Natural treatments, such as maintaining a healthy weight, focusing on an anti-inflammatory diet, and addressing the pain with physical therapy, massage therapy, and essential oils, may ease the symptoms and slow the degenerative progress of joint disease. Acupuncture and reflexology have also proven beneficial to some sufferers. Applying hot or cold packs—or alternating them—works for many people. An inclusive exercise program can be effective, helping you to keep loose, limber, and relatively pain-free. Getting enough vitamin D and calcium is also essential. Below are several more traditional options for easing joint and bone pain.

Turmeric root and powder. This orange-yellow ground spice is made by dry-grinding mature turmeric rhizomes.

TURMERIC A popular Asian culinary spice, turmeric *(Curcuma longa)* has also been used for eons as an analgesic. The active ingredient in turmeric is called curcumin. Curcumin is an antioxidant that is effective against both DJD and rheumatoid arthritis. Turmeric also lowers the levels of two enzymes that produce inflammation.

RESCUE REMEDY: *For a powerful pain-reducing tea, boil 2 cups of water, and add ½ teaspoon each of turmeric and ground ginger. Simmer for 10 to 15 minutes, and then strain. Drink as is, or add honey.*

DANDELION Many homeowners find dandelions *(Taraxacum officinale)* a nuisance, but these common springtime wildflowers are packed with amazing healing properties. The jagged leaves are high in vitamins A and C, and the essential fatty acids they contain can regulate immune responses and suppress inflammation, making them effective for treating rheumatoid arthritis.

> RESCUE REMEDY: *To make a zesty, healthful dandelion salad, combine a handful of fresh young dandelion leaves with an equal amount of baby spinach leaves, and top with a light dressing of extra virgin olive oil, lemon juice, and garlic. Older leaves can be sautéed with spinach or other greens as a side dish.*

PECTIN Extracted from fruit, pectin is added to homemade jams and jellies to help them set. It is also considered a home remedy for the treatment of arthritis, especially when combined with grape juice; it possibly works by making the synovial tissue in joints more elastic. Combine a tablespoon of liquid pectin with one glass of grape juice, and drink the mixture several times daily.

SUPPLEMENTS Glucosamine and chondroitin are believed to rebuild connective tissue and speed healing of wounds, making them effective options for treating osteoarthritis. Both can increase the risk of bleeding, however, so check with your doctor before taking them. Calcium is also necessary for healthy

Blackstrap molasses is a thick syrup made from sugar cane. A daily spoonful can help relieve joint pain.

bones—find it in dark leafy greens, dairy products, and almonds. Vitamin D improves our ability to absorb calcium; it occurs in fish, eggs, and sunlight.

BLACKSTRAP MOLASSES This dense dark molasses is a time-honored home remedy for arthritis. Rich in calcium, magnesium, and potassium, which regulate nerve and muscle function, this dietary supplement provides relief from joint pain. Take one tablespoon of blackstrap molasses in a cup of warm water once a day.

KEEP YOUR BONES STRONG AND HEALTHY

Osteoporosis is a disease that affects bone density, wherein the bones become brittle and fragile, making fractures a higher probability after a fall. The majority of sufferers are postmenopausal women with lowered estrogen levels, although smoking and heavy drinking are also factors. The disease can be diagnosed through a bone-density X-ray or a sonogram of the calcaneus (heel bone). Prescription medicines that slow bone loss are recommended, but they can be augmented with natural treatments like regular exercise and increased amounts of vitamin D, calcium, and magnesium.

Fibromyalgia is a disorder that causes widespread musculoskeletal pain accompanied by fatigue, sleep disorders, and memory and mood issues. It is believed that it increases the sensation of pain by altering the way the brain processes these signals. Other symptoms include tension headaches, TMJ, irritable bowel syndrome, and depression. Women are the main targets of the disorder, which has no cure, although exercise, yoga, and stress-reduction therapy are helpful.

Not all headaches are alike—the three categories are tension, cluster, and migraine headaches.

HEADACHE RELIEF

FIND HELP FOR THROBBING, PERSISTENT HEAD PAIN

The head is one of the most common sites for body pain. Even though the brain itself has no pain fibers, headache pain arises from the structures that surround the skull and the brain—the tissues, arteries, veins, and nerves—which can become inflamed or irritated. Headache pain is often difficult to describe; it might be a dull or sharp ache or a throbbing or squeezing, and the onset may be constant or intermittent, the levels mild or intense. Headaches are classified into primary and secondary groups. Secondary headaches are caused by structural problems in the head or neck, disease, or substance abuse, and also cranial neuralgia, facial pain, and other types of pain. The primary category includes tension, migraine, and cluster headaches.

> ### DID YOU KNOW?
>
> *Humans have been trying to alleviate headache pain for millennia. Early treatments included lashing a dead mole to the head, placing electric eels in the bath, and trepanning, the practice of drilling holes into the skull, which was practiced by early humans and revived with great gusto in the 17th century.*

The cause of a tension headache, the most frequently occurring kind, is not yet understood: one possibility is contractions of the muscles that cover the skull. Stressors that induce tension headaches may include prolonged manual labor, sitting at a computer and concentrating for long hours, and emotional stress. The main symptom is mild-to-moderate pain on both sides of the head.

Cluster headaches, which often run in families, tend to occur daily for a week or so, usually at the same time of day or night, and then disappear for months or even years. A sudden release of histamine and serotonin in the brain can trigger them, as well as a change in sleep patterns or certain medications. Sufferers describe the pain (typically located behind one eye) as excruciating. Cluster headaches are treated with oxygen inhalation and with triptan injections, lidocaine sprays, and other prescription medications.

Migraine headaches are the result of certain physiological changes in the brain. Symptoms can include warning indicators such as visual auras (flashing lights or blind spots) or a weakness on one side of the body, followed by debilitating throbbing or pounding pain, nausea, and sensitivity to light and sound. Triggers include red wine, aged cheese, the nitrates in smoked meats, some oral contraceptives, monosodium glutamate, sugar substitutes, alcohol, chocolate, and stress, as well as exposure to bright lights, loud noises, or strong smells. Attacks may last from 4 to 72 hours, and female sufferers outnumber males by three to one. Treatment includes over-the-counter and prescription drugs; preventative measures may include blood pressure, antiseizure, and antidepressant medications.

Healthy Solutions

Severe headaches require monitoring by a doctor, but tension headaches and early-stage migraines can sometimes be allayed by using natural treatments. Dietary changes—avoiding nitrates or MSG—can even forestall the onset of headaches. Traditional treatments for headaches include drinking plenty of water, increasing B-complex vitamins, detoxification therapy using two cups of apple cider vinegar in a hot bath, stretching exercises, and chiropractic treatments for improved posture.

CAYENNE PEPPER Applying cayenne pepper *(Capsicum annuum)* mixed with a dab of olive oil to the temples and neck can relieve headaches, relax muscles, and reduce inflammation—the capsaicin in the spice depletes substance P, a neuropeptide that causes headache pain, by evoking pain in another part of the body.

MAGNESIUM This safe, versatile mineral may prevent the brain-wave signaling that causes sensory changes, especially during migraines, and

GO GLUTEN FREE

Gluten, the protein found in wheat and other grains, may trigger headaches, especially migraines, in certain individuals. Research indicates that many headache sufferers found relief when they eliminated gluten from their diets. So if you are prone to headaches, try going gluten free for three weeks, and then slowly reintroduce foods that contain gluten until you find a good balance—your body will tell you how much gluten you can tolerate. Keeping a food diary will help you track your results.

block pain-transmitting chemicals in the brain. Taking 200 to 600 mg daily can reduce the frequency of attacks. Also increase your intake of beans, whole grains, seeds, nuts, leafy greens, and dairy products.

ESSENTIAL OILS Lavender essential oil is known as a mood stabilizer, and in studies with migraine sufferers, two-thirds benefited from inhaling this oil for 15 minutes. Cooling peppermint oil increases blood flow in the skin of the forehead, and it also helps soothe muscle contractions.

RESCUE REMEDY: *Rub a few drops of lavender or peppermint oil between your palms, and slowly work it into your forehead, temples, and neck. If necessary, dilute the oil with almond, grapeseed, or coconut oil.*

Lavender essential oil is available in small roll-on bottles, which allow you to directly target the source of your headache pain.

Replace stomach-irritating caffeinated coffee with a hot drink made from the roots of chicory *(Cichorium intybus).*

THE UPPER GI TRACT

SOOTHE STOMACH PROBLEMS AND IMPROVE DIGESTION

The upper gastrointestinal tract (or upper GI), begins with the mouth—where food is formed into a bolus (a small rounded mass) with help from the salivary glands before it is swallowed. Next is the pharynx, which is a membrane-lined cavity that compacted food passes through to the esophagus. The esophagus is a long muscular tube that transverses three regions of the body (neck, thorax, and abdomen). It is subsequently broken down into three sections: the cervical, thoracic, and abdominal. The stomach, a muscular bean-shaped pouch, is where major digestion takes place with the aid of acid and enzyme secretions. The stomach also secretes neutralizing mucus that protects its walls from the acid. Next comes the duodenum, the top of the small intestine. These organs are prone to acid reflux, indigestion, nausea,

> ### DID YOU KNOW?
>
> • *The heart and the stomach sit in close proximity. This is why people with indigestion sometimes fear that they are having a heart attack. Conversely, a heart attack can feel very much like gas (especially for women). If you have pain in your lower chest, think indigestion. If it emanates from your upper stomach, suspect a heart attack, and seek help.*

inflammation, and ulcers. Problems generally occur here when the nerves or muscles stop functioning properly. On the other hand, maintaining a balanced, nutrient-rich, high-fiber diet can help keep the upper GI tract in good working order.

GERD

Gastroesophageal reflux disease (GERD), or acid reflux, occurs when the sphincter that separates the esophagus from the stomach relaxes, allowing acidic stomach contents to splash into the esophagus. Symptoms may be a burning sensation, the taste of stomach fluids in the throat, a dry cough, and gas and pressure that can mimic a heart attack. Excess weight and tight-fitting clothing can aggravate symptoms. If left untreated, GERD can lead to serious complications that might eventually require surgery.

Healthy Solutions

Control GERD flare-ups through medication, diet, and natural remedies. Avoiding trigger foods, eating smaller meals, and not snacking close to bedtime are all helpful. Try eliminating tomatoes, citrus fruits, sugars, fatty or spicy foods, dairy products, caffeine, chocolate, and alcohol, and then reintroduce them gradually to see which ones cause an adverse reaction. Digestive enzyme supplements can help, as can a tablespoon of apple cider vinegar in four ounces of water taken before meals to support digestion.

INDIGESTION

If you end a rich meal feeling gassy, bloated, or nauseated, with pain in the chest, you may be suffering from acid indigestion with a side order of heartburn. Also known as dyspepsia, indigestion may be caused by overeating, consuming specific foods, pregnancy, gastritis, GERD, stress, nerves, or food poisoning.

Healthy Solutions

Neutralize stomach acid by mixing a teaspoon of baking soda (sodium bicarbonate) in a glass of water. Chicory root extract can increase the flow of bile and invigorate the whole digestive tract. Other proven stomach settlers include chamomile tea, a half cup of aloe juice, ginger supplements, candied ginger, or ginger tea. You can also chew on fennel or caraway seeds—the traditional Asian remedies for indigestion. Licorice supplements ease pain by coating the stomach lining. To relieve nausea, drink flat soda or coke syrup or try zesty peppermint tea. To banish heartburn, chew a piece of sugar-free gum for 20 minutes, or eat an apple or a banana.

RESCUE REMEDY: *To make stomach-soothing ginger tea, place 4 to 6 quarter-sized slices of fresh ginger in a pan with 2 cups of water. Cover, and simmer gently for 30 minutes. Strain—or not—and add honey or lemon to taste. Drink 20 minutes before mealtime.*

GASTRITIS

This is a group of conditions that all result in an inflammation of the stomach lining. Symptoms include a burning sensation in the pit of the stomach, nausea, vomiting, and abdominal pain. There are a number of causes, including vitamin B12 deficiency, and taking too many anti-inflammatory pain relievers, but the most prominent is the bacteria *Helicobacter pylori,* which also causes stomach ulcers.

Healthy Solutions

H. pylori typically needs to be treated with antibiotics, but natural remedies can also help ease gastritis symptoms. Neutralize stomach acid with baking soda, and avoid alcohol and spicy dishes. Other aids include chamomile or peppermint tea, ginger, yogurt, carom seeds, and strawberries, which can stop the inflammation of the stomach lining from ever beginning.

Try carom seeds for gastritis. Also known as ajwain or ajowan caraway, these are actually the fruits of the herb bishop's weed (*Trachyspermum ammi).*

LOSE THE BURN

Peptic ulcers are burns that form in the lining of the upper digestive tract; they occur as either stomach ulcers or duodenal ulcers. Although ulcers can result from stress, medications, diet, alcohol, smoking, or overuse of pain meds, roughly 70 percent are caused by the *H. pylori* bacteria. Burning pain from navel to sternum is the prevailing symptom; it can flare up at night and feel worse on an empty stomach. Treat ulcers with a diet that includes cabbage, bananas, coconut, and fenugreek. Aloe vera juice, licorice supplements, and probiotics (15 billion live organisms twice a day) can also help.

Up Close
THE POWER OF PROBIOTICS
CULTURED FOODS MAY COMBAT DIGESTIVES WOES

Kimchi is a traditional Korean dish of highly seasoned fermented vegetables, such as napa cabbage, daikon radish, ginger, cucumber, scallion, and garlic. Fermented foods can help you to keep your body supplied with healthy probiotic flora.

One key to maintaining good health is achieving proper balance in the body—of hormones or insulin, for example, as well as probiotics. Probiotics are the beneficial microorganisms—friendly bacteria—that are found in the digestive tract. The term *probiotic* comes from the Greek, meaning "for life," a definition embraced by many in the natural healing community, who believe in supplementing their own intestinal microbes with additional probiotics.

The notion that certain foods containing these microbes might bolster health, foster healing, and extend life was introduced in 1907 by a Russian scientist, Nobel laureate Elie Metchnikoff. He postulated that the extraordinary life span of certain Bulgarian and Russian peasants could be attributed to the fact that they consumed so much yogurt as part of their diet. He believed that the toxic result of

digestion in the large intestine, proteolytic bacteria, caused the physical affects of aging and that milk fermented with lactic-acid bacteria could combat these toxins by lowering the pH levels in the bowel.

In recent times, probiotics have been used to treat problems with the GI tract, including irritable bowel syndrome, belly bloat, and constipation. They can even aid in weight loss—participants in one study lost 5 percent of belly fat and more than 3 percent of subcutaneous fat by drinking a fermented milk beverage for three months.

Genetic Allies

These tiny warriors not only help the body to digest and assimilate food and produce vitamins, ongoing research indicates that they may also influence the activity of hundreds of our genes, enabling them to express in a manner that increases immunity and

Kefir is a drink that originated in the north Caucasus Mountains of Eurasia. Its taste is similar to yogurt, but in addition to probiotics, kefir also contains beneficial yeast, giving it incredible healing properties. A quart of homemade kefir contains more active bacteria than any probiotic supplement you can purchase and gives you a vitamin B12, biotin, calcium, magnesium, and folate boost, as well.

YOU WILL NEED:
  1 quart raw milk
  2 to 4 tablespoons kefir starter grains
  large glass jug with lid or cheesecloth cover

WHAT TO DO:
• Place the ingredients in the jug.
• Gently mix the kefir grains with the milk.
• Cover the jug with cheesecloth, and leave the jug out overnight at room temperature.
• Allow fermentation for at least 24 hours before straining out the grains.

Dairy and Food Options

Fermentation, the converting of carbohydrates to alcohol or organic acids using living organisms—yeasts or bacteria—was one of the earliest methods of preservation employed by our ancestors. Cheese, wine, and beer are all products of fermentation. Some dairy products contain cultures that help maintain or replenish the healthy microbes in the gut. These include yogurt, some cheeses (providing they are not pasteurized), and kefir, a cultured milk drink with a taste similar to yogurt. Fermented foods, like sauerkraut (cabbage), kimchi (mixed vegetables), natto (soybeans), and miso paste (soy, barley, and rice) will also furnish healthy digestive flora.

Your intake of probiotics—whether in food or as supplements—is especially important when traveling in foreign countries, after a course of antibiotics, or after a vaginal or urinary tract infection.

Milk kefir grains. Kefir grains are a combination of yeasts and bacteria that live in dairy foods. To make your own kefir, look for the grains at health food shops or online.

battles disease. Within the emerging medical field of epigenetics, it has been proposed that lifestyle plays a large role in how our genes are expressed—in other words, how the information in our DNA is converted into a functional product, such as protein. The once deeply held medical belief that our genes determine our health is being challenged. Some researchers feel that our genetic code is not set in stone; instead, it alters continuously—in large part based on diet and stress levels. It is therefore possible to lower the risk for some life-threatening diseases such as cancer by choosing foods like broccoli or onions that activate a tumor-suppressing gene. And if certain bacteria are able to support healthy genetic expression and strengthen the immune system, then it makes sense to incorporate these probiotics into your diet.

KNOW YOUR PROBIOTICS

The human digestive tract contains roughly 500 species of bacteria. *Lactobacillus acidophilus* resides in the small intestine and produces natural antibodies; *L. bulgaricus* produces lactic acid and creates a friendly environment for other species; *L. rhamnosis* tolerates less favorable environments and benefits infants and the elderly; and *Bifidobacterium bifidum* lives in the lining of the colon and protects it from pathogens.

THE LOWER GI TRACT

EASE THE CRAMPING AND DISCOMFORT OF BOWEL INFLAMMATION

The lower gastrointestinal (GI) tract comprises the small and large intestines. In the small intestine, food is broken down into nutrients—proteins into amino acids, fats into fatty acids, and carbohydrates into simple sugars—that are then absorbed. In the large intestine, or colon, waste is processed before being passed from the body as stools, and the remaining water and electrolytes are returned to the bloodstream. Many of the problems that afflict the bowel require medical oversight; however, some can be effectively treated with natural remedies.

CONSTIPATION

Constipation is a decrease in the frequency of bowel movements (fewer than three a week in most cases); the passage of hard, dry, often large stools; or bowel movements that are difficult or painful to push out. Constipation can be caused by a high-fat, low-fiber diet, insufficient hydration, lack of exercise, or stress and can be worsened by ignoring the symptoms when they first occur.

> **DID YOU KNOW?**
>
> • *Try pampering your insides with the BRAT diet whenever you feel intestinal woes. The BRAT acronym stands for bananas, rice, applesauce, and toast . . . all bland, soothing foods. Bananas and applesauce also provide pectin, a soluble fiber that absorbs excess water and slows down the passage of food.*

Fiber-rich dried fruits, including raisins, apricots, figs, gojis, prunes, pineapples, kiwi, papaya, and cranberries, are a tasty remedy for irregularity.

Healthy Solutions

Increase the amount of water you drink and your consumption of fruits and vegetables, and add fiber—whole grains, lentils, beans, and almonds—to your diet. Try drinking coffee, which stimulates the colon, or a cup of hot water with a spoonful of honey or a little lemon juice, a natural laxative. Other traditional remedies include oily sesame seeds, which moisturize the intestines, sprinkled on salads; a tablespoon of nutrient-rich blackstrap molasses taken at bedtime; mint or ginger tea; healthy fats like olive oil, nuts, and avocados; and dried fruit—like prunes, figs, or raisins—that contain fiber and digestive stimulants. Castor oil stimulates both the large and small intestines; swallow one or two teaspoons on an empty stomach. Taking probiotics to promote healthy gut bacteria and performing light exercise for 15 minutes each day should keep your plumbing humming.

DIARRHEA

Not usually serious, diarrhea, or loose, watery stools, is a common condition. It typically lasts for a few days and can be accompanied by painful cramping, bloating, and gas. Causes include food allergies, diabetes, medications, overactive thyroid, alcohol abuse, malabsorption, or an intestinal virus, or "flu." It may also follow a bout of constipation. If you suspect food poisoning as the cause, when cramping and diarrhea are severe and sometimes accompanied by vomiting, contact your doctor immediately.

Healthy Solutions

Even mild cases of diarrhea cause some discomfort and curtail activity, so most people seek a quick remedy. Natural cures include black tea with sugar and tannin-rich blackberries. Goldenseal capsules are believed to kill many types of harmful bacteria, including *E. coli*. You can also try eating a quarter cup of carrot or pumpkin puree each hour. Avoid spicy foods, beans, cabbage, caffeine, fruit, and alcohol for two days after symptoms are gone. You should also forgo any milk products for three days.

ELECTROLYTES Diarrhea can result in dehydration and loss of critical electrolytes—sodium, potassium, and chloride—so make sure to drink plenty of fluids. Some commercial sports or pediatric drinks contain electrolytes, but it is easy to make your own electrolyte-boosting beverage.

> RESCUE REMEDY: *Mix ½ teaspoon of salt and 4 teaspoons of sugar into 1 quart of water. Add a bit of orange or lemon juice or salt substitute to provide potassium. Drink the entire quart over the course of a day.*

Snip a few leaves from a home-grown mint plant to brew a soothing tea.

PSYLLIUM A form of fiber made from the husks of the seeds of the *Plantago ovata* plant, psyllium is also known as blond plantain, desert Indianwheat, and ispaghula. The ground seeds soak up excess fluid in the intestines and make stools bulkier. Take one to three tablespoons of psyllium in water each day until symptoms disappear.

IRRITABLE BOWEL SYNDROME

This chronic disorder of the colon includes cramping, gas, diarrhea, and constipation. It can be controlled in many cases by managing diet, lifestyle, and stress. Treatment often varies, however, from person to person. One common denominator might be dairy foods; possibly 70 percent of adults worldwide lack sufficient amounts of an enzyme (lactase) to digest the sugar (lactose) in milk products. IBS sufferers are especially prone to discomfort after eating dairy. Another culprit behind flare-ups is fat-heavy meals, which can cause the bowel to contract. These contractions are often very painful for IBS patients.

Healthy Solutions

Try portion control: eating smaller meals places a lighter burden on the lower GI tract. Increasing fiber is also beneficial: fiber creates larger stools that need fewer contractions to move through the colon—and that can sweep irritants out of the bowel before they cause cramping or gas. Fiber also alleviates both constipation and diarrhea.

LICORICE ROOT The sweet-tasting herb licorice (*Glycyrrhiza glabra*) is a natural anti-inflammatory and antispasmodic, and it can relieve irritation of the bowel. Licorice root can be taken as tea.

PEPPERMINT Studies have shown that IBS sufferers who took peppermint capsules eventually eliminated most, if not all, of their symptoms. The leaves of the peppermint plant (*Mentha × piperita*) can also be brewed into a soothing tea that offers effective lower GI relief.

URINARY TRACT HEALTH

AVOID BLADDER INFECTIONS AND REDUCE FREQUENCY AND URGENCY

There are several organs that make up the urinary tract. The kidneys, two bean-shaped organs filter waste from the blood to produce urine; the ureters are ducts that carry urine to the bladder; the muscular bladder holds urine; and the urethra is a tube that carries urine from the bladder and out of the body. When urinary health concerns arise, a cystoscopy—the insertion into the bladder of a pencil-thin tube with a tiny camera—may be recommended to determine the cause. Serious kidney ailments typically require a doctor's care, but some other urinary tract issues can be treated at home. Any sign of blood in the urine should also be checked by a doctor or specialist.

> **DID YOU KNOW?**
>
> *Large kidney stones, crystal formations that once had to pass painfully through the urinary tract to be expelled, can now be bombarded with extracorporeal shock waves and broken down into small fragments that pass relatively painlessly.*

A urinary tract infection (UTI) typically occurs when bacteria enter the through the urethra and then travel up the urinary tract, where they multiply in the bladder. UTIs may be a result of catheterization, holding in urine, or *E. coli* bacteria being transferred in some way from the anus to the urethra. Common symptoms of urinary tract infections include burning pain during urination and the sensation of still needing to pee after urination. A bacterial infection of the bladder is specifically known as cystitis.

Another urinary tract complication is frequent urination; that nagging need to urinate over and over is often a sign of a UTI. When irritation and swelling affect the bladder's ability to hold urine, even a small amount of fluid causes discomfort. Pregnancy, diabetes, prostate issues, radiation therapy, caffeine, spicy foods, and bladder problems can also cause more frequent urination.

You might also experience a feeling of urgency. That sudden sensation that sends you racing to the restroom can be caused by UTIs, alcohol, caffeine, an overactive bladder, bladder stones, enlarged prostate or urethral stricture, or neurological conditions such as stroke, MS, or Parkinson's disease.

Healthy Solutions

It is paramount that you increase your intake of water when suffering from a UTI; eight glasses a day at minimum are needed to flush out bacteria and increase the volume of urine. Add cucumbers to your diet: cucumbers are full of water and can supply extra fluid to your system. Ginger tea can prevent or reduce inflammation and ease pain. You should also avoid chocolate, citrus fruit, carbonated beverages, and caffeine, all of which can irritate the lining of the bladder. Placing a source of heat over your bladder can furnish major relief.

For a refreshing summertime beverage that will also keep urinary tract infections at bay, replace traditional lemonade with iced cucumber-and-mint-infused water.

Cranberries
(Vaccinium macrocarpon)

Cranberry juice is not the outstanding remedy it was once thought, but its acidity does help eliminate the bacteria that cling to the lining of the urethra. To be effective, however, three glasses a day are required—a lot of acid to process. A half cup of blueberries may provide the same effect.

BAKING SODA The chemical compound sodium bicarbonate is that pantry staple known as baking soda. Also called bicarbonate of soda, baking soda is an alkali, which means it can neutralize or lessen the acidity of your urine, which is what causes that burning sensation.

RESCUE REMEDY: *First thing in the morning, mix 1 tablespoon of baking soda with 1 cup of water, and drink the whole glass. Discontinue after one week.*

PARSLEY WATER This refreshing herbal remedy, made from the leaves of *Petroselinum crispum,* acts as a diuretic, increasing the amount of fluids you pass, helping to relieve any infection and speed up healing.

RESCUE REMEDY: *Add 1 cup of fresh parsley to 1 to 2 cups of boiling water. Let the mixture simmer for 6 to 10 minutes, and then strain and drink while hot. Or chill in the refrigerator for a parsley "iced tea." If you use dried parsley, place 2 tablespoons in 1 cup of boiling water, and steep for eight minutes before straining. Celery seeds, which can be chewed, have a similar diuretic effect.*

Flat-leaf parsley. Parsley can act as a natural diuretic.

COPING WITH INCONTINENCE

Urinary incontinence, the involuntary release of urine, can vary from a few drops to loss of bladder control. Nearly 25 million Americans suffer from some form of incontinence, the majority of them women. It is not a disease, but rather a symptom of an underlying condition and can be caused by loss of pelvic support of the bladder due to surgery or childbirth, an overactive bladder, menopause, neurological conditions, medications, UTIs, urinary stones, and constipation. Although medications and surgery are often prescribed, a number of natural treatments can help you regain some bladder control.

- Kegel exercises tighten the muscles of the pelvic floor. The kegel squeeze should be held for an 8 count, then relaxed for an 8 count. Do 8 to 12 repetitions three times daily.
- To treat incontinence, take 350 mg of magnesium hydroxide supplements twice a day for two weeks. Or try an Epsom salts soak for 20 minutes several times a week.
- Vitamin D, which maintains muscle strength, can be prompted into production by sunlight and is found in foods like fish, oysters, eggs yolks, and dairy products and as a supplement.
- Yoga exercises can help tighten the muscles that control the urethral sphincter; try positions like Root Lock, Chair Pose, Triangle Pose, and Squat Pose.
- Gosha-jinki-gan is a traditional Chinese herbal medicine that relieves urinary urgency and frequency.

THE ENDOCRINE SYSTEM
TREAT AND PREVENT GLANDULAR AILMENTS

This complex network of interconnected glands is responsible for how the heart beats and how bones and tissues grow. The endocrine system also controls our ability to turn calories from food into the energy that fuels our cells and organs. In addition to the reproductive ovaries and testes, their are several major glands. The pineal gland in the brain is likely linked to sleep patterns; the adrenal glands sit atop the kidneys and release the hormone cortisol; the thymus in the upper chest develops our immune system in early life; the four tiny parathyroid glands in the neck aid bone development; the hypothalamus, in the lower middle brain, instructs the pituitary to release hormones; the islet cells of the pancreas control the release of the hormones insulin and glucagon; and the thyroid, a butterfly-shaped gland located in the front of the throat controls metabolism. The pituitary gland at the base of the brain is often called the master gland—it influences many other glands, including the thyroid. It affects bone growth and female menstrual cycles.

This system is so closely linked that a small malfunction in one gland can throw off the balance of hormones in

> ### DID YOU KNOW?
>
> • *The trace mineral vanadyl sulfate, which regulates blood sugar levels, was discovered in France in the late 1800s. Vanadyl sulfate was the only treatment for diabetes prior to the development of insulin. It is still an option in the natural treatment of diabetes and can be taken in pill form as a supplement. It is also found in soybeans, shellfish, and mushrooms.*

the body, leading to endocrine disorders or diseases. Such problems will require the attention of an endocrinologist, but there are natural ways to keep this system healthy and to augment medical treatments.

DIABETES

This disease occurs when the body's response to the hormone insulin is impaired—carbohydrates are not metabolized properly, and glucose levels in blood and urine become elevated. Type I diabetes, which begins in childhood and can be life threatening, is treated with injections of insulin. Type II diabetes often occurs as we age. It can be treated with pills and dietary changes, as well as herbal medicines that control blood glucose levels.

Healthy Solutions

A healthy diet of low-fat, high-fiber foods and regular exercise are essential for diabetes patients. Mineral supplements that help normalize glucose levels include chromium picolinate, magnesium, potassium, and zinc. Herbal options that display antidiabetic properties include aloe, dandelion root, stinging nettle, eyebright, bilberry extract, bitter melon,

Momordica charantia is known as bitter melon, balsam-pear, bitter squash, or bitter gourd. In traditional Indian medicine, different parts of the plant are used to treat diabetes.

cinnamon, ginkgo biloba, burdock, evening primrose, fenugreek, ginger, goldenseal, alfalfa, kelp, and okra. Blueberry or huckleberry leaves are known to promote insulin production; to make a tasty tea, gather them before the fruit appears. Most of these herbs are safe to take with your existing medications, but check with your doctor first.

THYROID ISSUES

Ailments of this critical gland range from small goiters (harmless, enlarged glands) to cancer, but the most prevalent problems involve underproduction of hormones, called hypothyroidism, and overproduction, called hyperthyroidism. The former results in a sluggish metabolism with symptoms like fatigue, moodiness, weight gain, dry skin, and hair loss. It is estimated that perhaps 40 percent of the population has low thyroid function. Conversely, when an overactive thyroid is revving up your metabolism, you may suffer from anxiety, excess sweating, sleep disturbances, palpitations, and weight loss or gain.

A group of foods known as goitrogens can interrupt thyroid function and so should be taken in moderation—or steamed in the case of vegetables—if you suffer from thyroid issues. They include gluten, broccoli, cauliflower, radishes, cabbage, spinach, strawberries, peaches, peanuts, and soybeans.

Healthy Solutions

To boost an underactive thyroid, add wild-caught fish, coconut oil, and seaweed to your diet, as well as probiotic-rich products like kefir, kimchi, and miso. Try iodine-rich black walnuts, sprouted seeds, high-fiber foods, bone broth, and lots of fruits and non-cruciferous vegetables to boost hormone balance, brain function, and digestive health. Aerobic exercise is also recommended.

To treat an overactive thyroid, drink green smoothies made from kale, spinach, and spirulina (blue-green algae); flavor your meals with anti-inflammatory herbs like basil, rosemary, and oregano, protective herbs like bugleweed and lemon balm, and thyroid-regulating kelp like bladderwrack; increase B-complex vitamins; seek out fresh produce

Bladderwrack (*Fucus vesiculosus*), a seaweed abundant on the coasts of the Atlantic and Pacific, is rich in iodine and has an established history as a treatment for thyroid issues.

and lean proteins; and add immune-boosting ginger and detoxifying bone broth to your diet. Avoid gluten, processed foods, conventional dairy products, sugar, and artificial dyes or flavorings.

ESSENTIAL OILS Frankincense and myrrh are known to reduce stress and improve thyroid function. Simply place 2 drops of frankincense oil on the roof of the mouth daily, and massage 2 or 3 drops of myrrh oil onto the thyroid gland twice daily.

BOUNCE BACK FROM ADRENAL FATIGUE

If you are tired and dragging all the time, you may be suffering from adrenal fatigue syndrome. The adrenal glands produce cortisol—the hormone that deals with stress—and if they are functioning below normal levels due to elevated stress or in the aftermath of a serious infection, your energy will gradually disappear. To put the pep back in your step, try to reduce the stressors in your life and get plenty of sleep. Eat nutrient-dense foods like cruciferous veggies, kelp and seaweed, fatty fish, poultry, and nuts. Up your intake of vitamin B12 and C, and stay hydrated. Seek out herbs and minerals that support adrenal function, like ashwagandha, holy basil, magnesium, and zinc.

Symptoms of PMS include cramps, bloating, and headache.

FEMALE REPRODUCTIVE HEALTH

TREAT THE DISCOMFORTS OF PMS, MENOPAUSE, AND OTHER PROBLEMS

Most women experience one or more complaints of the reproductive system in their lifetime. These ailments can occur at the start of puberty—when the production of sex hormones increases, the reproductive organs (the uterus and ovaries) prepare for conception, and menstruation begins—until the onset of menopause and beyond. Naturally, serious conditions such as endometriosis, when uterine tissue forms outside that organ; fibroids, noncancerous tumors in the uterus; HIV/AIDS; and gynecological cancer all require the oversight of a physician, yet there are also conditions that can benefit from natural treatments at home.

MENSTRUAL COMPLICATIONS

During their monthly periods, many women may experience pain (dysmenorrhea), cramps, nausea, irregular cycles, and heavy flow.

Healthy Solutions

It's not surprising that for centuries women have turned to the natural world to find relief from

> **DID YOU KNOW?**
>
> • *If you suffer from pain or nausea and weakness as a side effect of your period, simply chew on a few fennel seeds. Fennel, a culinary herb of the Mediterranean, has been clinically proven to ease menstrual discomfort, plus it offers a safe, inexpensive alternative to medications.*

menstrual complaints—and have been pleased at the number of options afforded them. (If you are pregnant, check with your doctor before starting any herbal treatments.)

ANGELICA The sweet Chinese herb *Angelica sinesis*, known as angelica or dong quai, has a long history of easing menstrual and menopausal problems. It is high in vitamin B12 and contains ferulic acid, which relaxes muscles and relieves pain, and blood-thinning coumarins, which improve blood flow to the female reproductive organs.

BLUE COHOSH A traditional remedy for cramps, the herb blue cohosh (*Caulophyllum thalictroides*) contains methyl cytosine, an alkaloid believed to act as an antispasmodic. Although unrelated botanically, black cohosh (*Actaea racemosa*) is often used in conjunction with blue cohosh; it contains isoflavones that mimic hormonal activity and affect estrogen levels.

CHASTE TREE BERRY Also called chasteberry, Abraham's balm, lilac chastetree, and monk's pepper, chaste tree berry (*Vitex agnus-castus*), acts on the pituitary gland to affect hormone regulation; its use traces back to medieval monks, who found it curbed their sexual appetites. The flavonoids in the berries can slightly increase the production of progesterone in women, the lack of which can cause cramps, heavy bleeding, irregular periods, and infertility.

VAGINAL ISSUES

The warm, moist vaginal area is a prime location for irritations and the formation of yeast infections that can cause itching, burning, and dryness. Natural remedies abound, however, and many of them can be found right in your home.

Healthy Solutions

Dryness can be relieved by increasing your intake of fatty acids like vitamins A and B and beta-carotene and isoflavones like legumes, soy, flaxseed, nuts, and apples. You can also employ natural lubricants such as coconut or jojoba oil, aloe, or vitamin E suppositories. Or try adding a quarter cup of salt to your bath.

YOGURT The cultures in yogurt will help restore beneficial microbes, like *Lactobacillus acidophilus,* in your vagina. Probiotics can work in a similar manner.

> RESCUE REMEDY: *An effective way to combat stubborn yeast infections (vulvovaginal candidiasis) is to dip a tampon in active-culture yogurt and insert it for two hours, twice a day, until the symptoms are gone.*

REDUCE THE SYMPTOMS OF PMS

Premenstrual syndrome (PMS), which can occur just before your monthly period, often produces bloating, irritability, headaches, breast tenderness, sleep disturbance, and cravings. Causes may include hormonal imbalances (high estrogen-to-progesterone ratios), stress, and fluid retention. Some herbal remedies used for menstrual difficulties also work to ease PMS. These include maca root, chaste tree berry, dong quai, black cohosh, lemon balm, burdock, St. John's wort, and ginkgo.

Flowers of the chaste tree. Dried chaste tree berries can relieve the symptoms of PMS.

MENOPAUSE

The end of menses brings with it its own set of problems for many women—lowered libido, vaginal itching, painful intercourse, and mood swings.

Healthy Solutions

Once again, natural aids can help to ease these kinds of menopausal complaints; in particular, they can help to restore hormonal imbalances.

ASHWAGANDHA Also called Indian ginseng, poison gooseberry, or winter cherry, ashwagandha *(Withania somnifera)* is a key element in Ayurvedic medicine. This astringent member of the nightshade family can stimulate blood flow to the reproductive organs, increasing arousal and sensitivity, and relieve hot flashes, anxiety, and depression.

BLACK COHOSH The herb black cohosh addresses the problems of vaginal dryness and mental depression, as well as hot flashes.

MACA ROOT A popular South American herb, maca root *(Lepidium meyenii),* or Peruvian ginseng, is used to treat menopausal issues like hot flashes, sexual dysfunction, night sweats, and loss of libido.

OATS *Avena sativa,* commonly called oats or wild oats, is another libido enhancer favored by menopausal women; it stimulates the central nervous system and boosts the physical and emotional desire for sex.

MALE REPRODUCTIVE HEALTH

IMPROVE FERTILITY, CONQUER IMPOTENCE, AND PROTECT THE PROSTATE

This part of the male endocrine system includes the prostate gland, penis, and testicles. The testicles produce sperm (male reproductive cells) and hormones like testosterone. The penis ejaculates semen, the fluid that contains sperm. The prostate is a walnut-sized gland between the bladder and penis. It secretes a fluid that nourishes and protects the sperm; it is released as semen during ejaculation. Disorders of the testicles, penis, or prostate can affect sexual function and fertility, yet most of these issues are quite common, with many treatment options.

INFERTILITY

In roughly 1 in 5 cases in which couples are having trouble conceiving a child, male infertility is the culprit. One man in 20 has some issue involving a low sperm count; 1 in 100 has no sperm in his semen. Medical tests can determine if the problem is lack of sperm production or poor sperm transport. Two-thirds of infertile men have trouble making sperm in the testes. Other issues include a blockage in the tubes leading from the testes to the penis; the inability to maintain an erection or ejaculate sperm; low levels of pituitary hormones that affect the testes; and sperm antibodies.

Healthy Solutions

You can boost your level of fertility and improve sexual

A tasty kale smoothie enriched with vitamins A, C, and E is a quick way to boost male reproductive health.

> **DID YOU KNOW?**
>
> • *Acupuncture has been used in Asia for thousands of years to treat a variety of ailments. A recent study indicates it may have potential for treating erectile dysfunction—39 percent of the participants reported improvement in the quality of their erections as well as an increase in sexual activity.*

function in a number of natural ways. Increase sperm count and improve motility—quick, effective movement of sperm—by avoiding hot baths, tight underwear, cigarettes, excess alcohol, and radiation. Also consider avoiding exposure to xenoestrogens (DDT, PCB, dioxin) that mimic the effects of estrogen. These include plastic bottles and containers, chlorinated products, synthetic deodorants and cosmetics, and high-hormone dairy products like milk. It also helps to maintain a healthy weight; obesity is associated with low sperm count and impotence.

ANTIOXIDANTS These powerful compounds protect us from the free radicals that damage body tissues and can improve sperm quality. Eat a diet rich in carotenes and selenium and vitamins A, C, and E. Find these in foods such as leafy greens, carrots, citrus fruits, kale, broccoli, cauliflower, and yams.

VITAMINS These micronutrients can be the key to restoring fertility. Take 2,000 to 6,000 mg of vitamin C daily to keep sperm from clumping. Try 100 to 200 mg of zinc to increase testosterone levels, sperm count, and motility. Natural sources of zinc include oysters, turkey, wheat germ, legumes, and nuts.

ERECTILE DYSFUNCTION

Also known as impotence, erectile dysfunction (ED) is the inability to achieve or maintain an erection during sex. Symptoms can also include reduced sexual desire, or libido. ED can be caused by age, fatigue, stress, performance anxiety, relationship conflicts, hormonal or psychological

Rhodiola rosea, also known as golden root, appears to enhance sexual function. The dried root is used to make a tea or tincture, or it can be powdered and encapsulated.

problems, or alcohol. Medical issues like diabetes, heart disease, obesity, and enlarged prostate may also be at fault. Common treatments include medication, exercise, weight loss, reduced alcohol intake, and counseling.

Healthy Solutions

Although there are many prescription medications for ED, they all have some type of side effect, such as acne, breast enlargement, aching in the penis, or increased urination. They are also not recommended for men with low blood pressure or who have had a stroke. Natural remedies offer similar benefits with relatively few side effects.

HERBAL SUPPLEMENTS There are many herbs that can improve erectile function, as well as increase sexual desire and blood flow to the penis.

RESCUE REMEDIES: *Traditional herbs known for their ability to boost performance include* Panax ginseng *(take one to three 500-mg capsules daily);* saw palmetto berry *(one or two 80-mg capsules daily);*

muira puama *(three to six 500-mg capsules daily);* Ginkgo biloba *extract (one to three 250-mg capsules daily);* Rhodiola rosea *(one to three 500-mg capsules daily); and nutmeg (one 500-mg capsule daily). Because sperm formation can take up to three months, maintain your supplement regimen for at least that long.*

DHEA AND L-ARGININE Studies show that men with ED are more likely to have low levels of dehydroepiandrosterone (DHEA), a natural hormone produced by the adrenal glands that can be converted to both estrogen and testosterone. This dietary supplement is made from wild yam and soy. L-arginine is an amino acid that helps to make nitric oxide; nitric oxide relaxes blood vessels and facilitates an easier erection.

PROSTATE HEALTH

As men age, their prostate glands grow larger, which often causes urinary issues. Common symptoms include passing more urine during the day, an urgent need to urinate, decreased urine flow, a burning sensation, leakage, and urinating frequently at night. This condition, called benign prostatic hyperplasia (BPH), is not linked to cancer, although some symptoms are similar. (Always have your doctor investigate any prostate issues.)

Healthy Solutions

Modern medical treatments for prostate issues include drugs and surgery, but there are also some traditional options. Pumpkin seeds contain protective compounds called phytosterols that may help shrink the prostate gland. Saw palmetto berry extract can reduce the size of the prostate by altering certain hormone levels.

RESCUE REMEDIES: *The Amish make a useful tea by pouring 2 pints of boiling water over ¼ cup of watermelon seeds and letting it steep before straining. Other proven aids include stinging nettle, which is used in Europe for prostate problems; pygeum (African plum tree bark), an ancient urinary tract treatment; garlic extract, and beta-sitosterol capsules.*

ORAL AND DENTAL CARE
CHOOSE NATURAL HYGIENE FOR HEALTHY TEETH AND GUMS

Maintaining good oral and dental health is essential; the gums, tongue, and teeth are constantly at risk from the innumerable bacteria that live in the human mouth—a single tooth might host 500 million bacteria. These microbes, as well as viruses and fungi, are at the root of bad breath, tooth decay, canker sores, cold sores, gum disease, and thrush. You can fight back by regularly seeing a dentist, who will keep abreast of your dental needs and further advise you if you need treatment from an endodontist (a specialist in dental pulp), periodontist (a specialist in the structures around the teeth), or an oral surgeon (a specialist in tooth removal and mouth surgery). There are also many natural prophylactics you can employ to keep your mouth healthy, your breath fresh, and your smile beaming.

Your first defense is basic tooth care. We learned these steps as children, but how many of us still follow them today? Ideally, you should brush twice a day with a soft toothbrush, floss gently between the teeth to remove food particles, and then rinse with an antiseptic mouthwash. In addition, using a tongue scraper can freshen breath, and tooth-whitening strips can enhance your appearance.

> ### DID YOU KNOW?
> • *Oil pulling can prevent gum disease and bad breath. Simply swish two tablespoons of coconut oil—or any microbe-killing essential oil—in your mouth and between your teeth for 15 minutes. Make sure not to swallow the oil, which is now full of toxins. Afterward, spit it out, rinse with warm water, and brush your teeth as usual.*

TOOTH DECAY

Maintaining your teeth as an adult is especially important—as you age, extensive tooth loss can adversely impact how you masticate food or even dictate the foods you are still able to eat. Tooth cavities occur, in part, when carbohydrates left on the teeth nourish oral bacteria that then produce acids that eat into tooth enamel. Cavities tend to appear in children and teens, but no one is immune, especially when teeth are damaged or fillings are loose.

Healthy Solutions

The most effective way to ward off tooth decay is removing sugar from the diet. Opt for nutrient-rich and organic foods, and increase fat-soluble vitamins, such as A, D, E, and K, and minerals like calcium and magnesium. Also look for mineralizing toothpastes.

COLD SORES AND CANKER SORES

Unsightly cold sores, or fever blisters, which appear on the lips or mouth and can recur, are caused by the herpes simplex virus (HSV1). These sores are not only painful, they are also contagious and can be spread by kissing or other close contact. Canker sores (aphthous stomatitis) are small, painful mouth ulcers; their cause is not yet known.

Healthy Solutions

Calm a cold sore outbreak by applying aloe vera gel and zinc oxide cream on a sore, ease pain with icing, and speed healing time with a lip balm

Basic oral and dental care begins in childhood.

containing 1 percent lemon balm or a lemon balm tea compress. Regularly taking lysine supplements can also reduce the intensity of breakouts and prevent future ones. Stress may cause flare-ups, so practice calming protocols.

To soothe a canker sore, try placing a soaked chamomile teabag directly on the sore. You can also swish a tea made with two tablespoons dried sage inside your mouth, gargle with salt water, or eat yogurt to balance the bacteria in your mouth.

> RESCUE REMEDY: *Ease the pain of a canker sore with a homemade numbing spray. Just combine 9 drops each of peppermint essential oil and eucalyptus essential oil with 2 tablespoons of grapeseed oil in a spray bottle. Shake well, and spray directly on sores as needed.*

GUM DISEASE

An infection of the tissues of the mouth, gum disease (or periodontal disease), can result in tooth loss. It is caused by plaque, a sticky bacterial film that forms on the teeth. Warning signs include bleeding, swollen, or tender gums; bad breath; loose or separating teeth; and a change in bite patterns. Risk factors can be poor oral hygiene, pregnancy, smoking, genetics, and diabetes, as well as certain medicines.

Healthy Solutions

Natural remedies include rubbing essential oils—two drops of oil of cloves or tea tree oil in a carrier oil like grapeseed—along the gum line, eating lots of fresh garlic, boosting vitamin C with plenty of fresh veggies and fruit, and flossing after every meal.

THRUSH

Oral thrush, a yeast infection caused by the *Candida albicans* fungus, causes white lesions on the inner cheeks and tongue; severe cases may move to the throat or stomach. Thrush can be triggered by illness, compromised immunity, chemotherapy, pregnancy, medications, or smoking. Healthy treatments include a simple saltwater gargle; adding yogurt, cinnamon, raw garlic, coconut oil, cultured dairy, and fermented vegetables to your diet; and restoring immunity by taking vitamin C or milk thistle supplements.

> RESCUE REMEDY: *Mix a few drops of tea tree oil or oil of cloves with 1 tablespoon of carrier oil, and swish inside your mouth for 20 minutes before spitting out.*

Oil of cloves has a long history of use in dentistry, from helping to alleviate toothache pain to helping reduce the symptoms of oral or gum disease.

KEEP IT FRESH

Whether it emanates from the mouth or the stomach, bad breath can be a social liability and confidence destroyer. Healthy solutions include brushing after every meal, employing a tongue scraper, using a water pick (which shoots a stream of water against and in between the teeth to flush out bacteria), and keeping your mouth moist. Try chewing parsley, fennel, dill, cardamom, or anise seeds after you dine; suck on a cinnamon stick; or bite repeatedly on a whole clove to release antibacterial eugenol. And be sure to use a toothpaste containing tea tree oil, a natural oral disinfectant.

Jewelweed, or touch-me-not, can soothe the rashes caused by plant irritants like poison ivy and also calm insect bites.

FIRST AID FOR MINOR WOUNDS

TREAT CUTS, BITES, STINGS, BURNS, AND RASHES THE NATURAL WAY

Skin acts as a protective barrier against disease, warding off microbial and fungal invaders, and it does a remarkable job. But human skin is not invincible, and it can suffer from infected wounds, burns, insect bites and stings, and itchy rashes caused by exposure to poisonous plants.

INFECTIONS

Any insult to the epidermis that leaves an open wound can foster bacterial infections, especially from *Staphylococcus aureus* and beta-hemolytic *Streptococcus.* Cellulitis, an infection that involves the outer layers of skin, causes pain, swelling, tenderness, redness, and warmth. Antibiotics are typically prescribed for serious infections, but many home remedies are useful against minor infections.

Healthy Solutions

Try apple cider vinegar to help guard against infection. A slight dilution of this antibacterial and anti-inflammatory vinegar dabbed on a

> **DID YOU KNOW?**
>
> • *If you accidentally step on a nail, suffer a pet bite, or receive any deep puncture wound, it is critical to get a tetanus shot. Tetanus, also known as lockjaw, is a potentially fatal infection of the nervous system. Doctors recommend vaccination for infants and children, followed by a booster shot at least every 10 years.*

wound both restores pH balance and restricts bacterial growth. Aloe vera gel, taken directly from the leaves of the plant and applied to the skin, is another antibacterial option. You can also try a topical paste made of baking soda and water, which can regulate pH and speed healing. Along with its many other healthful properties, honey is a mild antiseptic, and you can apply it to cuts to keep bacteria from entering the wound. Take four or five cloves of garlic a day—or an equivalent supplement—to help guard against bacterial and fungal infections, especially those of the skin.

BURNS

Superficial or first-degree burns are painful, red, and swollen, but they do not penetrate below the top layer of skin. Second-degree burns display blisters and red or white splotches, along with pain and swelling. If smaller than three inches across, treat them as minor burns. Anything worse than that needs to be seen by a doctor.

Healthy Solutions

To soothe the pain of minor burns, try cold running water, fresh aloe vera gel, a soak made of black tea bags, or a slice of fresh potato to alleviate blisters. Once a burn has cooled, apply vitamin-rich coconut oil with a bit of lemon juice to encourage healing.

> RESCUE REMEDY: *Honey, with its antibacterial and anti-inflammatory properties, can disinfect a burn, help it heal, and also prevent hypertrophic scars. Spread honey on a length of gauze and place it over the burn. Change the dressing two or three times daily.*

OUTDOOR SKIN IRRITANTS

Spending a day outdoors can be healthful, but being outside does pose hazards . . . like stinging and biting insects and poisonous plants.

Itchy mosquito bites are best treated with a dab of aloe vera gel, apple cider vinegar, baking soda paste, or raw honey. Painful bee stings contain venom that needs to be neutralized. First remove the embedded stinger by flicking the edge of a playing card over it, and then wash with mild soap. Stings respond to icing, followed by applications of lavender essential oil, baking soda or Epsom salts paste, toothpaste, meat tenderizer (the enzyme papain breaks down toxins), honey, calamine lotion, or crushed basil leaves. Most spider bites are harmless, but some require a doctor's care. Learn to identify any poisonous spiders in your region. Clean a minor bite with mild soap, then use ice packs to reduce swelling. To draw out toxins, try a baking soda, aspirin, or activated charcoal paste; a sea salt compress; or a grated raw potato poultice. Obviously, anyone who is allergic to insect stings or is the victim of snakebite, needs immediate medical attention.

If you enjoy gardening or hiking, it helps to recognize—and avoid—toxic plants like poison ivy, oak, and sumac. The leaves, stems, and roots of these plants contain an oil called urushiol, which causes an allergic reaction, or histamine response, in 80 to 90 percent of the population. A rash may occur only hours after exposure and is characterized by red, swollen skin; weepy blisters; and severe itching. The rash is not contagious and usually subsides in one to three weeks. The oil, however, can linger on tools, clothing, and your pet's fur.

Healthy Solutions

Always wash with strong soap after suspected exposure to poisonous plants. Wear cloth gloves when gardening (urushiol may penetrate latex gloves), and wash them after use. If you do get a rash, cool the heat with a compress dampened with apple cider vinegar, witch hazel, or black tea, which has tannins that lower inflammatory reactions. Ease itching with bentonite clay, colloidal oatmeal baths, or a few drops of geranium, rose, or lavender oil on a compress. To lower histamine reactions, mix one part echinacea tincture to three parts water, and use on a compress.

JEWELWEED A traditional Native American herbal remedy for skin disorders, jewelweed *(Impatiens capensis)* is also known as spotted touch-me-not or orange balsam. It has shown to be effective in calming the irritating effects of poison oak, poison ivy, poison sumac, stinging nettle, and certain insect bites.

> RESCUE REMEDY: *Use the juice from the jewelweed plant directly on the infected area, or prepare an infusion from its chopped stems, leaves, and flowers.*

SPOT THE DANGER

The most natural solution is avoidance, so learn to distinguish these three potential threats from harmless wildflowers and weeds.

- Poison ivy *(Toxicodendron radicans):* Look for pointy-tipped leaves arranged in groups of three; green in spring and summer, reddish in fall.
- Poison oak *(T. diversilobum):* The leaves look like a cross between oak leaves and poison ivy. Some leaves form clusters of three; others grow in clusters of five, seven, or nine.
- Poison sumac *(T. vernix):* This woody shrub usually displays 7 to 13 leaflets arranged in pairs; leaves may show black or brownish spots.

NATURAL SKINCARE SOLUTIONS

REDUCE THE EFFECTS OF ACNE AND OTHER SKIN AILMENTS

The skin is the body's largest organ, covering 1.5 to 2 meters of surface area in the average adult and accounting for 12 to 15 percent of total body weight. It consists of two layers—the outermost epidermis acts as a waterproof barrier against the environment, protecting us from pathogens and preventing water loss. The second layer is the dermis, containing tough connective tissue, sweat glands, and hair follicles. A third layer, known as the hypodermis, contains fat and connective tissue but is not technically part of the skin. Human skin is prone to a number of conditions that can cause unsightly eruptions, pain, scarring, and even distressing social consequences. These include acne, psoriasis, atopic eczema, and rosacea. This organ is also home to small growths—moles, warts, and skin tags—that appear on our bodies with increasing frequency as we age. They are for the most part benign, but should be carefully monitored for any change in size, shape, or color.

DID YOU KNOW?

• *Apple cider vinegar is a powerful remedy for skin complaints like recurrent teenage acne and eczema. Look for skincare products that feature a "mother of vinegar" culture, which means that they are produced with a beneficial, antimicrobial fermenting bacteria, or acetobacter.*

back, and shoulders. The condition may occur only during puberty, come and go for many years, or last a lifetime. It is typically caused by excess facial oil—frequently caused by a sensitivity to testosterone—resulting in the buildup of skin bacteria. Severe acne suffered during the teen years can create emotional distress and confidence issues, while infected pimples can leave behind physical scars.

Healthy Solutions

Toning—meaning to remove excess oils and residue from the skin and to tighten the pores—is essential for healthy skin of all kinds. Fortunately, there are easy-to-make natural toners.

APPLE CIDER VINEGAR To tone an acne-prone complexion, you can dip a cotton ball in apple cider vinegar and dab it over the affected areas every morning and night. Vinegar contains magnesium and enzymes that kill harmful bacteria.

RESCUE REMEDY: *Any acne treatment should start with a clean face. Create your own healing vinegar-honey face wash by combining 1 tablespoon each of apple cider vinegar and coconut oil, 3 tablespoons honey, 15 to 20 drops of tea tree essential oil, and 2 capsules of live probiotics in a glass bottle. Dampen skin with water, massage mixture into face and neck, and then rinse. Gently blot dry with a soft towel.*

ACNE

A common skin problem, acne is also one of the most vexing. Acne consists of raised pimples called comedones—whiteheads or blackheads—and pus-filled pustules that form on the face, neck, chest,

MASKS A face mask can tone acne-prone skin, while also helping to tame breakouts and reducing the chance of future scarring.

RESCUE REMEDY: *Create an acne-fighting healing mask by mixing 2 tablespoons of raw honey,*

Use common pantry items like yogurt, oatmeal, and honey to mix your own face scrubs.

Scrubs are easy to make from ingredients like avocado, honey, brown sugar, and sea salt.

1 teaspoon coconut oil, and ½ teaspoon cinnamon. Smooth the mix over your face and neck, and leave on for 10 minutes before gently washing it off. Or try mixing the honey with 1 tablespoon of yogurt. Add a few drops of tea tree oil to the mask if breakouts are particularly bad.

SCRUBS Other healing resources include scrubs made from sea salt, brown sugar, or oatmeal combined with a base like honey, avocado, or yogurt; sweet basil tea to combat bacteria; and warm coconut or olive oil to moisturize skin and provide sun protection. Probiotic supplements and a diet of leafy greens, wild salmon, and hormone-free meat can also be beneficial.

CHRONIC SKIN INFLAMMATION

Potentially disfiguring, chronic skin problems like psoriasis and atopic eczema (also called atopic dermatitis) may require the care of a dermatologist, but there are natural ways to augment medications.

Healthy Solutions

Psoriasis, which causes raised, scaly, itchy patches, can be treated with warm baths containing Epsom salts, Dead Sea salts, mineral oil, or olive oil. For eczema—which causes redness, blistering, crusting, scaling, and oozing—moisturizing with coconut oil, toning with apple cider vinegar, and soothing with a honey mask are useful practices, as are oatmeal baths, aloe vera gel, and vitamin E oil.

DIMINISH THE EFFECTS OF ROSACEA

Rosacea is a disfiguring skin condition that predominantly affects women. Symptoms include redness on the cheeks; swollen, painful bumps; acnelike breakouts, and broken "spider" veins. Sunlight, medications, inflammatory reactions, or allergies may be the cause. There is no cure, but medications to control flare-ups are available, and special makeup can obscure redness. Natural remedies include green tea, soothing oatmeal or cucumber masks, and eating healthy fats, organic vegetables, "clean" proteins, and anti-inflammatory foods like onions, cruciferous vegetables, tomatoes, and turmeric. Also consider getting checked for food allergies.

Up Close
WHY SHUN THE SUN?
SUN WORSHIPERS RISK SKIN DAMAGE WHILE SEEKING THE PERFECT TAN

Beach day essentials: a sun-shading hat, sunblock, sunglasses (with UV protection), and a beverage. Staying hydrated is essential, and drinking plenty of water will help sun-damaged skin heal more quickly.

It has become a cliché—a sun-burnished couple walking hand-in-hand along a tropical beach, wearing only swimsuits and carrying umbrella drinks. It was magazine and TV advertisements like this, plus a host of popular movies and surfing songs, that encouraged baby boomers (and subsequent generations) to embrace beach culture with a vengeance. They had bathing suits, bathing trunks, bikinis, sunsuits, sundresses, surfer shorts, Hawaiian shirts, sandals, and sunglasses as they stretched out on beach towels or lounged in sand chairs. They had everything but what they really needed—an effective sunscreen. Boomers are the ones who are now lamenting all those hours spent basking in the sun basted with tanning oils. They are paying the price with crepey skin, loss of moisture and tone, facial wrinkles and creases, and age spots, as well as more serious aftereffects, such as skin cancer.

Unhealthy Rays

Sunlight seems so inviting—young children are told to go play outdoors on sunny days, and people who are deprived of sunlight for long stretches can actually become clinically depressed. We even associate some warmth in our complexions, as opposed to pallor, as a sign of good health. And although it is true that the sun's rays do stimulate production of vitamin D, those rays can also harm our skin if we are exposed to them for too long or suffer severe sunburn.

Sunlight contains ultraviolet (UV) light, producing radiation that damages the elastin fibers in our skin, reducing its ability to move back into place after it is stretched. UV rays make skin more likely to bruise or tear and take longer to heal; it also affects the melanin—the pigment in the skin—causing dark spots. And as we age, cumulative exposure can cause abnormal skin cell development that results in pre-cancerous lesions like actinic keratosis and skin cancers. Unfortunately, much of this damage does not show up on young skin; it is not evident until later in life, when it is too late to take preventative measures. Frequent use of tanning beds can have similar negative effects.

Undo Some of the Harm

These are a number of natural treatments that can help restore sun-damaged skin.

- Apply lemon juice to age spots for 30 minutes or overnight. The alpha-hydroxy acid in lemons causes cell turnover in the skin.
- Apple cider vinegar and onion juice (strained through a cheesecloth) also have skin-lightening properties when applied for 30 minutes.
- Castor oil has anti-inflammatory properties and can be used directly on the scaly lesions known as actinic keratoses.
- Coconut oil makes an excellent moisturizer for dry, sun-worn skin.

There are also many soothing natural remedies for treating acute sunburn.

- Aloe vera contains 150 minerals, vitamins, and trace elements and makes an excellent treatment for sunburn. Simply cut a leaf off a plant, open it up lengthwise, and rub the gel over your skin for quick relief. Reapply as needed.
- Add one cup of anti-inflammatory, antioxidant ground oatmeal to your bathwater, or make a paste from the powdered oatmeal with a quarter cup of milk and three teaspoons of honey. Apply it to your skin for 15 minutes before rinsing off. Or mix oatmeal powder and honey with pureed papaya, which contains healing enzymes.

> **MAKE IT YOURSELF**
> ## Almond-Coconut Sunscreen
>
> This natural sunblock offers an SPF of 4 or 5 and will keep for six months.
>
> YOU WILL NEED:
> ½ cup almond oil
> ¼ cup coconut oil
> ¼ cup beeswax
> 2 tablespoons non-nano zinc oxide powder
>
> WHAT TO DO:
> - Combine the first three ingredients in a pint glass jar with a loose cover, and place in a saucepan of water over medium heat.
> - Stir occasionally, and as the ingredients melt together, add the powdered zinc oxide.
> - Stir well, cool, and store in the refrigerator.

- Create a paste of cooling cucumbers in the blender. Leave it on the affected area for 20 minutes, and then rinse off.
- The tannic acid found in tea can pull the heat from sunburned skin. Dip a cloth compress in cooled brewed tea, apply wet tea bags directly to your skin, or add tea to your bathwater.

Cucumber paste

- Apply a washcloth soaked in apple cider vinegar, which will decrease inflammation, to any areas of painful skin. Leave the washcloth on for several minutes, and then moisturize the area with coconut oil.
- Add a few teaspoons of baking soda to a bowl of water, and then dampen a washcloth with the mixture to make a compress. Baking soda will restore skin's natural pH and promote healing.

SUNBLOCK BASICS

A commercial sunscreen with an SPF—sun protection factor—of 15 should be sufficient to safeguard most body parts from UV radiation. For use on the face and for young children and fair-skinned adults, move up to SPF 30 or 45. Apply sunscreen at least 15 minutes before exposure, and reapply every two hours and after water sports. Skiers or winter sports enthusiasts also need to apply protection. Sunblocks may lose strength after three years, so pay attention to expiration dates.

FACIAL SKINCARE

REVITALIZE YOUR COMPLEXION WITH NATURAL CLEANSERS AND LOTIONS

Maintaining your skin's appearance is a significant part of good health practices, one that can offer psychological benefits as well. It's not only women who need to pay attention to facial care—men are exposed to just as many pollutants and weathering factors as women; those with outdoor jobs may also be at risk from sun damage.

Facial skincare is a billion-dollar industry globally, but there is no reason for you to further enrich cosmetic and skincare companies, not when so many ingredients for creating natural cleansers, toners, moisturizers, and masks are available right in your pantry. Honey, yogurt, oatmeal, cucumbers, avocados, olive oil, vinegar, and lemons can all be

> ### DID YOU KNOW?
>
> • *Hyperpigmentation, those unsightly brown age spots that appear on the face and body, occurs when sun exposure increases melanocyte cell production. Solutions for these spots include dabbing on aloe vera gel, castor oil, or red onion juice mixed with honey; applications of almond paste, mashed papaya, or lemon juice; and a buttermilk rinse.*

transformed into luxurious agents of beauty. Some of the following recipes may also require a visit to your local health food store to purchase essential oils or other ingredients, but your ultimate cost will still be below what you'd pay for a similar product in a high-end department store or boutique.

Healthy Solutions

Your daily routine—performed morning and night—should include three steps—cleansing, toning, and moisturizing. You should also hypermoisturize and exfoliate once a week and spot-treat wrinkles and signs of hyperpigmentation.

CLEANSE The first step of your daily facial skincare regimen is thoroughly cleansing and detoxifying your face. Try one of these options.

- Massage a tablespoon of antimicrobial coconut oil into the face and neck, and then wrap in a warm towel to open pores. After 30 seconds, clean with a damp washcloth.
- Massage a tablespoon of plain yogurt into face, leave on for three minutes, and then rinse off with warm water. Yogurt is rich in protein and lactic acid, which work together to clear toxins from the skin and remove dead skin cells.

TONE Your second step is toning. A facial toner acts as an astringent; it not only removes dirt, old makeup, and other impurities on the skin, it also tightens the pores. Apply toner to a cotton ball, and dab it lightly over your face, except near your eyes. Never tug at or pull on tender skin. A toner made of two parts water and one part apple cider vinegar will clear clogged pores and restore your skin's pH level to a near ideal 5.5.

Pelargonium graveolens, one of the many varieties of the geranium flower, is the source of the essential oil. This oil has long been used as a base for facial moisturizers.

RESCUE REMEDY: *This simple recipe will provide you with an effective toner or a refreshing warm weather splash. Combine ¼ cup cucumber juice, ¼ cup green tea, and an optional tablespoon of vodka in a glass bottle. Store in the refrigerator.*

MOISTURIZE The final step of your daily skincare regimen involves restoring moisture that has been stripped from your complexion by a dry climate, winter weather, or forced hot air–heating. Moist skin is supple, elastic, and resists wrinkles.

- If you suffer from acne, consider moisturizing with hemp, safflower, or rose hip oil; these contain high levels of linoleic acid, which protects the skin's surface.
- For extra-dry skin, massage your face with macadamia, wheat germ, almond, or avocado oil, and then cover with a warm towel before rinsing with tepid water. These oils are rich in the fatty acids and polyphenols that nourish skin and combat aging.

RESCUE REMEDY: *Olive oil makes an excellent moisturizer, especially for dry skin or overnight use. Its antioxidant properties reduce free radicals and soothe irritated or sunburned skin and help lighten dark spots. Mix ½ cup olive oil, ¼ cup vinegar, and ¼ cup water, and massage into face. Or try oil of geranium, once the beauty secret of Egyptian royalty, diluted in a carrier oil.*

EXFOLIATE AND REVITALIZE As a supplement to your daily skincare regimen, once a week indulge in a restorative facial mask to exfoliate dead skin cells or replenish moisture.

- To create an anti-inflammatory exfoliating facial scrub, combine a half cup ground oatmeal with enough kefir and honey to make a paste. Apply

Homemade facial skincare products crafted from common kitchen items like lemon and honey or almond and coconut oils can help you see the same results as commercial creams—and save you money.

the paste to your face, leave on for 10 minutes, and then rinse thoroughly with warm water.

- To revitalize your complexion, smooth on a mixture of two tablespoons honey and one teaspoon lemon juice; let it dry before rinsing. The citric acid in the lemon kills bacteria and exfoliates, while the antibacterial, antioxidant honey prevents acne and slows signs of aging.
- To create a customized hydrating mask, combine any of the following: smashed bananas, which are full of potassium and vitamins A and B; plain yogurt, which nourishes dry skin with calcium and live cultures; egg whites, which are high in collagen, proteins, and vitamin A; honey, which is antibacterial; and fragrant hydrating oils, such as almond, jojoba, and coconut.

SMOOTH LINES AND WRINKLES

Wrinkles and creases can begin appearing as early as our twenties. Fight back by drinking plenty of water and treating trouble spots with applications of aloe vera gel; fenugreek oil or a puree of the leaves; vitamin E oil; a mask of mashed banana, papaya, pineapple, or avocado; sliced cucumber; a paste of rice powder, rosewater, and milk; or crushed strawberries with honey.

HEALTHY HAIR AND NAILS

RESTORE LUSTER, STRENGTH, AND SUPPLENESS WITH NATURAL REMEDIES

Both hair and nails are composed of the same substance: a protein called keratin. Although the keratinized cells in hair and nails are not alive, conditioners and moisturizers can improve the appearance of keratin damaged by dryness, heat, or chemical processes.

Dry, lusterless, thinning hair and brittle, splitting nails can both be indications of an underlying health issue. Like our skin, hair and nails act as a gauge of our overall well-being. In some cases, disease is to blame—thyroid problems and psoriasis can cause brittle nails, and severe eating disorders can result in wispy, fragile hair. Fish that might contain high levels of mercury, such as swordfish, can cause hair loss. Age is also a factor: hair and nails do tend to dry out as we grow older, but that simply means that they require a bit more care.

Healthy Solutions

There are several approaches for improving hair and nails. In addition to applying topical preparations that lessen existing damage, you can seek out keratin-friendly foods and mineral supplements to ensure that new hair growth will be shiny and sleek

DID YOU KNOW?

• *Nail biting is a nervous habit that damages nails, nail beds, and cuticles—and looks unsightly to boot. Try wearing light cotton gloves at night or during times when you tend to chew your nails at home. The bitter flavor of neem oil can keep you from nibbling, as might a pretty coat of fresh polish you won't want to bite off.*

and emerging nails will be smooth and strong. You might also eliminate unhealthy habits like binging on sweets or smoking, which reduces circulation and affects the amount of biotin—a hair and nail strengthener—in the bloodstream.

DIETARY OPTIONS Avoiding foods that damage hair and nails is as critical as choosing healthy options. Sugar and highly sweetened foods make blood sugar spike, which causes the body to raise levels of insulin and increase levels of androgen—a male hormone that makes hair follicles shrink in men and women, leading to hair loss. High-glycemic foods, those quickly broken down into sugars, produce the same response, so avoid starchy white breads, pastas, and cakes. Ultra-high doses of vitamin A and some prescription medications can also trigger hair thinning.

Vegetarians who consume little protein may suffer from brittle nails and dry hair. Alternate sources of protein include beans, lentils, tofu, and spinach. Fortunately, many foods improve the condition of hair and nails. Pork, broccoli, wheat germ, and red peppers contain a particular amino acid that actually creates keratin. Foods rich in omega-3 fatty acids—such as salmon, mackerel, tuna, walnuts, flaxseed, and eggs—act as a boon to hair and nails by keeping the body's keratinocytes healthy. Dark leafy green vegetables, rich in vitamins A and C, promote production of sebum, your hair's natural conditioner.

KEY SUPPLEMENTS The minerals zinc and iron are essential for keratin formation. Tiny white spots under your nails are likely signs of a zinc deficiency. Both zinc and iron are found in meat and seafood; vegetarians can find them in kidney beans and spinach. Calcium, that builder of strong bones, is also

Tame dry hair and fly-away ends with olive oil. You can also soak your nails in warm olive oil before a DIY manicure.

Flaxseeds, also called linseeds, are the small, brown seeds of the flax plant *(Linum usitatissimum)*. They are rich in omega-3 fatty acids, which promote healthy hair and strong nails. Try tossing a couple of tablespoons into a smoothie.

the architect of strong nails and hair. In order to make sure calcium is absorbed properly, take a vitamin D supplement, or drink horsetail tea or eat raw almonds or a can of tuna daily. Magnesium, the antistress mineral, can help prevent hair loss and eliminate the uneven ridges that appear on stressed nails; snack on pumpkin seeds or dark chocolate. Biotin, also called vitamin H, is a hair and nail strengthener often prescribed for those suffering from alopecia, an autoimmune disorder characterized by hair loss. You can find biotin in bananas, beans, and lentils.

TOPICAL FIXES Forget the mind-numbing array of hair- and nail-care products at your local superstore—effective remedies await you in your pantry. Natural nail treatments include massaging them with warm olive or coconut oil, soaking them in horsetail tea, or soaking them in a half-and-half apple cider vinegar and water bath. You can also apply a mix of a half teaspoon of vitamin E and a few drops of tea tree oil. Leave on for 30 minutes, and then rinse off.

There are scores of natural hair treatments that you can easily whip up in your kitchen. Create a vitamin-rich 30-minute hair mask with crushed avocado and one egg; an egg can also be added to shampoo for additional luster. Soak hair with black or green tea for natural shine; leave in for 10 minutes before shampooing. Before and after swimming, protect your hair from salt water or chlorine with a spritz made of one part apple cider vinegar and three parts water. Stop hair loss by mixing two tablespoons honey and onion juice and massaging into scalp; leave in for 40 minutes before shampooing. To curb flyaway strands, mix a few drops of sandalwood oil and olive oil in your palms, and then sleek them over the ends of your hair.

RESCUE REMEDY: *Rejuvenate damaged hair with this moisturizing conditioner. Combine 1 teaspoon apple cider vinegar with 2 tablespoons olive oil and 3 egg whites. Work through hair, wrap in a shower cap or plastic wrap for 30 minutes, and then shampoo and rinse. This shower cap method also works with coconut, almond, and jojoba oils.*

Vegetable-dyed pumice stones. These volcanic stones are the natural product of molten lava mixing with water and then hardening. Use one to smooth away calluses—the porous texture creates an abrasive surface that sloughs away hard skin.

NATURAL FOOT CARE

KEEP YOUR TOOTSIES ON THEIR TOES AND WALK HAPPY

The health of our feet is critical to every task we perform while standing upright, and if our feet are painful or compromised, they cannot easily convey us through our busy lives. Our feet take a repeated pounding every day in sweaty, confining footgear—stressors that can cause skin problems, joint issues, and fungal infections. Women are four times more likely as men to develop foot problems, and the damage caused by restrictive high-heeled shoes is frequently to blame.

CALLUSES AND CORNS

Common calluses are pads of thick, hardened skin caused by rubbing, friction, or pressure. They can form anywhere, but tend to appear on the side of the foot or the sole; plantar calluses form on the bottom of the foot. Small hard patches with a plug of skin at the center are called hard corns; they occur on the tops of toes or the outer side of the little toe. Soft corns are whitish and rubbery and grow between the toes. Seed corns form in small, tender clusters; they can be very painful when they occur on a weight-bearing part of the foot.

Healthy Solutions

To remove calluses, soak your feet for 15 minutes in a mix of hot soapy water and a cup of apple cider vinegar. This mix should soften them enough so that you can file them away with a pumice stone.

To remove corns, you can dab them with castor oil, rub them with the liquid inside a vitamin E or A capsule and cover with a white cotton sock, or soak an onion slice in white vinegar and bandage the slice over your corn while you sleep. Repeat this procedure until the corns disappear.

> **DID YOU KNOW?**
>
> • *Finding shoes that fit properly is more than a comfort issue. Ill-fitting footwear can rub or create pressure, leading to blisters, calluses, and corns and also aggravate bunions. If you have extra-wide or narrow feet, don't simply go up or down a size—shop for custom-width shoes in specialty stores or online.*

BUNIONS

A bunion, or *hallux valgus,* is a bony, jutting deformity that occurs at the base joint of the big toe. As it grows, it forces the big toe toward the other toes. Studies show that bunion sufferers are more likely to experience pain in the hip, knee, lower back, and foot. These growths also effect balance and gait and can increase the risk of falls (and make finding comfortable shoes a real chore). Their cause is unclear: they may run in families or be a result of wearing shoes with high heels or narrow toes.

Healthy Solutions

There are several remedies for bunion pain or tenderness. You can massage the bunion with warm olive, castor, or coconut oil for 15 minutes twice a day. You can also make a paste of a half teaspoon turmeric mixed with a little oil or soak in a footbath with a handful of Epsom salts. To improve toe flexibility, sit on a chair and roll your bare foot over a tennis ball or interlace your fingers between your toes and move them back and forth, and then up and down.

ATHLETE'S FOOT

The fungal infection known as tinea pedis is not restricted to the locker room. The main fungus that causes athlete's foot, *Trichophyton mentagrophytes,* will flourish in almost any moist, warm environment, even under your toenails. Symptoms include itching, stinging, and burning between the toes; painful blisters; peeling skin; white or scaly patches; and discolored or thick toenails. It is also contagious.

Healthy Solutions

For starters, always wearing flip-flops in wet places like public pools and locker rooms. To treat the symptoms,

Azadirachta indica, known as neem, nimtree, and Indian lilac. The oil pressed from the fruits and seeds of this plant can help relieve the symptoms of athlete's foot.

place slices of fresh garlic, a fungicide, between your toes for a day; apply neem oil to afflicted areas; or bathe feet in oregano tea or fresh ginger tea. Place baking soda in your shoes, dust on a layer of absorbent cornstarch before putting on your socks, and use a lemon juice and water rinse to control odor.

RESCUE REMEDY: *Treat outbreaks of athlete's foot with a footbath containing ½ cup apple cider vinegar and 2 tablespoons sea salt, and soak for 10 minutes. You can also add 40 drops of tea tree oil to your footbath.*

RELIEVE INGROWN TOENAILS

Onychocryptosis is a painful condition that causes the corner or side of the nail to grow into the skin of the big toe. It may be caused by genetics, trauma, athletics, bunions, improper trimming, fungal infections, or pressure from tight shoes. Try softening nails in an Epsom salts or castile soap bath for 20 minutes, and then gently push back swollen skin, and trim the nail straight across. Or place a length of dental floss under the nail to encourage growth in the proper direction.

CHAPTER 2

SOOTHE EMOTIONAL STRESS

Introduction
KEEP YOUR COOL
EASE BACK FROM DAILY PRESSURES AND EMOTIONAL ANXIETIES

Most of us who live in this fast-paced, complex world feel weighted down at times, overwhelmed by responsibilities to our families, jobs, and friends. We feel a nagging need to be the best we can be, to adhere to the edict, "never let them see you sweat." All this unrelenting pressure takes a cumulative toll on our health. Yet, many people shrug it off, getting by with food eaten on the run, cursory healthcare, and limited sleep. No wonder so many of us are battling—or trying unsuccessfully to ignore—the physical and mental fatigue brought on by stress.

Stress is the body's natural response to demands or threats—allowing us to prepare for a crisis with an energized response. Biologically, imminent danger releases a flood of stress hormones, including adrenaline and cortisol, throughout the body. Muscles tighten, the heart pounds, breath quickens, and blood pressure rises. Senses sharpen. In effect, you are now prepped with increased strength and stamina and a speedy reaction time. In small amounts, stress can be a performance enhancer or motivational tool. If accumulated stress is left untreated, however, it can have a very real physical impact. Studies have linked excess stress to heart disease, headaches, pain disorders, digestive disorders, autoimmune disease, eczema, ulcers, and reproductive issues.

We are also at risk for the psychological or mental effects of stress. Cognitive symptoms may include memory loss, fuzzy thinking, poor judgment, the inability to concentrate, and negative thinking. Emotional problems may manifest as moodiness, unhappiness, agitation, and feelings of isolation. If left unaddressed, emotional stress can escalate into chronic psychological problems such as anxiety, panic disorder, and depression. It can result in eating disorders like food addiction, bulimia, and anorexia. Unchecked stress can also lead to destructive habits like chain smoking, binge drinking, drug abuse, and compulsive gambling.

Recognize and Reduce Stress

One key aspect of coping with stress is recognizing when you are becoming stressed and taking steps to ease back from it. Learn to distinguish between normal, relatively low-impact daily stress—fractious kids or a cranky boss—and the kind that overloads your circuits—an IRS audit or serious family illness. Understand the factors that may exacerbate your reactions to stress. Finally, seek out ways to control stress, and investigate lifestyle changes that can lower stress levels. These include a balanced diet, regular exercise, mediation, acupuncture (which releases pleasure-inducing endorphins into the system), sensory therapy to stay grounded, and a support network of family and friends. You also need to look out for markers that your stress levels have gotten too high: sleeplessness, say, or a craving for carbs.

In the following chapter you will learn about the different manifestations of stress—insomnia, anxiety, depression, and smoking and other addictions—and how to address them with natural, healthy solutions.

(LEFT) Many herbs, such as rosemary, lavender, thyme, mint, and basil, can help relieve stress.

(OPPOSITE PAGE) Sharing a healthy meal with a friend can nourish both body and soul. If you do experience a low period, look to friends and family for comfort.

MAINTAIN MENTAL HEALTH

OVERCOME THE EMOTIONAL TOLL OF ANXIETY AND DEPRESSION

For most people, nervous agitation, moods swings, and the feeling of having "the blues" are a normal part of life. Yet, if they linger for weeks or months, these feelings can eventually lead to serious and debilitating psychological conditions such as anxiety disorders and depression. Thankfully, there are natural remedies that can help you beat the blues.

DID YOU KNOW?

- *One cup of unsalted pumpkin seeds consumed over the course of a day—sprinkled on cereal, then tossed with a salad or mixed with olive oil as a topping for baked fish—supplies an optimum amount of healthy fats and magnesium, both of which can improve your mood.*

ANXIETY

Anxiety is the body's normal reaction to stressful situations, making us pay attention and alerting us to dangers. But when anxiety, especially over the future, becomes excessive or turns to fear or panic, it becomes an anxiety disorder. It is calculated that 30 percent of adults will experience an anxiety disorder at some point in their lives. The classification of disorders includes general anxiety, panic, phobias, social anxiety, and separation anxiety.

Washing roots of the ashwagandha plant. Ashwagandha is an adaptogenic herb—a group of herbal ingredients used to improve the health of the body's adrenal system.

Healthy Solutions:

Anxiety disorders are traditionally treated with medication and counseling or therapy, yet there are natural substances that can also help to ease your sense of dread and calm your free-floating thoughts. The herb ashwagandha *(Withania somnifera)* reduces stress and eases the symptoms of anxiety. Kava *(Piper methysticum)* relieves panic attacks and calms anxiety; take 200 to 250 mg three times daily. The amino acid GABA acts to ease anxiety and is a muscle relaxer; take 500 mg three times daily. The calming neurotransmitter 5-HTP increases serotonin. Take 50 to 100 mg twice daily, but not with any prescription antianxiety meds.

LAVENDER The essential oil of a variety of lavender species (genus *Lavendula*) has been shown to reduce the symptoms of anxiety and depression.

> RESCUE REMEDY: *Place three drops of soothing lavender oil into your palms, and rub it onto your neck; or try a few drops of Roman chamomile oil to help you de-stress and calm down.*

DEPRESSION

A serious medical condition, depression—also known as major depressive disorder—allows negative thoughts to influence how you think, act, and feel. Causes can be chemical (an imbalance or lack of mood-elevating endorphins, such as serotonin, dopamine, and epinephrine), genetic (likely to run in families), personality based (especially for those with low self-esteem), or environmental (the result of neglect, violence, or abuse). The World Health Organization estimates that more than 300 million people worldwide suffer from this disorder, which is a leading cause of disability.

Healthy Solutions

As with anxiety, in addition to medication, psychological counseling is often advised for depression. This is not something anyone should be ashamed to consider. At this critical time, your therapist will become a valued member of your support team, helping you cope with emotional issues that could derail your normal life. These two tools can also be augmented with a number of natural aids and healthful diet decisions.

MOOD-ELEVATING FOODS Seek out foods that raise serotonin levels in the brain. These include coldwater fish like tuna and salmon that supply omega-3 fatty acids; healthy fats such as coconut and flaxseed oil; and eggs.

CAFFEINE-FREE BEVERAGES Although that jolt of caffeine might initially perk up your mood, you will quickly crash. Studies show that caffeine can affect serotonin synthesis in the brain: 5-HIA, a component of serotonin, has been found in the urine of coffee drinkers. Opt for decaffeinated coffee or herbal teas if you are feeling down.

GREEN TEA Try green tea as your morning drink. It does contain caffeine but also L-theanine, which works synergistically with caffeine, elevating your mood without that crashing effect afterward. L-theanine also reduces stress and boosts dopamine levels.

CHAMOMILE TEA Consider drinking this herbal tea later in the day. Sleeplessness is often a by-product of emotional distress, and chamomile (both *Matricaria recutita* and *Chamaemelum nobile*) contains a flavonoid that offers relaxing properties. Sipping a cup near bedtime with a bit of milk and honey should soon send you to dreamland.

ST. JOHN'S WORT A shrubby herb, St. John's wort *(Hypericum perforatum)* has been used for nervous disorders since the time of ancient Greece. It contains hypericin, a substance that appears to affect neurotransmitters in a manner similar to

> ### LET THERE BE LIGHT
>
> In winter, many people in northern climates—and especially women—suffer from seasonal affective disorder (SAD), a form of depression brought on by lack of sunlight. Sunlight is normally received by the retina, which transfers impulses to the hypothalamus to properly regulate our body clocks. During dark months, however, this sequence can be disrupted. Fortunately, specialized lights that are designed to provide a balanced spectrum of light similar to standing outside on a spring day are now available. This exposure to light reactivates the brain's circadian rhythms, which regulate human sleep cycles. And better sleep means a lower chance of depression.

selective serotonin reuptake inhibitors (SSRIs) such as Prozac or Paxil, which raise serotonin levels in the brain. It may interact with some medications, so check with your doctor first.

MAGNESIUM This mineral is critical to good mental health: it increases energy, synthesizes RNA and DNA, and stabilizes brain chemistry.

> RESCUE REMEDY: *Try adding magnesium-rich foods to your diet to improve mood and outlook: an ounce of dry-roasted almonds; ½ cup of black beans or boiled spinach, one medium banana, or 1 cup of soy milk.*

B VITAMINS The complex of B vitamins, especially B12 and B6, combat stress and produce endorphins in the brain. Adults with digestive disorders and some vegetarians may have difficulty getting enough. Try supplements, or increase your intake of B-rich foods like mackerel, turkey, cheese, shellfish, and spinach.

St. John's wort

Insomnia is not just a nuisance—a good night's sleep is essential for both physical and mental health.

INSOMNIA RELIEF
RESTORE NORMAL SLEEP PATTERNS AND REST EASY

Sleep provides humans with more than a rest at the end of the day. Countless studies have shown that getting adequate sleep plays a vital role in metabolism, memory, learning, and immunity function. Sleep is so necessary to your well-being, that your body regulates it the same way it does eating, drinking, and breathing.

Insomnia—an inability to fall asleep, remain asleep, or awaken refreshed—is a common sleep disorder. Over time, it can affect quality of life and job performance. Most adults need between eight to seven hours of sleep nightly, but a range of factors can cause these numbers to decrease, sometimes drastically. Sleep "bandits" include stress, anxiety, trauma, indigestion, pain, alcohol, caffeine, lack of physical activity, medications, hormonal changes, restless leg syndrome, and sleep apnea.

Healthy Solutions

Many people take prescription sleep aids for insomnia, but these are often habit-forming. The good news is that by changing your routine—and

> **DID YOU KNOW?**
>
> • *While you sleep, any fresh information you received that day is consolidated into your brain's long-term memory. So make sure to get a good night's sleep not only before studying or attending a critical lecture, but also after learning something new.*

opting for natural cures—you can gain control over your sleep issues. For instance, working out in the early evening will tire your body so that fretful thoughts do not intrude on your sleep cycle. Exercise also triggers an increase in body temperature, and the subsequent drop in temperature is believed to promote sleep.

TRYPTOPHAN There's an old adage that says, "First we eat, then we sleep," and it's certainly true that after a hearty meal our instinct is to nap. This is because the pancreas produces insulin during digestion, which in turn triggers the action of tryptophan, an essential amino acid in the brain that causes sleepiness. So try a bedtime snack to induce sleep, but keep it light—a glass of milk or a small piece of cheese—to avoid gas or bloating.

MELATONIN For years, scientists believed this hormone, which regulates sleep and wakefulness, was produced only by our pineal glands. We now know this natural sleep aid can be found in oats, sweet corn, barley, rice, ginger, and bananas. A bowl of oatmeal or a banana at bedtime will boost your melatonin and help you sleep.

VITAMINS AND MINERALS Studies show that a diet rich in certain vitamins and minerals is beneficial to maintaining sleep patterns.

- The B vitamins, which regulate many amino acids including tryptophan, can reduce insomnia; niacin in particular makes tryptophan work more efficiently.
- Individuals low in copper or iron often have trouble falling asleep. Try adding seafood to your diet—20 steamed clams offer 139 percent of your Daily Value (DV) of iron and 31 percent of your DV of copper. Lentils, nuts, and whole grains are also good sources of both minerals.
- Magnesium is another essential sleep nutrient that keeps the brain from overstimulation; find it in pinto and navy beans, spinach, Swiss chard, almonds, soybeans, and pumpkin seeds.

CHAMOMILE The flowering herb chamomile, both the Roman (Chamaemelum nobile) and German (Matricaria recutita) varieties, has been used for millennia to bring on sleep. Chamomile not only offers the healing properties of volatile oils and flavonoids, chamomile produces mildly sedative and muscle-relaxing benefits, acting as it does on the same parts of the brain and nervous system as antianxiety medications.

RESCUE REMEDY: *Brew a chamomile tea to foster relaxation, or add the essential oil to a bath as an aromatherapy agent and muscle relaxant. Add 10 drops of essential oil to a warm bath, and soak for five minutes before bedtime.*

VALERIAN This perennial flowering herb has been used since ancient times to treat insomnia and nervous disorders. It may even help to lower blood pressure in some cases. Valerian (Valeriana officinalis) works as a calming agent by increasing the levels of an amino acid neurotransmitter—gamma-amino butyric

acid (GABA)—in the brain, which then inhibits nerve transmissions and eases nervous activity.

RESCUE REMEDY: *To make valerian tea, pour 1 cup of boiling water over 1 teaspoon (2 to 3 grams) of dried valerian root and steep for 5 to 10 minutes. If sleep improves, continue with the tea for at least a month.*

BEDROOM MAKEOVER To help promote restful sleep, turn your bedroom into a sleep-friendly haven. Keep nighttime temperatures on the cool side. Hang room-darkening shades. Obscure any sources of light, like blinking laptop lights or luminous clocks. Change your pillows frequently, and use a mattress cover to avoid potential allergens. Use foam earplugs to reduce noise and a sleep mask to reduce light.

WHITE NOISE White noise is a random signal that has equal density at different frequencies, so consider a white noise machine to block out intrusive thoughts as you fall asleep. Or look into an ambient sound machine, which replicates the soothing sounds of rain, wind, traffic, the surf, and babbling streams. A quick noise-masking solution is to place a fan set on medium near your bed, but not blowing directly on you as you sleep.

Dried root of the valerian plant. Studies show that valerian root may reduce the amount of time it take you to fall asleep and once you are asleep, it allows you to sleep better.

Up Close
SOOTHING STRATEGIES
CREATE AN AURA OF CALM WITH TEAS, TISANES, AND A SPECIAL SPACE

You can choose from a vast array of herbs and spices when creating medicinal teas and tisanes.

You can shrug off stress and find peace and tranquility at home by treating yourself to teas and tisanes—a tisane is simply an herbal tea—and then enjoying them in a retreat of your own creation. You might want to designate a corner of a room for meditation or curl up in a comfortable chair near a window and sip your tea slowly, freeing your mind of troubling thoughts as you gaze outside or thumb through a picture book.

Steep Away Stress

Recent research shows that drinking certain teas can calm your nerves and relieve stress. This is due to two natural compounds: L-theanine, an amino acid found only in tea, and catechin, a flavonoid phytochemical found in green tea and, to a lesser extent, black tea. If you prefer caffeine-free brews, there are plenty of herbal tisanes, like valerian, lemon balm, or passionflower to soothe you.

Refresh Your Home

Your external setting is nearly as important as any internal remedy you ingest. Along with physical chaos, clutter can result in chaotic thoughts, weighing you down even when you are miles from home. If your living space is a bit of a disaster at the

A small investment in some luxury bath items like sea salts, essential oils, fluffy towels, and scented soap can turn your bathroom into a soothing retreat.

moment, here are some tips for cleaning up your act. Several suggestions incorporate feng shui—the Asian art of creating harmonious environments.

- To begin the decluttering process, label three boxes KEEP, GIVE AWAY, and THROW AWAY, and then sort your stuff into them. Toss out anything in the last box the same day you do the sorting, so that there's no chance to change your mind.
- Remove any objects that are blocking your doorways and find them a home.
- Color can affect mood and attitude. To create a calming space, change out any brightly colored throw pillows or area rugs for ones in soft, understated hues. Avoid reds and oranges, and think gentle neutrals like taupe and beige or muted pastel blues and greens.
- Find a space in one room large enough for a yoga mat, and dedicate this spot to meditation, yoga, or breathing exercises. Add incense, a small fountain, wind chimes, or an MP3 player with appropriately soothing music.
- Add large plants to your living areas. They release oxygen, neutralize off-gases from many products, and provide a sense of serenity.

- Do a "memory cleanse." If certain objects in your home have negative associations—photos of your ex, say, or a gift from a relative you dislike—remove them from sight.
- Conversely, display artwork, photos, or travel mementos that give your morale a boost.

Don't Forget the Bathroom

Turn your bathroom, however humble, into a day spa with the addition of bath sheets in subtle colors and mood lighting—like safe, flameless candles. Stock a tray with bath salts, hand-made soaps, and herbal shampoos and conditioners. Pamper yourself with an extra-soft bathrobe and comfy slippers. Give yourself a facial, a hot-oil hair treatment, or a pedicure, or linger in an Epsom salts bath for a restorative soak.

MAKE IT YOURSELF
Blended Tisane

Herbal tisanes don't have to be bland or medicinal—not if you prepare your own custom blends using a mix of herbs, spices, peel, bark, or fruit. Experiment until you find the blend that best suits your palette. These mixtures not only offer calming properties, they also offer piquant scents and delightful flavors. Pour them into a tall glass of ice cubes to enjoy them as delicious summer teas, too.

FOR A WARM AND SPICY BLEND, COMBINE TWO OR MORE OF THESE HERBS AND SPICES:
- twisted citrus peel or sliced ginger
- cinnamon stick, cloves, or cardamom
- vanilla bean, carob, or star anise
- rose hips or rose petals
- dried goji berries or dried mango

FOR A CRISP AND LIGHT BLEND, COMBINE TWO OR MORE OF THESE HERBS:
- dried mint or a handful of mint leaves
- dried valerian or red rooibos
- dried lemongrass or lemon verbena
- chamomile or passionflower
- dried lavender or calendula flowers
- dried bee balm leaves or flower

WHAT TO DO:
- Warm the teapot and cup first, and use a strainer to allow the ingredients to expand.
- Use roughly 2 teaspoons of mixture to 12 ounces of water, and steep for at least three minutes. Sweeten with honey if desired.

HEALTHY WEIGHT SOLUTIONS
REVERSE WEIGHT GAIN WITH SMART DIET AND EXERCISE CHOICES

Many of us who struggle to eliminate extra pounds find ourselves in the rebound-diet revolving door—where the weight comes off and then goes right back on again. The fact is, we need to change the way we eat every day, not just while dieting. Once sensible, healthy eating habits are established, they often become second nature. Our weight begins to regulate itself, and weight battles become small skirmishes.

Weight gain occurs when there is an increase in body fluid, muscle mass, or fat. An excessive weight gain resulting in more than 30.0 on the body mass index (BMI), which measures body fat based on height and weight, is considered obesity. An obese person is at high risk for heart disease, circulatory and digestive problems, diabetes, and many other

ailments. Obesity can be the result of poor diet and exercise choices, hormonal fluctuations, or genetic factors. Other possible culprits include a lack of sleep, which can leave us feeling less full after eating; the stress hormone cortisol, which increases our appetites when we feel pressure; depression (and certain antidepressants); an underactive thyroid, which slows metabolism; and quitting smoking, which increases food cravings and also slows metabolism. Menopause may lead to weight gain due to reduced activity and more "mood eating," and it can also redistribute fat around the waist.

Healthy Solutions

The fat in our bodies is considered stored energy, with calories being the measure of that potential energy. To lose weight, we need to expend more calories, or energy, than we take in; this causes the body to draw on its fat cell reserves, ultimately shrinking them. In consideration of this, weight-control programs typically take a two-pronged approach—the establishment of a lean, balanced diet and the inclusion of a regimented exercise program.

There is also a third factor for successful weight loss: lowering stress, which is one of the reasons people overeat, binge on junk food, or become chronically sedentary. One of the best ways to decrease daily stress is by admitting that it is there. We have a tendency to ignore it—at our peril, unfortunately. So acknowledge the stress, change your lifestyle to reduce the stressors, and deal with whatever is left over through exercise, meditation, and yoga or by taking up a relaxing hobby like knitting, puzzles, singing, or bird watching.

Dietary guidelines for losing weight recommend five or six small meals a day, providing most of the

A cup of cinnamon and star anise tea can help you lose weight by depressing appetite, eliminating retained fluids, burning fat, and balancing blood sugar.

calories come from grains, vegetables, and fruits, low-fat dairy, lean meat, poultry, and fish. Coconut oil makes a useful appetite suppressant; take one teaspoon before a meal to help cut portions. To maintain gut flora and process food more smoothly, resulting in fewer pounds, eat plain yogurt flavored with honey for breakfast or dessert. To aid digestion and reduce the production of fat cells, dilute the juice from half a lemon with a half cup of water and sprinkle with black pepper; drink after one meal every day. To burn off pounds, try green tea or exotic yerba mate tea made from the caffeine-rich leaves of *Ilex paraguariensis,* a South American holly tree.

RESCUE REMEDY: *Teas are a great choice to curb food cravings—they take the edge off your appetite and are easy to prepare. Try adding the following ingredients to a cup of boiling water: one cinnamon stick (or 1 teaspoon of ground cinnamon) and ½ teaspoon of star anise to balance blood sugar and depress appetite; 1 teaspoon green tea with ½ teaspoon ground ginger (or ½ inch of fresh grated ginger) to boost metabolism; 1 teaspoon chopped ginseng to increase energy; 1 teaspoon each of dried dandelion leaves and peppermint leaves for liver health; or a handful of chopped sage or 2 teaspoons dried sage to lower stress.*

You don't need elaborate gym equipment for your weight-loss regimen—a floor mat, resistance bands, and handheld dumbbells should suffice at first. Fat-burning strength moves, like squats, lunges, and curls, will shed weight, speed up metabolism, and increase muscle mass. (Enlarged muscles burn more calories, even after your workout ends.) You will then incorporate aerobic—cardiovascular—training, like walking, jogging, or bicycling, which elevates the heart rate, increases circulation, and boosts metabolism. More advanced gym workouts can allow you to target major muscles, but skip the boring 30-minute

UNDERSTAND EATING DISORDERS

Some people with abnormal eating habits may actually be suffering from a psychological disorder. These may include anorexia nervosa, involving inadequate food intake and fear of weight gain; bulimia nervosa, the consumption of large quantities of food followed by forced purging; and binge-eating disorder, consuming large amounts of food while feeling out of control and ashamed. Eating disorders evoke extreme emotions, and they may even be life threatening, so they require the care of a doctor or therapist.

treadmill or elliptical work; instead, try out a variety of "action" tools—barbells, kettlebells, battle ropes, BOSU and balance balls, and wobble boards.

RESCUE REMEDY: *This simple strength workout should be performed three times a week. Combine 20 body-weight squats, 20 walking lunges, 10 dumbbell (or milk jug) rows; a 30-second plank, and 30 jumping jacks, and repeat three times. Follow with a low-intensity cardio workout, such as walking or swimming for 30 minutes. You can gradually work up to interval cardio training, alternating periods of working out at different intensities.*

Taking classes like yoga or Pilates can help you regulate your weight in three ways: first by supplying you with a toning workout; second, by helping you to lower stress levels; and third, by plugging you into a supportive network.

KICK THE HABIT

NATURAL AND BEHAVIORAL AIDS TO HELP YOU QUIT SMOKING

Smoking the dried leaf of the tobacco plant was practiced as early as 5000 B.C. in the Americas. In the 16th century, tobacco traveled to the Old World, introduced to France from Spain by diplomat Jean Nicot, who lent his name to the actual plant, *Nicotiana tabacum.* Medicinal benefits were soon ascribed to tobacco— healing and drying, specifically—and smoking it quickly caught on worldwide. Centuries passed, and the tobacco industry flourished, especially in the American South. With the advent of cigarette-making machines in the late 1800s, fashionable people, including women, began to smoke in increasing numbers. Yet the early 20th century saw another statistical rise, a surprising increase in lung cancer, a previously rare disease.

Alas, modern smokers now understand the deadly effects of smoking, which is the leading cause of preventable illness in the United States. Cigars, cigarettes, and pipe and chewing tobacco all contain addictive nicotine, plus tar and carbon monoxide— more than 4,000 chemicals in total and 43 known cancer-causing agents. Even "natural" tobacco cigarettes with no commercial additives contain dozens of known carcinogens.

Damage from smoke inhalation can range from shortness of breath and wheezing, to COPD, emphysema, heart disease, and lung cancer.

It's not easy to quit smoking or give up other tobacco products, but the health benefits are well worth the effort.

> ### DID YOU KNOW?
>
> • *While you are quitting, it is critical to avoid others who smoke, not only in public spaces but also at home. Create a smoke-free zone, and post* NO SMOKING *signs in each room, on your deck or patio, and in your car. These signs will not only deter others, they will also remind you of your new healthy agenda.*

Healthy Solutions

Smoking cigarettes (or cigars) is not just about enjoying the taste of tobacco. There are psychological "rushes" and calming physical rituals associated with the act. Therefore it is not only the physical addiction to nicotine you must face, but also the loss of these pleasurable feelings and soothing rituals. Once you have determined to quit, however, there are plenty of proven remedies that can assist you. Some are behavioral aids; others are natural substances that will ease your transition from smoker to ex-smoker.

QUITTING GUIDELINES Follow these steps to get yourself mentally prepped for the big smoke-out.

- Make a list of the things you like about smoking. Then make a list of the reasons why quitting will be difficult—and think up a remedy for each one. If you write, "Nicotine is an addictive drug," counter with "There are replacements that allow me to withdraw gradually." For "Smoking helps me de-stress," write down "I will walk for 10 minutes when I feel pressured."

- Pick a quitting date, mark it on the calendar, and then write down all your reasons—including names of people—for making this decision.

- Carry only a few cigarettes with you in a small tin so you won't always have a supply on hand when the urge hits.

- To avoid the jitters, reduce caffeine intake for at least two months after quitting.

- Keep a smoking log to study when the craving most often hits. That way, when you quit you will know to distract yourself at those times. As alternative activities you can chew gum, walk, bike, bake, garden, craft, knit, play solitaire, meditate, have sex, or take a nap.

- Make sure you're in a good place mentally when you quit. If you're stressed or anxious, your cravings will increase.
- Change your diet to include plenty of fruits and vegetables, which can actually make cigarettes taste unpleasant.
- Give away any paraphernalia that reminds you of smoking—ashtrays, lighters, and match holders.
- Carry healthy snacks like carrot sticks, trail mix, pistachio nuts, sunflower seeds, or sugar-free gum or lozenges to replace cigarettes.
- After you quit, fill a jar with the money you are saving by not buying cigarettes. Then treat yourself to something nice you've always wanted—a mountain bike, spa weekend, high-end cookware, or garden fountain.
- Ultimately, gives yourself props: what you are doing may be great for your health, but at the same time it can be very difficult.

NATURAL ALLIES These herbal or natural aids should become part of your quitting protocol.

- Meditate or practice yoga or tai chi to regulate stress hormones and improve willpower.
- Try acupressure or acupuncture to the ear, which can curb the urge to smoke and ease withdrawal.
- Supplement with vitamins A, C, and E to expel toxins and reboot your system, making it easier to combat your urge to smoke.
- Take ginger capsules or tea to soothe the nausea you might feel as a result of quitting.
- Add a spoonful of ginseng powder to juices, cereal, or soup to suppress cravings.
- Try kava, St. John's wort, lemon balm, and lavender if quitting leads to insomnia.

- Take ginseng or ashwagandha if you feel your energy is flagging.
- Stay hydrated. Water acts as a detoxifier, flushing nicotine from your system and helping to counteract its harmful effects. For a potent detox, try grape juice. Its acids have the same cleansing results as water, but will work in less time.

RESCUE REMEDY: *Try this refreshing grape-cranberry slushie as a morning detox. Just combine ½ cup of frozen cranberries, ¾ cup of concord grape frozen juice concentrate, and ½ cup cold water in a blender or bullet.*

Try a cranberry-grape slushie to help cleanse your system.

COPING WITH ADDICTION

Those who are addicted to substances other than cigarettes, like drugs and alcohol, or are compulsively drawn to gambling, sex, shopping, or food, have found great solace and support—and many solutions—while attending group sessions lead by experienced therapists or reformed addicts. There are the 12-step recovery programs first popularized by Alcoholics Anonymous, as well as SMART, S.O.S., or Moderation Management programs. It is important to find a group that feels right for you. Your ability to remain clean in great part depends on the trust you have in your sponsors, mentors, and fellow group members.

CHAPTER 3

PREGNANCY AND INFANT HEALTH

Introduction
NATURAL CHOICES
GUIDELINES FOR PRENATAL HEALTH, DELIVERY, AND INFANT CARE

The nine months of pregnancy and the year that follows, of caring for and bonding with your new baby, are some of the most precious times in a mother's—and father's— life. And in spite of all the scientific advances that have been made to ensure that both mother and child are at low risk before, during, and after labor, many moms-to-be still yearn for something more personal, more enriching, as they prepare to give birth. The good news is that you now have options, alternatives to the formal clinical settings that were once de rigueur, including family-style rooms and birthing centers. These are part of the natural childbirth movement that first gained popularity in the 1960s and '70s and continues today.

Since the dawn of time, childbirth has been a most natural occurrence, but also one fraught with pain and risk. In aid of that, healers, shamans, and wise women created healing tonics from the ingredients they gathered from larder and woodland to ward off morning sickness, cramping, and early contractions and to ease birth itself. Some of these remedies are still being used today. In fact, it is during pregnancy that many women first seek out natural medicines, mainly because so many prescription drugs must be avoided. It's not surprising that even after the baby is born, these women continue to investigate natural options for themselves, their infants, and their families. Midwives, too, those trusted members of medieval communities who assisted women throughout their pregnancies—often with better success than early doctors—have again

become valued prenatal caretakers. There are also trained birthing assistants, called doulas, that you can enlist to ease your labor.

One thing that doctors and midwives know to be true is that every pregnancy is unique. As long as you have settled on a well-thought-out, holistic plan for your pregnancy and delivery, one that includes a medical backup in the case of complications, you should be able to face the upcoming birth with a sense of expectation and wonder. And once your bundle of joy is at home, you can continue to employ natural methods to treat minor infant ailments, like colic, teething pain, and diaper rash.

Herbs and Substances to Avoid
The majority of herbs and natural ingredients mentioned in the following chapter are beneficial and safe, but there are a number of medicinal herbs that pregnant women should avoid. Abortifacients, herbs that can induce miscarriage, include tansy, safflower, rue, mugwort, yarrow, Scotch broom, angelica, wormwood, and essential oil of pennyroyal. Teratogens, which can cause birth defects, include lupine, nicotiana, and sorghum, as well as alcohol. Alkaloids, chemical compounds that have diverse physiological effects on humans, include comfrey, borage, barberry, coltsfoot, goldenseal, and Oregon grape. Phytoestrogens, plant compounds that mimic hormones and may impact fetal development include soybeans, hops, red clover, and isoflavone extracts. If you are not sure if an herb or essential oil is safe, check first with your physician.

(LEFT) Herbs like mint are safe for pregnant women, but always check with your healthcare provider before using any natural remedy.

(OPPOSITE PAGE) From homemade foods to cloth diapers, parents have many natural options for baby care.

THE THREE TRIMESTERS

LEARN TO NURTURE YOURSELF AND YOUR GROWING BABY

While you are pregnant you will likely be mindful of what you are eating and drinking in terms of your baby's health. That is why a natural approach to diet and nutrition is especially important at this time. You will want to be sure you are consuming safe, wholesome, nutrient-rich foods and critical minerals as well as avoiding overprocessed, sugary, salty, or packaged foods.

During each of your three trimesters, specific fetal developments occur, and your own and your baby's nutritional requirements will change. By paying attention to these differing criteria, you can be assured of experiencing fewer digestive issues and potential health complications. Of course, this will all be unfamiliar terrain to new mothers, but keep in mind that women who follow through on prenatal care have healthier babies, with better outcomes, than women who don't.

FIRST TRIMESTER

This trimester extends from your last period through to week 12 of your pregnancy. Hormone levels change significantly at this time, your uterus begins

> **DID YOU KNOW?**
>
> • *The current wisdom is that pregnant women should avoid alcohol, which may lead to fetal alcohol syndrome, but some doctors believe a glass of red wine twice a week can be beneficial. A recent study showed that the offspring of moms-to-be who drank wine experienced better mental health than the kids of the moms who abstained.*

to enlarge, and your body increases its blood supply to support the circulation to the growing baby. You may suffer fatigue, morning sickness, headaches, and constipation, and your heart rate may also elevate.

Healthy Solutions

Treat constipation with prune juice, flaxseed, coffee, and fiber-rich foods. You can also double your water intake. Take folic acid supplements to facilitate fetal development—and start a year before conception if possible. Stop smoking and reduce alcohol consumption. This is when the risk of miscarriage is highest, so avoid harmful substances, follow a healthy diet, and take all your recommended supplements. Finally, check that none of your regular medications could impact the pregnancy.

SECOND TRIMESTER

This phase lasts from week 13 to week 27 and is considered the most comfortable trimester. Leg cramps, varicose veins, backache, and heartburn may surface, however. This is also when your baby will start moving and can recognize voices. At around week 20, an ultrasound scan will measure and assess the baby's organs and determine its gender. You should be tested for gestational diabetes around week 26 to 28.

Healthy Solutions

Treat leg cramps by taking a warm Epsom salts bath, icing the cramped leg, and making sure your electrolytes are balanced. Ease heartburn by chewing and swallowing fennel seeds or drinking ginger tea, or lemon water. Sometimes it helps to eat your main meal at midday. As for backaches, many pregnant women report that using a body pillow or pregnancy pillow to cradle or cushion them relieves back pain and eases other discomforts.

Iced ginger tea with lemon. Both ginger and lemon can help combat morning sickness and soothe an upset stomach.

Regular exercise, such as a daily 20-minute walk, can help you maintain a healthy weight. Walking can also relax your upper GI tract to help keep nausea at bay.

THIRD TRIMESTER

The final trimester runs from week 28 to birth of your baby. Weight gain at this time is normal—14 to 25 pounds, on average—but don't allow yourself to blossom too much. Those extra pounds will be harder to take off later, and an excess weight gain during pregnancy puts you at risk for complications like high blood pressure, preeclampsia, C-section delivery, and preterm birth. During this phase, your obstetrician will check your urine for protein, monitor your blood pressure and fetal heart rate, and check your hands and feet for swelling. The doctor will also determine fetal position and examine your cervix to see how your body is preparing for childbirth. This is also the perfect time to study up on labor and delivery or to join a birthing class with your partner.

Healthy Solutions

To curb weight gain, walk whenever possible; drink plenty of water; count calories (your onboard passenger requires only 50 calories a day during the first trimester and 300 a day at the end of the third); and eat lots of fiber—yellow and green vegetables and whole grains—which can also ease constipation and bloating. Also, get screened around week 35 to 37 for group B streptococcus, a bacteria that can seriously threaten newborns if passed on.

RESCUE REMEDY: *Improve the appearance of stretch marks with a citrus-sugar scrub. Combine 1 tablespoon of sugar with a few drops of lemon juice and almond oil. Massage into stretch marks to exfoliate and minimize unsightly lines; then rinse with warm water and pat dry. Continue for a month or until you see results. Other treatments include applying aloe vera gel, potato juice, olive oil, castor oil, cocoa butter, and whipped egg whites.*

BANISH MORNING SICKNESS

Pregnancy may be a delight, but throwing up every morning—and even during the day—is not. No one is sure what causes the nausea, but a likely culprit is the pregnancy hormone known as human chorionic gonadotropin (hCG). Fortunately, there are proven, traditional remedies that will calm your queasy stomach.

- Taking ginger in tea or seltzer is a time-honored cure for a troubled tummy.
- Eating or sniffing something mint flavored can ease nausea.
- Eating simple starches like saltines or toast will settle an upset stomach.
- Sucking a sour candy or drinking lemon water can relieve a sour stomach.
- Slightly increasing your intake of vitamin B6 helps combat nausea.
- Walking for at least a half hour often relaxes the upper GI tract.
- Going for acupuncture or acupressure treatments is effective for treating nausea.

THE BIRTHING JOURNEY
NATURAL CHILDBIRTH AND OTHER ALTERNATIVE CHOICES

In the decades since the counterculture movement of the 1960s, concerned women have sought alternative ways to experience the birthing process, options outside the cold, clinical atmosphere of a hospital delivery room. Some women choose to be attended by a midwife at home, and some undergo hypnotherapy or give birth in a wading pool surrounded by a support group. If, like these women, you want the birth of your child to be as natural as possible, there are many ways you can make the delivery less clinical and more personally meaningful.

Healthy Solutions

Pregnancy raises so many questions about the impact of bringing a new life into the world that some women forget to ask themselves how they want to give birth. For those who are inclined toward a more natural or holistic way of life, here are some suggestions and options.

> ### DID YOU KNOW?
>
> • *You may love snacking on chocolate bars, cinnamon buns, oranges, tacos, and onion rings. But if you are breastfeeding, be aware that those strong flavors may end up in your breast milk and either make your baby fussy or give him gas. Avoid chocolate, spices, citrus fruit, strawberries, "gassy" veggies, pineapple, and kiwi.*

A CAREFUL PLAN A month or so before your due date is the time to attend birthing classes and have your final prenatal visits with your healthcare provider. Continue your diet of nourishing foods, now amping up on eggs and meat for protein and iron; dairy foods for vitamin D; and water—at least 64 ounces daily—for hydration. You should also perform kegel exercises and pelvic tilts to strengthen your pelvic floor.

NATURAL CHILDBIRTH The term *natural childbirth* refers to experiencing labor with a minimum of invasive medical interventions or prescription painkillers. Instead, the mother utilizes breathing and relaxation techniques to block pain and is able to comfortably pace much of the delivery herself. In the United States, the two most common natural childbirth programs are the Lamaze technique and the Bradley method. Advocates proclaim them empowering and rewarding, plus the babies—with no drugs in their systems—are more alert afterward and more interested in breastfeeding.

MEDICATION-FREE DELIVERY You can work with a doula (also called a birth companion), who is a specially trained nonmedical person who assists you before, during, or after childbirth. She can greatly help reduce your pain by using a combination of physical and emotional support.

Water immersion during active labor can cut down significantly on pain because it relaxes and comforts the mother. Hypnobirthing (called calm birthing in Australia) uses relaxation, breathing therapy, and visualization to ease labor. Sometimes simply changing positions—moving from a bed to a stool or leaning forward on all fours with your legs spread, for example—can greatly lessen physical discomfort.

No matter the birthing method, the goal is the same for all mothers: delivering a healthy, thriving newborn.

RESCUE REMEDY: *Tender massage or comforting strokes from the woman's partner or her doula can help soothe away labor pain. Try using the calming essential oils of clary sage, peppermint, lavender, and myrrh. Use frankincense as the first stage of labor ends.*

THE MIDWIFE Midwives are trained healthcare professionals who consult on family planning, give prenatal exams and order tests, provide diet and exercise advice, deliver babies, and refer patients to doctors when necessary. They are also a valuable source of emotional and social support during all stages of pregnancy. When interviewing a midwife, ask about her experience, how many births she's attended, and the name of her backup obstetrician. Make sure she has been certified by the American Midwife Certification Board. If you have a friend who used a midwife, ask for a recommendation.

HOME BIRTH Home deliveries account for approximately 1 percent of births in the United States, but their numbers are on the rise. Women who make this choice appreciate delivering in a familiar setting and having some control over the birthing process. Risk of infant death is two or three times higher during home birth compared to hospital birth, however, so you need to balance the risks against the benefits. If you are experiencing an at-risk pregnancy, it is wiser to choose a hospital setting.

HOSPITAL OPTIONS Even if you decide against delivering at home, many hospitals now offer a range of more holistic birthing choices, including family-centered care, where your partner is at your side during delivery and the baby remains in the room after birth. Some hospitals even have homelike birthing centers for natural childbirth that feature

Storage jars, a feeding bottle, and a manual breast pump. Even working mothers can supply their babies with the numerous health benefits of natural breast milk.

birthing stools, birthing tubs, and midwife care. This way, if there are complications, the hospital facilities are only steps away.

BREASTFEEDING The practice of breastfeeding fell out of favor for a time, but it now has many advocates, including the World Health Organization, which recommends that a mother nurse her baby for a minimum of six months. Breast milk provides critical antibodies that defend the infant from infections and prevent allergies, and it is usually more easily digested than formula; as a result, babies are less gassy or constipated. Breastfeeding mothers generally have less blood loss after delivery, better uterus shrinkage, and greater weight loss—and also experience less postpartum depression. They also reduce the risk of breast cancer or cardiovascular disease.

Mothers who are not lactating regularly or whose babies need supplemental feedings may opt for commercial formula, which is safe, nourishing, and convenient. Just remember to burp the baby well after feeding him formula.

THE RIGHT POSITION

You can actually help to make sure your baby is in the optimum anterior position for delivery—head down, back along your belly, face toward your back—by avoiding lying down or leaning back. Instead sit up straight, sit cross-legged, walk, lie belly down on a body pillow, crawl, weed the garden, scrub the floor, swim using the breaststroke, and sleep on your left side.

Up Close
NATURAL BABY FOOD
PREPARE WHOLESOME, NUTRITIOUS "FIRST FOODS" AT HOME

By the time your baby approaches her first birthday, she will be eager to try new foods.

Health-conscious parents can be sure their infants and toddlers are not ingesting the additives and chemicals found in commercial baby foods simply by making their own supply. Commercial foods are increasingly geared toward healthier ingredients, but they still contain preservatives, sugar, and sodium.

Homemade baby food requires no additives and is far less expensive than store-bought versions. Simply set aside an hour a week to prepare the food, and then store it in small, lidded glass jars in the refrigerator. Most will keep for five or six days.

First Foods
Signs that your baby is ready for solid food—or first foods—can include waking more often at night or eating more meals than usual or even "cluster feeding" like a newborn. Six months is the optimal time to start introducing solid foods, and even if your baby is still on the breast or bottle, this additional nutrition will not go amiss. During the second half of their first year, babies require the nutrients found in animal fat and protein to foster brain, skeletal, and muscular growth, as well as iron, zinc, niacin, calcium, potassium, phosphorus, magnesium, vitamins A, B, B6, C, D, E and K, and omega-3 and omega-6 fats.

Stage-one baby foods, ideal for infants aged six to eight months, are soft cooked and easy to swallow, typically pureed in a blender or bullet, and then strained. Popular choices include cooked or steamed sweet potatoes, butternut squash, carrots, apples, peaches, and apricots, and raw bananas, mangoes, papaya, and avocados. Prepare a portion that fills a tablespoon, and offer it to your baby (some parents use a clean finger at first), and do not fret if your baby does not finish the "meal." This is all new territory. It also helps to introduce one food at a time, three or four days apart.

SIMPLE CEREAL Cooked rice, bran, or oat cereal is a versatile meal option for babies; serve it alone or mix with formula, breast milk, or fruit puree. Add a quarter cup brown rice powder or bran powder (ground in the blender) to a cup of boiling water, then simmer and stir evenly for 10 minutes. You can also mix a quarter cup ground (not instant) oats in three-quarters of a cup of water. Serve warm.

PUREED FRUIT Add a pound of dried unsulphured apricots to two cups of white grape juice, pear juice, or apple juice, and bring mixture to a boil. Simmer for 15 minutes, and then puree until thin and smooth. Peeled apple slices can simply be boiled and then mashed or pureed; try adding mashed bananas, and sprinkle with wheat germ (for eight months or older).

Organic green broccoli and spinach puree. Many fruits and vegetables are easy to whip into healthful, natural baby food. Glass storage jars are readily available online.

Stage-2 Meals

As your baby matures at around 8 to 12 months—and masters the art of eating—you can start offering transitional stage-2 foods, those with more substance and that contain actual pieces. At this point, babies will try almost anything you place in front of them.

Once your baby is handling chunkier foods, you can broaden your shopping list and combine ingredients. Try cottage cheese mixed with quinoa or scrambled eggs; broiled grapefruit with a drizzle of syrup and cinnamon served with yogurt; canned lentils added to organic tomato soup and topped with melted cheese; steamed salmon flaked and added to mashed sweet potato; uncooked pastina boiled in low-sodium chicken broth; or veggie burgers topped with mashed avocado.

FISH STICK FAVORITES Slice a half pound of cod, halibut, or salmon fillets into inch-thick strips, and then cover in whole wheat flour, and dredge in a mixture made of two eggs and two tablespoons of milk. Cover the strips with ground organic potato chips, and bake on a greased baking sheet for six or seven minutes on each side.

BABY-FRIENDLY FIRST FOODS

These nourishing foods are perfect for your six-to-eight-month-old baby.

- Cooked and blended red meat furnishes iron, zinc, and B12.
- Bone broth contains gelatin, calcium, magnesium, and phosphorus.
- Egg yolks provide healthy fat, choline, and cholesterol, and they are great for eye and brain development.
- Boiled butternut squash contains vitamins A and C and the minerals magnesium, potassium, and manganese.
- Avocados supply healthy fats, niacin, and vitamins B, E, and K.
- Bananas are an excellent source of potassium, magnesium, manganese, and vitamins B6 and C.
- Cultured or fermented foods like yogurt or kefir supply probiotics to the GI tract.

THE HEALTHY BABY

NATURAL SOLUTIONS TO TREAT INFANT AILMENTS AND KEEP YOUR BABY HAPPY

It's not surprising that a lot of new parents freak out a little once they get their baby home. There are so many things to learn—even diapering can be a challenge—and scary responsibilities that they don't want to get wrong: What if the baby's fever spikes, or he develops a weird rash? And what's with all that crying? These questions, and more, plague new parents and keep them up at night—even after the baby finally drifts off to sleep. Your go-to for any suspected illness should be a healthcare provider, but it also helps to have an experienced parent, relative, or friend on call during those first weeks to share their knowledge. You'll see first-hand how to ease a colicky baby or treat a stuffy cold.

Healthy Solutions

Of course you will contact your physician if something serious or persistent presents with your infant, but there are certain minor ailments that babies are prone to that you can treat naturally at home without an emergency call to the doctor.

> ### DID YOU KNOW?
>
> • *If your baby is ailing or feeling out of sorts, fill and prepare a hot water bottle according to directions, and swaddle it in a soft towel to use as a comforting pillow for baby to cuddle. Place the wrapped bottle next to a sore tummy, achy ear, or congested chest. Or use it to warm chilly toes after a winter outing in the stroller.*

CONGESTION When your baby gets a stuffy nose or a mild cough, take her into the bathroom with the shower running hot enough to steam up the room. Or leave a sliced onion next to the crib—the sulfur content in the onion will draw out the mucus and fluids causing the congestion.

FEVER To reduce a baby's mild fever, slice a lemon over a bowl of warm water, and then use a washcloth to sponge his body and limbs with the lemon water. The fruit's aromatic oils and the evaporating water will cool the skin. A one-to-two dilution of apple cider vinegar and water will have a similar effect

COLIC A gassy, unsettled stomach is often the culprit when babies cry and cry. Sometimes a pacifier works to soothe colic, or try sustained movement—rocking the crib, cuddling or walking the baby and singing, or a ride in the car. You could also ask your doctor about adding more fiber to her diet.

RESCUE REMEDY: *Chamomile can soothe your baby's upset stomach. Steep three chamomile tea bags in a bowl of hot water, and then prepare a warm—not hot—compress, and apply it to baby's abdomen for 10 or 15 minutes. To keep the compress warm, top with a swaddled hot water bottle.*

TEETHING As babies cut their first teeth, the pain can make them miserable, and parents quickly learn that a finger massage of the gums can help. Plastic or rubber teething toys contain harmful chemicals, so opt for teethers made of organic cotton or hardwoods finished with beeswax; some baby-approved versions combine both materials.

Relieve baby's teething pain with natural wood teethers finished with beeswax.

Add mashed bananas to your baby's diet to help relieve diarrhea, and be sure to keep him hydrated.

ITCHY SKIN Many babies are prone to dry, itchy skin, especially in winter. Half a cup of oatmeal, finely ground in the blender and added to bath water, makes an effective treatment for babies who are suffering from skin problems. The protein in the oatmeal soothes skin and preserves its natural barrier. Let baby soak for 15 minutes twice a day. Oatmeal is also effective for treating diaper rash.

CONSTIPATION Babies poop. A lot. And they are rarely neat about it. Yet, as much as parents dread those diaper loads, the opposite—an empty diaper or dry, hard stools—can be alarming. You can restore your baby's regularity by adding chopped organic prunes to solid food. Prunes contain sorbitol, a type of sugar alcohol that is believed to have a mild laxative effect.

DIARRHEA Loose stool in infants will often respond to mashed bananas, which are binding. Otherwise, stick to a normal diet with the addition of plenty of fluids—water, extra formula or breast milk, or chicken or vegetable broth—to prevent dehydration.

DIAPER RASH This red, inflamed, blistery rash is found on the buttocks, thighs, and genital area. Causes include exposure to urine or stool, food allergies, yeast infections, and bacteria. Dissolve two teaspoons of healing baking soda in four cups of water and sponge it on baby's bottom, and then gently pat dry. An application of petroleum jelly, coconut oil, or shea butter can protect the skin from the irritating effects of urine and feces. You can also sprinkle on absorbent cornstarch to keep the diaper area dry and prevent friction.

RESCUE REMEDY: *A weak dilution of white vinegar— 1 teaspoon to 1 cup of water—makes an effective baby wipe to neutralize urine and resist yeast. You can also rinse laundered cloth diapers in a bucket of water mixed with ½ cup vinegar to remove any residual soap and eliminate urine odor.*

DIAPER NEWS

Many eco-conscious parents who choose cloth diapers over disposable ones have started using pocket-style diapers that hold super-absorbent inserts. The colorful covers or wraps have hook-and-loop or snap closures. They are fun, easy to put on and take off, and don't require pins or fasteners. Another plus is that they are easy to make at home for those who are handy with a sewing machine.

CHAPTER 4

AGING AND WELLNESS

Introduction
GETTING BETTER, NOT OLDER
ASSESS YOUR EVOLVING NEEDS AND TAKE ACTION

People are living longer, healthier lives than ever before . . . and they are looking a lot better doing it. Much of this is due to improved medical care and a better understanding of nutrition—how power foods and vitamins, minerals, and other supplements can increase longevity. There is a heightened awareness of how fitness and exercise can impact and improve senior health. It's encouraging, too, that researchers are studying memory loss, sleep deprivation, fuzzy thinking, and other psychological or brain-related ailments that trouble an aging population. Plus, there is now a focus on how physical appearance affects mood and outlook. And let us not forget that many people—including many seniors—are leading cleaner, healthier, relatively toxin-free lives by incorporating natural health boosters and remedies and natural practices into their daily routines.

As we grow older, it helps to be aware of how the body is changing—especially if it's changing for the worse. Are your joints beginning to creak? Is a once-mild backache generating chronic pain? Do you experience shortness of breath when you climb stairs? Are your cholesterol or blood sugar levels increasing? Is your blood pressure high? These signs don't necessarily mean that you are over the hill, but rather they are indications of potential problems you need to address. And that is the next step, determining what you can realistically do to hold back the incursions of time and make lifestyle alterations to stave off deterioration and disease.

Eat Right and Stay Fit

Your diet is the first factor you need to examine—and it may be the easiest one to correct. By implementing a balanced eating regimen, with an emphasis on high fiber and low fat, you can start to lose weight, speed up your metabolism, regulate your blood pressure, and lower blood sugar and cholesterol levels. Adding certain healing herbs, spices, and other plants to your recipes will also boost your immune system and improve your mood, digestion, circulation, joint health, and skin tone. And speaking of skin tone, there are plenty of natural methods for stopping your looks from fading and keeping your complexion and body well moisturized.

Remaining active is the key to sustained health as we age; start out by walking—three brisk 20-minute walks a week are a reasonable, low-impact way to begin—or swimming and bicycling, before graduating to more aerobic, heart-healthy exercises and workouts either at home or at a health club. This might be the time to investigate natural joint supplements and herbal energy boosters. And don't forget to check out the variety of herbs and natural substances that keep your memory in good working order and augment brain function.

(LEFT) Now is the time to investigate memory boosters, such as *Ginkgo biloba* supplements.

(OPPOSITE PAGE) Keep fit with thrice-weekly walks.

Garlic bulbs, fresh picked from the garden. Add this pungent herb to your diet to gain its heart-healthy benefits.

EAT FOR LONGEVITY

MAINTAIN VITALITY WITH SOUND FOOD CHOICES AND HEALTHFUL HERBS

Our bodies experience a host of changes as we age, but our nutritional needs don't alter all that much. We still need those lean proteins, high-fiber whole grains, richly colored fruits and vegetables, healthy fats, and low-fat dairy products. But most seniors need fewer calories because their metabolism has slowed; taking in too many may result in excess weight that impedes mobility and causes complications for those suffering with diabetes or heart disease. Other dietary questions that occur as we grow older may include what foods raise energy levels, which herbs combat illness, and what to eat to live a long, vigorous life.

Healthy Solutions

The answers to many of our dietary health questions can be found in nature. As advocates of natural cures will tell you, any number of herbs, spices, nutrients,

and foods have the ability to aid weight loss, eliminate fatigue, ward off illness, and increase quality of life, as well as lifespan.

NUTRIENT SUPPLEMENTS Older adults should consider increasing the nutrients that seniors often lack; look for foods or supplements that supply vitamin B12, folic acid, calcium, vitamin D, potassium, magnesium, fiber, or omega-3 fatty acids.

WEIGHT- LOSS AIDS Keeping at a healthy weight is optimal, especially as we age. Any extra pounds put undue strain on our ankles, knees, and hips and can lead to circulatory, respiratory, and digestive issues. To eat wisely—at any age—try following the U.S. government's new online graphic guideline called MyPlate, which shows how the five basic food—fruits, grains, vegetables, protein, and dairy—should rate on the plate. Certain herbs can help you drop pounds by boosting metabolism and offering fat-burning, or thermogenic, properties. These include cumin (one teaspoon a day can help you burn up to three times the body fat), black pepper, turmeric, ginger, garlic, and cayenne. Cinnamon balances blood sugar and eases cravings, and vitamin-rich dandelions can reduce bloat.

FATIGUE FIGHTERS Many herbs are known for their calming qualities, but some have the opposite effect. Rosemary is used in Chinese medicine to stimulate alertness and cognitive function as it protects the body from cell-damaging free radicals; Siberian ginseng is used to treat fatigue, as well as joint pain and insomnia; nettle promotes vitality; astragalus energizes *chi* (core strength); and bee pollen provides a burst of energy.

HERBS FOR LIFE A surprising number of plants can combat illness and even prolong life by heightening immunity and providing a powerful defense against debilitating conditions and disease. These miracle workers include the following herbs and spices.

- Astragalus root (genus *Astragalus)* boosts the immune system, protects against heart disease, and can slow aging at the cellular level.
- Goji berry (genus *Lycium)* can slow macular degeneration and boost sexual function.
- Cloves *(Syzygium aromaticum)* are full of antioxidants; they promote long life by reducing cell damage and cleansing toxins from the body.
- Garlic *(Allium sativum)* improves cardiac health by lowering cholesterol levels and blood pressure.
- Milk thistle *(Silybum marianum)* has been used for millennia to treat liver ailments; this herb might also lower cholesterol.
- Oregano *(Origanum vulgare)* is renowned for empowering the immune system
- Sage *(Salvia officinalis)* works to increase lifespan with its antioxidant, antibacterial, antifungal, and antiviral properties.
- Cayenne and other hot peppers (genus *Capsicum)* contain capsaicin, an anti-inflammatory that relieves joint pain and cluster headaches.

Antioxidant haldi doodh. This healthful drink is made with fresh or ground turmeric, which gives it its golden color.

MAKE IT YOURSELF
Haldi Doodh

You can enjoy the multiple health benefits of turmeric with this version of haldi doodh—also called "golden milk"—a traditional Ayurvedic beverage in India. The drink's anti-inflammatory properties can reduce the painful swelling of arthritis, ease a sore throat, and help improve muscle flexibility.

YOU WILL NEED:
 1 cup organic milk
 1 teaspoon organic coconut oil
 ½-inch to 1-inch piece of turmeric
  or ¼ teaspoon ground turmeric
 honey
 cinnamon

WHAT TO DO:
- Combine the milk, coconut oil, and turmeric in a saucepan.
- Heat the mixture on medium, stirring constantly. Do not allow the mixture to boil.
- Add honey to taste, sprinkle with cinnamon, and then serve warm or chilled.

- Ginger *(Zingiber officinale)* reduces inflammation throughout the body and eases arthritis pain.
- Turmeric *(Curcuma longa)* has a long history as a medicinal spice. Its active ingredient, curcumin, promotes longevity with antioxidants and helps prevent inflammation and tumors.
- Cinnamon *(Cinnamomum verum)* has both antioxidant and anti-inflammatory properties.

FOREVER YOUNG

NATURAL SKINCARE CAN ERASE YEARS FROM YOUR APPEARANCE

Feeling attractive can play a major role in maintaining self-esteem for just about everyone, and it remains a factor as we get older. It is therefore important to preserve and protect aging skin—if only because it has probably already seen its share of damage. Unfortunately the harsh (and dangerous) effects of the sun's UV rays on human skin were downplayed and even unrecognized during the youth of today's seniors. Many of them were once sun-worshiping baby boomers, slathering on the suntan oil and disdaining sunscreens. Older skin, even without the lines and wrinkles caused by aging, sun damage, or smoking, tends to be dry, thin, and less resilient. It may also sag, develop a crepelike appearance, and show brownish age spots.

DID YOU KNOW?

• *Even if you are doing your body a favor by carrying around a water bottle, beauty experts warn against drinking straight from it—all that pursing of your lips can create lines around the mouth and add to existing ones. Instead, use a bottle with a spout so you can squirt water into your mouth.*

Healthy Solutions

If you're a senior, to replenish your skin you need to follow a different set of skincare guidelines than you did in your youth. Dry, crepey skin needs extra moisturizing, while lines and wrinkles can benefit from lotions that actually plump up the skin. There are ways to care for aging skin and protect it from further damage, starting with sun protection. Stick with an SPF 30 sunscreen that has broad spectrum UVA/UVB protection. And whenever you head outside, be sure to don a broad-rimmed hat and sunglasses. How you clean your skin also matters. To hydrate skin, keep showers and baths short—sustained exposure to water leaches away moisture. Also use only warm water—hot water strips natural oils from face and body.

Shea butter, extracted from the nut of the African shea tree. You can use this skin-smoothing moisturizer as a base in many homemade skincare products, such as body bars, lip balms, whipped body butters, and liquid creme foundations.

FACIAL SKINCARE Your face needs extra care as you get older. Be sure to clean your face with gentle cleansers; avoid antiaging creams that contain irritants like retinoids or alpha-hydroxy acid. To deep clean, try a clarifying facial mask.

Try natural ingredients like avocado and honey to make your own moisturizer.

RESCUE REMEDY: *To make a clarifying facial mask, blend three parts olive oil with one part castor oil, and massage it over your face. Dampen a washcloth in comfortably hot water, place it over your face for a few minutes, and then use it to gently remove the oil, along with dirt and impurities. Rinse with warm water.*

WRINKLE FIRST AID There are plenty of commercial skincare products that replace the oils our faces lose, but most contain added fragrances and a host of chemicals. For a natural antiwrinkle cream, simply dab anti-inflammatory extra virgin olive oil on problem areas—the corners of the eyes, under the chin, and around the mouth.

RESCUE REMEDY: *This avocado-honey facial moisturizer leaves your skin looking and feeling youthful and dewy. And by helping your skin retain moisture and acting as a temporary filler for wrinkles, it makes your complexion plump out and appear smooth. In a blender, combine 3 tablespoons of fresh dairy cream, ¼ ripe avocado, and 1 tablespoon honey. Puree the ingredients into a creamy consistency. Apply the lotion to your face, neck, and décolletage, leave it on for an hour, and then rinse it off with warm water.*

BODY CARE To care for your whole body, while you are still damp from a shower, moisturize with a lotion that contains glycerin, mineral oil, or hyaluronic acid to lock in moisture. Your body deserves some pampering too, so why not try a nourishing, luxurious whipped body butter after stepping from the bath?

RESCUE REMEDY: *To make an aromatic whipped body butter, first bring a small pan holding a couple of inches of water to a simmer. Place ½ cup each shea butter, cocoa butter, and coconut oil with ½ cup almond oil in a heat-proof glass bowl, and sit it just inside the pot of simmering water. Stir until the mixture melts together. Let it cool slightly, add 10 to 30 drops of your favorite essential oils, and then cool in the refrigerator. Whip with a hand mixer until fluffy, and place in a lidded glass jar. Store at room temperature or in the fridge.*

AGE SPOT ELIMINATOR

Hands say a lot about us—especially when they are sprinkled with dark spots. These spots, known as age spots, appear most often on sun-exposed areas, so along with the hands, you may find them on your face, shoulders, and arms. To remove some of the pigment of age spots, try exfoliating with this natural scrub. In a bowl, combine a half cup of cooked rice with a tablespoon each of agave nectar and lemon juice, and blend well. The rice exfoliates dead skin, the agave offers hydration, and the lemon juice helps lighten skin and also sloughs away dead cells Apply the mixture to dry hands with a firm, circular motion for one to two minutes. You can also rub it on the palms or soles of the feet to soften calluses.

Find a group yoga class or practice in the park with friends. This low-impact form of exercise can help keep your joints strong.

FIT AT ANY AGE

EXERCISE CAN BE THE KEY TO INCREASED FLEXIBILITY AND MOBILITY

Physiological studies indicate that the *more* people move, the more they *can* move. This is especially true for our aging population. It is therefore critical that, as we get older, we do not fall prey to the sedentary lifestyles that pervade our modern world. Habitual lack of exercise can lead to weight gain, circulatory or respiratory problems, heart disease, and diabetes, and being a couch potato can exacerbate arthritis pain and joint issues. So to avoid spending your golden years in discomfort and distress, you need to get up, get fit, and get strong.

Healthy Solutions

Okay, so you might not be as spry as you once were, but you can always find ways to exercise. Even while sitting down, you can lift hand weights or a broom

> **DID YOU KNOW?**
>
> • *Some gyms offer trained senior-fitness pros who will customize workouts that won't overtax vulnerable areas like the back and neck, and who can keep clients motivated with routines that are fun and challenging. Another option is the "Silver Sneaker" classes found at many gyms that are geared to the needs of the over-55 set.*

handle. Why not start by taking brisk walks outdoors or at the mall, joining a YMCA swim class, or biking to a nearby store? Try working out at home using kitchen counters or chairs for balance and towels as resistance bands. You can invest in a few pieces of home gym equipment or join a health club. The level of intensity you seek is up to you, but the two most important factors under your control are the decision to begin and the determination to stick with it. (Naturally, check with you doctor before beginning any strenuous exercise plan.)

SHOW UP! One of the most depressing statistics in the fitness industry is the large number of people who join a gym or health club and then rarely, if ever, actually go. There's something, at least initially, about belonging to a gym that seems to increase inertia rather than combat it. If you feel you need something to prod you out the door, then the following tips might help you get cracking.

- Dress casual. You don't need to be the gym fashionista with sleek new athletic wear and designer sneakers. Just don a pair of comfortable shorts or stretch-fabric pants, a T-shirt, and some type of athletic shoe. After you become a regular attendee, then it's time to shop for all that fancy gym gear.

- Ask a buddy or relative to join with you so that you can encourage each other when that urge to make excuses and stay home strikes. If you have a senior parent who resists exercise, offer to become a gym member, too.

- Sign up with a trainer for a month or two. Having an actual appointment at the gym each week should compel you to go there. Or join an exercise or dance class that looks like enough fun to stir up your enthusiasm.

- Don't overdo your early workouts so much that you're too achy to return to the gym for weeks. Go slowly until you build up strength and stamina.

- Don't try to emulate the rugged calisthenics routines you learned in school all those decades ago. Instead, explore modern modes of exercise, which offer a wider range of health benefits and are less likely to result in injury.

PROTECT BONES AND JOINTS Exercise is important for "loading" the bones, taxing them to make them strong, and for flexing the joints, keeping them supple. Before you embark on any exercise program, however, consider a bone density scan to check for osteopenia—low bone density, or osteoporosis—very low bone density. It may be time

Opt for high-energy snacks like almonds and cashew nuts, pumpkin and sunflower seeds, and raisin and dried cranberries, rather than high-carb cookies and cakes.

to increase your intake of bone-building calcium and vitamin D, which allows calcium to be absorbed properly. Also consider natural supplements, like glucosamine and chondroitin, that lubricate joints. And be aware that moderate strength exercises, like lifting weights, build up your muscles and protect the joints they support.

INVESTIGATE YOGA AND TAI CHI Both these venerable Asian disciplines offer low-impact, senior-friendly options for exercise and, at the same time, allow participants to reduce stress. Check online or in your local newspaper for the location of classes.

EAT RIGHT TO MAINTAIN ENERGY

The proper diet becomes increasingly important as your workouts expand. To keep your energy high, focus on high-quality protein like fish, beans, and eggs. Reduce your intake of processed carbohydrates like cookies, cakes, and pizza and instead snack on nuts and seeds. And don't forget about hydration, making sure that you drink enough before, during, and after a workout.

Up Close

IT'S ALL ABOUT ATTITUDE

DON'T LET YOUR AGE DEFINE YOU OR CURTAIL YOUR ACTIVITIES

You need to keep connected, so stay in touch with old friends or take a class to make new ones of all ages.

For many seniors—especially those who have recently retired—the "golden years" can seem more like a time of isolation and loneliness. Some older adults may believe their useful or productive days are behind them, others may feel abandoned when second- and third-generation family members move away. Some seniors are mourning the loss of a spouse or life partner. Even the death of a beloved pet can be a blow. If left unaddressed, these despondent or melancholy feelings can turn into depression, which is a common problem in older adults. Yet, it often manifests without the expected feelings of sadness. Rather, patients experience a lack of motivation, low energy, and an increase in physical problems, such as arthritis flare-ups or painful headaches. If you suspect depression in yourself or an aging loved one, don't wait to seek out a counselor or therapist.

Open the Door

Psychologically, it's vital for alienated or depressed seniors to re-engage with their lives and attempt greater social outreach. Their immediate goal should be to renew their interest in the world around them, discover new vistas, and explore fresh challenges. From a medicinal standpoint, there are a number of herbs and nutrients that can boost production of mood-elevating endorphins that may have been depleted by improper diets, excess stress, and toxic environmental factors. Here are some simple, effective suggestions for rejoining the human race.

- Volunteer. Offer to conduct a children's reading hour at your library, help plant a community garden, or work at a soup kitchen or food pantry. Nothing reduces our own woes like helping other people deal with theirs. Volunteering can also expand your social network.

- Go outside. Breathing fresh air and relaxing in nature are excellent curatives, so ride a bike, bird watch, sketch, beachcomb, walk to the park, or plan a picnic along a scenic byway.
- Reconnect with old friends. Social media can put you in touch with former schoolmates, coworkers, club members, and distant relatives. Or use it to make new friends.
- Adopt a pet. Studies verify that the affection of dogs and cats can actually lower your blood pressure; dogs also provide opportunities for daily exercise and social interaction.
- Learn new skills. Have you always wanted to learn to knit, play chess, or cook Chinese food? Now is the perfect time to find a class.
- Cut carbs. Minimize mood swings by reducing sugary or starchy foods, which make blood sugar levels rise and then crash, adversely affecting your emotional state.

Nature's Uplifters

Humans have been using natural remedies to banish the blues and raise their spirits since the earliest civilizations. Herbs and supplements that combat depression—or any loss of interest in life—include the following remedies.

- Ginseng (genus *Panax*) is an adaptogenic—an herb or compound that helps manage stress—known for improving mood, attention span, and memory and raising energy levels.
- Lemon balm *(Melissa officinalis)* is a mild sedative that relieves feelings of depression, nervousness, insomnia, and headaches.
- St. John's wort *(Hypericum perforatum)* is considered a natural antidepressant and may be used to replace prescription medicines in cases of moderate depression.
- Passionflower *(Passiflora incarnata)* contains mild narcotic compounds that result in restful sleep and a reduction of daytime anxiety.
- Golden root *(Rhodiola rosea)* helps regulate the response to stress, overcome feelings of melancholy or depression, and improve mental energy and mood.

GET CONNECTED

Recent studies show that seniors who interact with electronic devices—in other words, learn to use cell phones, laptop computers, and tablets—have better self-esteem and greater social outreach than those who don't. Although impairments of vision, hearing, or manual dexterity might be issues for older users, certain manufacturers now produce "senior" phones with oversize control keys and laptops with extra-bright screens or keyboards that light up. Useful technologies seniors should consider include Skype and other live computer video exchanges via the Internet; e-readers, which can hold thousands of books and have the option for enlarging print; video and computer games, which can improve cognition and mental agility; and health-tracking software.

- Kava *(Piper methysticum)* can ease nervous tension and anxiety, especially in social settings.
- L-tyrosine, an amino acid that enhances mood, sleep, and emotional well-being, supports the production of endorphins like dopamine.
- SAM-e (S-adenosylmethionine) is the synthetic form of a molecule made in our bodies. SAM-e supplements can be used to relieve depression and alleviate arthritis pain.
- High-potency multivitamins, especially those with zinc, vitamin B6, and folate, can help the body synthesize mood-improving neurotransmitters.

Golden root tea or supplements can help regulate mood.

MAINTAIN MEMORY

KEEP YOUR FACULTIES SHARP WITH THE RIGHT FOODS AND SUPPLEMENTS

In addition to the physical toll aging takes on our bodies, there are also mental side effects most of us will at some time experience. These can include memory loss, cognitive impairment, and fuzzy thinking—the inability to concentrate, even on familiar tasks. Although stress, depression, medications, thyroid issues, and vitamin deficiencies can be responsible for these problems, three physical factors are often the cause. First, the hippocampus, the region of the brain where information is stored and accessed, can deteriorate with age. Second, the hormones and proteins that foster brain cells and stimulate neural growth diminish as we get older. Finally, seniors often suffer decreased blood flow to the brain, which can affect memory and cognitive function.

> ### DID YOU KNOW?
>
> • *If you chronically lose or misplace things—your keys, your cell phone, the dog's leash—slow down and stop multitasking. It takes about eight seconds to commit information to memory, and if you're doing three things at once, it's no wonder you can't remember where you left your glasses.*

Healthy Solutions

Forgetful behaviors like misplacing your keys or blanking on someone's name are not necessarily a cause for alarm; as we grow older, there is bound to be some sketchy recall. Yet major memory loss is not a normal part of aging. Studies indicate that lifestyle choices are the key to how healthy the brain remains as we grow older. If minor-to-moderate memory problems trouble you, there are ways to build up your brain and tricks for keeping track of your life. And, naturally, there are supplements and herbs that can help keep your brain functioning in top form.

VITAMIN D Low levels of vitamin D in older adults have been associated with inferior brain function, including negative effects on planning, processing information, and the formation of new memories. If you are unable to access vitamin D by appropriate exposure to sunlight (UV light triggers our bodies to produce it), then take a D3 supplement.

BACOPA Scientific studies on humans have confirmed that *Bacopa monnieri*, an aquatic flowering plant, can improve a number of mental functions, including recollection, clarity, verbal learning abilities, speed of information processing, and memory.

GINSENG This popular Asian herb (genus *Panax)* is often prescribed to treat fatigue and improve quality of life. When used in conjunction with *Ginkgo biloba,* it is believed to activate certain neurotransmitters in the brain to enhance memory function.

GINKGO Studies bear out that this reputed memory enhancer indeed has the ability to improve recall, raise cognitive function and learning skills, and reduce depression. *Ginkgo biloba* can also increase blood circulation along the nervous system, promoting brain development.

To help keep your memory sharp, don't forget to pour yourself a cup of antioxidant-rich green tea.

ROSEMARY This culinary herb possesses antioxidant properties that can neutralize cell-damaging free radicals. When used in aromatherapy, the scent of rosemary *(Rosmarinus officinalis)* lowers cortisol levels, increases concentration, and reduces anxiety, which can interfere with memory.

BLUEBERRIES This juicy dark-colored fruit is chock full of flavonoids, which have anti-inflammatory and antioxidant properties, making them vital for improving brain function, warding off cognitive decline, and preventing memory loss.

GREEN TEA The extracts in green tea are full of antioxidants, which help shield lipids and proteins from age-related issues due to oxidation. They can also protect the hippocampus—the seat of our memories—from the deleterious effects of aging.

BRAIN FITNESS GUIDELINES Follow these simple tips and watch your memory regain its vigor.

- Stay social. Interacting with others keeps the brain stimulated and challenges verbal skills.
- Walk. Recent research shows that walking six to nine miles a week can prevent brain shrinkage and memory loss.
- Don't smoke. Smoking can constrict the flow of blood to the brain.

Nutrient-dense smoothies are a great way for seniors to get the vitamins they need. This mix of brain-healthy nuts, berries, and bananas provides a potent memory boost.

- Avoid alcohol. Overconsumption of alcohol actually shrinks the brain of adults.
- Opt for antioxidants and omega-3 fats. Fruits, veggies, green tea, seafood, and walnuts can keep the brain from "rusting" due to free radicals.
- Get enough sleep. While we sleep, each day's memories are consolidated, formed, and stored for later retrieval.
- Make lists to jog your memory. Efficiency experts say that we all should do this to stay on track.
- Stretch your brain. Turn to word games, books, online blogs, newspapers, and magazines, to keep the gray matter fit.
- Learn new things. Taking classes, studying a language, or discovering new driving routes all engage the brain.
- Use mnemonic devices to remember names and places. When you meet Jack Horsley, picture a car jack holding up a horse. Or use a rhyme: Susan Greer has eyes like a deer.

MAKE IT YOURSELF
Nutty Banana-Berry Smoothie

This delicious brain-boosting breakfast treat or afternoon snack features antioxidant berries, potassium-rich banana, and walnuts, a great source of omega-3 fats.

YOU WILL NEED:
1 cup almond milk
1 ripe banana
1½ cups fresh or frozen blueberries
½ cup fresh or frozen strawberries
¼ cup raw walnuts, soaked and drained

WHAT TO DO:
- Blend the almond milk with the banana.
- Add the other ingredients to the blender and puree until smooth. Serves two.

PART II

NATURE'S
PHARMACOPOEIA

CHAPTER 5

MEDICINAL HERBS

Introduction
DISCOVER NATURE'S GIFTS
LEARN THE MEDICINAL SECRETS OF HERBS AND HEALING PLANTS

Herbs are described as plants with leaves, seeds, or flowers that are used to flavor food, treat disease, and provide scent. Medical care based on the administration of herbs is known as herbal or botanical medicine or phytomedicine. Healing plants are also valued for their medicinal qualities, but, unlike herbs, they are not usually a food source. With both herbs and healing plants, some or all parts may be used—root, stem, leaf, flower, fruit, or seed—and especially the essential oils distilled from the plant, which contain beneficial compounds, vitamins, or minerals.

From humankind's earliest beginnings, herbs have been valued for their ability to combat disease. The fossil records show that *Ginkgo biloba* has been on the planet since the Paleozoic period—and doubtless became a remedy used by early humans. Remains of rose hips, which are powerful antioxidants, have been found near prehistoric camps. Egyptians penned the Ebers Papyrus around 1500 B.C., which—along with records of more than 700 magic formulas and incantations—contains many legitimate herbal cures. People then may not have understood the science behind these cures, but it's likely that through trial and error they began to realize that consuming some plants made them feel better than when they ingested others. Herbal medicine has been practiced by almost every culture all over the world. The cures were lauded by the Greeks and Romans, detailed in the journals of Chinese doctors, utilized throughout the Middle East, venerated in Indian Ayurvedic medicine, and incorporated into the healing ceremonies of the indigenous people of Africa, Australia, Oceania, North America, and South America.

For millennia, herbs ruled as the medicines of choice to cure or prevent disease, ease pain, boost immunity, calm the nerves, and elevate the spirits. But as science advanced and more complex remedies were formulated in the laboratory, most herbal cures were relegated to the realm of quackery—fake medicines and questionable tonics mostly made up of alcohol and who knew what else.

Modern Times, New Attitudes

Yet science was not through with herbs. Some life-threatening diseases, like cancer or HIV/AIDS, still resisted attempts at finding a cure—or even medications to ward them off—so researchers began to look back on those early herbal remedies and wonder if there was any validity to their claims. The medicine chests of the ancient apothecaries were once again opened—and science was surprised, and probably a little peeved, that many herbs showed surprisingly effective results when employed against the diseases that currently plague modern society.

Herbal medicines will surely continue to become more mainstream, especially as the advances in research and testing demonstrate their value for treating and preventing increasing numbers of diseases and conditions. So read on, and acquaint yourself with the herbs and healing plants that are once again being deployed in the ongoing battle against illness. You never know which one might become the next medical wonder.

(LEFT) Early humans may have used rose hips as herbal medicine.

(OPPOSITE PAGE) There is a rich variety of healing herbs, and many parts of the plants are used, including the flowers.

ALFALFA
REDUCE CHOLESTEROL LEVELS, FLUSH TOXINS, AND RELIEVE ACHES

A perennial flowering plant, alfalfa *(Medicago sativa)* is a member of the pea family (or Leguminosae, also known as the legume or bean family) that originated in Asia. It is now grown in many parts of the temperate world as a nutritionally rich forage crop—used for grazing, hay, and silage, as well as a cover crop. The ancient Greeks and Romans fed it to their livestock, as did the Arabs, who reserved it for their cherished horses and named it *al-fac-facah,* or "father of all foods." Known as lucerne in the United Kingdom, this plant, with its trifoliate leaves, resembles clover when young. As the plant matures, the leaflets elongate, and clusters of small blue-violet flowers appear that are soon followed by small yellow-green fruits.

DID YOU KNOW?

• *This beneficial legume has some amazing properties—it can be harvested up to 11 times per year without affecting the plant's ability to regrow, and although its average lifespan is 4 to 8 years, depending on the variety of alfalfa and the climate, some plants can live more than 20 years.*

Health Benefits

Traditional medicinal uses for alfalfa include treating the kidneys, bladder, and prostate and flushing the bowels of toxins, and leaf preparations have been cited for their antiarthritic, antidiabetic, and antiasthmatic properties. Current lab studies have shown that the plant's saponins—soaplike chemical compounds—and fiber bind significant quantities of cholesterol, and one human study indicated that the herb might be useful in reducing cholesterol levels. It is also reported to be effective for treating sore joints and headaches and building up the immune system. Nutritionally, alfalfa contains chlorophyll, carotene, protein, a host of minerals (including calcium, iron, and magnesium), all the B vitamins, and vitamins C, D, E, and K.

You can drink alfalfa brewed alone or with other herbs in tea or take it in capsule form. Dried alfalfa is just as effective as fresh. With its mild flavor, you can add it to soups, salads, or other dishes. Alfalfa sprouts, which are sold at most supermarkets, are high in vitamins and minerals and can be included in salads or munched on as an easy, healthy snack.

Alfalfa sprouts

RESCUE REMEDY: *Packaged raw sprouts can contain bacteria, so heating them is recommended. Just spread them on a tray, and place them in the oven for a minute or two to "toast" them. Toss them into a salad, layer them in a sandwich, or munch them as a crispy-textured treat.*

BEE-BOTHERING PLANTS

A lfalfa nectar is a great favorite with our endangered honeybees. Yet, the configuration of the alfalfa flower results in the pistil and stamens hitting a foraging bee on the head. Older, more experienced bees soon learn to draw nectar from the sides of the flowers. This does not expose them to pollen, however. Beekeepers, looking to pollinate fields of alfalfa, try to place as many young bees as possible on site, mainly because the youngsters haven't been bonked on the head enough times to use the sideways maneuver.

ALOE VERA

SOOTHE BURNS AND MOISTURIZE AND HEAL THE SKIN

One of the many aloe species, *Aloe vera* is a member of the Asphodelaceae family of flowering plants. This stemless succulent grows wild in tropical regions around the globe; the thick, fleshy, spearlike leaves are usually green or gray-green and possess marginal serrations with small white teeth. In summer, pendulous yellow blossoms appear on tall spikes. Like other aloes—and numberless other species of plants—aloe vera forms arbuscular mycorrhiza fungi in a symbiosis that allows the plant to access increased minerals from the soil. Aloe vera is often cultivated for agricultural or medicinal purposes, and it also makes an attractive garden or house plant. Because it can survive with little rainfall, aloe is also popular in xeriscapes—drought-friendly gardens and landscapes. Aloe is used commercially in skin lotions, cosmetics, and healing ointments, as well as in yogurts, beverages, and some desserts.

DID YOU KNOW?

* *Aloe vera was known by many names throughout its long history as a natural treatment for burns and skin irritation. The ancient Egyptians called it the plant of immortality, the ancient Chinese referred to it as harmonic remedy, Arab traders named it the desert lily, and to Hindu doctors it was the silent healer.*

claims, that aloe can heal wounds or that intravenous treatments of aloe can relieve phlebitis, have either been disproved or need more clinical study. Still, there are more than 75 active compounds in aloe, including vitamins, minerals, enzymes, sugars, amino acids, and fatty acids, and currently the plant's phytochemicals are being studied for possible bioactivity, with a view to future medical applications.

RESCUE REMEDY: *Aloe vera can be a nongreasy makeup remover, and with its antibacterial properties, makes a superior face mask, especially for those with sensitive skin, acne, or rosacea. Mix 1 tablespoon of gel with 1 teaspoon each of almond milk and lemon juice. Apply to your face, leave on for three minutes, and rinse. For an antiaging facial cleanser, combine 1 tablespoon of aloe gel with 1 teaspoon of coconut oil. Massage in your hands until warm, and then use to wash your face.*

Health Benefits

This plant has been intrinsic to the healing traditions of many countries for millennia, primarily for soothing burns and irritations or moisturizing the skin. In Ayurvedic medicine, extracts of aloe, along with agave, are recommended as a skin treatment and are called *kathalai*. Written reports of usage go back to the Ebers Papyrus of the 16th century B.C., and in the first century A.D., Pliny the Elder described the plant's properties in *Naturalis Historia (Natural History)*.

As with many herbal remedies, some controversy surrounds the plant's effectiveness. Claims that fresh aloe gel can soothe first-degree or second-degree burns have been supported by research. Topical applications have also been proven effective against outbreaks of genital herpes and psoriasis. Other

Aloe vera gel can be used directly from the plant. There are also many commercial aloe vera gel products available.

ANGELICA

CONTROL PMS, REGULATE HEART RHYTHM, AND ENHANCE THE IMMUNE SYSTEM

The genus *Angelica* features tall, robust, aromatic biennial and perennial plants that are part of the family Apiaceae. It likely originated in the temperate and subarctic regions of the Northern Hemisphere and is typically found in ravines, damp meadows, and coastal regions. The plants grow from three to nine feet in height and display large bipinnate leaves and white or greenish white flowers that form large compound umbels. The flowers have a sweet, musky scent, making them enormously attractive to honeybees and many other winged pollinators.

> **DID YOU KNOW?**
>
> *According to a European legend, the plant's name comes from a monk's tale that an angel came to him in a dream and revealed that this plant was able to cure the plague—and thus it was christened "angelica." In truth, angelica does have antimicrobial properties and may have actually been effective against the bubonic plague bacillus.*

Healing Benefits

Over the centuries, angelica has remained a favorite of healers from many cultures. A number of species have been used in alternative medicine. One of the most common is *Angelica archangelica,* or garden angelica. The roots, leaves, and seeds of this plant all have medicinal value, and European healers often prescribed it for colds, coughs, bronchial and urinary ailments, indigestion, to calm anxiety, and to increase appetite. During the 16th and 17th centuries, angelica was combined with other herbs in a tonic called Carmelite water, which was believed to cure headaches, reduce agitation, promote long life, and protect against poisons and evil spells.

Another species, *A. sinensis* is used in traditional Chinese medicine, where it is called dong quai. Dong quai is reputed to increase red blood cell count, strengthen the heart and lungs, and improve liver function. Also nicknamed "female ginseng," dong quai is frequently used to treat reproductive problems, such as cramps or hot flashes and is also reportedly an effective aphrodisiac.

Modern research reveals that dong quai demonstrates properties that may translate into reduction of pain, dilation of blood vessels, and stimulation or relaxation of uterine muscles. Lab studies with animals also indicate some potential for treating abnormal heart rhythm, preventing accumulation of the platelets in blood vessels that form plaque, and protecting the liver. Angelica contains carotene, which helps the liver to produce vitamin A; valeric acid, known to calm the nerves; and plant sterols, which enhance the immune system. In conjunction with other herbs, especially black cohosh, angelica is an effective treatment for PMS. An infusion of the herb used as a gargle is good for easing sore throats and soothing mouth wounds. Dried angelica root is rich in nutrients, including vitamin B12, zinc, thiamine, riboflavin, potassium, magnesium, iron, fructose, glucose, and trace minerals, although the root is toxic when fresh.

RESCUE REMEDY: *To combat a cold, mix 4 teaspoons dried root and rootstock and 3 cups water. Let stand for eight hours, and then strain. Take 1 to 1½ cups per day.*

Dried angelica root and slices. Known as dong quai, *Angelica sinensis* is one of the medicinal species of this herb.

ASTRAGALUS

TREAT COLDS, FLU, AND VIRUSES AND STRENGTHEN THE LIVER, LUNGS, AND SPLEEN

Also known as Mongolian milkvetch, astragalus is a perennial member of the Leguminosae (the pea, bean, or legume family). It originated in Asia and is indigenous to northern and eastern China, and parts of Korea and Mongolia. The plant has green pinnate leaves and produces the lipped flowers typical of the pea family in pinkish or yellowish hues. The healing portion of the plant derives from the yellow core of its firm, fibrous root.

DID YOU KNOW?

• *There are more than 2,000 species of astragalus worldwide, but in China only two types are used medicinally:* Astragalus membranaceus *(which is known as* huáng qí) *and* A. mongholicus. *They are often combined with other herbs, like ginseng, angelica, or licorice, for the synergistic benefits they create.*

Health Benefits

Astragalus root (*Astragalus membranaceus)* has been used as a medicinal herb for more than 2,000 years. Known as *huáng qí,* it is one of the 50 fundamental herbs of traditional Chinese medicine. In the West, it is perhaps best known as an immunity booster—according to researchers, TA-65, a proprietary extract of the root, is linked to age-reversal effects in the immune system. Astragalus is also valued by natural healers as a major tonic and nourishing "superfood" that provides the following benefits:

• Wards off bacteria and viruses
• Treats colds and flu
• Promotes the growth of new tissue
• Benefits the liver, lungs, and spleen

Formal medical research has only recently begun on the healing potential of this herb, but according to the National Institutes of Health there are indications that it can—alone or in combination with other herbs—affect the immune system, the heart, and the liver. There is also the possibility that in conjunction with conventional medicines, astragalus can be useful for treating cancer. The Natural Medicine Comprehensive Database reports that long-term usage may prevent colds and, when taken for six weeks, it can reduce the symptoms of seasonal allergies, such as a runny nose and itchy eyes. The flavonoids the herb contains could explain its cardioprotective qualities, while its anti-inflammatory polysaccharides may allow it to reduce cholesterol levels. The herb is also an adaptogen, meaning it contains properties that can protect the body from the effects of mental, physical, and emotional stress.

Astragalus root

WHERE TO SHOP FOR ASTRAGALUS

You can buy slices of dried astragalus in Chinese or Asian groceries. These can either be simmered in tea—it lends the beverage a sweet taste—or in soups. The herb can also be found in health food stores as an extract, capsule, tablet, or purchased in tea bags. It is also adaptable to be grown in many parts of the United States; the roots, which look like tongue depressors, can be harvested in four or five years.

BACOPA

TREAT DEPRESSION AND ANXIETY, MAINTAIN MEMORY, AND SUPPORT LIVER FUNCTION

An aquatic or semiaquatic plant, bacopa *(Bacopa monnieri)* is a low-growing ground cover that forms dense mats in wetlands. A member of the Plantaginaceae, or plantain family, it is found in tropical or subtropical regions around the world. With its succulent leaves and white or pink flowers it is an appealing plant, and some species can be seen floating in aquariums or backyard ponds.

Bacopa has a 3,000-year history as a medicinal plant, and has been used primarily as an aid to mental functioning. As a healing herb and staple of Ayurvedic medicine—it is known as *brahmi* in India—bacopa is believed to improve mental abilities, namely comprehension or acquisition *(Dhi)*, memory or retention *(Dhriti)*, and recollection or recall *(Smriti)*.

Health Benefits

Experts estimate that as many as 90 percent of primary care visits are for ailments related to stress. Stress is certainly a significant factor in loss of productivity in the workplace, as well as in digestive complaints and recurring back and neck pain. Yet advocates of natural remedies know that this unassuming plant is a powerful adaptogen—an herb that enables the body to adapt to stress or unfamiliar

> ### DID YOU KNOW?
> * *This is a global herb—it is known as* brahmi *in Hindu,* niirpirami *in Tamil,* phak mi *in Thai,* timare *in Kannada,* lunawila *in Sri Lankan,* 'ae'ae *in Hawaiian,* rau dang *in Vietnamese,* kleines fettblatt *in German, and as water hyssop, moneywort, or herb of grace in English.*

situations by increasing certain chemicals in the brain.

Bacopa can also help treat depression and anxiety by regulating the mood-elevating endorphins seratonin and dopamine. It may also improve some measure of memory in healthy older adults and in children aged six to eight years. It is currently under study as a possible treatment for dementia. Compounds found in bacopa, known as bacosides, may have the ability to influence human brain cells and even promote regeneration of brain tissue. Bacosides are also reported to increase the effect and decrease the "high" when used with addictive opioids like morphine and oxycodone, thus reducing the risk of drug dependency. Bacopa supports liver function, the body's main detoxifying organ. Bacopa supplements are available in liquid extract, tablets, or encapsulated powder. It is fat soluble and is best taken with a meal. As with any supplement, start with a low dosage, and gradually increase if needed.

> ### STAYING FOCUSED AND ALERT
> Children or teens who suffer from attention deficit hyperactive disorder (ADHD), a behavioral disorder marked by trouble focusing or paying attention and impulsive or disruptive behavior, are often prescribed Adderall. This drug counteracts the symptoms of ADHD by boosting alertness, attention, and energy levels, but it is also highly addictive. Bacopa may be an effective Adderall alternative, replicating many of these benefits, including fostering focus, learning, and memory, and improving cognitive function—without the risk of opioid dependency. On the downside, it can take as many as 10 or 12 weeks before patients begin to report feelings of improvement.

Bacopa leaves

Mixed cultivars of basil, including a purple. Basil's rich scent makes it both an effective culinary herb and medicinal plant.

BASIL

AID DIGESTION, ENHANCE APPETITE, AND TREAT RESPIRATORY AILMENTS

An herbal plant associated with the Mediterranean region, basil (Ocimum basilicum), is often referred to as the "king of herbs." Its spicy-sweet flavor, earthy scent, and versatility in recipes has certainly earned it its place among the preeminent culinary herbs in the world.

This annual member of the mint family, with its spikes of small white, pink, or purple flowers, originated in India, Africa, and Asia. In India, it was used to protect the dead from evil spirits, and it still grows on the grounds of many Hindu temples. It is now found worldwide, thriving in outdoor gardens in semitropical or temperate regions and on windowsills in climates that don't support tender herbs.

Health Benefits

In the realm of ancient herbal healing, basil was employed to purify the mind, open the heart, and even cure malaria. Today it is used to aid intestinal problems such as indigestion, nausea, and gas. It is the herb's

> **DID YOU KNOW?**
>
> • *Fresh basil can be frozen for use all year long. Puree the leaves in a blender, and freeze in an ice cube tray covered with a little water. When a recipe calls for fresh basil, simply defrost and use. Always add fresh basil to a dish just before serving to preserve its taste and health benefits.*

antispasmodic properties that make it so effective for treating flatulence and stomach irritations. Its pungent flavor triggers saliva production, which can aid digestion. It also acts as an appetite enhancer and increases the flow of bile. By stimulating the cilia in the nose, it helps to clear nasal passages of mucous and harmful bacteria, making it beneficial for treating respiratory ailments. It is also prescribed to ease motion sickness.

The therapeutic power of this herb lies in its essential oil, mainly methyl chavicol. Fresh basil also contains carotenoids—pigments that act as antioxidants, protecting us against chronic diseases—and folic acid, one of the B vitamins that helps the body make healthy new cells. Dried basil provides the minerals calcium, magnesium, and iron.

RESCUE REMEDY: *Try basil wine as a digestive aid. To prepare it, steep a bunch of basil leaves in a bottle of white wine for one day. Strain, and then refrigerate. Drink a 4-ounce glass after meals to improve digestion.*

Up Close
INDOOR GARDENS
YOUR GUIDE TO ENJOYING HERBS ALL YEAR ROUND

You don't need a lot of backyard acreage to have your own herb garden. Many herbs will thrive indoors.

One way to ensure a steady supply of fresh or freshly dried herbs throughout the year is to grow them yourself at home. Many herbs need only a south- or southwest-facing windowsill with good natural light (at least four hours a day) to perform their best, and if you stagger planting times, you can rely on having a fresh crop to harvest almost continuously.

Windowsill Favorites

Some medicinal herbs that do well in the home are as follows. Most of them can be grown indoors from seeds or cuttings or started outside during the warmer months, and then transplanted indoors as the weather cools. Miniature greenhouses make it easier to keep the humidity high, but a daily spritz of water from a spray bottle is almost as effective. If a plant does start to dry out, you can water it, and then bag it up in a clear plastic bag until it perks up.

LAVENDER Fragrant lavender (genus *Lavendula*) has many uses: it is a culinary herb, a crafting material, and a medicinal aromatic. To grow it indoors, find a breezy spot with natural sunlight. Lavender requires plenty of bright light and a refreshing airflow to thrive.

OREGANO A Mediterranean culinary favorite, oregano (*Origanum vulgare*) offers rich flavor and the medicinal benefits of volatile oils thymol and carvacrol, which inhibit bacterial growth. Plant the tip of an outdoor plant in a pot of starter soil and place in a south-facing window.

SAGE Savory-tasting sage *(Salvia officinalis)* captures the essence of Thanksgiving. Used to treat mouth and throat ailments, this wiry herb will tolerate the dry indoor air. Grow from a cutting—the tip of an outdoor plant, say—in the strong sun of a southern windowsill.

ROSEMARY A pungent culinary herb, rosemary (*Rosmarinus officinalis*) is part of the famous bouquet garni used in Continental cookery, but it is also a versatile medicinal plant, easing stress, gastric problems, and pain. Start from cuttings in a southern window, and keep soil moist until the stalks root.

TARRAGON The perfect accompaniment to seafood, poultry, and eggs, tarragon (*Artemisia dracunculus*) is also a powerful scavenger of harmful free radicals. To be grown indoors, tarragon requires a dormant period. Pot a garden specimen in fall, and then allow the leaves to die back. Place the plant in your coolest indoor spot for several days, and then move it to a south-facing window. Feed with liquid organic fertilizer to keep it thriving.

THYME A venerable cooking herb, thyme (*Thymus vulgaris*) also contains antioxidants and many volatile oils that provide healthy fats to the brain, kidneys and heart membrane. Begin indoors using a soft tip from a garden plant or repotting an outdoor plant. Thyme enjoys full sun, but it will tolerate partial sun in an east- or west-facing window.

CHIVES This zesty member of the onion family offers both antibiotic and anti-inflammatory benefits. Like thyme, a chive plant (*Allium schoenoprasum*) needs a dormant stage. Dig up a clump of chives and repot them. Leave the pot outside until the leaves die back, and then place the pot in a cold interior spot, perhaps the basement, for a few days before setting in your sunniest window.

Rosemary makes a good choice for a window garden, and with its needlelike leaves is a candidate for home drying.

BASIL A staple of Italian cookery, basil (*Ocimum basilicum*) is an antibacterial and antimicrobial herb. It needs only sunlight and warmth to flourish. Grow from seeds, and snip off flowers before they bloom to keep the leaves from becoming bitter.

PARSLEY This mild culinary herb not only offers tumor-repressing volatile oils and cell-protecting flavonoid antioxidants, but it will also grow steadily in an east- or west-facing window. Start parsley plants (*Petroselinum crispum*) from seeds, or transplant a small clump from your garden.

BAY LEAF The leaves of the bay laurel (*Laurus nobilis*) flavor sauces and soups, and their essential oil relieves bruising and body aches. Bay laurel is actually a tree, but it does well indoors in a pot with well-draining soil. Place in an east-facing or west-facing window; just make sure that there is space for air to circulate around it.

DRY YOUR OWN HERBS

Although the piquant flavors of freshly harvested herbs are hard to beat, many recipes—and remedies—call for dried herbs. Fortunately, the process of drying herbs is simple to perform at home. If you are gathering herbs from your indoor pots, simply snip them off at the stem. Outdoor herbs should be gathered in mid- to late morning, after the dew has dried. Herbalists suggest that just before flowering is the best time to pick. After rinsing your herbs and patting them dry, secure the stems with a twist tie (so you can tighten it as stems shrink) and hang the bundle upside down inside a pierced paper bag in a warm, dry spot. Ideal herbs for drying include bay leaves, rosemary, thyme, and sage. Tender-leafed plants like basil, parsley, mint, tarragon, and lemon balm may need rapid drying in a low oven to prevent mold.

Arctium lappa flowers and burrs. This species is also known as greater burdock.

BURDOCK

REDUCE BLOOD PRESSURE, REGULATE INSULIN, AND BOOST THE IMMUNE SYSTEM

Burdock *(Arctium lappa)* is a common wildflower that offers a number of uncommon health benefits. This member of the thistle family originated in Europe and Asia and was transported to the Americas with French and English colonists. The tall, stout, green plant displays large, wavy, wedge-shaped leaves and purple flowers that mature into rounded thistly fruits, with burrs that cling relentlessly to the fur, feathers, or clothing of any passing creature. (These burrs were the inspiration behind the creation of hook-and-loop fasteners.) Burdock prefers rough habitats—vacant lots, fallow fields, roadside ditches, hedgerows, and riverbanks. The long root, which can reach two or three feet in length, is sometimes prepared as a vegetable, and the delicate young stalks can be peeled and then boiled.

Health Benefits

Burdock has been a reliable healing herb for hundreds of years, used by cultures all over the world. Typically, it is the dried first-year root that is utilized, but some herbalists also employ the leaves and fruits. It has been used alone or combined with yellow dock and sarsaparilla as a blood purifier or to treat skin infections, such as boils and abscesses, and skin diseases like acne, psoriasis, and eczema. Burdock may also increase circulation to the skin and promote

> **DID YOU KNOW?**
>
> • *Burdock has a host of colorful folk names, including lappa, fox's clote, thorny burr, beggar's buttons, cockle buttons, love leaves, philanthropium, personata, happy major, and clot-bur. Its genus name, Arctium, comes from the Greek word for "bear," a reference to the rough, furlike appearance of the plant's burrs.*

perspiration, thus detoxifying epidermal tissues. A poultice of the leaves can reportedly bring down the painful swelling of gout.

Medical research indicates that burdock root contains a high concentration of a carbohydrate called inulin. Inulin works to strengthen the liver, and, along with its high concentrations of mucilage, has a soothing effect on the GI tract. The plant also possesses polyacetylenes that furnish antibacterial and antifungal properties. Burdock's medicinal qualities also include the following.

- The plant's high levels of potassium, a vasodilator, can reduce blood pressure and relieve tension within the cardiovascular system.
- The inulin—a type of fiber—found in burdock is particularly effective at regulating the balance of insulin and glucose in the body and may reduce the severity of diabetes or prevent its onset.
- With its high levels of antioxidant vitamins C and E, burdock significantly boosts the immune system's ability to eliminate free radicals.
- In research studies, burdock's organic compounds have been linked to improving the detoxifying function of the liver. It can also restore hormonal balance by helping the liver metabolize certain hormones, such as estrogen, allowing hormonal levels to normalize.

CALENDULA

HEAL WOUNDS, SOOTHE SKIN, TREAT INFECTION, AND RELIEVE ABDOMINAL DISCOMFORT

Also known as pot marigold, calendula (*Calendula officinalis*), is a member of the Compositae (the aster or daisy family). Native to Micronesia, southwestern Asia, and the Mediterranean region, it is now naturalized in most temperate locations and is a favorite with gardeners everywhere. It is currently cultivated for commercial purposes in the Mediterranean region, the Balkans, Germany, India, Poland, Hungary, North America, Chile, Australia, and New Zealand. The name comes from the Latin for "little calendar," because the plant was thought to bloom on the *calend*, the first day of the new moon cycle; the name *marigold* is a reference to the Virgin Mary or "Mary's gold." The noted 11th-century nun and gardener Saint Hildegard of Bingen is believed to be the first to cultivate the herb, which became a mainstay of European herbal studies.

Health Benefits

Most herbalists would agree that this popular flower is also one of the top plants when it comes to healing wounds and providing anti-inflammatory, antiviral, and antimicrobial properties. For centuries, calendula has been relied on as a remedy for abdominal cramps, constipation, women's reproductive issues, and chapped lips or split skin. In Ayurvedic medicine the herb, which is considered energetically cooling, is used on minor wounds, eye irritations, and bee stings. Called *jin zhan ju* in Chinese medicine, calendula is considered energetically neutral and drying and is used to support healthy skin.

Herbal calendula appears in a variety of forms: as a healing lotion, oil, gel, compress, tincture, or tea; as a soothing bath soak or gentle facial cream; and as a germ-fighting ingredient in toothpaste and

> **DID YOU KNOW?**
>
> • The early Greeks and Romans used calendula for numerous rituals, even wearing them in garlands. In India, it is a sacred flower that's been used to decorate the statues of Hindu deities for millennia. At festive celebrations, the vibrant orange blossoms are strung together and hung up as decorations.

mouthwash—not to mention that those gorgeous deep orange petals can be eaten in salads, soups, and stews, especially in Middle Eastern or Mediterranean dishes. The petals are also dried and used to color cheeses or as a substitute for saffron.

Calendula's powerful flavonoids and linoleic acid provide it with amazing anti-inflammatory qualities, which protect cells from inflammatory compounds. This makes it one of the go-to herbs for treating sore throats, diaper rash (especially if used with coconut oil), dermatitis, and ear infections. One study also showed that the herb relaxes spontaneous muscle contractions, while other studies indicate that calendula-based gels and lotions help speed up slow-healing wounds and exposed ulcers, along with hemorrhoids, possibly by increasing blood flow and oxygen to the affected areas. The best time to harvest the flowers for medicinal purposes is during the heat of the day in summer, when the resins are high.

The whole calendula plant, but especially the blossoms and the leaves, has a wide variety of medicinal uses.

CHAMOMILE

REDUCE STOMACH ACIDS, TREAT COLIC, AND REDUCE INFLAMMATION

A member of the Compositae (the aster or daisy family), chamomile, is best known for its stomach-calming or sleep-inducing capabilities, but it can provide a range of health benefits. *Matricaria recutita,* known as German, Italian, and Hungarian chamomile; scented mayweed; or wild chamomile, is the species most often used by herbalists. It originated in Europe, Asia, and North Africa and grows as an annual that reaches about two feet in height. It has green feathery leaves and small white flowers arranged as florets. *Chamaemelum nobile,* familiar as Roman, English, or garden chamomile, also has multiple medicinal uses.

Health Benefits

The ancient Egyptians were among the first to value chamomile, using it as both a medicine and a cosmetic aid. They dedicated it to the sun and honored it above all other herbs. The Greeks prescribed it for fever and female disorders, and, of course, the blossoms have been used for many centuries to make a relaxing tea. Chamomile is the fifth herb mentioned in the "Nine Herbs Charm" found in the early Anglo-Saxon *Lacnunga* (see opposite page). It has also been used to treat hay fever, muscle spasms, respiratory issues, inflammation, migraine headaches, menstrual disorders, gastrointestinal disorders, skin irritations, and hemorrhoids.

Among chamomile's many chemical compounds, two are notable: apigenin, which demonstrates chemoprotective effects against cancer in lab studies, and alpha-bisabolol, which has antiseptic and anti-inflammatory properties and reduces pepsin secretion without changing the secretion of stomach acids. In studies, chamomile extracts have shown inhibitory effects on cancer cells in vitro, but have minimal effect on normal cells. The bisabolol and flavonoids in the herb have displayed antispasmodic effects on animals; in human studies, chamomile (in combination with herbs like vervain, licorice, fennel, and lemon balm) proved an effective treatment for colic. Due to its emollient and anti-inflammatory qualities, it is often added to commercial skin treatments; its appealing apple scent makes it a natural for use in the perfume and aromatherapy trades (the plant's name derives from the Greek *khamaimelon,* meaning "earth apple"). Therapeutically, the herb can be taken in the form of teas, tinctures, lotions, capsules, or drops.

> **DID YOU KNOW?**
>
> • *Chamomile has had some unusual applications over the years. In ancient Egypt, this herb was part of the mummification process. Early gardeners found it useful because it had the ability to stimulate the growth of other plants, even sickly ones. A chamomile tea rinse can enhance the color of blond hair.*

RESCUE REMEDY: *A soothing tisane made from fresh or dried chamomile steeped in hot water is ideal for bathing skin irritations, chickenpox, eczema, psoriasis, or sunburn. Dip a small cloth compress into comfortably hot tea, and press it against the affected area until the cloth cools. Repeat several times a day.*

German chamomile (*Matricaria recutita*). Both *M. recutita* and *Chamaemelum nobile* feature petite daisylike flowers.

CHERVIL

HEAL SKIN WOUNDS, RELIEVE CRAMPS, AND EASE JOINT INFLAMMATION

This culinary herb has a medicinal history that dates back to ancient Rome. Also known as garden chervil or French parsley, chervil *(Anthriscus cerefolium),* is a member of the Apiaceae, also known as the parsley, carrot, or celery family. The herb originated in the Caucasus Mountains and was spread by Roman troops throughout most of Europe. The plant typically grows from 16 to 28 inches in height with tripinnate eaves and small white flowers that form umbels. A staple of French cooking, chervil is part of the flavorful fines herbes—along with parsley, chives, and tarragon—used to add earthy but delicate tastes and scents to chicken, egg, and fish recipes. The fresh leaves, known as cicily, have a slight licorice-lemon taste and make a delicious addition to salads, dips, or finger sandwiches.

DID YOU KNOW?

One reason chervil may not be popular in American gardens is its resemblance to cow parsley (Anthriscus sylvestris), *an invasive British weed. It also looks a lot like a poisonous plant called hemlock—the one responsible for the death of Socrates—so chervil should never be picked in the wild.*

Health Benefits

Romans were so pleased about the discovery of chervil in the Caucasus region that they named it the "herb of rejoicing," taken from the Greek word *chaerophyllon.* Not only did they relish it in their cooking, they also valued it as a diuretic and for its stimulating and blood-purifying properties. It was also believed to be an aphrodisiac and a sexual tonic for older men and said to inspire cheerfulness and sharp wit. Subsequent European cultures used chervil as an aid to digestion, for lowering blood pressure, and, in an infusion with vinegar, as a cure for the hiccups. Bathing the face with water in which chervil had been boiled was believed by ladies of the French court to preserve the complexion. Yet in spite of these multiple applications, many early herbalists did not favor the plant—perhaps thinking its mild taste meant that it possessed weak curative powers.

Modern research has shown chervil to be an excellent source of antioxidants, which help to stabilize cell membranes and reduce inflammation. Today, it is recommended as an eyewash and as a tea to ease menstrual cramps. Crumpled leaves can be placed on wounds, insect bites, or burns to speed healing, and a warm chervil poultice can be applied to ease joints swollen by arthritis or injury.

Use fresh chervil in your recipes to reap its antioxidant benefits. Mix it with goat cheese, salt, and pepper to use as a cracker spread. Blend it with a little bit of chives and breadcrumbs to top grilled oysters. Or add it to sautéed mushrooms or whipped potatoes.

Potted chervil

THE NINE SACRED HERBS

Chervil is the eighth herb mentioned in the "Nine Herbs Charm," which is found in the early Anglo-Saxon *Lacnunga.* The *Lacnunga* (or *Remedies)* manuscript, dating from the 10th to 11th centuries, is a collection of nearly 200 mostly herbal remedies, prayers, and charms. Translations of the original Old English list of the nine sacred herbs vary, but the general consensus has mugwort, plantain, watercress, betony, chamomile, stinging nettle, crabapple, and fennel rounding out the ingredients of this remedial charm.

CLARY SAGE

IMPROVE MOOD, PREVENT INFECTION, AND TREAT PAIN, COUGHS, AND WOUNDS

A member of the Lamiaceae, or mint family, clary sage (*Salvia sclarea*) is a close relative of the garden sage of culinary fame (*S. officinalis*). This perennial or biennial herb originated in the northern Mediterranean region along with North Africa and Central Asia. It grows to three or four feet in height, with sturdy, hairy stems and clumping flowers in shades of pale purple or mauve. When distilled, the essential oil is used to flavor liqueurs, vermouth, and wines, especially muscatel.

Health Benefits

Clary sage has been a favorite of natural healers since the Middle Ages, when it was employed as an eyewash or aid to clear sight (thus the name). Doctors often recommended placing a mucilaginous seed into an inflamed eye to attract the irritant. Yet it was also valued for treating a wide number of disorders—and it remains valued today.

Modern research reveals that among the herb's chief chemical components are sclareol, which in recent studies has shown potential in fighting

> ### DID YOU KNOW?
>
> *Clary sage boasts both anti-inflammatory and antioxidant properties, making it a natural cholesterol fighter that helps the body to reduce plaque in the bloodstream that can build up on arterial walls and increase the risk of heart attack or stroke. It also addresses two other risk factors—stress and poor circulation.*

leukemia, and linalyl acetate, which reduces skin irritations and rashes. It also contains alpha terpineol, geraniol, linalool, caryophyllene, neryl acetate, and germacrene. It is most often employed as an essential oil, with a multitude of medicinal properties that include the following.

- Antispasmodic—Treats coughs, headaches, and stomachaches
- Antidepressant—Boosts self-esteem and mental strength
- Aphrodisiac—Increases libido
- Antibacterial—Treats infection, especially in regard to the colon, intestines, and urinary tract
- Antiseptic—Prevents wounds from becoming septic or contracting tetanus
- Astringent—Helps strengthen the gums and tones, heals, or rejuvenates skin

Due to its phytoestrogens—plant-derived estrogens—clary sage is one of the best herbs to balance the body's hormones. It is reported to relieve menstrual cramping and discomfort, as well as prevent postmenopausal issues, such hot flashes, and uterine problems, such as bleeding, tumors, and pain. The essential oil of clary sage is a known calmative and sleep aid, with related benefits that include easing anxiety, vertigo, and stress. It is also used as a digestive and as an anticonvulsive.

Clary sage flowers, leaves, and essential oil

RESCUE REMEDY: *The versatile essential oil can be used in several ways. To inhale it, add 2 or 3 drops to a diffuser, or add 3 to 5 drops to a warm tub. You can also apply it topically to relieve pain or cramping. To use it as a facial treatment, combine 5 drops of clary sage oil with 5 drops of a carrier oil, and massage into the affected area. To take the oil internally, use only the highest quality oil available, and dilute a drop of oil in a glass of water, add it to honey, or stir it into a smoothie.*

COMFREY

SOOTHE RASHES AND SHALLOW WOUNDS AND TREAT SKIN CONDITIONS

This perennial herb has a long history as an herbal medicine and a garden booster. The variety most frequently used is Russian comfrey (*Symphytum* x *uplandicum*), a cross between common comfrey (*S. officinale*) and rough comfrey (*S. asperum*). This member of the family Boraginaceae is native to Europe but is now found all over North America and in western Asia. It prefers damp grassy locations like riverbanks, ditches, marshes, and bogs. The plant bears broad, hairy leaves and small bell-like flowers, typically in cream or purple, which are often striped. The root is black and turniplike. Many gardeners report that this plant is a boon to their plots, not only as an effective fertilizer, but also as an attractant to soil nutrients that enrich nearby plants.

> ### DID YOU KNOW?
>
> • *In addition to being a medicinal herb, comfrey is valued as a fertilizer in organic farming. The plant's roots initially mine nutrients from the soil, and then, as the leaves decompose, they can be placed as mulch around plants or used to add nitrogen to the compost heap.*

Popular as a curative since Roman times, comfrey was once known as boneset and knitbone, leading to its genus name, *symphis,* from the Greek for "bones growing together" and *phyon,* for "plant."

Health Benefits

With its genus name, it is no surprise that the herb was once widely used to treat broken bones, sprains, strains, and arthritis. (It is still used to "set" bones, especially those that cannot be placed in a cast, such as rib bones.) It was also employed for bronchial problems, gastric distress, and varicose ulcers. Its mucilaginous properties made it useful against acne, burns, bug bites, and other skin conditions and for preventing or treating scars.

Modern science reveals that the herb contains allantoin, a small, organic molecule that may stimulate skin cell growth and reduce inflammation, as well rosmarinic acid and tannins, making it ideal for treating rashes and shallow wounds. It should only be used topically as a salve, in a poultice or compress, or as an essential oil.

> ### MAKE IT YOURSELF
> ## *Soothing Comfrey Salve*
>
> Comfrey can help relieve the discomfort of rashes or small wounds. It is not recommended that it be ingested—it contains dangerous levels of hepatotoxic pyrrolizidine alkaloids (PAs) that can cause liver damage. To use it topically, try this recipe for a soothing salve.
>
> **YOU WILL NEED:**
> ½ cup dried comfrey leaves
> ½ cup dried plantain
> 1½ cups grapeseed, almond, or olive oil
> 4 teaspoons beeswax pastilles
> 20 drops rosemary essential oil
>
> **WHAT TO DO:**
> • Infuse herbs in oil in a Crock-Pot for three hours or in a glass jar for two or three weeks.
> • Warm up the infused oil, and strain through a cheesecloth into a pint mason jar.
> • Add beeswax to warm oil, and stir to melt.
> • Mix in 20 drops of rosemary oil, and pour into lidded storage container.

Filtering an infusion of comfrey leaves. Comfrey, which should only be used externally, can be the base of a comforting topical ointment or salve.

The dandelion was imported to the New World as a food crop. As a medicinal, you can eat it or take it as a supplement.

DANDELION

CONTROL DIABETES AND PROMOTE GALL BLADDER, HEART, AND URINARY HEALTH

t is increasingly apparent with each passing year—and with each new medical study—that a plant once dismissed as a nuisance weed in reality possesses powerful disease-fighting properties. Yes, the humble dandelion *(Taraxacum officinale),* that bane of many a landscaper, is full of vitamins and other nutrients, as well as healing agents. This member of the family Compositae originated roughly 30 million years ago in Eurasia. It now flourishes in most temperate parts of the globe. Dandelions prefer moist soil and are found on roadsides and riverbanks and in lawns and meadows.

The plant ranges in height from 2 to 16 inches, with oblong, jagged leaves that can grow upright or spread out to the side—and inspired the name *dent de lion,* or "lion's tooth" in French. A hollow stem rises above the leaves and bears tiny yellow florets, that combine into one large flower head. The dried florets form "blowballs" or "clocks," made up of fruits with silver-tufted parachutes called pappi, which are easily dispersed. This plant, like many in its genus, is able to reproduce asexually using apomixis—the fruits are produced without a pollinator—in most cases making the offspring genetically identical to the parent plant.

DID YOU KNOW?

* *The dandelion has been given many common names in England and America, including: blowball, lion's tooth, milk witch, cankerwort, yellow gowan, Irish daisy, swine's snout, monkshead, priest's crown, puffball, faceclock, pee-a-bed, wet-a-bed, white endive, and wild endive.*

Health Benefits

Dandelions leaves, or greens, if gathered while the plant is young, make a savory addition to salads, with a tangy taste similar to mustard greens. The leaves are valuable detoxifiers, high in beta-carotene, fiber, vitamin C, and potassium—and they actually provide more iron and calcium than spinach. The blossoms are frequently made into wine and jam. The milky latex in the leaves and stem has been used to repel mosquitoes and remove warts.

The plant was long popular with healers in Europe, North America, and China for treating infections and liver problems, as a diuretic and laxative, to increase appetite, and to improve digestion. Modern research confirms many of the plant's healing applications. It contains a number of flavonoids, including luteolin (an antioxidant that benefits the liver) and apigenin, which offers anti-inflammatory and antitumor properties, as well as a variety of other immunity-boosting compounds. These components give it the potential to reduce the risk of cancer, control diabetes, aid weight loss, and treat gall bladder disorders. Its diuretic properties make it effective for lowering high blood pressure and treating urinary infections.

ECHINACEA

SUPPORT RESPIRATORY HEALTH AND REDUCE INFLAMMATION, PAIN, AND ANXIETY

This longtime herbal remedy, *Echinacea purpurea,* known as the purple coneflower, also adorns many summer gardens and perennial borders. The plant is native to North America—for centuries the Great Plains Indian tribes utilized its antibiotic and pain-relieving properties. A member of the Compositae, it can reach 47 inches in height. It displays coarse, often hairy lanceolate or ovate leaves and cone-shaped heads with rays, or petals, in shades of purple on long, sturdy stems. The flowers are hermaphroditic and are pollinated by butterflies and bees. Echinacea prefers wild habitats like dry, sparse woodlands and prairies, but it also performs well in cultivated beds.

Health Benefits

Echinacea has a long history as a natural curative and wellness tonic. In addition to *E. purpurea,* other medicinal species are *E. angustifolia* (narrow-leaved purple coneflower) and *E. pallida* (pale purple coneflower). All parts of the plant—flowers, leaves, and roots—are used in herbal medicine, although the aboveground portions are believed to be the most effective, containing polysaccharides that stimulate immune function. In fact, most of the plant's chemical constituents—essential oils, inulin, flavonoids, and vitamin C—can augment immunity. The herb is also known for treating respiratory ailments and is effective against colds, flu, sinusitis, strep throat, and whooping cough. Taking echinacea regularly may cut your chance of contracting a cold by nearly 60 percent and reduce its duration by a day and a half. Other potential health benefits include the following:

- The National Institutes of Health reports that its phytochemicals could be valuable tools for combating brain cancer tumors.

> **DID YOU KNOW?**
>
> - *Echinacea gained its common name from the flower's spiky brownish central disk—the word* echinacea *derives from the Greek* ekhinos, *or "hedgehog," because the plant's center resembles that spiny animal.*

- Echinacea's anti-inflammatory properties make it useful against acute or chronic inflammations, including rheumatoid arthritis.
- Echinacea benefits the skin, and it has been used to heal rashes, spider bites, eczema, stings, infections, and wounds, and to regenerate skin.
- It is effective against several types of pain, including bowel pain, stomach distress, headaches, herpes, sore throats, and toothache. It can be taken as a supplement or drunk in tea or a paste can be made of the ground herb and applied directly to the affected area.
- As a treatment for mental disorders, especially ADD/ADHD, *E. angustifolia* has been shown to quell emotional disturbances, social phobias, anxiety, and depression. (Take no more than 20 mg per dose to avoid negating the effects.)

RESCUE REMEDY: *Echinacea makes a safe, mild, natural laxative. A cup of tea daily can keep you regular; drink two cups if you become constipated.*

Echinacea in bloom. These plants are as useful as they are attractive—just about all parts have medicinal value.

ELDER

BOLSTER THE IMMUNE SYSTEM, TREAT INFECTIONS, AND EASE ALLERGIES

Native to Europe and North America, elder (a deciduous member of the Adoxaceae, or moschatel family) grows in sunny locations in either wet or dry soil. The species most often used by herbalists, *Sambucus nigra,* is a large bush or shrub with pinnate, serrated leaves and a flattish top, where it displays masses of creamy, fragrant blossoms followed by drooping bunches of juicy, deep purple berries. The genus name was adapted from the Greek *sambuca,* or "sackbut," an ancient stringed instrument favored by the Romans that was possibly made from hardy elder wood.

> ### DID YOU KNOW?
>
> • *The name* elder *comes from the Anglo-Saxon* aeld, *or "fire." In earlier times, the hollowed stems of the elder tree were used to build up fires—the soft pith of young branches is easily removed so that the remaining tubes can be used as pipes to blow air onto a flame. The plant was soon known as pipe tree or bore-tree.*

Health Benefits

As a curative herb, elder was often referred to as the "medicine chest of the country people." Healers used the flowers and berries to make healthful cordials and teas and for treating respiratory and digestive ailments, constipation, and urinary tract issues. The bruised leaves were used as an insect repellent.

Modern research has revealed elder's antiseptic, antibacterial, anti-inflammatory, and antiviral properties and bears out its medicinal value, especially against respiratory viruses. In a study by the American Botanical Council, a group suffering from flu were treated with elderberry and recovered in half the time of the placebo group. This might be due to the anthocyanins in the plant, which inhibit the growth of hemagglutinin, spiky proteins that a flu virus uses to attach itself to healthy cells and invade them. The herb then increases production of lymphocytes that bolster the immune system. Elder has also shown to be an effective killer of many hospital pathogens, such as *Staphylococcus aureus.* It contains potent antioxidant, anticancer bioflavonoids, as well as chlorogenic acids, which can ease allergies and regulate blood glucose levels. The triterpenoids found in elder offer analgesic, anti-inflammatory, and anticancer benefits.

Elder can be taken as a supplement as dried flowers, or in tea, pill, or tincture form. Elderberries of any color need to be cooked prior to use to avoid possible gastrointestinal complaints.

Elderberries. Elder fruit and flowers are used to make teas, jams, cordials, and wines. Other parts of the plant are toxic.

ELDER IN LEGEND AND LORE

Elder was the medieval symbol of sorrow and death; it has also figured in myths and legends—Judas Iscariot reputedly hung himself from an elder tree, and European lore insisted it was bad luck to cut branches from an elder and thus displease the spirit of the tree. Conversely, it was believed that Jesus Christ was crucified on a cross made from a giant elder tree.

The leaves, flowers, and seeds of *Eucalyptus globulus*, known as the Tasmanian blue gum or just blue gum. This species is the primary source of commercial essential oils.

EUCALYPTUS

TREAT WOUNDS AND BURNS, COLDS, MUSCLE AND JOINT PAIN, AND MENTAL EXHAUSTION

The eucalyptus, or gum tree, dominates the forests of Australia with more than 700 species, many offering nutritional support to koalas and other marsupials. Oddly, genus *Eucalyptus* originated in South America, where it is no longer native. Of the 15 species found in other parts of the world, only 9 are exclusively non-Australian. Today, they are cultivated in Asia, North America, Europe, and Africa, as fast-growing sources of wood and of oils used for cleaning and as natural insecticides. The trees are also water guzzlers that can be used to drain swamplands. Like other members of the myrtle family (Myrtaceae), these are mostly evergreen; generally the leaves are lanceolate, petiolate, and alternate, and a waxy or glossy green. The flowers have no petals, but multiple fluffy stamens in white, cream, yellow, pink, or red and woody, cone-shaped fruits that release waxy, rod-shaped seeds. The bark may be stringy, rough and furrowed, flaky, short-fibered, or ribbonlike. Eucalyptus is known for its camphorlike odor and pungent flavor; a distinctive honey is made from its flowers.

Health Benefits

The antiseptic essential oils that are steam-distilled from the plant are used for deodorizing surfaces and cleansing the air. In small quantities, the oil flavors sweets, cough drops, toothpaste, and decongestants.

DID YOU KNOW?

• *Many species of eucalyptus are known as gum trees because they exude kino, or plant gum, from any breaks in the bark or stalks. This substance looks like red currant jelly but dries into an amberlike material that is used in medicines, in the leather tanning process, and to make dyes.*

Natural healers use it for treating wounds, muscle aches, joint pain, mental exhaustion, and skincare. With its antimicrobial, antibacterial, and anti-inflammatory properties, the oil is effective for treating cuts, scrapes, burns, stings, and abrasions. It is a powerful ally against colds, flu, and sinus infections when inhaled from a diffuser; it also works as an expectorant to rid the body of toxins. It can even be used on pets, if kept away from the eyes and open wounds.

The trees contain an organic compound originally known as eucalyptol, now called cineole, which offers a range of medicinal benefits, including reducing inflammation and pain and even destroying leukemia cells. More than a thousand research studies have been dedicated to unlocking the potential of this compound. Cineole and other terpenoids found in the trees often form a smoglike vapor over eucalyptus woodlands; this haze was responsible for the naming of Australia's Blue Mountains.

RESCUE REMEDY: *Eucalyptus oil can work wonders for rejuvenating your hair and hands. To restore luster to you hair, combine a few drops of eucalyptus oil with olive or coconut oil, and work through your hair before shampooing. To clean grimy hands—or stimulate hands and feet in the bath—mix a few drops of the oil with Epsom salts and sea salt, and use as a scrub.*

FENNEL

CONTROL ANEMIA, SOOTHE INDIGESTION, AND PROMOTE HEART HEALTH

An aromatic flowering plant, fennel (*Foeniculum vulgare*) is employed both in the kitchen as an aromatic herb and in the sickroom as a healing herb. This member of the celery, carrot, or parsley family (Apiaceae) originated in the Mediterranean and was spread across Europe by Roman armies. Over time, it naturalized in many locations, especially in areas with dry soil near seacoasts or rivers. It is now widely cultivated for its tasty leaves and fruits.

The fennel plant is a hardy perennial with sleek, sturdy stems, feathery leaves, and tiny yellow flowers that form umbels. These plants are garden behemoths that can even reach heights of eight feet. The attractive licorice flavor of fennel comes from the presence of anethole, an aromatic compound also found in anise and star anise.

Health Benefits

Over the centuries, natural healers have used fennel to relieve colic, treat ulcers, promote milk flow in nursing mothers, and expel wind. Today, we know that fennel contains a number of beneficial volatile oils, among them anethole, limonene, anisic aldehyde, pinene, myrcene, cineole, fenchone, and chavicol, which are responsible for the plant's healing properties. The

herb—whether taken fresh in salads or soups, as a tea, as dried seeds, or in supplement form—is effective in treating a number of serious conditions. These include anemia (fennel contains both iron, the main constituent of hemoglobin, and histidene, an amino acid that stimulates production of hemoglobin), indigestion (the essential oils stimulate the secretion of gastric juices and reduce stomach inflammation), flatulence (the aspartic acid found in the plant reduces gas), high blood pressure (the herb's potassium acts as a vasodilator, facilitating blood flow), and high cholesterol (its high fiber helps to maintain healthy cholesterol levels and to eliminate damaging LDL cholesterol). The seeds are also a good source of dietary fiber. In addition to flavonoid antioxidants that battle free radicals, fennel contains vitamins A, B complex, C, and D, as well as copper, iron, calcium, potassium, manganese, and magnesium.

MAKE IT YOURSELF
Flavorful Fennel Soup

Enjoy the anise/onion taste of braised fennel in this quick and easy—and healthful—soup.

YOU WILL NEED:
  5 fennel bulbs
  ¼ cup butter
  32 ounces of low-sodium vegetable broth
  1 garlic clove, minced
  Kosher salt and black pepper

WHAT TO DO:
• Melt butter in a skillet over medium heat.
• Trim and quarter the fennel bulbs, and add them to the butter; sauté until caramelized, about 10 minutes.
• Add broth, and simmer for an additional 20 minutes or until fennel is soft.
• Stir in minced garlic, and season to taste.

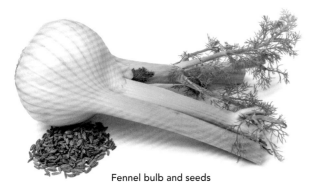

Fennel bulb and seeds

GINKGO

EASE MIGRAINE PAIN, TREAT VITILIGO, AND IMPROVE COGNITIVE FUNCTION

The venerable ginkgo tree (*Ginkgo biloba*) shows up in fossil remains dating back to 270 million years ago. It is the only remaining species in the division Ginkgophyta—all its other relatives are now extinct. Also known as the maidenhair tree, the fossil tree, kew tree, or silver apricot (which translate into *gin kyo* in Japanese), the ginkgo originated in China. There, a few old-growth stands in the wild, and certain trees planted beside temples are known to be more than 1,500 years old. In addition to China, the trees are cultivated in North America and Europe, though they have naturalized in neither place. Ginkgos prefer open, sunny ground and semi-wild sites, including rocky mountainsides, riverbanks, disturbed ground, and cliff edges.

The trees can reach heights of 66 to 115 feet and have distinctive fan-shaped leaves. A female tree produces slender flowers and then seeds—often not until it is 40 years old. Four months later, a male displays small cones that contain pollen. The wrinkled, cherry-sized seeds give off a foul smell if they decay. The seed meats are eaten in China, often as part of celebrations such as weddings and Chinese New Year. In large quantities these seeds can be toxic.

Health Benefits

One of the mainstays of Chinese herbal medicine for thousands of years, ginkgo was considered a versatile curative and tonic as well as an aphrodisiac. According to modern research, however, the jury is still out on its actual healing effects. In spite of that proviso, *Ginkgo biloba* is one of the best-selling health supplements in North America and Europe. Advocates insist on its efficacy, and some studies do bear out their claims. The herb has been successfully used to treat vitiligo, a

> ### DID YOU KNOW?
>
> • *In several European studies, a condition called tinnitus, or ringing in the ears, was successfully treated with ginkgo. In a German study, ginkgo proved superior to the placebo in reducing symptoms in a group of 60 sufferers. In a French study, 103 patients received the herb and all of them reported improvement.*

disorder in which the melanocytes that give skin its color are destroyed, resulting in white patches of skin; it has helped reduce the uncontrolled movements that can result from antipsychotic drugs; and it has been shown to ease migraine pain and improve concentration in children with ADHD. Perhaps most significantly, in an analysis published in the *Journal of Alzheimer's Disease*, ginkgo was able to stabilize or slow the mental decline associated with Alzheimer's, dementia, and cognitive impairment. Recent evidence also shows that the extract contains two constituents, flavonoids and terpenoids, that provide powerful antioxidant benefits. It also boosts platelet formation and circulation, and it offers anti-inflammatory properties. Research is ongoing, as scientists study the effects of this venerable herb on more than 100 different diseases.

Boiled ginkgo nuts. These "nuts" are actually the seeds of the ginkgo tree. In Asian cookery, these yellow seeds are used in both desserts and main courses.

GINSENG

TREAT HIGH BLOOD PRESSURE, DIABETES, HYPERLIPIDEMIA, AND HEART FAILURE

Among the world's most popular healing herbs, *Panax ginseng*—known as Asian, Chinese, or Korean ginseng—has a history thousands of years long. A slow-growing perennial, it is a member of the Araliaceae (aralia, ivy, or ginseng family). Ginseng is native to the Manchurian mountains in China but can now be found in many cooler temperate regions. The plant typically reaches no more than 18 inches high; single stems hold three to five serrated leaflets and small greenish flowers that mature to red berries. It is the pale, fleshy root that provides most of the plant's medicinal properties; it contains ginsenosides and gintonin, compounds that benefit the cardiovascular system, central nervous system, and immune system when tested in cell cultures or animal models.

Ginseng's genus name, *Panax,* comes from the Greek for "all-healing," an indicator of how much early civilizations valued this herb. In the early 1700s, when the Western world's demand for Asian ginseng became greater than the available supply, merchants began seeking new sources. Imagine the surprise when a Canadian Jesuit priest, who was searching for a replacement herb, found what he sought growing in French Canada. What came to be called American ginseng (*P. quinquefolius*) was already popular with Native Americans, who for many years had used it to treat headaches, fevers, coughs, and wounds. When the herb was also discovered growing wild throughout much of the eastern United States, the country began exporting its own species of ginseng to China.

> ### DID YOU KNOW?
> • *This plant's distinctive root, with its forked legs, gave ginseng its common name: in Chinese,* renshen *is a combination of the words for "man" or "person" and "plant root." Ginseng's strengthening powers and its human shape soon became an inspiring symbol of divine harmony on earth.*

Health Benefits

Considered a rejuvenative by early Manchurian physicians and a bestower of great strength by healers in India, ginseng also reputedly has the ability to improve physical performance and boost memory and, as well as act as an aphrodisiac when used in aromatherapy.

In spite of the herb's reputation for medicinal versatility, modern scientific findings often run counter to the claims of traditional healers, and some researchers question many of the powers attributed to the herb. Another issue that affects its effectiveness is that non-Asian users generally use a tenth of the dose traditionally taken in China and Korea. There is some clinical evidence that the herb is beneficial when used to treat high blood pressure, diabetes, hyperlipidemia, and heart failure—but only when administered in the higher Asian doses. Its vaunted benefits as an antidote to fatigue and as a memory booster have been born out in some studies, but better-quality clinical trials on humans are needed. There is also some controversy about whether health warnings involving the herb are valid or not.

Asian ginseng. With a root that looks like a human body and stringy shoots that resemble arms and legs, it has earned its genus name that translates as "person plant root."

GOJI BERRY

INCREASE VIGOR, FIGHT DISEASE, AND IMPROVE MOOD AND GENERAL HEALTH

In one small, colorful package, these edible berries offer powerhouse protection—including major antioxidant and anti-inflammatory benefits. Goji comes from two closely related species of boxthorn, *Lycium barbarum* and *L. chinense*. Also known as wolfberry, these deciduous members of the Solanaceae, or nightshade family, originated in Asia but are also grown commercially in Europe, the United States, and Australia. The bright red berries, with their sweetly tart flavor, are often sold in a dried form, like raisins. The perennial plants range in height from 3 to 10 feet, with small lanceolate or ovate leaves and trumpet-shaped flowers in shades of pink or purple.

DID YOU KNOW?

• *China is the main exporter of goji berries worldwide; plantations of the nutritious scarlet fruit cover 200,000 acres, primarily in the Ningxia Hui and Xinjiang Uyghur regions. Ningxia berries, known as "red diamonds," have been grown along the same fertile flood plains of the Yellow River for 700 years.*

Health Benefits

Goji berries recently took the health food world by storm, even though they have been part of traditional Chinese medicine for millennia. They were—and are—valued for their ability to increase vigor, fight disease, and improve mood. Modern research confirms their effectiveness on the gastrointestinal and urinary tract and the cardiovascular, respiratory, and musculoskeletal systems. Their beta-carotene is a boon to skin and eye health, while another antioxidant, zeaxanthin, gives these berries (along with saffron and bell peppers) their color. Goji contains vitamins A and C, zinc, iron, and fiber, and it supplies complex carbohydrates that elevate blood sugar slowly, rather than causing it to peak and crash. Surprisingly, these berries provide protein: 10 percent of your daily requirement in a four-ounce serving.

Goji berries have several other potential medicinal applications. For example, in lab tests, goji increased the effectiveness of flu vaccines in aged mice, an important plus for seniors who don't receive full immunity from their flu shots. And according to one Chinese study, a chemical in goji (beta-sitosterol) can help decrease overgrown cells and cause tumor cells to undergo apoptosis, or "cell suicide." Further study is needed to confirm this benefit.

For centuries, this fruit was linked with sexual fertility, and animal studies with rats showed that goji significantly increased sperm quantity and movement; shortened erection, capture, and ejaculation response; and aided recovery of testosterone levels. They may even be a natural option for treating erectile dysfunction. Other potential benefits look promising: people who drink goji berry juice report increased energy, athletic performance, ability to concentrate, quality of sleep, and feelings of well-being.

RESCUE REMEDY: *A great option if you need a portable, low-calorie, low-fat snack is a ¼ cup of goji berries; eat them alone or mix with nuts. (Larger portions may supply too much vitamin A.) You can also sprinkle goji over salads, yogurt, or cereal, or add it to smoothies.*

Dried goji. With their chewy raisinlike texture, these red berries can be added to both sweet and savory dishes.

GOLDENSEAL

BOOST IMMUNITY AND PROMOTE HEART, REPRODUCTIVE, AND DIGESTIVE HEALTH

Considered a natural antibiotic and an anticancer agent, goldenseal (*Hydrastatis canadensis*) is one of the five top-selling herbs in the United States. Part of the buttercup family (Ranunculaceae), it is believed to be the only living species in its genus.

This woodland plant is native to southeastern Canada and the eastern United States, where the Cherokee and Iroquois Indians had used it for centuries, both as a remedy for infections and as a yellow colorant. This may explain one of its folk names—Indian dye. It has also been known as orangeroot, yellowroot, yellow puccoon, ground raspberry, yellow paint, wild curcuma, eye root, eye-balm, wild turmeric, and yellow eye.

Goldenseal grows to roughly 8 to 14 inches in height and produces a single hairy stem with two large-toothed, palmate leaves with five to seven lobes and small white flowers that mature into fruit that resemble raspberries. All parts of the herb have

> ### DID YOU KNOW?
>
> • *Goldenseal's reputation as a versatile curative may still be awaiting solid clinical proof, but it does appear to have the ability to boost the efficacy of other herbs with which it is formulated or blended. One example is a mix of goldenseal and echinacea taken to prevent or lessen the effect of colds.*

medicinal potential, but it is the thick, knotted, yellow rhizome that is most often utilized by healers.

Goldenseal prefers shady locations with rich soil. It once grew wild in many locations, but as its popularity as a folk medicine increased during the 18th century, its numbers dwindled. By 1905, overharvesting and habitat destruction made the wild herb increasingly difficult to find. As a result, it is now an endangered species, federally protected from harvesting on public lands, although an approximate 60 million plants are picked each year without being replaced. Today, most goldenseal is cultivated commercially and harvested in a sustainable manner.

Health Benefits

The plant reputedly possesses many healthful applications—boosting immunity, controlling muscle spasms, acting as an astringent, stimulating the heart, raising low blood pressure, easing digestive disorders and painful menstruation, reducing swelling and edema, and treating infections. Natural healers have also prescribed it for colds, allergies, eye disorders, bowel issues, and even cancer. The herb does contain an alkaloid called berberine that in laboratory tests destroyed many types of bacteria—including those that cause diarrhea—as well as candida-causing yeasts and parasites like tapeworms and giardia. There is, however, no conclusive research on how it affects humans. Some studies suggest goldenseal should be avoided by pregnant women and infants.

Goldenseal leaves and flower. Goldenseal comes as a powder of the dried leaf or root and as a tablet, oil, tincture, or salve.

HEARTSEASE

LOWER CHOLESTEROL, EASE CONSTIPATION, AND BOOST THE DIGESTIVE TRACT

Familiar to some gardeners as the colorful wildflower Johnny-jump-up, heartsease *(Viola tricolor)* is also a long-venerated herbal medicine. The plant originated in Europe and has since spread to North America, where it is found in acid-rich grasslands and wastelands offering partial shade. This small creeping annual—or short-lived perennial—typically reaches five inches in height. The flowers, which range in color from purple and blue to yellow and white, have two basic color patterns: a single color with dark "pencil" lines radiating from its center; or a combination of blue, purple, white, or yellow that features a "face"—a dark center that ranges in expression from happy to sad. These blossoms are self-fertile hermaphrodites and are pollinated by bees. Heartsease is the progenitor of the cultivated pansy gardeners grow today and is sometimes called wild pansy. A small commercial variety of pansy is also known as Johnny-jump-up.

Health Benefits

Heartsease has been employed medicinally for thousands of years—the Greek poet Homer advised its use to cool anger, and the Roman botanist Pliny recommended it for headaches and to relieve dizziness. Medieval folk healers favored it, both internally and topically, for treating epilepsy, ulcers, and skin diseases, while North American Indians applied it to boils and swelling. With its expectorant properties, the plant was a logical curative for respiratory ailments, like colds, asthma, bronchitis, and whooping cough. Its diuretic qualities make it useful when treating rheumatism and cystitis.

Modern research has indicated that these delicate wildflowers may pose a threat to some serious illnesses. Heartsease contains cyclotides, small peptides that are useful in the development of drugs because their size and structure lend them great stability. Many of the cyclotides found in *Viola tricolor* are cytotoxic, meaning they could be directed to destroy cancer cells. The whole plant, especially the edible flowers, contains antioxidants, and some extracts are antimicrobial or anti-inflammatory. Heartsease is also so mild it can be given to children.

Heartsease contains saponin (a soaplike compound that can lower cholesterol and risk of heart disease), mucilage (gel-like soluble fiber that can also lower cholesterol, ease constipation, protect the digestive tract, and stabilize blood sugar), and carotenoids (pigments that act as antioxidants, offering protection from chronic disease).

RESCUE REMEDY: *Heartsease is often taken as a tea; it makes an excellent spring tonic hot or cold, benefiting the kidneys and easing gout. To prepare an infusion, mix 1 tablespoon heartsease in 1 cup boiling water and steep for 15 minutes, and then strain. Drink three times weekly. Heartsease can also be blended with other teas.*

Dainty heartsease, whether a wildflower or cultivated garden plant, has powerful medicinal properties.

A couple of days after a hibiscus bloom shrivels up, the ripe calyx will be closed, and it will feel solid when squeezed—a sign that it is ready for harvesting.

HIBISCUS

PROMOTE HEART HEALTH, EASE DIGESTIVE ISSUES, AND BOOST THE IMMUNE SYSTEM

A colorful member of the mallow family, hibiscus (*Hibiscus sabdariffa*) likely originated in Egypt or Angola, but it now grows in many tropical and subtropical regions of the world. It is also known as rose mallow, roselle, Jamaican sorrel, Indian sorrel, red sorrel, maleate, and vinuela. For centuries in North Africa and the Middle East, the large, showy flower petals have been used, along with the bark and the calyces (dark red, cup-shaped sepals of the flower), to make a healthful sour tea. Hibiscus may also be taken internally as a syrup, a powdered extract, or capsule supplement. Hibiscus is the key ingredient in the popular Caribbean liqueur roselle.

Health Benefits

Among its many benefits are the following.

- Supplies multiple antioxidants and vitamin C
- Maintains healthy blood pressure and cholesterol levels
- Eases digestive issues
- Boosts the immune system
- Treats inflammatory problems
- Combats liver disease
- Speeds up the metabolism, offering a healthy way to gradually lose weight

DID YOU KNOW?

- *The healthful hibiscus is also utilized in other ways: in Polynesia, the bark fibers are used to make grass skirts; in China, the "shoe flower" is used to polish shoes; and in Tahiti, single women wear a hibiscus blossom behind their right ear, while married women wear it behind the left ear.*

In Egypt and the Sudan, tangy sour tea—served hot or cold—has long been used to regulate fluid balance and body temperature and aid heart health. In North Africa, the tea is drunk to encourage respiratory and throat health and to improve the quality of skin. Iranians are known for drinking sour tea to maintain normal blood pressure, a benefit that has been confirmed by several recent studies. In Europe, the herb is considered beneficial to respiratory health and circulation and is used to alleviate constipation. When combined with lemon balm and St. John's wort, it can ease restlessness and insomnia.

The hibiscus plant contains 15 to 30 percent plant acids—citric acid, malic acid, and tartaric acid—and one that is unique to the plant, allo-hydroxycitric acid lactone. Clinical trials on controlling cholesterol have for the most part indicated that a dose of 1,000 mg taken thrice daily can maintain levels of LDL and HDL cholesterol that are already in a healthy range.

RESCUE REMEDY: *To maintain healthy cholesterol levels, take 1,000 mg of the dried herb three times daily, or drink a cup of sour tea twice a day. To make it, add ½ cup of the dried flowers to 3 cups of boiling water, and then let the tea steep for 15 to 20 minutes.*

HOPS

TREAT ACNE AND PROMOTE REPRODUCTIVE AND DIGESTIVE HEALTH

Technically, hops are the female flowers or seed cones (called strabiles) of the hop plant (*Humulus lupulus*). Not only has this plant become highly valued for its ability to flavor and stabilize beer, but it has also been used by traditional healers to ease anxiety, relieve stomach disorders, and reduce menstrual cramps. The hop plant is a vigorous grower with bines (not vines) that can reach more than 20 feet in length and will climb up any support—a wall, trellis, or rope line. The hop's green cones, or bracts, contain medicinal polyphenols, while the interior offers aromatic lupulin glands that have the appearance of yellowish pollen.

It is believed that the hop plant was originally cultivated in Germany some time around the 8th century, but it was not added to beer until many years later. Beer is an alcoholic beverage created by the fermentation of starch into sugar and using malted grain, brewer's yeast, and water; the Chinese first brewed it around 9500 B.C. The addition of aromatic hops, possibly in the 10th century, not only added some needed bitterness to the sweet brew, but the antimicrobials found in the plant also retarded spoilage—a major problem for brewers.

Health Benefits

As anyone who has nodded off after a few glasses of beer will not be surprised to learn, hops have often been used in the past—sometimes combined with valerian (*Valeriana officinalis*)—to induce sleep and relaxation. Modern research has discovered this soporific effect is due to dimethylvinyl carbinol, an alcoholic compound found in the plant.

From the time of the early Greeks and Romans, healers have used hops as a spring tonic and to treat infections, women's problems, and dandruff—even

> ### DID YOU KNOW?
>
> • *Ever wonder where the bubbles in beer come from? Fermentation is the process wherein yeast, which is a microorganism, metabolizes the sugars extracted from the grains used to brew beer and produces alcohol and carbon dioxide gas. The CO_2 is what provides the carbonation and creamy head beloved by enthusiasts.*

leprosy and the plague. Recent studies of *Humulus lupulus* have revealed that this plant possesses a flavonoid compound called xanthohumol. Xanthohumol may have antiviral, anticlotting, anti-inflammatory, and antitumor activity. Researchers became particularly interested in that last property after a 2008 study revealed that the compound inhibited cell lines in a common type of liver cancer. It has other benefits as well.

- Hops extract is loaded with antioxidants, making it an effective acne treatment.
- Hops also contain phytoestrogens that mimic the effects of a woman's own estrogen, balancing the sex hormones and keeping the libido healthy. They can also ease periodic pain, relieve PMS, and reduce the effects of menopause.
- Hops tea can stimulate the stomach to increase production of digestive acids, while its antibacterial qualities—bitter acids called lupulone and humulone—make it beneficial for bladder and urinary tract infections.

Both herbalists and brewers harvest the flowers of hops.

LAVENDER

TREAT MOOD DISORDERS AND DIGESTIVE PROBLEMS AND REDUCE PAIN AND INFLAMMATION

This lovely perennial adorns the garden and the home with its vibrant colors, and it offers a restful scent that repels insects. Lavender also lends a taste of Provence to recipes and as a medicinal oil possesses calmative, digestive, and analgesic properties. Within the 47 species of this plant, two of the most popular are English lavender (*Lavendula angustifolia*) and French lavender (*L. stoechas* or *L. dentata*). Native to the Mediterranean, it is now found nearly worldwide. This perennial prefers sunny, well-drained soil. English lavender is a hardy, evergreen shrub that can reach 6.6 feet in height. The gray-green leaves are narrow, and the purple flowers bloom on spikes.

In the kitchen, lavender's scent reminds the cook that it is cousin to mint, marjoram, thyme, and sage and can be used in similar ways. It adds an earthy flavor to meat dishes and salads and a unique herbal profile to custards, jams, cookies, and teas. It is easily harvested from field or garden and can be bundled and hung upside down to dry for later use.

> **AT A GLANCE**
> • *If you buy lavender for culinary or medicinal purposes, always purchase it from a reputable health food store or food market. Craft stores often carry dried lavender to use in flower arrangements, but it is likely treated with chemical preservatives.*

Health Benefits

Lavender has been prized since the days of the pharaohs, when the Egyptians used this fragrant herb as a perfume and as part of the process of mummification. The ancient Romans bathed with it, cooked with it, and used it to scent the air. Early healers called it spikenard, or nard, from the Greek name for the herb, *naardus*.

Contemporary research reveals that lavender oil contains more than 100 constituents including linalool, camphor, coumarins, tannins, cineole, and flavonoids. Used topically or inhaled, it is effective against insomnia, anxiety, and depression, digestive problems, headache pain, toothaches, sprains, and skin conditions and for healing burns and reducing inflammation. It may slow the effects of aging due to its antioxidant properties. Chinese research reports that this oil helps the body manufacture three key antioxidants—glutathione, catalase, and SOD—within one day of using it. Diffused lavender oil may prevent cellular damage that can lead to cancer. According to a study in Tunisia, the oil protects the body from the components of diabetes, including increased blood sugar, weight gain, and liver and kidney dysfunction.

Iced lavender lemonade. This summer beverage is not only easy on the eyes, it is also a healthful drink containing beneficial antioxidants.

RESCUE REMEDY: *Lavender lemonade is tart and refreshing and contains powerful antioxidants to boost the immune system. To prepare, bring 2 cups of water to a boil, remove from heat, and stir in ¾ cup honey. Add ¼ cup fresh crushed lavender flowers, cover, and steep for 20 minutes. Strain the beverage, pour into a pitcher, and stir in 1 cup lemon juice. Add another 2 cups of water, stir, and chill. Serve with fresh lemon slices and lavender sprigs.*

LEMON BALM

TREAT INSOMNIA, SOOTHE THE SKIN, AND INCREASE MENTAL ACUITY

This tartly aromatic herb has been lauded for centuries for its ability to calm the nerves, boost mental vigor, and increase longevity. Perennial lemon balm *(Melissa officinalis)* is a member of the mint or deadnettle family (Lamiaceae). It originated in south-central Europe and soon spread to the Mediterranean basin and Central Asia. It has now naturalized in many other regions, including North America. Major commercial producers are Hungary, Egypt, Italy, and Ireland. The plant reaches heights of 59 inches, and the green, serrated leaves have an appealing minty lemon scent. In summer, the small white flowers are full of nectar, drawing bees by the score. (Lemon balm's generic name, *Melissa,* comes from the Greek word for "honeybee.") It grows in clumps and can spread either vegetatively or by seeds.

With its light lemony notes, it is used to flavor ice creams, fruit dishes, and candies, as well as hot and iced teas. Lemon balm is also often used as a complement to peppermint tea. As a culinary herb, it can be made into pesto or added to fish and poultry dishes for a touch of zest.

Health Benefits

Since before the Middle Ages, traditional healers have relied on lemon balm to reduce anxiety, increase appetite, ease pain, and support thyroid, liver, and digestive health. Current research on its chemical constituents reveals that it contains the powerful antioxidants rosmarinic acid, eugenol, tannins, and terpenes, which counteract harmful free radicals.

- The essential oil is well regarded for treating insomnia, allowing restless sleepers—including children—to slumber through the night. A trial on menopausal women that treated them with

> ### DID YOU KNOW?
>
> • *Lemon balm's value goes beyond its healing and culinary properties—it also has several commercial applications. Beekeepers cultivate it to attract bees for honey production; it is grown in quantity by perfumeries for its aromatic citrus-scented oil; and the cosmetic industry includes it in many skincare and beauty products.*

lemon balm and valerian extract found the herbs provided restful sleep in the majority of cases.

- In the 14th century, the queen of Hungary successfully used lemon balm to treat facial wrinkles; you can use it to smooth the skin and reduce fine lines. This benefit derives from the plant's volatile compounds (p-coumaric, caffeic, and rosmarinic acids), which boost the body's response to harmful organisms that affect the complexion.

- In an Australian study, the herb was shown to increase mental alertness, sharpen problem-solving skills, and improve mood. When combined with acupuncture, its antioxidant eugenol helped test subjects recover functions related to memory. Eugenol is also known to protect brain cells from free radicals.

RESCUE REMEDY: *Lemon balm lends itself to many beneficial modes. For a relaxing, scented soak, fill a sachet with the dried herb, and float it in your bathwater. Add citrus character to a pitcher of cucumber water by placing fresh lemon balm leaves and a few lemon wedges in with the sliced cucumbers.*

You can use the fresh leaves of lemon balm—or the herb's essential oils—for a variety of medicinal purposes.

MILK THISTLE

DETOX THE LIVER, IMPROVE DIGESTION, AND SLOW THE AGING PROCESS

Often considered a noxious weed, milk thistle (*Silybum marianum*) redeems itself as an herb that supports liver function. This member of the Compositae (the aster or daisy family), was native to the Mediterranean, but is now found worldwide. It thrives in dry, rocky soil and grows in places most plants eschew—abandoned pastures, empty lots, and disturbed ground. An annual or biennial plant, it can reach heights of up to 10 feet. The pale green leaves are flocked with hairs and bear sharp spines along the margins. The flowers, which form spiky red or purple crowns, are a favorite of songbirds like goldfinches when their blooms go to seed in late summer.

DID YOU KNOW?

• *The plant's common name comes from the milky white fluid released from the crushed leaves—or possibly the milky patches on the leaves. Other folk names include blessed milk thistle, Marian thistle, Saint Mary's thistle, Mediterranean milk thistle, variegated thistle, and Scotch thistle— although the latter is another plant altogether, Onopardum acanthium.*

Milk thistle is edible: the roots can be parboiled, roasted, or eaten raw. Once the tender new shoots have their woolly hairs rubbed off, they can be boiled and served with butter. The leaves, also deprived of prickles, make a fine addition to salads.

Health Benefits

For more than two millennia, milk thistle was used for treating canker sores, headaches, vertigo, jaundice, baldness, and even the plague, but this herb was most renowned for its effectiveness against disorders of the liver and gall bladder. Greek physician Dioscorides was among the first to detail the plant's curative powers in A.D. 40.

The scientific community now recognizes milk thistle for its ability to decrease or even reverse liver damage caused by pollution, certain medications, and exposure to heavy metals. It may work by drawing toxins from the body, making it ideal for treating kidney stones, gallstones, high cholesterol, skin damage, and the draining effects of chemotherapy, as well as impeding the development of cancer cells. It is also able to improve digestive function by encouraging the formation of enzymes, increasing bile production, decreasing gut inflammation, and soothing mucous membranes. The plant contains high levels of anti-inflammatories and antioxidants and is rich in vitamins C and E, which may slow the aging process. Milk thistle can be taken as a pill, powder, tincture, extract, or tea. The seeds can be eaten, but they are so small that they furnish relatively few health benefits.

Prickly milk thistle collected for medicinal purposes

RESCUE REMEDY: *Drinking a health shake containing milk thistle before you head out for a night on the town and again the next morning can prevent a hangover—the herb not only protects the liver from alcohol, it also prompts the generation of new hepatic cells.*

MINT

PROMOTE DIGESTIVE HEALTH AND RELIEVE NAUSEA, HEADACHES, AND COLDS

Mints, of the genus *Mentha* in the family Lamiaceae, encompass a number of medicinal herbs within the 15 to 20 extant species. Two outstanding examples are spearmint (*M. spicata*), a favorite in European convent gardens, with its carvone (or carawaylike) scent and long history as a curative, and peppermint (*M. x piperita*), with its menthol scent and reputation as a versatile medicinal resource. Peppermint, a hybrid cross between spearmint and water mint (*M. aquatica*), can quickly become an overgrown garden nuisance, so always keep it in a container. Mints typically have square stems and green serrated leaves and produce delicate pinkish or lavender flowers. They are beloved of bees and butterflies.

As a culinary herb, mint leaves can be mixed with other salad greens for a bit of extra zing, and they also make a tasty, soothing tea. (For a quick hit of mint in summer, freeze fresh leaves in ice cube trays, and then use them in iced tea whenever you want.) Mint is used commercially to flavor ice creams, chocolate candies, gum, cough drops, liqueurs, and soft drinks and as an ingredient in cosmetics, skincare products, medications, inhalers, toothpaste, mouthwash, and breath fresheners.

Health Benefits

Since the time of the ancient Greeks, healers have used mints to treat a wide range of ailments, and their popularity continues today. Mints make excellent appetite stimulants and palate cleansers. They can calm indigestion and heartburn—the aroma of the herbs activates the salivary glands, causing them to release digestive enzymes that ease that gassy feeling. Any drops or lozenges that contains mint flavoring will have the same settling

> **DID YOU KNOW?**
>
> • *There is one digestive condition that precludes the use of soothing peppermint: acid reflux disease, in which stomach acid leaks into the esophagus, causing pain and possible scarring. Because peppermint can relax the sphincter at the base of the esophagus, it may allow harmful acid to enter the space.*

effect. For travelers, the menthol found in the peppermint can likewise relieve the nausea and discomfort of air or motion sickness. The aroma and cool sensation of mint found in certain balms can banish the pain of headaches when applied to the forehead or nose. The herb's pungent odor can also help to clear up the congestion and coughing brought on by colds, flu, bronchitis, and other respiratory complications. For asthma patients, mint not only clears congestion, it also serves as a relaxant.

The scent of mint-based essential oil is also a natural stimulant, recharging the brain, reviving the memory, and overcoming feelings of sluggishness, depression, or fatigue. And for those who suffer from acne or skin irritations, mint is a natural antiseptic and an excellent skin cleanser. Mint oils can be ingested, applied topically as a salve, or inhaled with a diffuser. You can even place a few drops in a pillow or hankie and let the oil soothe you while you sleep.

RESCUE REMEDY: *Want the benefits of both mint and mustard? Drizzle the goodness of mint-Dijon dressing over your favorite salad. Simply whisk together ⅓ cup lemon juice, 1 tablespoon Dijon mustard, ½ teaspoon honey, ⅓ cup chopped mint leaves, ⅓ cup extra virgin olive oil, and 1 minced garlic clove, and add salt and pepper to taste.*

Spearmint leaves

Up Close

Up Close

GIFTS FROM THE SEA

DISCOVER THE AMAZING HEALTH PROPERTIES OF MARINE VEGETABLES

Spirulina, usually sold in powdered form, mixes well with spinach and blueberries to make a nutrient-rich smoothie.

For thousands of years, many coastal cultures—including the Japanese, Chinese, and Korean—have relied on harvesting seaweed and algae for food. It is only recently that the natural health community became aware of the nutritional benefits of these marine vegetables. Seaweed and kelp might not sound very appetizing, based on the slimy green stuff you see washed up on the beach. And alga? Well, let's just say something that forms pond scum can't possibly be a food, right? The truth is, these water-born plants are richer in nutrients than any land vegetables, and they are also low in calories—a cup of raw kelp has fewer than 20 calories.

What Are Seaweed and Algae?

There are several types of edible plants that inhabit aquatic environments. Alga—one of the most primitive organisms on earth, with fossils dating back more than three million years—happens to be one of them. Collectively algae produce energy through photosynthesis and will form in salt water, freshwater, or brackish water, near shore or out to sea. They are simple in cellular structure, and even the gigantic ocean kelps have no complex organs as terrestrial plants do. There are countless species of alga, with more than 320,000 collected specimens. Edible seaweed (some forms are inedible or toxic) is a multicellular, marine form of algae that generally inhabits shallow water. Kelp, a subgroup of seaweed, is also the largest form of seaweed.

As a food source, seaweed can be consumed fresh or dried, (the dried form retains all the nutritional value). Fresh algae do not keep well, so they are typically sold as a dried powder or as tablet supplements. The powder makes a healthy addition to soups, salad dressings, stir-fries, salsa, guacamole, and smoothies.

Below are some of the most popular edible seaweeds and algae. Most can be found in health food or specialty stores or Asian markets.

SPIRULINA This popular genus of blue-green alga is rich in beta-carotene and all essential amino acids; it is roughly 60 percent protein.

CHLORELLA This genus of blue-green alga provides a great source of the detoxifying plant pigment chlorophyll, which removes heavy metals from the body. Chlorella also enhances immune function and encourages tissue repair.

KELP This class of brown alga (Phaeophyceae) contains iodine and high levels of calcium; its antioxidant properties improve insulin resistance and metabolize fat more efficiently.

WAKAME This sweet seaweed's high levels of magnesium improve heart function and regulate blood pressure. Wakame (*Undaria pinnatifida*) also acts as a diuretic.

NORI Familiar as sushi wrapping, this red alga (genus *Pyropia*) is high in protein and fiber.

DULSE This red alga (*Palmaria palmata*) offers high protein and a wealth of minerals.

Among its many health benefits, seaweed can aid in weight loss and improve blood sugar levels—its fiber helps control weight and balance blood sugar, plus the carotenoid fucoxanthin found in brown algae enhanced fat burning in animal studies. Seaweed can regulate the gut—a fiber found in kelp called alginate forms a gel when it enters the stomach, slowing digestion, increasing the sense of fullness, and causing blood sugars to rise slowly after meals. Based on animal research, seaweed has antioxidant, anti-inflammatory, and blood-thinning properties, all of which can help lower the risk of heart disease. Seaweed's high levels of omega-3 fatty acids are also a boon to cardiovascular health. Cultures that regularly consume marine vegetables have lower instances of cancer, according to *Nutrition Reviews*, possibly because of the reputed ability of fucoxanthin to inhibit the growth of tumor cells. Seaweed consumption is also linked to lower estrogen levels in women, which can decrease the risk of breast cancer.

Nutrients

Seaweed is a good source of B-complex vitamins and vitamins A, C, and K. A cup of kelp provides nearly one quarter of the daily requirement for vitamin K, a fat-soluble nutrient that communicates with the platelets that form blood clots. Seaweed also provides calcium, selenium, and zinc. Many marine veggies also supply iron, which provides energy and nourishes the circulatory system.

Gunkan chuka. This Japanese sushi packs a double dose of nutrition, with a nori wrap topped with wakame salad.

ENJOY A "SEAFOOD" SALAD, SOUP, OR SANDWICH

To make a healthful salad with sea vegetables, combine a cup and a half of kelp or wakame with some sesame oil, freshly grated ginger, and top with a sprinkling of roasted sesame seeds. Kelp and wakame can be added to miso soup along with marinated cubes of tofu for a probiotic boost. Protein-rich spirulina can be added to soups, salads, or smoothies or mixed into hummus to use as a sandwich spread.

A spike of mullein

MULLEIN

CONTROL RESPIRATORY AILMENTS AND ALLEVIATE PAIN AND INFLAMMATION

Common mullein (*Verbascum thapsus*) wears several hats—this tall-stalked wildflower, often found in vacant lots and on scrub ground, is also a cultivated garden favorite and a valued medicinal plant. This species is a member of the figwort family, or Scrophulariaceae, and its genus contains from 210 to 250 species. Also known as great mullein or the velvet plant—due to its densely fuzzy leaves—it is native to Europe and Asia, with the widest diversity appearing around the Mediterranean. European settlers carried it to North America, where it naturalized and was used by Native Americans for skin and respiratory conditions. It is now found in many temperate and semitropical climates.

Biennial mullein can reach heights of more than nine feet, though three or four feet is more usual. First-year plants form a base, a rosette of large pale green leaves, and then the following year send up a spike that produces yellow flowers that whirl upward from the bottom of the spike. These plants are known to flower for long periods of time, as long as three months, with an individual blossom opening only part of the day, while another opens earlier or later. The fruit capsule contains a multitude of tiny seeds.

Health Benefits

This herb was a popular curative during ancient times: in the first century, Greek physician Dioscorides recommended it for treating hemorrhoids and

> ### DID YOU KNOW?
>
> • *For those who enjoy back-to-basics camping, keep mullein in mind. The stems are said to make excellent drills for starting fires using the hand-drill method in which a long stick is held between the palms and rapidly rotated against the notch in a wooden fireboard until it ignites.*

Roman botanist Pliny (along with later medieval healers) for treating arthritis. The flowers have been used to cure ringworm and ease burns and were a regular part of traditional Austrian medicine, prepared as a tea or ointment. The leaves, with their expectorant properties, proved an effective traditional remedy for the symptoms of tuberculosis, colds, flu, pneumonia, allergies, and sore throats.

This herb might just be coming into its own again—recent research in Ireland bears out many of these traditional medicinal claims. The leaf extract contains antiviral, antitumor, antifungal, and antibacterial qualities. To further gain respect, it has also been recognized as anti-inflammatory and antispasmodic. Nutritionally, mullein contains the B vitamins B2, B5, B6, and B12, as well as vitamin D, and other beneficial compounds.

> ### THE NAME GAME
>
> Mullein has gathered some of the most fanciful wildflower names—clown's lungwort, Bullock's lungwort, Our Lady's flannel, Adam's flannel, beggar's blanket, blanket herb, wild ice leaf, Aaron's rod, Jupiter's staff, Peter's staff, Jacob's staff, shepherd's staff, Cuddy's lungs, feltwort, fluffweed, hare's beard, and old man's beard. It is also called candlewick plant or hag's taper because the stalks could be dipped in tallow to make torches.

OREGANO

REDUCE STRESS, FIGHT INFECTION, AND ENHANCE DIGESTIVE HEALTH

A deeply aromatic staple of the modern Latin kitchen, oregano (*Origanum vulgare*) is also prized by herbalists for its healing properties. This member of the Lamiaceae, or mint family, is native to western and southwestern Eurasia and the Mediterranean region and is now found in the cuisine of many regions, especially Latin America and the Philippines. It is sometimes called wild marjoram and is, indeed, a close cousin to sweet marjoram (*O. majorana*). The common name probably derives from the Greek *origanon,* meaning "acrid herb," or possibly from *oros,* "mountain" and *ganos,* "brightness," referring to the plant's zesty flavor.

This flowering perennial herb ranges in height from 8 to 30 inches, with spade-shaped olive green leaves and small pink or purple flowers produced on long spikes. The blooms are favorites of bees and butterflies, and the plants host other beneficial insects. The flavorful leaves are used for culinary applications—they are even more intense when dried—for their aroma, warmth, and slightly bitter taste. The herb, fresh or dried, is a mainstay of Italian cooking, perhaps most famously to flavor pizza.

Health Benefits

For thousands of years, this herb was believed to boost the body's immunity to disease and was used to treat digestive issues, skin ailments, and fatigue.

Today, many alternative healers continue to prescribe oregano for a range of ailments. The research to support these curative claims is still ongoing, however. What is known is that oregano contains a number of beneficial compounds, among them rosmarinic acid and eugenol, powerful antioxidants that are known to relieve the effects of stress. The herb also possesses antibacterial

> ### DID YOU KNOW?
>
> • *Prior to World War II, American cooks had little experience with earthy, aromatic oregano. It was U.S. soldiers, returning from the war in Italy, who first introduced the savory plant to their wives—who quickly embraced this herb that gave a sunny taste of the Mediterranean to soups, salads, and main dishes.*

qualities, allowing it to defend the body from infections in the digestive tract, urinary tract, and skin. Its fiber content also eases digestion and enhances bowel health. Nutritionally, oregano boasts vitamins A, B6, C, E, and K, as well as fiber, folate, iron, copper, calcium, magnesium, potassium, manganese, and tryptophan. The minerals found in the plant help to maintain strong bones and may protect older adults from the effects of osteoporosis. The herb is also a natural source of the omega-3 fatty acids that are so vital to heart health, balancing cholesterol levels, and reducing cardiovascular inflammation that can lead to heart attacks and strokes. Finally, the herb's rich mix of nutrients aids the liver to detoxify the body of pollutants and may even speed up the process.

Oregano in bloom. This plant is easy to grow at home in a medicinal herb garden or in pots in a windowsill garden.

The blossom and leaves of the passionflower vine. This herb is available as capsules, tablets, tinctures, and essential oils.

PASSIONFLOWER

CONTROL ANXIETY AND DEPRESSION AND COUNTER INSOMNIA

The distinctive passionflower vine (*Passiflora incarnata*) brings an exotic presence to even the humblest yards. Yet it is also a medicinal herb, used as a calmative and antispasmodic. A member of the family Passifloraceae, the plant is native to the southeastern regions of North America. It is a perennial in the south, but it is treated as an annual farther north and is cultivated around the world as a garden ornamental. In the wild, it likes acidic, sandy soil in full sun and is found growing in thickets, at the edges of woodlands, and along fence lines. Its vines can reach lengths of 10 to 20 feet, and it uses its coiled tendrils to climb trees, bushes, or other fixed objects. The green leaves are deeply lobed, and the large, frilled flowers, are a striking purple and white. The yellow-orange fruit—not to be confused with commercial passion fruit—is the size of a chicken's egg and contains many seeds.

Health Benefits

Native Americans once used passionflower to heal cuts and bruises, and the Incas brewed a tonic tea from it. The Eclectics of the 19th century, a group predating today's naturopaths, touted it as a remedy for insomnia, indigestion, diarrhea, menstrual problems, epilepsy, and whooping cough, and they used the juice to soothe burns, scalds, and toothaches.

DID YOU KNOW?

* Passionflower's name did not arise from any romantic notion, but rather from early Jesuit missionaries who believed that the plant's structure evoked the "passion," or crucifixion of Christ: the three nail-like stamens, the five anthers as the five wounds, and the threadlike corona as the crown of thorns.

Many studies have verified its sedative, antispasmodic, and antianxiety properties—one found it to be as effective for anxiety as the psychoactive drug benzodiazepine—yet researchers were often unable to attribute those beneficial effects to any specific chemical compounds. One alkaloid, harmaline, was shown to be the active ingredient responsible for the plant's sedative qualities. Harmaline may have a cumulative effect, however, when combined with anxiety medications or other herbs, such as valerian or St. John's wort.

Until 1978, passionflower was available as an over-the-counter remedy for anxiety and insomnia. But stricter drug laws—and a lack of hardcore data on the herb's safety and effectiveness—caused it to be pulled. Still, research continued, with some gratifying results. Opium addicts undergoing treatment reported lowered levels of anxiety when they took passionflower extract along with prescription clonidine. And in a 2008 study, it reduced the anxiety of pre-op patients when given an hour and a half before surgery.

RESCUE REMEDY: *Make a relaxing tea by steeping a handful of leaves and flowers in 4 cups of boiling water.*

PATCHOULI

TREAT SKIN AND HAIR PROBLEMS, ELEVATE MOOD, AND FIGHT INFECTION

Evocative of love-ins, peace marches, and outdoor folk concerts, patchouli can be said to truly be the scent of the Woodstock generation. But baby boomers aren't its only fans: many herbalists value it as a remedy for skin ailments, depression, and low sex drive. Patchouli (Pogostemon cablin) is an evergreen perennial shrub in the mint family that displays serrated leaves and small pinkish white flowers. The common name comes from the ancient Tamil words patchai and ellai, meaning "green leaf." Originally a native of Southeast Asia, it is now found in many tropical regions, but primarily in Indonesia, Malaysia, China, Brazil, and India.

The plant is known for its pungent odor—described as warm, rich, fruity, exotic, or balsamic. Commercially, patchouli is used as a perfume base in at least a third of perfumes and fragrances because it is able to blend so well with other scents. (The plant also provides a high yield of essential oils, up to 3.5 percent, compared to most other herbs.) Additional uses include potpourri, incense, air fresheners, insect repellent, soap, detergents, deodorants, paper towels, and cosmetics.

Health Benefits

For thousands of years, this herb was a valued resource of traditional healers, especially in Malaysia, Japan, and China. Egypt's King Tutankhamun was entombed with 10 gallons of the oil, and the Romans used it to stimulate their appetites. At one point, the oil was so highly valued by European traders that a pound of patchouli was worth a pound of gold. The steam-distilled oil can be used to treat skin problems, such as dermatitis, acne, dandruff, and eczema, and to heal wounds and reduce scarring. Its scent

> ### DID YOU KNOW?
>
> • *As a signature scent, patchouli can be somewhat polarizing. Advocates admire its complex musky notes, like something straight from a Middle Eastern bazaar, while its detractors find it acrid and insist it reminds them of cat urine. So if it's your scent of choice, use it sparingly.*

also offers mood-lifting and libido-enhancing effects. This versatility is not surprising: the essential oil possesses antiseptic, antidepressant, astringent, and aphrodisiac properties. In an Indian study, the plant's antibacterial and antifungal qualities were vindicated when it destroyed 20 out of 22 bacterial strains and all 12 fungal strains in lab tests. At home, there are a number of ways you can benefit from the oil.

- To treat oily hair or dandruff, add a few drops of patchouli oil to your shampoo; leave on for two minutes before rinsing.
- Dilute the oil in a carrier oil, such as olive or almond oil, and massage it into your skin to prevent wrinkles or improve the look of cellulite.
- A few drops placed on your wrists and ankles or on your sheets, can keep away ants, bedbugs, and other insect pests.
- Use the essential oil to treat cuts, scrapes, insect bites, sores, and burns.
- Place a few dabs of patchouli oil under your arms to act as a deodorant.

Patchouli leaves. The essential oil of patchouli has multiple uses, from aromatherapy to medicinal and cosmetic treatments.

They may be small, but psyllium seeds and their husks pack a powerful punch, helping to regulate your lower GI tract.

PSYLLIUM

PROMOTE DIGESTIVE HEALTH, CONTROL CHOLESTEROL, AND AID WEIGHT LOSS

The natural health community—and subsequently the food industry—is always looking for the next big health-boosting phenomenon, and when it turned its focus to the many benefits of fiber during the last decade, there was humble psyllium, ready for its close-up. Psyllium (*Plantago psyllium*), also known as ispaghula, is the common name given to several plants in the Plantaginaceae, or plantain family, that has mucilage-producing seeds. Psyllium is native to northern India and Iran and is now also cultivated in the Mediterranean region, Europe, North Africa, Pakistan, and western Asia, as well in the southwestern United States. It prefers cool, dry climates, sandy soil, and sunny locations. The plant is a small annual with long narrow leaves and a foot-long stalk that produces clusters of tiny white flowers that are pollinated by the wind. These flowers mature into small, dark, glossy seed capsules that often show a reddish tint. The mucilage, a thick, colorless gelling agent, produced by these seeds and husks is commercially used as a thickener for ice cream and other frozen desserts.

Health Benefits

Psyllium has been part of Old World and Asian medicine for centuries, and it is believed the Aztecs may have used it as a food source. As it still is today,

> **DID YOU KNOW?**
>
> • *Tiny psyllium seeds are harvested through a process called thrashing and winnowing. Once the seeds are ripe and brittle, the plants are cut off halfway up the stalk and the tops are bound and dried. They are then ground with stones and sifted. Finally the seeds are sieved through increasingly finer mesh.*

psyllium was employed as a bulk-forming laxative by early healers. The plant's seeds are a soluble fiber, passing through the digestive tract without being completely broken down or absorbed. The mucilage the seeds produce absorbs excess water in the intestines, helping to soften stools and stimulate normal bowel movements. It is this gentle emetic effect that also makes the plant helpful in cases of irritable bowel syndrome, hemorrhoids, and other bowel-related ailments. Psyllium fiber can also help control diarrhea.

Recent research has expanded the medicinal role of the plant and earned it newfound respect. Psyllium is now also believed to lower triglycerides and blood glucose, control cholesterol, and aid in weight loss. In studies, psyllium fiber lowered levels of low-density lipoprotein, LDL (what is sometimes called "bad" cholesterol), in the blood. As such, it may provide a cholesterol medication that does not negatively affect weight, blood pressure, or levels of glucose, iron, or zinc. Research also indicates that psyllium can lower blood glucose levels enough to reduce the requirements of those who are insulin dependent; it may also prevent diabetes for those who are vulnerable to the disease. Additional research is needed, however, until the effects of including psyllium fiber in a long-term diet have been fully determined.

ROSE HIPS

BOLSTER THE HEALTH OF THE IMMUNE SYSTEM, RESPIRATORY TRACT, HEART, AND JOINTS

With powerful antioxidant benefits, the fruits of the rose plant have been a popular folk remedy for many centuries. Also known as rose haws or rose heps, rose hips are most often red or orange in color but can a be a deep purple or black. The rose plant—in its many incarnations—is a perennial, woody flowering plant in the Rosaceae family. Most roses are native to Asia but are also found around the world. After pollination in spring or early summer, the bloom produces a rounded hip that ripens during the late summer or fall. Not all roses produce marketable hips, but some species that do include *Rosa canina* (the dog rose found in English hedgerows) and *R. majalis* (the cinnamon rose).

Rose hips are used to make commercial herbal supplements, herbal teas, jellies, jams, marmalades, beverages, syrup, pie fillings, and wine. In Sweden, a rose hip soup called *nyponsoppa* is quite popular, as is *rhodomel,* a type of mead made from the hips and petals. In Hungary, rose hips are the main ingredient in *palinka,* a type of fruit brandy. The hips are also the main ingredient in *cockta,* the national soft drink of Slovenia. As a tea, rose hips are often blended with hibiscus, and in craft shops, they are sold for use in dried flower arrangements and to make potpourri.

Health Benefits

These nutrient-packed fruits have been used for thousands of years—by prehistoric cave dwellers, early Asian and European cultures, and possibly civilizations in the Americas. Most of their medicinal effects come from high amounts of vitamin C, carotenoids, flavonoids, and polyphenols. Rose hips are currently being researched for their ability to supply the following biological benefits.

DID YOU KNOW?

* *Throughout history, rose petals, not just the hips, were thought to have medicinal value. Roses were widely cultivated in the Middle Ages, and the petals were used for treating sores, coughs, colds, eye inflammations, diarrhea, painful joints, anxiety, lethargy, and many other ailments. They were also believed to stanch blood.*

* Rose hips' high levels of vitamin C allow them to give the immune system a boost and stimulate white blood cells, which fosters the treatment of respiratory problems and helps prevent asthma.

* The organic compounds and antioxidants found in the hips are able to reduce cholesterol levels, lowering the chances of suffering a heart attack or stroke.

* Rose hips are known as strict regulators of blood glucose levels, making them ideal for preventing the blood sugar spikes and plunges that can be so dangerous for diabetics.

* By eliminating free radicals in the body, rose hips can keep these harmful by-products of cellular metabolism from damaging healthy cells, either by causing their mutation into cancer cells or simply killing them off.

* Studies on the potential of rose hip extracts for treating arthritis pain resulted in small improvements that require further investigation.

The bright red hips of *Rosa canina,* which are useful for making a healthful and tart tea, rich in vitamin C. This rose species is a preferred source of aromatic essential oils.

ROSEMARY

SHARPEN THE BRAIN, RAISE THE SPIRITS, FIGHT INFECTION, AND MAINTAIN REGULARITY

This popular culinary herb was once a mainstay in the pharmacopoeias of early herbalists and healers. Rosemary *(Rosmarinis officinalis)* is a woody perennial in the mint family, Lamiaceae, that originated in the Mediterranean region and is now cultivated worldwide in temperate seaside locations. The plant can reach a height of five feet and displays pungent, evergreen, needlelike leaves and flowers in white, pink, purple, or blue. The name comes from the Latin *rosmarinus,* or "dew of the sea." Legend says that the Virgin Mary laid her blue cloak upon the plant, turning white flowers blue, and rosemary is sometimes referred to as "Rose of Mary." It is among the most popular kitchen herbs, used to flavor stuffing, meat dishes, and grilled vegetables. In the garden, rosemary acts as a pest control. Commercially, it is used in incense, perfumes, shampoo, and cleansers.

DID YOU KNOW?

• *Use rosemary to make an effective mouthwash that can improve your oral health. Simply steep some leaves in a glass of hot water, and then gargle with it or swish the water through your teeth for several minutes. Rosemary's active compounds will kill the bacteria in your mouth and give you naturally fresh breath.*

Health Benefits

Sacred to the Egyptians, Greeks, and Romans, venerable rosemary was used to treat memory loss, sour stomach, and pain. Researchers now know that many of the plant's medicinal properties stem from its powerful phytochemicals—rosmarinic acid, camphor, caffeic acid, betulic acid, carnosic, and carnosol. The benefits of this herb are many.

• Once used to improve recall and sharpen mental focus, in recent studies, the herb has been found to stimulate brain activity in older adults, even those with more advanced cognitive disorders like Alzheimer's disease or dementia.

• The sweet, earthy aroma can raise the spirits of those suffering from anxiety or stress, whether the leaves are ingested or applied topically.

• Rosemary's antioxidant, anti-inflammatory, and anticarcinogenic properties pose a triple threat to diseases that could affect the immune system.

• It is an effective agent against bacterial infections, especially against the staph infections that kill thousands every year and *Helicobacter pylori,* the pathogen that causes stomach ulcers.

• Add rosemary to your weekly diet to maintain regularity—it treats stomach disorders like indigestion, constipation, diarrhea, and bloating.

The herb is also known to stimulate blood flow, rushing necessary oxygen to all parts of the body, ensuring proper metabolic activity; and to ease the pain of injury or inflammation. A paste or salve is effective for external pain, while consuming the herb works to relieve internal pain, such as migraines. As a supplement, it is inexpensive and available in most pharmacies. It can also be grown in the garden or on a windowsill for home use and is extremely beneficial when included as a regular part of the diet.

The woody scent of rosemary essential oil is often used in aromatherapy as an energizer and cognitive booster.

SAGE

TREAT DIARRHEA, RESPIRATORY AILMENTS, HOT FLASHES, AND EXCESS PERSPIRATION

This kitchen favorite was highly valued by early healers as a digestive, gargle, nerve tonic, and poultice. Sage *(Salvia officinalis)* is a small, perennial, evergreen shrub in the mint family, Lamiaceae. It originated in the Mediterranean region, especially along the Adriatic coast, where it still grows wild. It is now found in most parts of the temperate world and is cultivated commercially in the United States, Canada, Argentina, Germany, and France. The plant typically reaches two feet in height, with woolly leaves of gray-green and flowers of blue, lilac, cream, or white that form two lips, similar to an open mouth. Bees flock to this herb with its lemony, slightly bitter scent.

DID YOU KNOW?

Sage is an ingredient in a concoction called Four Thieves Vinegar, which also contains wine or vinegar infused with spices and garlic. This drink was believed to ward off bubonic plague, a deadly flea-born pestilence that in the 1300s wiped out one-fifth of the world's population.

Health Benefit

The ancient Egyptians revered sage's power as a fertility drug, and the Greeks applied it to bleeding wounds and used it to treat sore throats and tuberculosis. The Romans considered the plant sacred—both its common and generic names come from the Latin *salvere,* or "to be saved"—and used it as a local anesthetic and a diuretic. Many medieval monasteries cultivated it as well. The herb was even found among the healing traditions of India—Ayurvedic, Siddha, and Unani—as treatment for indigestion and sore throats. Healers from antiquity to the Middle Ages advised it for snakebite, increasing fertility, strengthening the sinews, curing palsy, and as a tonic for the "head and brain." In the 19th century, it was a folk treatment for insect bites, damaged hair, mental or nervous conditions, mouth infections, and fevers.

Modern research validates the herb's antibacterial, antifungal, antiviral, and astringent properties and reveals that the essential oil contains alpha- and beta-thujone, camphor, and cineole. Herbalists recommend it for treating diarrhea, colds, throat infections, hot flashes, and excess perspiration. Studies on herpes patients who used sage resulted in a reduction of the number, size, and severity of oral or genital sores and decreased frequency of outbreaks. Sage might also be effective against Alzheimer's disease—it has been shown to be an acetylcholinesterase inhibitor, the only type of drugs approved to treat the disease by the U.S. Food and Drug Administration.

MAKE IT YOURSELF
Savory Sage Rub

Sage makes a tasty rub for grilled meats, while also offering a variety of health benefits.

YOU WILL NEED:
1 tablespoon dried sage
¼ cup dried rosemary
2 tablespoons dried oregano
2 cloves of garlic, minced
Kosher salt and pepper to taste

WHAT TO DO:
• Apply to dry steak, chops, or poultry.
• Chill overnight, and then grill or oven broil.

Sage leaves can be recognized by the fine silvery bloom that covers them.

Chewing the leaves of salad burnet, which is also known as garden burnet or small burnet, is said to aid digestion.

SALAD BURNET

EASE DIGESTION AND DIARRHEA, SHRINK HEMORRHOIDS, AND BOLSTER WOMEN'S HEALTH

A culinary herb used in salads and dressings, salad burnet (*Sanguisorba minor*) provides astringent medicinal qualities. This perennial member of the rose family (Rosaceae) is native to western, central, and southern Europe as well southwestern Asia. It came to the New World with settlers—Thomas Jefferson even made note of it—and it has since naturalized across most of North America. A denizen of dry, grassy meadows, it prefers limestone soils and lots of sun. It tends to grow in clumps and can reach from 16 to 36 inches in height. The rounded green leaves have lacy, toothed edges, and the small, dense, purple flowers grow on spikes.

In the kitchen, the tender young leaves add a fresh cucumber flavor to salads, dressings, finger sandwiches, and soups, and it can be used in many of the same recipes that call for mint. The leaves and flowers are found in Asian dishes. Salad burnet is a good plant to raise in containers, offering fresh produce throughout the growing season, even for those with limited space.

Health Benefits

In past centuries, salad burnet was used to ward off the bubonic plague, treat rheumatism and gout, and

> ### DID YOU KNOW?
>
> • *During the 17th century, English scientist and philosopher Francis Bacon recommended the planting of salad burnet underfoot on walkways, along with thyme and water mint. Bacon wrote that the scent of the herbs would "perfume the air most delightfully, being trodden on and crushed."*

to control heavy bleeding—the Latin genus name, *Sanguisorba*, roughly translates to "soaking up blood." In China, the plant was employed to increase sexual potency and, again, to stop gastrointestinal bleeding. The leaves are known to have astringent (contracting) and anti-inflammatory properties, making them effective for combating the organisms that cause stomach ailments, while both the leaves and the root can ease digestion, cure diarrhea, and shrink hemorrhoids. The herb is also used as a supplement for women's health. Research indicates that the plants contain medically beneficial glycosides, antivirals, tannins, ellagitannins, saponins, and beta-sisterol. These compounds stimulate the immune system, help lower cholesterol, and can slow the growth of cancerous tumors. Traces of the antioxidants quercetin, kaempferol, and rutin are found in the stems and leaves. Nutritionally the plant contains vitamins A, B, and C and the minerals iron and potassium.

RESCUE REMEDY: *Enjoy the minty cool taste of salad burnet—and gain the health benefits of this antioxidant herb—by adding fresh leaves to iced tea, sparkling water, or your favorite summer cocktail.*

SORREL

TREAT A HOST OF CONDITIONS FROM HEART DISEASE TO SKIN AILMENTS

This pleasant-tasting lemony garden herb also offers immunity-boosting benefits. Sorrel *(Rumex acetosa)*, known as common or garden sorrel, is a perennial herb in the Polygonaceae (the smartweed family). A close relative, French sorrel *(R. scutatus)*, developed in France and Italy and has a milder flavor than its cousin. Sorrel was originally a popular English herb that spread to the Continent, where it was cultivated in gardens and grew wild in fields and meadows. It is now also found in Central Asia and appears in North America as an introduced species. The plant reaches 24 inches in height, with deep roots, fleshy stems, and arrow-shaped leaves. It displays whorled spikes that bear reddish green flowers, which may become purplish as they mature. Sorrel is dioecious—having two sexes—with stamens and pistils on separate plants.

Sorrel was once a popular culinary herb in Europe. In the English country kitchen, French sorrel was mashed into a pulp with vinegar and sugar and served as "greensauce" over cold meats. French chefs used sorrel to make *soupe aux herbes* and added it to fricassees. Modern cooks are only just beginning to rediscover the herb.

> **DID YOU KNOW?**
>
> • *Yellow dock* (Rumex crispus), *a wild cousin of sorrel, was popular in the Middle Ages for treating respiratory ailments, skin conditions, and liver problems, as well as for its mild laxative effect. These days, experts advise caution when consuming it—always cook it, and avoid it entirely if you have urinary tract issues, rheumatism, or gout.*

Health Benefits

Renaissance herbalists believed that sorrel has cooling properties, making it effective against "hot" ailments— inflammations, pestilential or choleric agues, and violent moods. It was also prescribed to stimulate the appetite, kill worms, and open boils. Modern research indicates that it contains healthful flavonoids, antioxidants, and anthocyanins, making it a potential treatment for high blood pressure, heart disease, diabetes, and cancer. The herb's tannins clear nasal passages and help combat sinusitis. It is also used to improve eyesight, boost immunity, strengthen bones, heal skin ailments, increase appetite, and slow aging. The plant is also rich in vitamin C—sorrel was once given to sailors at sea to prevent scurvy, a disease that arises from lack of citric acid—as well as vitamins A and B9 and the minerals potassium, magnesium, sodium, calcium, and iron.

> **MAKE IT YOURSELF**
> ### *Fresh Sorrel Juice*
>
> Try this healthy and tasty sorrel tonic, which is packed with vitamins and minerals.
>
> YOU WILL NEED:
> 2 pounds carrots, cleaned
> 2 stalks celery, washed
> 1 apple, cored and cut into eighths
> ½ to 1 bunch sorrel
>
> WHAT TO DO:
> • Run two of the carrots through a juicer or bullet blender.
> • Add celery and sorrel, and then alternate adding in carrots and apple slices.
> • Strain through cheesecloth, and drink chilled.

Fresh sorrel. Toss these arrow-shaped leaves into juice or a smoothie or tear them into pieces to add to a salad.

STEVIA

LOWER HIGH BLOOD PRESSURE AND REGULATE CHOLESTEROL AND BLOOD SUGAR LEVELS

When the world went looking for a low-calorie alternative to sugar, a small tropical shrub stepped up to fill the gap. Stevia (*Stevia rebaudiana*), a member of the Compositae (the aster or daisy family), is native to Paraguay and Brazil. The plant can reach three feet in height and has slender branched stems, serrated green leaves, and tiny white flowers that bloom in fall. It is grown commercially in Japan, Thailand, Paraguay, and Brazil, with China being the leading exporter.

Health Benefits

The Guarani people of Paraguay have been using what they call *ka'a he'ê*, or sweet herb, for more than 1,500 years to sweeten teas and medicines and to treat wounds and inflammations, reduce swelling, and relieve depression. Natural healers often recommend the plant as a remedy for colic, burns, dandruff, skin ailments, and wrinkles.

Its flavor has been compared to honeysuckle nectar, and its active compounds, called steviol glycosides (mainly stevioside and rebaudioside), provide up to 40 times the sweetness of sugar with almost no calories. It also has a negligible effect on blood glucose levels, making it ideal for individuals on carbohydrate-controlled diets. The plant contains antioxidant tannins and flavonoids—especially kaemferol, which in tests was able to reduce the risk of pancreatic cancer by 23 percent. These phytonutrients also make stevia useful for lowering high blood pressure and regulating cholesterol and blood sugar levels. It is a noncarbohydrate sweeteners, so it does not promote the growth of *Streptococcus mutans* in the mouth—thus reducing the incidence of cavities; certain compounds in stevia may actually lower the quantity of oral bacteria. Unlike sugar, which is nearly nutritionally bankrupt, stevia contains proteins, fiber, iron, carbohydrates, phosphorus, calcium, sodium, potassium, magnesium, zinc, and vitamins A and C.

Stevia granules and leaves. The granules are made from high-purity steviol glycosides extracted from the plant.

SEEKING APPROVAL

Stevia was banned as a food additive in the United States in 1991, when early studies indicated that it might cause cancer. As of 2008, the U.S. Food and Drug Administration has approved stevia extracts—high-purity steviol glycosides—to be lawfully marketed and added to food products. (Keep in mind that the leaves and crude stevia extracts do not have FDA approval for use in food.) In 2008, the FDA also approved the stevia extract known as rebiana as a food additive. Rebiana is now part of a widely marketed product called Truvia. Critics complain, however, that Truvia offers few of the health benefits provided by stevia. Meanwhile, the European Union approved stevia in 2011, while Japan has been safely using it for many years.

The stinging hairs on nettle leaves have inspired other common names, such as burn weed and burn nettle.

STINGING NETTLE

STIMULATE THE BLOOD, CONTROL PMS, BENEFIT THE KIDNEYS, AND EASE PAIN

In spite of its threatening name, this plant has long been used as a food source, as well as a detoxifying herb and industrial fiber. Stinging nettle (*Urtica dioica*) is often considered an invasive weed, and five of the six subspecies are capable of inflicting painful stings with their hypodermic-like trichomes, fine hairs that inject histamines and other chemicals into the skin. The plant is found in ditches, wastelands, and abandoned gardens.

Once the stinging chemicals in the leaves have been neutralized in boiling water, the plant can be brewed into a healthful tea. Nettle soup is a mainstay of some cultures, including the mountain villages of Nepal.

Health Benefits

For many centuries, the stinging parts of nettle served as a counterirritant—flogging with the plant was once a popular cure for arthritis pain. Healers used the herb to treat coughs, congestion, allergies, and urinary tract disorders. Modern research reveals the presence of flavonoids, histamines, and seratonin in the plant. Current applications of the herb are varied.

> **DID YOU KNOW?**
>
> • *Stinging nettle, called* stiðe *by the Anglo Saxons, has a long history, both in herbal and in practical use. It was part of the early medieval Nine Herbs Charm, and burial shrouds made from cloth woven from the spun stem fibers have been found in Denmark that date back 5,000 years or more.*

• It can reduce the cramping and bloating of PMS, minimize blood flow during menstruation, and address the physiological problems associated with menopause.

• Stinging nettle tea is recommended to ease pain for women who are experiencing prolonged labor. The herb acts as a coagulant, so it can also prevent excessive bleeding, and it can even aid new mothers by stimulating milk production.

• Compounds found in the herb act as detoxifiers. As an alterative, it improves the nutrient uptake of the stomach, and as a diuretic, it ensures that the neutralized toxins are quickly eliminated.

• It contains high levels of vitamin C and iron.

• As a stimulant, stinging nettle tea has been proven effective for treating inflammatory conditions like arthritis, gout, and chronic muscle pain.

• The boron found in the herb can help maintain the calcium content in bones.

Exercise caution when working with this herb's extremely potent essential oil, always mixing nettle extracts with a neutral carrier oil.

Up Close

DARK HERBS

THE HEALING POTENTIAL OF POISONOUS PLANTS

In magical lore, foxglove is a baneful herb associated with the underworld and used for communing with the fairies. It is now used by the pharmaceutical industry to formulate heart medications that treat cardiac arrhythmias.

Natural healers or shamans did not always deal with harmless, ingestible herbs. Sometimes they utilized more dangerous plants that offered curative medicinal properties, administering them in tiny doses. The highly poisonous plants mandrake, henbane, hemlock, and opium were all used for centuries to numb patients prior to surgery. Other herbs could induce abortion, kill intestinal parasites (like hellebores), or even regulate heartbeat (foxglove), but they, too, had to be used with great caution.

From Bane to Benefit

As medical science continued to look for cures for life-threatening diseases, some of these poisonous plants fell under scrutiny. These plants were powerful and intimidating, with complex mechanisms. Yet with the aid of sophisticated modern research methods, might not some poisonous or questionable "cures" from the past prove to have a valid place in modern medicine? The answer was a resounding "Yes!" For instance, deadly plant neurotoxins that disrupt messages to the muscles in the heart or lungs can have fatal results. But what if nonlethal doses of the same substance could halt tremors or keep pain from registering? Essentially, poisons alter or stop things from occurring in the body, just as medicines do. It became just a matter of harnessing that power for good. Some toxic plants that currently have medicinal applications are listed here.

- The entire yew tree (genus *Taxus)* is poisonous to humans, yet research in the 1960s indicated that an ingredient in the bark of the Pacific yew (*T. brevifolia)* could be used to inhibit some cancers. A derivative called paclitaxel is now an effective weapon against breast, lung, and other cancers, as well as AIDS-related Kaposi's sarcoma.

- Sweet wormwood *(Artemisia annua),* which contains the potentially poisonous chemical thujone, is the source of the antimalarial drug artimisinin, which is also garnering praise as a powerful treatment for breast cancer.
- All parts of foxglove *(Digitalis purpurea)* are poisonous, yet it was often used successfully in past centuries to treat dropsy, what we now call congestive heart failure. Yet, no one knew why it worked. Then around 1785, Dr. William Withering discovered digitalin, an active ingredient in the plant that increases blood flow, strengthens the heartbeat by increasing the amount of calcium in the heart's cells, corrects cardiac arrhythmia, and reduces swelling of hands and ankles. It is the source of digoxin, a drug used today to treat a variety of heart-related conditions.
- The opium poppy *(Papaver somniferum)* was the source of morphine, an anesthetic that revolutionized the treatment of pain. (Alas, it also gave rise to the destructive, addictive street drug heroin and other opiates.)
- Madagascar periwinkle *(Vinca rosea)* contains toxic alkaloids in its tissues; these alkaloids are now used to cure leukemia and other cancers.

An illustration of deadly nightshade from *Flora von Deutschland* by Otto Wilhelm Thomé, published in 1885

THE HERBAL ROGUE'S GALLERY

Some plants were used by practitioners of the dark arts and blended into potions that they believed could bring about good or ill results: charms to create love or guarantee a bountiful harvest, or curses to defeat an enemy or cause a rival's downfall. The rogue's gallery of dark herbs includes some substances that actually have a hallucinatory effect if ingested.

- **Deadly nightshade** *(Atropa belladonna)* was believed to induce psychic visions and was a key ingredient in witches' "flying ointment."
- **Wolfsbane** (genus *Aconitum*), or monkshood, was worn for protection against werewolves and vampires.
- **Hemlock** *(Conium maculatum),* a deadly poison, was regarded as a "cure" for overcrowded prisons.
- **Mandrake** *(Mandragora officinarum)* was employed as a protective home charm that increased fertility in women and cured impotency in men.
- **Mistletoe** *(Viscum album)* was worn for protection or to attract love.
- **Henbane** *(Hyoscyamus niger),* included in witches' flying ointment, was also carried to attract love.
- **Cherry laurel** *(Prunus laurocerasus)* leaves were crushed and used in killing jars to preserve insects.
- **Rue** *(Ruta graveolens)* was thought to prevent illness, purify ritual spaces, and clear the mind.
- **Sweet wormwood** *(Artemisia annua)* offered protection from spirits and aided divination.
- **Mugwort** *(Artemisia vulgaris)* was thought to induce psychic dreams and astral projection.
- **Opium poppy** *(Papaver somniferum)* was smoked to provide insightful visions.
- **Yew** (genus *Taxus*), held sacred by Druids, represented everlasting life.

ST. JOHN'S WORT

TREAT ANXIETY, INSOMNIA, HYPOTHYROIDISM, BLADDER ISSUES, PMS, AND NERVE PAIN

This plant is often viewed as an invasive weed, but it offers a time-tested treatment for depression. St. John's wort (*Hypericum perforatum*) is a flowering plant in the Hypericaceae family. It is native to the temperate regions of Europe and Asia and has naturalized in the United States and Australia. It can be found growing in sun or slight shade, especially in open meadows, along roadsides, and at the edges of woodlands. The plant normally reaches two feet in height and bears erect, woody-based stems and yellow, five-petaled flowers. As its common name indicates, the plant has a long association with St. John the Baptist—it traditionally flowers on St. John's Day, June 24, and the flowers are said to bleed red bloodlike oil on August 29, the day of the saint's beheading.

DID YOU KNOW?

• *European folklore attributes amazing powers to St. John's wort—the ability to ward off thunderbolts and lightning and demons and witches. The genus name* Hypericum, *meaning "over a picture," refers to the tradition of hanging the herb over religious images on Midsummer's Day to keep away evil.*

Health Benefits

Ancient cultures used the herb to treat sores, burns, sprains, nerve pain, and inflammation. It was made into a calming tonic and also recommended for colds, flu, and coughs, as well as stomach and bowel problems, fatigue, and epilepsy. It was frequently used to stanch deep wounds; in the Middle Ages, a plant's healing specialty was supposedly indicated by its shape or texture, so this usage was based on the small oil glands on the leaves that looked like wounds. During this time, the herb was employed to cure jaundice, dysentery, bed-wetting, hysteria, and lung complaints. The Eclectics in the 1800s valued it for treating anxiety, nervous complaints, and depression, which are still some of its chief benefits. The hypericum oil extracted from the plant was a popular rub for healing bruises, swelling, and wounds, but by the turn of the 20th century the herb had fallen from favor.

The recent revival of interest in this potent herb occurred when research validated its effect on mild-to-moderate depression. This effect is possibly due to the compound hyperforin, although the plant also contains tannins, flavonoids, and another compound called hypericin that displays antiviral activity against HIV, herpes, and hepatitis. In studies, the herb showed some ability to aid nicotine withdrawal and lower alcohol cravings. Currently, it is used to treat anxiety, insomnia, seasonal affective disorder, shingles, hypothyroidism, bladder issues, PMS and menopausal symptoms, and nerve pain.

RESCUE REMEDY: *To make a healing balm for skin or lips, combine 5 tablespoons St. John's wart oil with 2 teaspoons beeswax in a pan, and blend over a pot of simmering water. Add 5 drops of your favorite essential oil, and transfer to a tin or container before it thickens.*

St. John's wort in bloom. As an herbal remedy, this plant can be taken in the form of a tea, tincture, or tablet.

You can grow summer savory in a backyard garden or windowsill and then dry it to use later in teas and other remedies.

SUMMER SAVORY

REGULATE CHOLESTEROL LEVELS, FIGHT INFECTION, AND TREAT GAS AND JOINT PAIN

Versatile summer savory (*Satureja hortensis*) offers culinary, aromatic, and medicinal applications. A member of the Lamiaceae, or mint family, this hardy annual plant is native to southeastern Europe and the Mediterranean, where it has been used in food preparation for more than 2,000 years. It is now found in many temperate regions of the planet. It reaches a height of one to two feet and bears narrow, aromatic leaves and tubular lilac-colored flowers. They should be harvested for drying during blooming season, from July to September.

Similar in culinary usage to its perennial cousin, winter savory, summer savory has a spicy, peppery taste and is included in the classic bouquet garni and fines herbes. It blends well in recipes with thyme, marjoram, and oregano and is often used to flavor sausage meat. In the Middle Ages, the herb added pungency to cakes and pies.

Health Benefits

Summer savory's medicinal use goes back at least to ancient Egypt, where the powdered plant was used in love potions and to treat sore throats, poor vision, palsy, sciatica, and numerous intestinal problems. Roman poet Virgil noted its fragrant aroma and recommended it be planted near beehives. Over the years, it has been used as a general health tonic, an expectorant for respiratory problems, and a digestive aid to cure diarrhea and reduce flatulence. Rubbing a sprig of it on a bee or wasp sting was also believed to relieve pain.

We now know that the plant's leaves and shoots contain a variety of chemical compounds with antioxidant properties, including linalool, camphene, terpinol, myrcene, and other terpenoids. Its dietary fiber helps to reduce levels of bad cholesterol and increase levels of the good. The herb's essential volatile oils include antiseptic, antifungal thymol, as well as carvacol, which inhibits the growth of many bacterial strains. Nutritionally, it offers vitamins A, B6, and C, niacin, and thiamine, as well as impressive amounts of potassium, iron, calcium, magnesium, manganese, zinc, and selenium. These healing properties enable the herb to treat superficial wounds, aid digestion, ease intestinal gas, help clear up mucous, and reduce joint pain.

> **DID YOU KNOW?**
>
> • *Summer savory, a mint relative of lavender, sage, and thyme, has a long history of medicinal use. Famed 17th-century English botanist Nicholas Culpeper praised summer savory as a "cure-all" and advised that it always be kept on hand.*

RESCUE REMEDY: *Dry your own summer savory by trimming off the top 6 inches of the plant just before or during blooming. Spread small pieces out to dry on a screen or paper at room temperature. Separate dried leaves from stems, and store in a sealed glass container in a cool, dark location.*

TARRAGON
STIMULATE APPETITE AND REMEDY INDIGESTION, FLATULENCE, HICCUPS, AND INSOMNIA

A favorite of French chefs that offers multiple medical benefits, tarragon is a major player in the culinary stakes. Also known as French tarragon, dragon wort, or estragon, tarragon (*Artemisia dracunculus*) is a member of the daisy family. It originated in Siberia and western Asia and is now cultivated in many temperate or semitropical regions and can still be found growing wild in Eurasia and North America. Tarragon matures into a shrub that will reach four or five feet in height, with lanceolate, glossy green leaves, thin woody stems, and tiny greenish or yellowish white blooms. When preparing recipes, most cooks advise going easy on the tarragon—its sweet, aniselike flavor can dominate other less robust herbs. Russian tarragon (*A. dracunculoides*) has a milder flavor and is less often used in cooking.

Health Benefits

Natural healers found this to be a versatile herb, prescribing it to stimulate appetite and to remedy indigestion, flatulence, hiccups, and anorexia.

> **DID YOU KNOW?**
>
> • *Considered one of the top providers of antioxidants among common herbs, tarragon is known as a free radical scavenger, helping our bodies to get rid of those harmful by-products of metabolism that can negatively affect RNA, DNA, cellular membrane, proteins, vitamins, and carbohydrates and cause premature aging, inflammation, and cancer.*

Tarragon is an outstanding source of antioxidants, and it also contains valuable phytonutrients and the essential oils methyl chavicol, cineol, ocimene, and phellandrene.

Compounds in the herb extract can lower bad cholesterol by keeping platelets from aggregating and adhering to the walls of blood vessels, thus helping to prevent heart attack and stroke. Tarragon provides vitamin A, C, and antioxidant B-complex group vitamins like folate, pyridoxine, niacin, and riboflavin. It is also a source of the minerals calcium, copper, potassium, and zinc manganese—utilized by the body as a cofactor for an antioxidant enzyme called superoxide dismutase—and iron, which is necessary for cellular respiration and blood cell production.

The following list includes some of tarragon's medicinal applications. The herb can be eaten fresh, taken dried, steeped in water as tea, or used as an infused or essential oil.

- A few drops of the essential oil are able to fight bad breath, destroy microbes on the skin, and reduce body odor.
- Tarragon tea can help overcome insomnia and relieve anxiety.
- Unless a women is pregnant or nursing, she can employ this herb to maintain reproductive health.
- Tarragon eases digestion by aiding the production of bile by the liver.
- Research indicates that it can promote muscle growth by increasing the absorption of creatine, an organic acid that helps to build strength.

RESCUE REMEDY: *Eugenol, an essential oil found in tarragon, has long been used in dentistry as a local anesthetic and to reduce toothache pain. Simply chewing the leaves can ease oral discomfort.*

Fresh tarragon has both culinary and medicinal uses.

TEA

PREVENT BREAST CANCER, STRENGTHEN THE HEART, AND TREAT ASTHMA AND OTHER AILMENTS

This evergreen shrub or small tree not only furnishes a beverage staple enjoyed around the world, it also offers a range of health benefits. A member of the Theaceae family, the tea plant *(Camellia sinensis)* comes in two types: a narrow-leaf variety *(C. sinensis* var. *sinensis),* grows in the cool mountains of central China and Japan; the broad-leaf variety *(C. sinensis* var. *assamica),* prefers the moist, tropical climates found in northeast India and the Szechuan and Yunnan provinces of China. Both display glossy green leaves and small white flowers.

Health Benefits

The first black tea—Lapsang Souchong—was produced in the late 1500s, during China's Ming Dynasty, and healers adopted it to treat a variety of ailments. The Dutch introduced the drink to Europe around 1610.

Tea contains high levels of antioxidant polyphenols; in a study at Tufts University, well-steeped black and green teas scored higher than the top-ranked fruits and vegetables for antioxidant content. Tea also provides beneficial compounds theaflavins and thearubigens, as well as sodium, proteins, and carbohydrates.

Tea is used to treat a range of complaints. Its theaflavins can help destroy abnormal cells; it is possible both black and green tea can prevent breast cancer in premenopausal women. It is also heart healthy—according to the American Heart Association, people

> ### DID YOU KNOW?
> • *The tea plant has a growth phase and a dormant phase. In cool climates, the dormant phase usually coincides with winter. The new shoots, or "flushes," picked as they emerge in spring, make the best tea.*

who drink three to four cups of black tea daily are at lower risk for strokes and heart attacks. Boston School of Medicine studies show that it can also correct the abnormal functioning of blood vessels, possibly averting stroke and fatal heart attacks. For asthma sufferers, drinking hot tea can open airways, allowing them to breathe more easily. Tea can alleviate diarrhea, too; its tannins have a soothing effect on intestinal irritation. These tannins are also astringent, and comfortably hot teabags can relieve the itch and pain of poison ivy, sunburn, and insect bites. You can also press wet teabags against swollen gums or boils, and tea's flavonoids help treat cold sores by suppressing the growth of the herpes virus.

RESCUE REMEDY: *Ease inflamed, dry, or irritated eyes by soaking two teabags in warm water for 10 minutes. Squeeze out excess moisture, and place them over your eyes.*

A tea plantation in Munnar, India, growing *Camellia sinensis* var. *assamica.* There are four main tea types: black, green, oolong, and white. How the plant is harvested and how the leaves are processed determines the type.

TEA TREE

FIGHT ACNE, TREAT SKIN CONDITIONS, AND CONTROL FOOT ODOR

A tree or tall shrub in the Myrtaceae, or myrtle family, the tea tree (*Melaleuca alternifolia*) yields essential oils that possess medicinal properties, but it also has applications as an antiseptic cleaner. The plant is endemic to Australia. It prefers full sun at the edges of streams and in marshy flatlands, where it often dominates the surrounding terrain. The trees reach an average height of 20 feet and feature a bushy crown and papery whitish bark. The oil-rich leaves are long, smooth, and soft. In spring and summer, the trees display masses of cream or white flowers on spikes. Their fluffy appearance accounts for the common name snow-in-summer. Other names for it include narrow-leaved paperbark and narrow-leaved ti-tree.

Health Benefits

For more than a century, tea tree has been used in Australia to treat fungal nail infections and skin problems like acne and psoriasis, as well as lice, scabies, and ringworm. The plant was originally a bush medicine of the indigenous Bundjalung people of eastern Australia, who inhaled the oil's vapors to treat coughs and colds, made it into an infusion for skin ailments, and applied the crushed leaves to wounds before covering them with a poultice. Today, natural healers from all over the world are discovering the benefits of this versatile essential oil.

The essential oil is recognized as a powerful antiseptic with antibacterial, antifungal, antiviral, and antimicrobial properties. Research indicates that a 5 percent solution of the oil works as effectively on acne outbreaks as the popular drugstore remedy benzoil peroxide, and it is gentler on the skin. Simply add a few drops of the oil to 30 drops of witch hazel, and then apply with a cotton ball. If you're looking for a gentle makeup remover that can control acne outbreaks, simply mix a quarter cup of canola oil with 10 drops tea tree oil in a small, lidded glass jar, and shake well. Apply with a swab, rinse with warm water, and finish with a mild toner. Tea tree oil is also effective against foot odor, for relieving chicken pox rash and cold sores, for treating athlete's foot and jock itch, and it has recently gained popularity in the practice of aromatherapy. It should never be ingested.

> ### DID YOU KNOW?
>
> • *Melaleuca alternifolia is the source of commercial tea tree oils, but related plants also yield oils that are used in similar ways.* M. cajuputs *(white samet) is the source of cajuput oil, and* M. quinquenervia *(broad-leaved paperbark) yields niaouli oil.*

Tea tree oil and leaves.
The source species of the oil is usually called narrow-leaved paperbark.

> ### MAKE IT YOURSELF
> ## Mani-Pedi Massage
>
> To soften dry cuticles, prepare this emollient mixture of carrier and aromatic healing oils.
>
> YOU WILL NEED:
> 10 drops tea tree oil
> 10 drops lavender oil
> 1 tablespoon jojoba oil
> 1 tablespoon avocado oil
>
> WHAT TO DO:
> • Combine jojoba oil and avocado oil in a dark-colored glass jar.
> • Add tea tree and lavender oils, and shake well.
> • Massage a few drops into the cuticles of your fingernails and toenails.

THYME

PROMOTE CARDIOVASCULAR, CIRCULATORY, EYE, AND RESPIRATORY HEALTH

This evergreen herb offers a trifecta of medicinal, culinary, and ornamental uses. Thyme *(Thymus vulgaris),* a member of the mint family, Lamiaceae, is also a close relative of oregano. Native to the Mediterranean and parts of Africa, the plant is now found in sunny locations in many parts of the world. It is a bushy, woody shrub that reaches a foot in height and is often used as a ground cover. It displays small, aromatic gray-green leaves and pink or purple clusters of flowers.

In the kitchen, thyme lends a spicy, sweet flavor to dishes and is an ingredient in both the bouquet garni and herbes de Provence. Dried thyme is known for retaining its flavor better than most other herbs. It is also used to flavor liqueurs, cheeses, and mouthwash and is an ingredient in hand sanitizers.

Health Benefits

The Egyptians were among the first to use thyme medicinally, including as an overall health booster and in the embalming process. The Greeks sprinkled it in their baths and burned it as incense during religious rituals. Roman legions spread the herb throughout Europe, where it was quickly adopted for both table and medicine chest. It has been in continual use as a healing herb since then.

Scientific research indicates that thyme's main active ingredient, thymol, acts as an antifungal and antiviral, helping to ease the burden on the immune system when disease strikes. Its impressive concentrations of antioxidants, among the highest in any herb, allow thyme to prevent oxidative stress to the body's organs and neural pathways. These antioxidants include lutein, zeaxanthin, and thymonin. High levels of iron and other vital minerals in the herb stimulate production of red blood cells—

> ### DID YOU KNOW?
>
> • *During the Middle Ages, thyme, already an established healing herb, was also placed under the pillow to ward off nightmares and given to knights by noble ladies to bring on courage during tournaments or before battle. It was sometimes placed in coffins to assure passage into the next life.*

boosting circulation and oxygenation of the organs and extremities. The herb's potassium and manganese support cardio function by relaxing blood vessels and lowering blood pressure, while its carotenoids and vitamin A make thyme a boon to eye health. Thyme's mucous-busting expectorant properties and anti-inflammatory qualities make it ideal for treating respiratory problems such as colds, flu, bronchitis, sinus infections, chronic asthma, or seasonal allergies, especially when delivered in the form of a potent, powerful tea. In addition to a beneficial tea, the leaves can be used in a decoction with carrier oils or creams for topical applications. An excess intake of the herb might cause gastric distress.

A honeybee sips the nectar of a thyme bloom. This aromatic herb will attract pollinators to your yard. Beekeepers plant thyme to produce a flavorful honey.

VALERIAN

RELIEVE INSOMNIA, HIGH BLOOD PRESSURE, ANXIETY, AND MUSCLE CRAMPS

This flowering perennial's use as a healing herb goes back to ancient Greece and Rome. Valerian (*Valeriana officinalis*), a member of the Caprifoliaceae family, is also known as garden valerian, garden heliotrope (no relation to true *Heliotropium,* though), setwell and all-heal, the latter two names bearing testimony to the plant's earlier medicinal use. During early centuries the herb was also called nard, amantilla, or baldrian. The plant's generic name comes from the Latin word *valere,* meaning "to be strong and healthy." It is native to Europe and some regions of Asia. It can reach heights of five feet and bears deeply toothed green leaves and sweetly scented flowers with pink or white heads, which make it a popular garden ornamental.

This herb is sometimes used to flavor foods and drinks such as root beer. In the 16th century, the aromatic flowers were used to produce perfumes, but the other parts of the plant, especially the root, are said to smell like dirty socks or stinky cheese.

Health Benefits

Valerian's role as a medicinal herb goes back to the early Greeks and Romans, who used it as a remedy

DID YOU KNOW?

• *Valerian is considered an invasive species—one that proliferates and puts native plants at risk—in many locations, including the state of Connecticut, where it is banned, and in New Brunswick, Canada, where it is listed as a plant of concern. Check with your local cooperative extension before planting this herb.*

for insomnia, anxiety, indigestion, urinary infections, and liver complaints. Arab, Indian, and Chinese physicians also refer to its curative powers in their records. Seventeenth-century English botanist Nicholas Culpeper wrote that valerian fell under the influence of the planet Mercury and that it was possessed of a "warming faculty."

Today, medicinal preparations are made from the plant's roots, rhizomes, and stolons, which are dried and sold in capsule form. The fresh leaves can also be used to prepare a mildly sedative tea.

Contemporary natural healers employ valerian as a sleep inducer, an antiseptic, an anticonvulsive, a migraine treatment, or a pain reliever and use it to treat insomnia, high blood pressure, anxiety, stress, and muscle cramps. Its many active compounds, including alkaloids, isovaleric acid, iridoids, sesquiterpenes, and flavanones, are believed to contribute to its effectiveness. Of most interest to researchers is gamma-aminobutyric acid (GABA), a receptor that interacts with its other constituents. So far, however, studies on the herb's mechanism of action, and its use as a sedative, have been inconclusive.

RESCUE REMEDY: *Combat insomnia with valerian tea mixed with lemon balm, which helps brighten the musky taste of valerian root. To make this tea, in the morning, mix 1 teaspoon of ground valerian root in 1 cup warm water, and let it stand all day before straining. Before dinner, pour 1 cup of boiling water over one or two fresh lemon balm leaves. Steep for 10 minutes, and add to the strained valerian tea. Add 1 teaspoon of honey, and drink a cup after dinner and a cup before bedtime.*

Valerian tea with flowers and roots

WATER CHESTNUT

TREAT SKIN INFECTIONS, RESTORE HEART HEALTH, PROMOTE SLEEP, AND EASE MIGRAINES

Chinese water chestnut, or simply water chestnut (*Eleocharis dulcis*) has a history in Indian medicine and is a favored ingredient in Chinese stir-fry recipes. This perennial member of the Cyperaceae, or sedge family, is native to Asia, Australia, tropical Africa, and islands in the Pacific and Indian Oceans. Other names include bush nut, water nut, spike rush, and ground chestnut.

The water chestnut is not a true nut, but rather the fruit, or corm, of a tuberous sedge—an aquatic plant that grows in ponds, marshes, and lakes. Roughly two-thirds of the plant remains submerged, but the tall stemlike leaves float above the surface. It is under these that the edible water chestnuts—triangular, white-fleshed, papery brown-skinned corms—appear. They are harvested as seasonal vegetables, but canning makes them available throughout the year. Water chestnuts are known for their remarkable crunchiness, which does not diminish after being cooked or tinned. The sweet, delicate flavor is similar to a combination of apple, coconut, and sweet chestnut. The corms are often used in the manufacture of starch flour.

Health Benefits

Water chestnuts are part of both Ayurvedic and Unani traditions of natural medicine; the outsides of the corms were once crushed by aboriginal healers to treat wounds. Research verifies that these vegetables offer a range of nutrients—including dietary fiber, vitamin E, B-complex vitamins, potassium, copper, manganese, and zinc. They also provide antibiotic, antibacterial, antiviral, antioxidant, and anticancer properties, making them useful as remedies for skin infections, restoring vigor, curing sleeplessness, easing migraines, and even combating cancer. Adding water

> **DID YOU KNOW?**
>
> • *Don't confuse Chinese water chestnuts with another group of water chestnuts* (Trapa natans, T. bicornis), *which are also known as water caltrop, buffalo nut, bat nut, and devil pod. These water chestnuts bear ornately shaped edible fruit, but they are not economically important. They are also unrelated to sweet chestnut* (Castanea sativa).

chestnuts to your diet could provide the following health benefits.

- The potassium in the corms can help lower high blood pressure and normalize an irregular heartbeat.
- The vitamin B1 in the plant has shown some potential for slowing down the progression of Alzheimer's disease.
- This waterborne vegetable is low in calories and nearly fatless—half a cup contains only 0.1 gram of fat.
- The minerals manganese, copper, and zinc present in the corms of water chestnuts may help reduce bone loss in postmenopausal women.
- Eaten raw, water chestnuts make a great tonic for the body and act as detoxifying agents, especially for those suffering from jaundice.
- The corms help cool the body by stimulating production of saliva and quenching thirst.
- The extract is effective against indigestion and nausea. It can also stimulate the appetite.

Peeled water chestnuts reveal crunchy white flesh.

WATERCRESS

PROMOTE EYE HEALTH, MAINTAIN HEART HEALTH, AND BUILD BONE STRENGTH

This aquatic plant makes a piquant addition to salads and sandwiches and it also has numerous medicinal applications. Watercress (*Nasturtium officinale*) is a rapidly growing perennial that is native to Europe and Asia and is found in meandering streams. A member of the Brassicaceae family, watercress is related to mustard, radish, and wasabi, which all share its sharp, peppery flavor. In spite of its botanical name, watercress is only distantly related to the flowering plants called nasturtiums (family Tropaeolum). Due to its hollow stems, watercress is able to float, making it ideal for commercial hydroponic cultivation. The rounded, scalloped leaves are a bright green, and the small white flowers appear in clusters.

You cannot dry this plant's leaves for later use, but you can find fresh watercress in farmer's markets, green grocers, supermarkets, and health food stores.

> ### DID YOU KNOW?
>
> • *Watercress is so popular that two cities actually lay claim to it. Alresford, England, is considered the watercress capital of the United Kingdom; its annual Watercress Festival brings in 15,000 visitors each year. Back in the 1940s, Huntsville, Alabama, was known as the "watercress capital of the world."*

Health Benefits

Watercress may be the oldest known vegetable to be consumed by humans. The early Greeks and Romans eagerly sought it as a flavorful food source, and they also employed it for treating respiratory ailments, constipation, parasitic worms, goiter, tuberculosis, cancer, and baldness. It was used to make a healthful spring tonic, to stimulate the appetite, and to improve sexual performance. When applied topically, watercress was said to cure warts, scabies, arthritis, rheumatism, and eczema.

Today, herbalists prescribe the plant for eye health, regulation of cholesterol and blood pressure levels, maintaining the heart, and building bone strength. Recent studies indicate that its phytonutrients are instrumental in its ability to fight off infection, maintain connective tissue, keep bones strong, and prevent iron deficiency. A study at the University of Ulster reported that daily intake of watercress could reduce the damage to DNA caused by free radicals. Another study at the University of Southampton found that a compound in the plant, phenethyl isothiocyanate (PEITC), displayed anticancer properties, especially against breast cancer. This effect may arise from the ability of PEITCs to starve tumors of blood, thus triggering a "turn off" signal. Watercress is rich in vitamin K and supplies impressive amounts of vitamin A, vitamin C, riboflavin, vitamin B6, calcium, manganese, and folate. It is low in carbohydrates and fats; a half-cup serving contains a scant 11 calories.

RESCUE REMEDY: *To benefit from watercress's many healthy properties, add five or six leaves to a slice of multigrain bread spread with reduced-fat cream cheese. Place a slice of pumpernickel on top, remove the crusts, cut into quarters and, voilà!, instant finger sandwiches.*

The taste of healthful watercress has a peppery zing.

WINTERGREEN

RELIEVE PAIN, TREAT INDIGESTION AND RESPIRATORY AILMENTS, AND STAY ALERT

Years ago, plants that did not lose their leaves and maintained photosynthesis during the colder months were referred to as "wintergreen." More recently, that word came to be replaced by the term *evergreen*. One group of aromatic plants in the genus *Gaultheria* kept the name, however. The most prevalent species in North America, the American wintergreen *(G. procumbens),* is also known by a host of folk names, including eastern teaberry, American mountain tea, Canada tea, checkerberry, squaw vine, wax clusters, spiceberry, and boxberry. This low-growing shrub is a member of the Ericaceae family; it prefers pine or hardwood forests and is often part of an oak-heath forest. It grows from a shallow rhizome, producing aromatic elliptic or ovate leaves, bell-shaped white flowers, and a berrylike red fruit. The leaves and berries are edible and are winter favorites of white-tailed deer, wild turkey, ring-necked pheasant, black bear, and red fox.

DID YOU KNOW?

* *Wintergreen is used to flavor chewing gum, mints, and tobacco, as well as dental products like toothpaste and mouthwash. It is also a component in the American soft drink root beer, with the result that many non-Americans who try the drink for the first time, complain that it tastes like toothpaste.*

Health Benefits

Native Americans used wintergreen leaves to brew a healing tea to treat rheumatism, fever, sore throat, headaches, and body aches. The plant's effectiveness at easing pain is not surprising—wintergreen contains an aromatic compound called menthyl salicylate, and its main metabolite is salicylic acid, a renowned painkiller. (It is also the primary metabolite of acetylsalicylic acid, or aspirin.)

The plant's beneficial properties can be attributed to its two main components—the aforementioned menthyl salicylate, along with gaultherilene. The distilled oil of wintergreen is a popular remedy for a number of ailments, even for people outside the natural health community. The following are some ways that you might benefit. (Bear in mind that wintergreen oil can be toxic and should never be taken internally.)

- To combat respiratory distress, mix a few drops of wintergreen oil with a small amount of coconut oil, and massage it on your throat, chest, and upper back.
- Place an open container of the oil on your desk to keep you awake and alert as you work.
- To relieve overworked muscles or aching joints, combine one part wintergreen oil with four parts carrier oil, and massage into affected areas. Or ease indigestion or bloating by rubbing the oil on your abdomen in a circular motion.
- After a sweaty run, give your hot feet a cooling blast by applying a mixture of wintergreen, coconut, and peppermint oils.

RESCUE REMEDY: *Add a few drops of wintergreen oil to a spray bottle filled with distilled water for a powerful antibacterial spritz to use on your shower shoes, yoga mat, or other workout equipment.*

Low-growing *Gaultheria procumbens* bears bright red berries. During the American Revolution, when tea leaves were hard to come by, colonists found that wintergreen made a tasty substitute, hence it is often called teaberry.

WINTER SAVORY

FIGHT INFECTION, INCREASE LIBIDO, AND PROMOTE HEART AND DIGESTIVE HEALTH

An attractive border or edging plant in sunny locations, this culinary herb also excels in the sickroom. Winter savory (*Satureja montana*), a member of the Lamiaceae family, is a perennial, semi-evergreen plant native to the Mediterranean region. The Roman legions enjoyed cooking with it and introduced it to northern Europe during their campaigns. The plant tops off at 16 inches in height and displays oval-lanceolate glossy green leaves and clouds of small white flowers.

It is often grown along with its cousin, summer savory, but in the kitchen, winter savory projects a slightly stronger flavor with a touch of bitterness in comparison. As a companion plant in the garden, it protects beans from harmful weevils and keeps aphids and mildew away from roses.

Health Benefits

Traditional herbalists believed winter savory could inhibit sexual desire, while summer savory was supposed to increase it. Botanist Nicholas Culpeper recommended it for colic in the 1600s, and a tea made from the herb was used to treat intestinal problems like cramping, nausea, diarrhea, and gas. Winter savory contains the antibacterial and

> **DID YOU KNOW?**
>
> • *In a 2015 Polish study, winter savory was one of the therapeutic essential oils used to inhibit the growth of* Candida albicans, *a yeast that can cause oral thrush and vaginitis, especially in individuals with HIV or cancer, or patients who have recently undergone surgery.*

antifungal volatile oils carvacrol—which gives a tangy taste, similar to marjoram, to the herb, and antiseptic thymol—even more thymol than is found in summer savory. Both the shoots and leaves contain disease-fighting antioxidants and fiber, which helps control bad cholesterol (LDL) and boost good cholesterol (HDL). The tea is known to be effective for treating stomach woes and sore throats, as well as improving the function of the liver and kidneys. The oil is also used in lotions for treating baldness and ointments for easing arthritis and joint pain.

The herb contains notable amounts of vitamin A, vitamin C, niacin, thiamine, and pyridoxine—which combats stress by keeping up levels of the soothing neurotransmitter GABA in the brain—and the minerals potassium, iron, calcium, magnesium, manganese, selenium, and zinc.

> **MAKE IT YOURSELF**
> ## Winter Savory and Beans
>
> This lemony bean side dish seasoned with winter savory is hearty *and* heart healthy.
>
> YOU WILL NEED:
> 2 sprigs of winter savory
> 1 16-ounce can white butter beans
> 1 tablespoon olive oil
> 1 stalk celery, chopped fine
> 1 red onion, chopped fine
> 3½ ounces of vegetable stock
> zest and juice of ½ lemon
>
> WHAT TO DO:
> • Combine oil, onions, and celery in a pan, and heat on low until vegetables are soft.
> • Add beans and winter savory, and stir.
> • Add stock, and simmer for 15 minutes or until liquid reduces.
> • Add salt and pepper to taste; top with lemon zest and a squeeze of lemon juice.

A sprig of winter savory can be rubbed on bee or wasp stings for instant relief from the pain.

YERBA MATE

BOOST ENERGY, MOOD, AND MEMORY, TREAT ALLERGIES, AND REGULATE BLOOD SUGAR

This member of the holly family, Aquifoliaceae, is the source of a popular South American hot beverage, which is said to have the "strength of coffee, the health benefits of tea, and the euphoria of chocolate." Yerba mate *(Ilex paraguariensis)* originated in the equatorial rain forests of South America and is often still found there. The plant develops from a shrub into a tree that can reach nearly 50 feet in height. It bears oval, bright green leaves and clusters of greenish white flowers with four petals, which mature into a red fruit, or drupe.

The common name comes from *yerba,* Spanish for "herb," and the Quechua word *mati,* which can mean "drink container" or "gourd." In precolonial Brazil the drink was enjoyed by the indigenous Guarani people. It then spread to the Tupi people of Paraguay, and by the 17th century was found in Argentina, Bolivia, Chile, and Peru. Today, yerba mate is grown commercially on plantations in Brazil, Argentina, Paraguay, and Uruguay.

Health Benefits

This herb has an ongoing history as a tonic used to sharpen the mind, increase mental stamina, provide a balanced energy boost, and elevate mood. Research reveals it is useful for treating allergies, and in studies with mice, it reduced the risk of diabetes and high blood sugar. It suppresses the appetite, so it may be effective for weight loss—its high levels of polyphenols, such as flavonoids and phenolic acids, work by inhibiting the enzymes that play a role in metabolizing fat. The herb also slows the emptying of the stomach, making dieters feel more satiated.

> **DID YOU KNOW?**
>
> • *The beverage brewed from this plant is called* mate *in Spanish and* chimarrão *in Portuguese. Friends often pass a gourd around, sipping the tea with a metal straw; sharing it has the cultural significance of a Japanese tea ceremony. Pope Francis, a native of Argentina, has even been photographed drinking yerba mate.*

Since 2011, studies have tried to determine the herb's effect on chronic diseases. The results point to the legitimacy of many claims, especially in regard to reduction of fat cells, inflammation, and LDL cholesterol levels. Yerba mate was also found to have the highest antioxidant levels of any *Ilex* species. Nutritionally, the plant provides vitamins A, C, and E, B-complex vitamins, and the minerals calcium, iron, potassium magnesium, manganese, phosphorus, and zinc. On the negative side, there is a possibility the hot drink may be associated with cancer of the mouth, larynx, and esophagus, but more research is needed.

RESCUE REMEDY: *To prepare yerba mate tea, fill a large mug (ideally, a calabash gourd or wooden mate cup) three-quarters full with dry leaves and twigs, and then top it off with hot, not boiling, water. Sip the brew and occasionally refresh the hot water.*

Dried yerba mate leaves and calabash cup. This traditional Argentine energy beverage is served in special mate cups, which are usually crafted from gourds or wood and feature a *bombilla,* or metal straw.

CHAPTER 6

BENEFICIAL SPICES

Introduction
THE SPICE SAGA
THESE AROMATIC SEASONINGS HAVE A LONG MEDICINAL HISTORY

Few foods have as storied a past as the dried plants and herbs we call spices. Evidence suggests that early humans were no strangers to their use—hunter/gatherers likely wrapped meats and vegetables in leaves to cook them, and then realized the taste of certain plants affected the flavor of what they ate. This led to experimenting with other plant matter, perhaps adding nuts, seeds, berries, and bark to their food. Medicinal use of spices soon followed—if an individual was suffering from an ailment, yet improved after eating a specific spice, it was then earmarked as a remedy.

In early civilizations, certain spices were so prized that they became items of trade or tribute—the Bible mentions the visiting Queen of Sheba offering King Solomon "many spices and precious stones." In China, around 2700 B.C., Shen Nung wrote *Pen Ts'ao Ching,* or the *Classic Herbal.* Egyptian papyrus records from 1555 B.C. listed fennel, garlic, juniper, cumin, coriander, and thyme as curative spices. Mesopotamian scrolls lauded aromatic spices such as saffron, poppy, garlic, cumin, anise, and coriander. Indian cooks created rich, complex flavors with spices like black pepper, cinnamon, turmeric, cardamom, and ginger. The ancient Greeks imported eastern spices like cassia, pepper, cinnamon, and ginger to augment their own Mediterranean herbs—oregano, basil, marjoram—for both kitchen and dispensary. Arab cultures excelled at cooking with spices, and it was Arab traders who first brought the rare spices of Asia to ancient Rome. Their caravans carved out the

silk routes to the East—the famous Silk Road—still used today. The Arabs also mastered the art of distilling essential oils from herbs and aromatic plants.

From Rare Treat to Modern Medicinal
In Europe during the early Middle Ages, only the very wealthy could afford spices. With the advent of the Crusades in the Near East, trade with that region opened up . . . and spice prices went down. Spices were used as preservatives, to mask the taste of spoiled food, and to flavor wine. Apothecaries employed exotic spices as medicine, with many of their recipes based on Arab formulas. Both Marco Polo and Christopher Columbus revealed a host of new spices—and potential medicines—with their explorations of China and the Americas, respectively. In Colonial America, healthcare was rooted in plant-based medicine—from Native American shamans to village midwives—while seagoing merchants bartered for prized preservatives like black pepper.

Spices are still prized in the kitchen, but they are hardly rare—modern transportation methods have made global trading a reality and even the most obscure examples are available at ethnic markets or online. And as the natural health revival expanded, spices again became popular for their medicinal benefits. Meanwhile, science vindicated those early healers by revealing that many spices *do* work as remedies and also the mechanics of *how* they work. So if you are seeking new ways to improve your health, read on, and discover the healing properties offered by these versatile spices.

(LEFT) Star anise, nutmeg, and cinnamon

(OPPOSITE PAGE) A young practitioner of Ayurvedic medicine preparing spices like turmeric, ginger, pepper, and cardamom in the traditional manner.

BLACK PEPPER

EASE RESPIRATORY AILMENTS AND SOOTHE JOINT PAIN

This familiar hot culinary seasoning—so popular it has at times been called the "master spice" or the "king of spices"—is also a mood elevator, preservative, and healing remedy. Black pepper (*Piper nigrum*) originated in the southwestern Indian state of Kerala, but demand for it soon grew so great that merchants sent expeditions eastward, seeking new sources. The plant, a member the Piperaceae family, is a woody vine that may reach 30 feet in length. It matures at about four years, when the vine produces clusters of small white flowers, which in turn form the small red berries known as peppercorns. Black, green, or white peppercorns come from the same plant—their color depends on when they are picked or how they are processed. Black peppercorns offer the most intense flavor.

Health Benefits

Traditional healers once used black pepper to treat worldwide scourges such as scarlet fever, typhus, dysentery, smallpox, cholera, and bubonic plague. Today, it is employed to stimulate circulation, ease respiratory symptoms, and boost the immune system. Black pepper contains piperine, which is similar in composition to morphine (derived from the opium poppy) and acts as a painkiller. It also contains antioxidants such as vitamin C, flavonoids, and carotenes that combat free radicals and protect the body from cancer and phytonutrients that aid weight loss by breaking down fat cells and boosting metabolism. As a treatment for anxiety, it creates a sensation of heat on the tongue that stimulates the brain to produce "feel-good" endorphins, which results in a sense of well-being.

This warm pungency comes from the alkaloid capsaicin, which increases sweating and urination—speeding up the removal of toxins from the body. Black pepper is an excellent gargle for sore throats and an effective expectorant for congested lungs, and it can break up the mucous of stuffed-up noses. Studies also indicate that it can reduce the tendency to form blood clots and lower levels of bad cholesterol. When applied topically, added to ointments or liniments, black pepper can bring inflammation to the surface and ease joint or muscle pain. It can also be used as an antiseptic for dressing wounds.

> **DID YOU KNOW?**
>
> • *Black pepper was once so valuable it was used as a form of money—even demanded by Attila the Hun to ransom the conquered city of Rome. In the Middle Ages, a pound of black pepper was equal in worth to a pound of gold.*

Peppercorns and vine. To retain its health benefits, grind pepper fresh, and add it at the end of the cooking process.

> **MAKE IT YOURSELF**
> ### Black Pepper Tonic
>
> Prepare this invigorating peppery tea to combat fatigue or sooth anxiety.
>
> YOU WILL NEED:
>   2 cups fresh water
>   1 teaspoon freshly ground black pepper
>   1 tablespoon honey
>   1 teaspoon lemon juice
>
> WHAT TO DO:
> • Boil water.
> • Add all ingredients except honey, and allow the mixture to steep for 5 minutes.
> • Add honey, and strain into two mugs.

CARDAMOM

AID DIGESTION AND WARD OFF INFECTION WITH THIS NUTRIENT-RICH SPICE

This aromatic tropical spice is the seed from several plants in the Zingiberaceae family that were native to India, Bhutan, Indonesia, and Nepal. There are two main types: true, or green, cardamom, and black cardamom. True or green cardamom *(Elettaria cardamomum)* has a sweet flavor and is distributed from India to Malaysia as well as Guatemala and Tanzania. This perennial plant, which can reach six feet in height, has long pointed leaves and pale lilac flowers. Black cardamom *(Amomum subulatum),* also called brown, greater, or Nepal cardamom, is grown in eastern Nepal, Sikkim, and the Darjeeling district in India and southern Bhutan. It has a smoky, dark flavor. Both plants produce small pods with black seeds.

This spice is naturally a large part of Indian cuisine, but it is also used in Sweden and Finland to flavor holiday breads. In the Middle East, ground cardamom is traditionally added to coffee and tea.

DID YOU KNOW?

• If pungent black pepper is the king of spices, then sweet, mellow cardamom is the queen. One of the most expensive spices, it places third behind saffron and vanilla. In India, it is often chewed at the end of a meal to ensure pleasant breath.

Health Benefits

Cardamom is mentioned in regard to trade in 12th-century Ceylon (Sri Lanka), and it was part of both Ayurvedic and Chinese traditional medicine, especially as a remedy for teeth and gum infections, throat ailments, lung congestion, inflamed eyelids, stomach problems, and gallstones. Today, we know that many of these early applications have been borne out by research—cardamom can treat dental infections, control cholesterol levels, protect the gastrointestinal tract, relieve urinary tract infections, and alleviate respiratory ailments. It contains vitamins A, C, and B6, riboflavin, niacin, thiamine, sodium, potassium, iron, calcium, copper, manganese, zinc, and phosphorus.

Both kinds of cardamom can offer the following health benefits.

• Recent experiments with cardamom at the King Saud University in Saudi Arabia indicate that the spice can help control muscle spasms and reduce inflammation—and they also found that it possesses cancer-fighting potential.

• Its antimicrobial properties enable it to inhibit the growth and spread of harmful microbes, including those that cause food poisoning.

• When inhaled during aromatherapy, this spice eases the symptoms of asthma and bronchitis by increasing blood circulation to the lungs.

• Cardamom has aphrodisiac properties and can be used to treat impotence.

• Cardamom is also administered as a general health tonic and taken to cure nausea.

• Use this spice rather than antibiotics to treat oral ailments—cardamom does not interfere with the "friendly" bacteria in the intestines.

RESCUE REMEDY: *To make a gargle to relieve a sore throat, add ½ teaspoon each of ground cardamom and cinnamon to 1 cup of water, and bring to a boil.*

Green and black cardamom pods. A third type, white cardamom, is actually a bleached version of the green.

To make the spice, fresh chili peppers are dried and ground. Cayenne has antibacterial properties, which is why many cultures found it useful as a preservative.

CAYENNE

RELIEVE ACHING MUSCLES, STIMULATE METABOLISM, AND IMPROVE CIRCULATION

This fiery spice of the American tropics also offers a long list of health benefits. Cayenne peppers, which are dried and ground into the spice, are the fruit of the chili plant (Capsicum annuum). The wild bird pepper of the American southwest and Central America was the original source of a diverse group of cultivars, ranging from the mild bell pepper to five-alarm scotch bonnets, with cayenne on the very hot end of the spectrum at 30,000 to 50,000 Scoville units—the measure of a pepper's heat. The chili plant is a small perennial shrub of the Solanaceae family, with off-white or purplish flowers that mature into fruit (berries) of red, green, or yellow.

Based on evidence found in caves, human beings in the Western Hemisphere were eating hot peppers around 7000 B.C. and started growing them between 5000 and 3400 B.C., making them among the oldest cultivated plants. The chili pepper was introduced to Europe by Peter Martyr, a historian who voyaged with Columbus. Not long after, cayenne made its way to China and India—and was quickly incorporated into their respective cuisines.

Health Benefits

The indigenous people of South and Central American used medicinal cayenne to treat

> **DID YOU KNOW?**
>
> • *This seasoning was once known as cow-horn pepper, red hot chili pepper, aleva, and bird pepper. English botanist Nicholas Culpeper called it Guinea pepper— an erroneous Old World name applied to a New World spice. Its common name comes from the city of Cayenne, the capital of French Guiana.*

heartburn, fever, sore throat, tremors, gout, paralysis, flatulence, hemorrhoids, and nausea. Cayenne contains high levels of capsaicin, a molecular compound with analgesic properties that works by depleting the amount of substance P, a pain-causing neurotransmitter in the nerve endings. In animal studies, capsaicin also reduced heart arrhythmias and stimulated blood flow. It has been shown to reduce the growth of prostate cancer cells and, according to a study at UCLA School of Medicine, may actually be able to destroy them.

Cayenne also contains a beneficial compound called CAY-1, which suppresses more than 16 fungal strains, yet does no harm to animal cells. Cayenne can aid digestion by increasing production of saliva, digestive enzymes, and gastric juices, all of which help the body metabolize food. It benefits the circulatory system by reducing atherosclerosis (hardening of the arteries) and may help prevent the formation of blood clots. When taken at breakfast, cayenne is known to decrease appetite, making it useful for weight loss. A recent study of half a million people concluded that those who regularly eat spicy foods have a 14 percent chance of living longer than those who don't. Although the spice is typically used in tiny amounts, it does contain vitamins A, B6, E, and C, riboflavin, potassium, and manganese.

CINNAMON
TREAT COLDS AND COUGHS, LOWER CHOLESTEROL, AND REDUCE INFLAMMATION

This distinctive spice, with its sweet, warm flavor, comes from the inner bark of several tree species in the genus *Cinnamomum*. The two most common varieties are Ceylon cinnamon *(C. verum)*, also known as true cinnamon, and cassia or Chinese cinnamon *(C. aromaticum)*, which comes from southern China and is less expensive than the Ceylon species. As a result it is often used in commercial baking. The cinnamon tree, native to the Caribbean, South America, and Southeast Asia, is an evergreen member of the Laurelaceae family that can reach 60 feet in height. Cultivated trees are traditionally coppiced—cut short and covered with soil—so that they will spread out, producing multiple limbs for harvesting the bark. When the bark is stripped and dried, it curls into tight rolls called cinnamon sticks. With its pleasing, earthy scent, cinnamon has been used for centuries in the processing of perfumes and for making scented oils for religious rituals.

Health Benefits
Early use of cinnamon dates back to at least 2000 B.C., when the Egyptians prized it as culinary seasoning, a universal cure-all, and as part of the embalming process. From the days of ancient Greece to the Middle Ages, doctors prescribed it for coughs, sore throats, to ease arthritis pain, to improve circulation, and as a general tonic.

Research on this spice's medicinal properties is ongoing, but there is evidence that it is effective for treating muscle spasms, vomiting, diarrhea, colds, infections, loss of appetite and erectile dysfunction. It is even richer in antioxidants than superfoods like garlic and oregano. These antioxidants help to reduce chronic inflammation. Cinnamon is also being studied for its ability to lower blood pressure and cholesterol and triglyceride levels, which can all contribute to heart disease.

> **DID YOU KNOW?**
> • *Next to black pepper, cinnamon is considered the second-most popular spice in the United States and Europe. The current craze for warm, sticky cinnamon buns no doubt helped it achieve that rank, but it has always been a kitchen favorite in both sweet and savory recipes.*

Cinnamon is available as a ground spice or as bark sticks.

CINNAMON UNDER THE MICROSCOPE
This spice's medicinal benefits have been the subject of many recent studies. According to *Diabetes Care*, a heaping teaspoon (6 grams) of cinnamon a day can improve glucose and lipid levels in those suffering type 2 diabetes. The National Institutes of Health reports that a chemical found in the cassia variety, cinnamaldehyde, could be useful against bacterial and fungal infections, and at Tel Aviv University, researchers discovered that an extract found in cinnamon bark called CEppt might hinder the development of Alzheimer's disease. In a study of Indian medicinal plants, cassia bark extracts showed effectiveness at combating HIV-1 and HIV-2, and according to the Rush University Medical Center, cinnamon may help stop the destructive processes associated with multiple sclerosis.

Up Close
OVERCOME YOUR CRAVINGS
THE TRUTH ABOUT THOSE SWEET TREATS AND SALTY SNACKS

A favorite sweetener of vegans, natural maple syrup has fewer calories per serving than cane sugar.

For millennia, few spices or seasonings were as sought after as sugar and salt, their rarity making them the province of nobles and kings. Sugar, that builder of empires, was formed into hard, conical sugar loafs that were locked away, the sweet scrapings carefully doled out. Salt was mined, traded—and guarded—like gold. It was so valuable that Roman legionnaires were often paid with it, their "salary" proving that they were "worth their salt." And it was not only used to intensify flavors—salt was also an effective preservative for meat in the days before refrigeration.

This level of desirability is understandable—sugar and salt are two of the five taste sensations that human beings crave, along with sour, bitter, and umami (meaty/savory). Is it any wonder that after all those centuries, when populations yearned for the sweet and the salty, that our modern food industry fills our processed foods with disproportionate amounts of sugar or salt, or both? Overindulging in either substance can be potentially damaging.

The excess consumption of sugar can lead to obesity, heart disease, and elevated cholesterol levels. In addition to being addictive, sugar causes tooth decay, creates insulin resistance, and can even result in cancer. Too much salt can lead to kidney stones, gastric ulcers, and osteoporosis. It causes water retention, affecting blood pressure, the heart and arteries, and kidney and brain function, putting us at risk for heart attack, stroke, dementia, and kidney disease. Fortunately, there are now palatable substitutes for sugar and salt—either natural or chemical alternatives, or combinations of herbs and spices that mimic the tastes we crave.

A rich mix of herbs and spices can help you kick the salt habit.

The Sugar Rush

Sugar is detrimental to the body in so many ways. Yet whether it is refined sugar, cane sugar, corn syrup, or the host of other sugars available, Americans, on average, consume nearly 66 pounds of added sugars yearly. (USDA guidelines advise that added sugars should account for no more than 10 percent of total daily calories.)

Saccharine, the first low-calorie sweetener, was developed in 1879, but it did not become popular until dieters in the 1960s discovered it. When it was linked with cancer in the 1970s (findings that have since been overturned), the next generation of substitutes appeared, including aspartame (Equal, Nutrasweet), sucralose (Splenda), and neotame (Newtame). But they, too, raised questions of safety. Another recent alternative is Truvia, which is made from an extract of the stevia plant, but is cloyingly sweet. Alcohol sweeteners like xylitol and sorbitol have only a slight effect on blood sugar levels, making them a healthy option for diabetics.

Some alternatives to refined sugar come directly from nature—like honey, which offers mild antioxidant benefits, and maple syrup, which has fewer calories than cane sugar. Blackstrap molasses

does derive from cane sugar, but it is rich in minerals. And finally, there is the fructose found in fruit; it is twice as sweet as refined sugar, so you ideally need less of it to satisfy your taste buds.

The Salt Fix

Sodium chloride is the chemical name for common table salt. Like sugar, it has no real nutrient value, but it does have some health applications. Sodium is necessary for the proper functioning of the body's nerves and muscles. Salt also possesses antibiotic qualities, making it beneficial for some skin ailments and as a gargle for sore throats. Yet the Mayo Clinics calls salt "the silent threat," and the fact remains that most of us take in too much—and 77 percent of it comes from processed foods.

Anyone who has been medically advised to reduce their salt intake needs to start reading package labels—the World Health Organization recommends that adults ingest no more than five grams of sodium per day—and considering alternatives to table salt. Potassium chloride offers a salty flavor, but it has a somewhat bitter taste and is often marketed with sodium chloride. Pungent or peppery spices like cumin, cardamom, black pepper, or cinnamon; or savory herbs like garlic, chives, cayenne pepper, or ginger; or a commercial mix like Mrs. Dash, can all please the palate with none of salt's side effects.

MAKE IT YOURSELF
Savory Salt Substitute

This simple mix makes a zesty, healthful seasoning that can help quell salt cravings.

YOU WILL NEED:
1 teaspoon chili powder
2 teaspoons black pepper
2 teaspoons dried oregano
1 tablespoon garlic powder
2 tablespoons dried mustard
3 tablespoons paprika

WHAT TO DO:
• Combine ingredients in a glass shaker bottle.
• Sprinkle over meat, poultry, veggies, or salads in place of added salt.

CLOVES

BUILD UP YOUR IMMUNE SYSTEM, EASE DIGESTION, AND RELIEVE PAIN

Often thought of as a warming fall and winter spice, cloves *(Syzygium aromaticum)* offer their many health benefits throughout the year. The clove itself is the unopened bud of the pink flower of the clove tree, an evergreen that grows from 25 to 50 feet in height and has smooth bark and scented yellow-green foliage. It is a member of the Myrtaceae, or myrtle family, and native to the Maluku Islands of Indonesia. The spice's common name comes the Latin word *clavus,* which means "nail," because the bud has a round head and long tapered stem, like a nail.

Health Benefits

For thousands of years, cloves have been treasured for their medicinal benefits: by the Chinese, who considered them aphrodisiacs, and by Ayurvedic doctors, who used them to treat tooth decay and bad breath. Traditional healers utilized not only the buds, but also the stems and leaves to create remedies. The distilled oil of cloves is still renowned for its

DID YOU KNOW?

• *From the Middle Ages onward, the value of cloves escalated, to the point that actual wars were fought to control their home islands, the Malukus, even into the modern era. Today, Zanzibar in East Africa is the largest exporter of cloves worldwide.*

effectiveness as a pain reliever, but it must be diluted in carrier oils.

Bioactive compounds that have been isolated in the spice's extracts include flavonoids, hexane, thymol, methylene, chloride, ethanol, eugenol, and benzene. These are likely responsible for the spice's potent antioxidant, anti-inflammatory, and antimicrobial properties. The antioxidant qualities are particularly useful for protecting the organs, especially the liver, from free radicals. Because cloves stimulate the secretion of digestive enzymes, they are excellent for treating stomach ailments, gas, gastric irritability, and nausea. The eugenol and its derivatives are valuable for maintaining bone density and strengthening the skeletal system, lowering risk of GI tract cancers, and easing joint pain. The buds also contain compounds that boost the immune system by increasing the number of disease-fighting white blood cells. Some studies indicate that certain clove extracts mimic insulin and can help control blood sugar levels. Cloves provide vitamins A, C, D, E, and K, as well as B6, B12, thiamine, riboflavin, niacin, and folate and the minerals calcium, iron, magnesium, phosphorus, potassium, sodium, and zinc.

Citrus-clove pomanders

RESCUE REMEDY: *For a refreshing and antibacterial mouthwash, pour a cup of boiling water over 1 tablespoon of whole cloves in a glass canning jar, and then strain after cooling. Gargle with 1 teaspoon morning and night. Will keep for a week.*

THE SCENT OF CLOVES

You can make an attractive, aromatic pomander that will add a citrus-clove essence to your home and also repel flying insects. Simply "nail" spikes of whole cloves into an orange or lemon, forming a pleasing pattern. Place the scented pomander in a small bowl or hang it from a decorative ribbon or cord.

CORIANDER

FIGHT INFECTIONS, EASE ALLERGIC REACTIONS, AND TREAT COLIC IN CHILDREN

The annual cilantro plant (*Coriandrum sativum*) produces both the herb cilantro (the fresh leaves) and the spice coriander (the dried seeds). The plant itself is sometimes called coriander or Chinese parsley. It is a member the Apiaceae family and originated in southern Europe, Northern Africa, and southwestern Asia. The plant grows to roughly 20 inches in height, with leaves that are broad near the base and more feathery near the top and small white or pale pink flowers. The spice's name derives from the ancient Greek *koriannon,* or "bedbug," because the plant's dank smell was similar to that insect pest. Small amounts of coriander were found in Tutankhamen's tomb, indicating that the early Egyptians cultivated this non-native plant. For centuries, it played a major role in South Asian cooking, and after it was introduced to the New World in 1670, it also became a fixture in Mexican cuisine.

DID YOU KNOW?

Both cilantro and coriander have fans and detractors—many people believe the herb and the spice are essential parts of Mexican, Indian, and Asian cooking, while others think they smell like dirty socks and taste like laundry soap—a result of the saponins contained in the plant.

Health Benefits

It is suspected that the plant's pungent smell first recommended it as a remedy— the logic being that anything that smelled that bad had to be strong medicine. The Greeks and Romans both praised it as a remedy, and early Britons combined it with cumin and vinegar to preserve meat. During the Renaissance, it was mixed into love potions. The seeds were once eaten in quantity for their slightly narcotic effect, which led to the name "dizzycorn."

Coriander seeds have fewer nutrients than cilantro leaves, but they still contain fiber, calcium, selenium, iron, magnesium, and manganese. And this spice offers a wealth of other beneficial qualities.

- The oil of coriander soothes allergic skin reactions, such as hives, that are the result of exposure to plants, foods, and insects. The spice has proven antihistamine properties to help control seasonal allergies.
- When they are crushed, coriander seeds give off a lemony flavor due to the organic compounds— terpenes, linalool, pinene, and limonene—they contain. The spice's antiseptic properties make it useful for treating mouth ulcers, and its antioxidants can help prevent eye diseases and treat conjunctivitis.
- The seeds contain dodecenal, a compound that is twice as powerful as some antibiotics for combating salmonella-based ailments.
- When inhaled, the essential oils can stimulate the secretion of digestive enzymes and juices and also relieve colic in small children.
- Coriander essential oil has been shown to inhibit both gram-positive and gram-negative bacteria, including *Staphylococcus aureus,* a leading cause of infections.

The seeds and leaves of *Coriandrum sativum.* The dried seeds are ground to make the spice coriander. The leaves are known as the herb cilantro.

CUMIN

HEAL SKIN OUTBREAKS, SUPPORT DIGESTION, AND TREAT CONGESTION

Based on worldwide usage, cumin (*Cuminum cyminum*) is the second-most popular spice after black pepper. Now, a growing awareness of international spices—and the accolades of the natural health movement—has leveraged this pungent favorite into American kitchens as well.

Cumin is a small, slender-stemmed member of the Apiaceae family. The plant reaches 20 inches in height and produces white and pink clusters of flowers. The seeds that are the source of the spice are oval and yellowish brown with paler ridges. Cumin is native to the Mediterranean; it was cultivated by the Egyptians, both for culinary and embalming use, as long as 5,000 years ago. India adopted the spice—*jeera* in Hindi—as the perfect addition to curries, kormas, masalas, and soups.

Health Benefits

According to the Bible, cumin's value was once so high it was used as currency. During the Middle Ages, the plant was accessible to most Europeans, unlike exotic and expensive Asian spices, and could be found in the medicinal gardens of many monasteries.

Today, this powerful antioxidant is used to treat a range of ailments. Skin outbreaks like acne, rashes, and boils respond to cumin's detoxifying components

> ### DID YOU KNOW?
>
> • *The flavor of this spice was so admired that ancient Greeks kept a container of cumin on their dinner tables, as most Americans do today with salt and pepper. If you dine out in Morocco, you will find a similar container of cumin awaiting your meal.*

such as cuminaldehyde, thymol, and phosphorus. The presence of vitamin E also keeps the complexion healthy and combats the onset of wrinkles, age spots, and sagging skin. A facial mask of one part turmeric to three parts cumin blended into honey or yogurt will leave skin exfoliated and glowing. Cumin's essential oils lend it antimicrobial and antifungal properties; it acts as a natural laxative, thus eliminating the chief cause of hemorrhoids. Those same essential oils also activate the salivary glands and the production of digestive enzymes, all necessary for proper functioning of the stomach. The presence of caffeine allows the spice to break up respiratory congestion, while other properties speed up secretion of anticarcinogenic and detoxifying enzymes. Nutritionally, the spice contains vitamins B1, B2, B3, C, and E, and it is high in dietary fiber and iron—making it useful for treating anemia, improving blood flow, and sharpening concentration.

Ground cumin and the dried seeds

> ### MAKE IT YOURSELF
> ## Cumin Grilling Rub
>
> Ground cumin works well as an ingredient of a dry rub for most meats—beef, pork, or chicken—imparting a smoky, peppery flavor, as well as many health benefits.
>
> YOU WILL NEED:
> 5 tablespoons dried cumin
> 2 tablespoons ground coriander
> 2 tablespoons dry mustard
> 1 tablespoon kosher salt
> 1 tablespoon paprika
> 1 teaspoon black pepper
>
> WHAT TO DO:
> • Combine all ingredients, and store mixture in an airtight container.
> • Apply a tablespoon of blend per serving. Dab onto both sides of meat, and grill. Do not let spices burn.

GINGER

CLEAR CONGESTION, RELIEVE GASTRIC DISTRESS, AND DECREASE INFLAMMATION

This aromatic, zesty mainstay of Asian and Indian cuisine is not limited to culinary applications—it is also a potent medicine once known as the "gift from the gods." Ginger (*Zingiber officinale*) is a tall, flowering perennial, and a member of the Zingiberaceae family along with its spicy cousins cardamom and turmeric. Originally native to the rain forests of Southern Asia, it was imported to Europe in the first century A.D. and greatly favored by the Romans. It is now produced commercially in India, Jamaica, Fiji, Indonesia, and Australia. Ginger is an attractive plant often used by landscapers; it grows to three or four feet in height and features narrow, reedlike green foliage and pink and white buds that mature into yellow flowers. The knobby root—or rhizome—is fleshy and juicy; it is harvested for culinary and medicinal purposes and can be eaten raw or cooked. The generic name derives from the Sanskrit *srngaveram*, or "horn body," based on the shape of the root.

Health Benefits

Natural healers in Asia have turned to ginger to calm upset stomachs and to relieve the congestion of colds and influenza for more than 3,000 years. Researchers now know that the phenolic compounds in the ginger plant relieve gastric irritation, stimulate the production of saliva and bile, and ease intestinal contractions. The root's inflammation-fighting gingerols and shaogals kill the rhinoviruses that cause respiratory ailments. They thin mucous to break up chest and nasal congestion and relieve coughing and

> **DID YOU KNOW?**
>
> • *Ginger acquired some unusual uses in its long history—early Chinese sailors used the vitamin C-rich spice to prevent the disease scurvy; in Victorian England, pub customers sprinkled ground ginger on their ale—an early version of ginger ale; and for millennia the spice has been used as an aphrodisiac.*

sore throats. Ginger is also diaphoretic—meaning it works to warm the body from within. As an anti-inflammatory agent, ginger root can ease inflammation in the colon, thus decreasing the risk of colon cancer, and in clinical trials it was effective for treating the inflammation associated with osteoarthritis.

The most recent scientific studies of the plant focus on its potential for treating serious conditions like heart disease, diabetes, and obesity and its ability to increase energy and foster healthy skin and hair. Its nutritional profile includes dietary fiber, vitamins C and B6, folate, niacin, riboflavin, calcium, iron, potassium, magnesium, phosphorus, and zinc.

RESCUE REMEDY: *An ancient recipe for sweating out the toxins of a cold involves putting 1 teaspoon of cayenne pepper and 1 teaspoon of ground ginger in your socks and then walking as much as possible. You can also place five slices of ginger in your bathwater and breathe deeply to open nasal passages. Healing ginger tea, best with honey and lemon, simply involves steeping a few ginger slices in boiling water, and then straining.*

Ginger is available as a ground spice and also as the fresh or dried root.

JUNIPER BERRY

FLUSH OUT BACTERIA, REDUCE BLOATING, AND FIGHT FATIGUE

Juniper berries are not berries at all. They are actually the female seed cones of various species of junipers, most commonly *Juniperus communis*. In addition to seasoning European game dishes and gin, juniper berries offer a number of medicinal properties, which in some cultures overshadow their role as a spice. The tree is an evergreen cypress (family Cupressaceae) that originated in Asia, Canada, northern Europe, Scandinavia, and Siberia. It ranges in size from a dense shrub to an erect tree of 33 to 52 feet in height. The early-maturing green berries are used to flavor gin, while older purple-black berries are used in cooking. The flavor profile of the berry offers the resinous taste of aromatic compounds called pinenes; as it matures, it incorporates more citrus or "green-fresh" notes. The berries are crushed slightly before processing and can be used fresh or dried.

DID YOU KNOW?

• *Juniper berries are perhaps best known for flavoring the alcoholic beverage gin. When vintners of the Middle Ages wanted to improve the unpleasant taste of malt wine they added herbs and spices, including juniper berries. This led to the drink being called* jenever, *from the Dutch for "juniper."*

Health Benefits

This spice dates back at least to ancient Egypt—imported berries, likely from Greece, were found in the tombs of pharaohs. The Greeks themselves used the berries to enhance the abilities of athletes competing in the Olympic games. The Romans valued the berries as an inexpensive substitute for rare black pepper.

Among their proven health benefits are the host of disease-fighting components they contain. Their antimicrobial and antifungal properties allow them to destroy pervasive gram-positive and gram-negative bacteria. As a diuretic, they can relieve bloating, lower blood pressure, and remove extra salts. They can also treat urinary tract infections by flushing out bacteria and toxins. Studies show that the spice contains high levels of antioxidants that can help combat cancer, arthritis, and heart disease, as well as help maintain a youthful appearance. The essential oil's stimulating effect can treat dizziness, depression, and fatigue and can be used as an antiseptic on wounds. The oil can also be used to detoxify the blood of harmful heavy metals and undesirable compounds produced by the body itself. Until there is further research on the spice's side effects, it should be avoided by pregnant woman.

Ripe and unripe seed cones, or berries, of *Juniperus communis*. Juniper berries can be taken medicinally in either tincture form or as a flavoring for meats and sauces.

A BITTER SOLUTION

Because of their acrid flavor, juniper berries are among a category of plants known as bitters, or astringents. According to studies at the University of Michigan, bitters can improve digestion and ease heartburn by causing the body to produce saliva and secrete extra digestive enzymes and stomach acids, increasing the fluids that are needed to break down food.

MUSTARD

CLEAR CONGESTION, CONTROL BLOOD PRESSURE, AND RELIEVE MUSCLE ACHES

Humble mustard plants with their bright yellow flowers are not only the sources of a spice and a condiment, but the greens are also a favored side dish in the American South—and have earned the title of "superfood" from nutritionists. These member of the Brassicaceae family are still found growing wild in Europe and western Asia with their cousins the wild turnip and radish. There are three main varieties: mild white mustards *(Sinapis alba, Brassica alba, and B. hirta)* are found in North Africa, the Middle East, and the Mediterranean. They are often used as green manures, crops that are left to wither in the field to restore nutrients to the soil. Spicy brown or oriental mustard *(B. juncea)* likely came from the Himalayan foothills. It is the source of Dijon mustard. Intense black mustard *(B. nigra)* originated in southern Europe and south Asia. At present, Nepal and Canada produce the most mustard seed—nearly 60 percent of the world crop.

The spice possibly dates back to Stone Age settlements or to around 5000 or 4000 B.C. in China. Noble Egyptians were buried with the seeds, and the Romans were the first to grind them and make a paste with unfermented grape juice, called must. It was they who introduced the spice to France and later to the British Isles.

Health Benefits

Early healers once mixed mustard with ginger and mint as a libido boost for bored wives and used the spice in restorative baths and as a treatment for chilblains. The spice was also used to treat colds and sinus problems—and it is still an effective decongestant and expectorant. The old-fashioned mustard plaster—powdered mustard spread inside a bandage—can provide relief to aching muscles.

> ### DID YOU KNOW?
>
> • *Energy researchers are looking into the possibility of using mustard oil to create biodiesel—a renewable fuel that is similar to diesel. In tests, it showed good flow properties in cold climates, plus the meal that is left after pressing has proven to be useful as a pesticide.*

Modern science reveals that these seeds possess beneficial phenolic components and are a rich source of vitamin A, folate, magnesium, phosphorus, calcium, and potassium. The seeds' selenium content allows them to reduce the severity of asthma and rheumatoid arthritis. Their magnesium helps lower high blood pressure and reduce the frequency of migraines. Certain phytonutrients, called isothiocyanates, have been shown to inhibit the growth of stomach, colon, and cervical cancers. The seeds can stimulate production of the enzymes that protect the skin against psoriasis, a chronic inflammatory autoimmune disorder, and help to heal the lesions.

RESCUE REMEDY: *To encourage hair growth and minimize its loss, massage 1 tablespoon of mustard seed oil into your scalp, cover hair with plastic wrap, and wait for 30 minutes. Then shampoo and style as usual. Repeat treatment once a week.*

Brown and yellow mustard seeds, along with powdered and prepared yellow mustards

NUTMEG

CONQUER INSOMNIA, FLUSH TOXINS, AND FRESHEN YOUR BREATH

Warm, pungent nutmeg is one of two spices harvested from the nutmeg tree (*Myristica fragrans*). Nutmeg is the dried seed or kernel of the tree's fruit, and mace comes from the waxy, lacy, red covering of the seed called the aril. The evergreen nutmeg tree, a member of the Myristicaceae family, is native to the Banda Islands, part of the Maluku Islands in Indonesia, where cloves were first discovered. Not surprisingly the Malukus are often referred to as the Spice Islands. The trees are now cultivated in Malaysia, Grenada, and southern India. Trees can reach 50 feet in height and produce large, glossy, oval leaves and apricotlike drupes, or fruit.

Health Benefits

Healers in the Middle East, India, and China have employed nutmeg as a medicinal spice since ancient times. The Greeks and Romans valued it as a brain tonic and for treating depression and anxiety. The Chinese prescribed it for abdominal pain and inflammation. Its use in Europe goes back to the Middle Ages, when Arab traders introduced it to the Venetians. It was soon found in the larders of cooks and the dispensaries of physicians.

Natural healers prize nutmeg for its versatility. With its naturally calming effect, it has the ability to treat sleeplessness, and courtesy of this sedative effect, it can stop muscle and joint pain. It also eases nausea and indigestion—nutmeg oil reduces the amount of gas in the intestines and can also boost the appetite. Another use is as a cleansing agent for ridding the body of toxins built up by stress, diet, pollution, and tobacco—especially where the liver and kidneys are concerned. Nutmeg oil, diluted in a carrier oil, is effective against toothache pain. Its antibacterial properties help it to kill germs in the mouth; this is why it's often found as an ingredient in toothpaste.

Recent studies have determined that nutmeg contains the compounds myristicin and macelignan, which are known to shield the brain from degenerative diseases like Alzheimer's.

Nutritionally, nutmeg contains potassium, which improves circulation, as well as calcium, iron, and manganese. Note that, if taken in excess, grated nutmeg or nutmeg oil can have a narcotic effect.

RESCUE REMEDY: *To combat insomnia, grate some nutmeg into in a cup of milk at bedtime. To cleanse oily skin, a mild facial scrub made from nutmeg powder and honey can help eliminate blackheads and heal acne scars.*

> ### DID YOU KNOW?
>
> • *The nutmeg tree is the only tropical plant that is the source of two spices obtained from two separate parts of the plant. (Cilantro and coriander come from the same plant, but it is not tropical in origin.) The tree also produces essential oils, oleoresin, and nutmeg butter.*

Myristica fragrans fruits split open show the brown kernels—the spice nutmeg—with the waxy red covering that is ground into mace.

SAFFRON

LOWER STRESS LEVELS, BOOST IMMUNITY, AND STRENGTHEN YOUR HEART

This delicate spice, once known as red gold, is harvested from the fall-blooming saffron crocus (*Crocus sativus*), a small flower in the Iridaceae, or iris family. The saffron crocus, native to southwestern Asia, is no longer found in the wild; it is now grown in Eurasia, North Africa, North America, and Oceania, with Iran the current leading exporter. The plant ranges from 8 to 12 inches in height and bears narrow green leaves with a white stripe and up to four pale purple flowers. The three stigmas are a bright red-orange. The saffron plant is sterile and does not produce viable seeds: for reproduction, humans must dig up the corms, separate the smaller "cormlets," and then replant them.

The spice's fragrance has been described as "haylike," which is due to the chemicals picrocrocin and safranal. The plant also contains crocin, a golden yellow pigment that is used to color foods and textiles.

Health Benefits

Saffron is an ancient curative—a 3,500-year-old fresco on the Greek island of Thera shows a goddess presiding over the preparation of medicine from the saffron flower. Modern researchers now know the spice contains more than 150 volatile compounds, including carotenoids, antioxidants, and other biochemicals.

Natural healers use saffron to treat a range of health problems. Saffron can ease mild depression and reduce stress; this is due to safranal, which has sedative properties, and other compounds that stimulate the release of mood-elevating hormones. Saffron is also an effective aphrodisiac for women with low libido. The sedative effect is useful for soothing upset stomachs and excessive gas. When applied topically, the spice's anti-inflammatory properties can reduce the pain of sports injuries or

> **DID YOU KNOW?**
>
> • *The spice is made from the stigmas and styles—or threads—of the saffron crocus, which need to be harvested by hand. This process is so labor-intensive —it can take 75,000 threads to make a single pound— that saffron is considered the most expensive spice in the world by weight.*

arthritis. New research has added appetite suppression to the list of saffron's benefits.

Saffron also contains many micronutrients—its vitamin C content helps to produce immunity-boosting white blood cells and the collagen necessary for healing wounds. A high concentration of iron allows the spice to increase circulation and oxygenation for a healthier metabolism and higher energy levels. Its potassium dilates blood vessels and arteries, thus decreasing blood pressure and reducing the risk of heart attack or stroke. Its manganese can help the body regulate blood sugar levels and may prevent the development of type 2 diabetes or help to control it in those with the disease. High levels of vitamin B6 help the nervous system to function properly. Other minerals found in the spice include copper, selenium, zinc, and magnesium. Saffron can be taken with food or as a supplement. It has a number of side effects if consumed in large amounts.

The red-orange stigmas of the saffron crocus, the world's most precious spice. They are also the source of dyes that yield hues from vibrant yellow-oranges to deep scarlets.

The dried fruit of star anise

STAR ANISE

LOOSEN CHEST CONGESTION, CONTROL CRAMPING, AND BOOST IMMUNITY

Often treated as a garnish, this attractive, anise-flavored spice adds its pungency to baked dishes and has the power to relieve upper respiratory and digestive ailments. Star anise *(Illicum verum)* comes from a medium-sized evergreen tree native to southern China and northeast Vietnam; it is now cultivated in Laos, Korea, Japan, Taiwan, and the Philippines. A member of the Schisandraceae family, the tree displays large, glossy green leaves and decorative white flowers. The dark brown pods, with eight carpels radiating out like a star, are actually the dried fruits—each carpel bears an elongated seed. Although their flavors are similar, intense aniseseed *(Pimpinella anisum)* is more often used in European cooking, while Asian chefs prefer subtle star anise. It is also found in Chinese five-spice powder, along with cloves, fennel seeds, Chinese cinnamon, and Sichuan pepper.

Health Benefits

For centuries, Chinese physicians used this spice as a stimulant and to treat coughs and colic. European healers prescribed star anise tea for easing the pain of rheumatism and menstrual cramps and for increasing libido. Current research reveals that the essential oil contains thymol, terpineol, and anethole—the latter responsible for its distinctive scent, as well as shikimic acid, which is a key ingredient in the virus-fighting medication Tamiflu. It also provides two major antioxidants, linalool and vitamin C, which protect cells from environmental toxins and free radicals. Extracts of the plant are being used to treat the invasive yeast *Candida albicans* and in lab tests have reduced tumor growth in animal subjects. Meanwhile, researchers in Taiwan reported that four antimicrobial compounds derived from star anise had proven effective against nearly 70 strains of drug-resistant bacteria.

Natural healers recommend this spice for treating colds, coughs, and flu, soothing sore throats, and reducing abdominal cramping and nausea. When taken as a tea after meals, star anise controls bloating, gas, indigestion, and constipation. The anethole found in the spice is known to have an estrogenic effect that may help regulate hormone function in women, and nursing mothers will find that it increases the production of breast milk.

> **DID YOU KNOW?**
>
> • *With its sweet, distinctive taste, star anise has many commercial applications, including use as a flavoring for meat, vegetables, curries, marinades, confections, baked goods, mouthwash, toothpaste, beverages, and liqueurs—especially Galliano and sambuca. It is also used to manufacture perfumes, in pickling, and for aromatherapy.*

THE LICORICE CONNECTION

Star anise shares its flavor not only with aniseseed, but also with the herb licorice root *(Glycyerrhiza glabra)*, which is made into candy. The root possesses anti-inflammatory properties and has been used to treat asthma, protect the stomach from ulcers, and fend off viruses. If eaten to excess, licorice root can cause water retention and elevate blood pressure, but most "licorice" candies today are flavored with anise.

TURMERIC

PURGE FREE RADICALS, REDUCE INFLAMMATION, AND FIGHT INFECTION

A recently rediscovered "old" spice—along with cumin—turmeric (*Curcuma longa*) brings the taste of the Middle East and India into Western kitchens—and offers amazing medicinal potential. The spice is processed from the yellow root of a perennial rhizomous plant in the Zingiberaceae family. Native to southern Asia, it can reach four feet in height and produces large, oval, upright leaves on sturdy stems and pale pink or white flowers on spikes.

Valued as a seasoning for thousands of years, turmeric is what gives curry its distinctive color and warm, earthy flavor. It is grown throughout the tropics, but India remains the largest exporter of the spice, which is also called Indian saffron. It is used to dye foods like mustard and margarine and fabric, most notably the saffron-hued robes of Buddhist monks.

Health Benefits

Healers have used this spice for more than 4,500 years, especially practitioners of Ayurvedic medicine. Turmeric contains curcumin, a powerful antioxidant that scavenges the free radicals that can damage cell membranes. The spice lowers the levels of two enzymes that cause inflammation, and it can also prevent platelets from clumping together to form blood clots. These properties make it especially useful for addressing the following concerns.

- Curcumin stimulates the gall bladder to produce more bile, which can aid digestion. In one study, patients who were in remission from ulcerative colitis and who took turmeric, had fewer relapses than those taking a placebo.
- In some animal studies, turmeric extracts were able to lower levels of bad cholesterol (LDL) and also kept it from building up on blood vessels.

DID YOU KNOW?

- *Turmeric holds deep religious significance for Hindus—who view it as sacred and auspicious. During wedding ceremonies, the groom ties a string dyed with turmeric around the neck of the bride. This* mangala sutra *indicates that she is now a married woman, capable of overseeing a household.*

- Based on test-tube studies, turmeric combats infections by destroying bacteria and viruses.
- Research is in its early stages, but there are indications that curcumin can inhibit or prevent certain cancers, including cancer of the prostate, skin, breast, and colon.
- A 2012 study indicated that curcumin may be able to prevent subsequent heart attacks in bypass surgery patients.

The piperine in black pepper greatly increases the absorption and effects of turmeric when they are taken together, while bromelain is known to increases its anti-inflammatory effects.

RESCUE REMEDY: *To include more turmeric to your diet, mix 3 tablespoons into a cup of honey in a lidded jar. Use it to give an antioxidant boost to tea or to relieve a sore throat or cough. Or entice your kids to take a spoonful of the healthful "golden" honey on their cereal. Store in your pantry; both ingredients are shelf stable.*

You can use the bright orange rhizomes of turmeric or the rich gold powdered form for cooking or medicinal uses.

Up Close
SWEET SURPRISES
THE HEALTH BENEFITS OF CHOCOLATE AND CAROB

Dark chocolate with almonds. In moderation, this sweet treat can be a healthy indulgence.

Chocolate has gotten a bad rap for years. So much so that people who continued to consume it called it their "guilty pleasure" or styled themselves as "chocoholics." Carob is a health food store alternative to the dark deliciousness of the cacao bean, but it never really challenged chocolate's status. Yet both substances are full of healthful compounds and nutrients and can help treat a number of ailments. They deserve to be reexamined beyond their current roles as an indulgence (chocolate) and a lackluster mimic (carob).

Chocolate
Chocolate is made from the fruit of the cacao plant *(Theobroma cacao),* which is native to the rain forests of Central America. This small evergreen tree, a member of the Malvaceae, has lobeless leaves and produces clustered flowers right along the trunk. These mature into a pod filled with a viscous pulp and 20 or 30 seeds—the cocoa beans. The name comes from the classical Nahuatl word *chocolātl.*

Fermented medicinal beverages made from cacao date back to 1900 B.C., to the Olmecs in Mesoamerica. The drink was sacred to the Mayan culture of the Yucatan, while the Aztecs believed it was a "gift of Quetzalcoatl." Consumption of the drink was reserved for warriors and the ruling class, and the pods were sometimes used as currency. The original drink was bitter, laced with spices and chili peppers, but when chocolate arrived at the courts of Europe in the 1500s, sugar was added. The hot beverage was soon enjoyed by all levels of society, and chocolate—as a drink, candy, or baking ingredient—has remained a favorite treat ever since.

Due to the fat content of the cocoa bean, chocolate was vilified for decades and often cited as a contributing factor in acne, obesity, diabetes, heart disease, and high blood pressure. A host of recent studies, however, have revealed that chocolate contains biologically active phenolic compounds—powerful antioxidants—and offers anti-inflammatory properties. These findings spurred research into its effects on aging, oxidative stress, blood pressure, and hardening of the arteries. Chocolates that contain plant sterols and cocoa flavonols can control blood sugar; some may be able to delay or halt cognitive decline, lower cholesterol levels, and relieve stress. The higher the cacao content—and the lower the sugar content—the more health benefits chocolate can offer. Opt for dark over milk chocolate varieties, which have added milk solids, sugar, and cream.

Carob

Also known as St. John's bread, locust bean, or locust-tree, the carob tree (Ceratonia siliqua) is the source of sweet, edible pods that possess medicinal applications. This flowering evergreen shrub or tree (a member of the Leguminosae, also known as the pea, legume, or bean family), is also a popular choice of garden landscapers. Native to the Mediterranean region—southern Europe, North Africa, and the Middle East—the tree can reach nearly 50 feet in height. It produces long, pinnate leaves and numerous small flowers that form racemes that slowly mature into narrow, deep brown pods that can reach a foot in length. These pods are ground into a powder that resembles cocoa in taste and has been used as a sweetener and a curative for at least 4,000 years.

In addition to being a low-fat, caffeine-free alternative to chocolate, carob has been employed medicinally since ancient Greece. It is high in fiber, pectin, protein, and antioxidants, contains no gluten and is naturally

sweet. It can replace chocolate in recipes on a one to one ratio. It also offers twice as much calcium as cocoa, as well as vitamin A and B-complex vitamins, copper, manganese, potassium, and magnesium, and it does not trigger migraines as chocolate can. The plant's tannins make it useful for treating stomach distress, and its natural thickeners can help relieve diarrhea. As a weight-loss aid, its fiber inhibits production of a hormone that signals hunger. In studies, the fiber in carob also reduced bad cholesterol (LDL) and triglyceride levels. Carob gum, processed from the seeds, is found in many skincare products and medications.

The rich brown pods of the carob tree are both flavorful and healthful.

Dried vanilla pods and flower

VANILLA

IMPROVE HEART HEALTH, LOWER STRESS, AND RESTORE YOUR COMPLEXION

The sweet, creamy flavor of vanilla entices the palate while furnishing a number of healthy benefits. The vanilla bean comes from a species of orchid (Vanilla planifolia) in the family Orchidaceae. Native to Mexico, the orchids are now cultivated commercially in Madagascar, Indonesia, Mexico, Tahiti, and India, each region offering its own distinct flavor profile. The orchid vines typically grow on trees or poles and bear oval green leaves and waxy, delicate, greenish yellow flowers that are pollinated only by Melipona bees. The flowers give way to narrow six-inch podlike fruits, wherein lie small black seeds.

Like chili peppers and tobacco, vanilla was another remarkable New World discovery sent back to the courts of Europe, where it was used to sweeten hot chocolate. It wasn't until the royal apothecary of Elizabeth I suggested using it as a solo flavoring that its popularity took off. Because it must be pollinated by hand outside of Mexico, it is the second-most expensive spice after saffron.

Health Benefits

The indigenous Totonaco people of pre-Columbian Mexico first used vanilla to induce relaxation and treat indigestion. More recently, the spice's main flavor compound, vanillin, has been shown to

DID YOU KNOW?

• *The word* vanilla *comes from the Spanish* vanilla, *meaning "little pod." When the Spaniards first encountered the spice in the 15th century, it was a favorite of the Aztecs, who had conquered the original cultivators—the Totonaco Indians of Mexico—and named the fruit* tlilxochitl, *or "black flower."*

measurably reduce cholesterol levels in the body, thereby preventing hardening or inflammation of the arteries and the formation of blood clots. The spice also offers high levels of antioxidants, lending it the ability to heal damaged cells and stimulate cell regrowth. It further protects the immune system, making it easier to bounce back from injury or disease. Vanillin can also help diminish the damaging effects of free radicals, including cancer and chronic ailments. In test tubes, it has been effective against the blood disease sickle cell anemia, and there is hope it will soon work on human subjects.

When inhaled during an aromatherapy session, the essential oil of vanilla can directly impact the brain and bring on a sense of tranquility, making the spice an ally against anxiety and stress. The scent can relieve nausea, and vanilla-infused tea is known to calm stomach inflammation and control cramping, diarrhea, and vomiting.

RESCUE REMEDY: *Enlist the plant's antibacterial properties and healing B vitamins to combat outbreaks of acne or to diminish scarring from previous outbreaks. Simply combine 5 drops of vanilla extract with 1 teaspoon honey and 1 teaspoon yogurt in a small bowl. Massage onto face with a cotton ball, and leave on for 10 to 15 minutes before rinsing with cool water.*

WILLOW BARK

RELIEVE PAIN, REDUCE INFLAMMATION, AND SOOTHE STOMACH UPSETS

This ancient pain remedy, perhaps the oldest known to humans, is derived from the bark of the willow tree. Willows, member of the Salicaceae family, can range in size from tall trees to spreading shrubs and are native to Europe, Central Asia, and parts of North America. They are hardy trees and constitute a successful species in most of their chosen habitats—so that the harvesting of their bark has not significantly affected their numbers. Not all willows accumulate sufficient amounts of an analgesic substance called salicin: the species most often used for therapeutic harvesting is the white willow *(Salix alba),* followed by the purple willow *(S. purpurea)* and the crack willow *(S. fragilis).* Willow trees typically produce thin, lanceolate leaves and tubular, bristling flowers called catkins—yellow on the males, green on the females.

Health Benefits

Recorded use of willow bark as a medicine goes back to ancient Egyptian texts, and Chinese healers recommended it more than 2,500 years ago. Around 400 B.C., Greek physician Hippocrates advised chewing the bark to lower a fever and decrease inflammation. Its use as an analgesic doubtless goes back even further, when the earliest civilizations discovered that the bark could alleviate the pain of injuries, childbirth, headache, and toothache.

The pain-killing benefits are due to salicin, a compound similar to aspirin (acetylsalicylic acid). Salicin (as well as aspirin) works by blocking an enzyme called COX-2, which manufactures a chemical, prostaglandin, that races to the brain after an injury and stimulates pain and swelling in the afflicted area. In the late 19th century, salicin was used to create aspirin. Research studies show that

> ### DID YOU KNOW?
>
> • *White willow has both an inner and outer bark, each containing different concentrations of compounds, with certain ones more effective for treating particular ailments. This is why it takes a trained herbalist or skilled alternative health practitioner to prepare willow bark supplements or powders.*

willow bark also contains high levels of flavonoids and polyphenols, which offer anti-inflammatory, antiseptic, fever-reducing, and immunity-supporting properties.

Today, willow bark is an effective alternative to over-the-counter pain medicines, strong enough to treat the severe discomfort of migraine headaches, lower-back spasms, and menstrual cramps. As an anti-inflammatory, it can soothe stomach upsets or irritable bowel syndrome; lower fever; reduce the swelling of tendinitis, bursitis, and, to some extent, rheumatoid arthritis and osteoarthritis. As a complexion brightener, the plant's antioxidants increase blood flow to facial skin and reduce the appearance of wrinkles and age spots; its astringents help to combat acne.

Willow bark can be chewed as bark chips, or taken as a decoction, tea, powder, liquid extract, or in pill form. Due to potential health complications, children under 18 should avoid willow bark.

White willow bark prepared for medicinal use

CHAPTER 7

ESSENTIAL OILS

Introduction
THERAPEUTIC AND SENSUAL
HEALING ESSENTIAL OILS HAVE AGAIN SURGED IN POPULARITY

Essential oils are complex chemical compounds that are extracted from natural sources—usually plants—and used as wellness aids and remedies. The term *essential oils* is actually a truncation of "quintessential oils," referring to Aristotle's fifth element, quintessence—life force or spirit, which he added to his four basic elements (fire, air, earth, and water). The processes of distillation and evaporation were once believed to release the spirit of a plant, which gave rise to the term *spirits* for distilled alcoholic beverages.

There are several methods for isolating essential oils: Distillation uses water, steam, or a combination of both. Examples of distilled plants include nutmeg and lavender. (Herbal distillates, also known as floral waters, are the aqueous products left behind after essential oils are removed. They are used in cosmetics and toiletries.) Expression, or cold pressing, used for citrus peel, is another isolation method, as are resin tapping and maceration/distillation. Here, plant matter is macerated in warm water until the enzyme-bound essential oils are released; examples are garlic, wintergreen, and bitter almond. Essential oils concentrate the healing properties of plants, so they can be far more powerful than their source botanicals and often need to be diluted in carrier oils such as olive, jojoba, or almond. Plants store their essential oils in several ways—near the surface, where the merest touch elicits a scent; within the internal structure, where the leaf or seed must be broken to release the odor or oil; or within the actual plant tissue. External secretions are contained in glandular trichomes, which can attract pollinators or deter pests. This surface scent occurs in the herbs basil, lavender, marjoram, oregano, peppermint, and rosemary. Internal oils are found in intercellular spaces—round secretory cavities that occur in citrus plants, eucalyptus, cloves, and resinous trees—and oval secretory ducts that are found in dill, angelica, caraway, fennel, cedar, pine, and juniper. Oil cells contained within plant tissue occur in bay laurel, black pepper, cardamom, nutmeg, and patchouli.

Ancient Methods

A crude version of steam distillation was practiced for more than 5,000 years, primarily to create the floral or aromatic waters used as tonics and in cooking and perfumes. The early civilizations of Asia and the Mediterranean made a substance similar to essential oil by warming plant matter in fat to cause separation. Persian philosopher-scientist Avicenna refined the art of distillation around A.D. 900 and produced true essential oils. Throughout the Middle Ages, these oils were valued for their antibacterial, antiviral, antifungal, anti-inflammatory, sedative, and analgesic properties, as well as for their scents and flavors.

Contemporary natural healers use essential oils to maintain health, treat diseases, provide emotional balance, reduce stress, relieve pain, cleanse the home, enhance appearance, and eliminate insect pests. Continue reading to discover in more detail the many uses and benefits of essential oils, as well as how to prepare your own blends at home, and the secrets of aromatherapy.

(LEFT) Many herbs, such as marjoram, bear scent structures close to the surface. Essential oils are typically delivered through inhalation, ingestion, or topical application.

(OPPOSITE PAGE) There are many ways to disperse the scent of essential oil, including reed diffusers and aroma burners.

BOTANICAL SOURCES

THE WIDE SPECTRUM OF ESSENTIAL OILS CAN PROVIDE TARGETED RELIEF

Whether you want to raise your spirits or lower a fever—or whatever your healthcare requirement—there is surely an herbal remedy that can accomplish it. Likewise, there is probably an equivalent essential oil that can supply the same benefit. One advantage of essential oils over herbs is that they are concentrated for quicker, more effective results. They are also easy to obtain—even the more exotic examples can be found online.

Healthy Solutions

There are so many plant essences available that it should be relatively simple to find the right botanical oil to treat your specific healthcare, skincare, or home-cleaning needs.

IMPROVE YOUR HEALTH This may be the top reason most people turn to essential oils: to treat illness, relieve pain, or control weight. Consequently, there are numerous essential oils intended to target

> **DID YOU KNOW?**
>
> *• Essential oils are extreme concentrations of plant extracts—one drop of peppermint oil is equal to 28 cups of peppermint tea. It takes 5,000 pounds of rose petals to distill a pound of pure rose oil. This explains the cost of some oils—price is based on how much raw material is needed.*

particular health problems—and whether they are supplying antioxidant, anti-inflammatory, or analgesic properties—the following oils can help.

- Anise aids digestion, relieves cramps, and eases joint pain.
- Oregano improves digestion, fights germs, and eliminates fungus.
- Lime acts as a restorative and tonic.
- Lemon helps you to shed pounds and boosts energy levels.
- Lemongrass treats fevers and infections.
- Bay laurel treats colds, flu, and sprains.
- Peppermint soothes aching muscles.
- Eucalyptus clears congestion and kills bacteria.
- Tea tree is antibacterial, antiseptic, and antiviral.
- Grapefruit activates enzymes that break down brown body fat.
- Cumin aids digestion and kills bacteria, and it is used in veterinary medicines.
- Myrrh has antimicrobial, astringent, expectorant, and antifungal properties.

REBALANCE YOUR EMOTIONS Smell is the most powerful of our senses, and it can strongly evoke memories and feelings. Everyone has a particular scent that they associate with childhood or a loved one: a whiff can conjure up an emotional reaction. You can use that innate response to control your mood in the present. Inhaling the following essential oils through diffusion, baths, or massage can restore peace and balance to a stress-filled life, calm nervous anxiety, raise depressed spirits, and trigger memories that can reconnect you to your "life stream."

- Lavender and chamomile are calming and can induce sleep.
- Bay laurel can help you overcome insomnia.
- Eucalyptus promotes relaxation.
- Peppermint cools and calms the body.

The fragrant yellow flowers of the cananga tree *(Cananga odorata)* are the source of its calming essential oil.

- Rose, ylang-ylang, frankincense, and bergamot orange relieve anxiety.
- Orange, bergamot orange, kaffir lime, and jasmine combat depression.

INCREASE SPIRITUAL AWARENESS

For thousands of years, aromatic oils and incense have been a part of religious rituals and ceremonies, often signifying transcendence from the earthly to the divine, as their scents were carried up through the ether. Many advocates of meditation, yoga, tai chi, and other spiritual practices find that essential oils—diffused, inhaled, or applied topically—can enhance their experience and increase their ability to seek an inward direction. Studies show that certain essential oils, like those listed below, activate the brain's limbic system, which is associated with memory, emotion, and state of mind.

- Angelica can induce spiritual awareness and create a sensation of peace.
- Vetiver can help ground a nervous person.
- Frankincense is able to deeply touch the soul.
- Rose offers comfort, dissolves sorrow, and creates a path to forgiveness.
- Patchouli symbolizes new beginnings, fosters inspiration, and eases nervous exhaustion.

ENHANCE YOUR SKINCARE ROUTINE

Even those without sensitive skin should take care to shun drying facial soaps, oil-stripping shampoos, and chemical-laden skincare products. These essential oils—once the secret weapon of legendary beauties throughout history—can clear blemishes, help erase lines and wrinkles, soften rough patches on elbows, knees, and feet, and promote healthy, shining hair.

- Tea tree treats psoriasis and other skin conditions.
- Lavender, mixed with a carrier, can soothe sunburn and heal minor wounds.
- Myrrh improves the appearance of dry skin.
- Frankincense is an astringent that opens pores and tightens skin.
- Lemon is antibacterial and antiviral.
- Coconut conditions skin, hair, and nails.

Kaffir lime *(Citrus hystrix)* yields two kinds of essential oil. The leaf oil has a strong, green aroma. The rind oil, often called Thai bergamot, produces a tarter citrusy scent.

CLEANSE THE HOME It hardly makes sense to practice natural healing if you are still using harsh chemicals or toxic cleaning products to disinfect your home, launder your clothing, or keep insect pests at bay. Try the alternatives listed here.

- Tea tree, lavender, peppermint, and eucalyptus are all antibacterial.
- Lemon has a clean scent and acts as a disinfectant.
- Rosemary and cinnamon are both effective antibacterials and antiseptics.
- Thyme fights household germs.
- Wild orange cuts grease on dishes.
- Citronella effectively repels flying insects.
- Pennyroyal repels fleas on dogs and cats.

Rose oil is extracted from the flower's fragrant petals. The damask rose *(Rosa damascena)* and the cabbage rose *(R. centifolia)* are two of the most common sources.

Up Close

MIX YOUR OWN ESSENTIAL OILS

CREATE BENEFICIAL CURATIVES AND AROMATIC RESTORATIVES AT HOME

A blend of essential oils from several sources can be more effective than using a single scent.

Once you have familiarized yourself with the various health benefits and distinctive scents of different essential oils, it might be time to consider making your own customized blends. You can find the perfect formula to treat colds, soothe coughs, heal wounds, rejuvenate your spirits, or improve the look of your complexion and hair. Blended oils can be used in diffusers, on scent pillows or sachets, in the bath, or for massage, and they also make great gifts. In general, they should not be ingested.

Before you start, you will need several dark glass bottles with airtight lids, an eyedropper, and a carrier medium to dilute the oils. Carriers usually consist of oils like olive, jojoba, grapeseed, sweet almond, or coconut, but they can include vodka, unscented castile soap, beeswax, and uncooked rice, beans, or buckwheat hulls to fill scent pillows. For the recipes below, unless stated, dilute in two ounces of carrier oil. Finally, you will need a selection of essential oils.

Medicinal Blends

Most illnesses rarely present with a single symptom—for example, colds come with coughs, sore throats, and chest congestion, and stomachaches are often accompanied by diarrhea or nausea. Now you can create a blend of essential oils that can target all or most of the symptoms you experience. You can also combine several oils that are effective against one pervasive symptom, a cough, say, that lingers after the flu has passed.

RESPIRATORY AIDS To control congestion, combine 30 drops eucalyptus oil, 26 drops ravensara oil, and 4 drops peppermint oil (no carrier required). Apply 3 drops to a cotton ball, and inhale. To control stubborn coughs, heat half a pot of water until steaming (do not bring it to a boil), remove from heat, and add 3 drops eucalyptus oil and 3 drops lavender oil. Cover your head and the pot with a towel, and inhale for 10 minutes.

STOMACH RELIEF To ease indigestion, gas, and cramping, blend two or three of the following—2 drops peppermint, 3 drops each of ginger, caraway, anise, coriander, tarragon, thyme, or citrus oils in carrier oil, and massage into abdomen or place in diffuser.

PENETRATING MUSCLE MASSAGE To make a massage blend, mix 20 drops Roman chamomile and 4 drops black pepper; or 5 drops ginger, 8 drops peppermint, and 10 drops eucalyptus in carrier oil.

HAIR CONDITIONER To make this hair moisturizer, mix 1 tablespoon jojoba carrier, 3 drops rosemary, and 1 drop lavender. Massage conditioner into damp hair; leave on for 20 minutes before shampooing.

SKIN Rx Blend 8 ounces unscented hand or body lotion, 10 drops patchouli, 15 drops sandalwood, and 5 drops carrot seed. Dispense from a plastic bottle.

Soothing Aromatic Blends

Perfumers refer to "notes" to describe the full spectrum of a scent. The top note is the prevailing scent that is first encountered; it is sharp but does not last long. The middle note, or body, is considered the heart of the aroma; it can last up to two hours. The base note, or fixative, can be detected a few hours—or even a day—after the initial scents. Test a combination of scents by dabbing different oils on paper strips and sampling two or three at a time until you achieve the balance you desire. Remember that a powerful scent, such as chamomile, may overpower a subtler scent like lavender, so calculate the ratio of your ingredients accordingly. All the blends here should be mixed with two ounces of carrier oil and used with a diffuser or placed in a scent pillow.

Neroli oil, also called orange blossom oil, has a citrusy floral scent that helps elevate mood. It takes about 1,000 pounds of the hand-picked blossoms of the bitter orange tree *(Citrus aurantium)* to steam-distill the essential oil.

CALMING FLORAL BLEND Mix 2 drops lavender, 2 drops rose, 4 drops mandarin, and 2 drops vetiver.

ANXIETY RELIEF Use any combination of the following—4 drops bergamot, 6 drops clary sage, 2 drops frankincense, 5 drops sandalwood, 5 drops lavender, and 4 drops lemon.

ANTI-STRESS BLEND Mix 12 drops clary sage, 4 drops lemon, and 6 drops lavender.

PIQUANT BOUQUET Use 8 drops bergamot orange, 4 drops anise, 4 drops geranium, 6 drops jasmine, and 5 drops sandalwood.

REFRESHING HERBAL BLEND Mix 5 drops basil, 4 drops peppermint, 4 drops rosemary, and 3 drops pine, 3 drops rue, and 3 drops vetiver.

BRIGHT CITRUS BLEND Mix 5 drops grapefruit, 6 drops orange, 5 drops ginger, and 4 drops cypress.

A NOTE ON OTHER BLENDS
Essential oils are usually complex mixtures of hundreds of individual aroma compounds. They are distinct from aroma oils, which are essential oils and aroma compounds in an oily solvent; infusions, a carrier oils permeated with one or more herbs; absolutes, oily mixtures extracted from plants using chemical solvents; and concretes, which are semi-solid masses collected from fresh plants through solvent extraction.

AROMATHERAPY
BENEFIT BODY AND SPIRIT WITH DIFFUSED ESSENTIAL OILS

The practice of aromatherapy promotes healing and relaxation through the inhalation or application of volatile oils extracted from plants. The benefits of these oils can be delivered by diffusion (releasing a fine mist into the air), by inhaling the vapors directly, or during massage. Aromatherapy's use as a natural health aid has recently gained enormous popularity, and a major industry has sprung up around it.

The concept of scenting the air for improved health began 6,000 years ago in China, when healers burned certain herbs to induce feelings of well-being. The Egyptians employed incense and bath and massage oils as health aids but were best known for using oils in the embalming process. Greek physician Hippocrates was said to rid Athens of the plague by employing aromatic fumigation. The Arabs mastered the art of perfumery for personal enhancement and healing—and Crusaders brought these oils back to Europe with them. When the Catholic Church banned all natural remedies, healing oils fell out of favor for centuries.

The term *aromatherapy* comes from French chemist Rene Maurice Gattefossé. In 1910, he was burned during an explosion in his family's perfume lab and prevented gas gangrene by quickly rinsing the burns with lavender essence. He soon began to experiment with healing oils and then worked with wounded soldiers during World War I.

Diffusers are the most popular way to benefit from aromatherapy. The simplest is the reed diffuser: you just insert channeled reeds into the oil, which is then sucked to the top of the reeds, dispersing the scent. Aroma burners use a candle to warm the upper bowl of a vessel filled with essential oils and a bit of water. Electric heat diffusers warm up absorbent pads containing essential oils and allow them to evaporate into the air. Ultrasonic diffusers use water with the essential oils to create a cool mist. A cool-air nebulizing diffuser uses air pressure to break down the oils into fine particles before releasing them into the air. They offer maximum therapeutic benefits, but need frequent cleaning.

> ### DID YOU KNOW?
>
> • *Although no "love potion" can guarantee the affection of another person, there are quite a few essential oils used in aromatherapy that are believed to stimulate attraction or improve sexual performance. These include jasmine, neroli, rose, ylang-ylang, vanilla, clary sage, clove, patchouli, and vetiver.*

Healthy Solutions

The essential oils used in aromatherapy can benefit several systems in the human body. Perhaps their greatest and most direct pharmacological effect is on the blood supply to the brain. They also provide indirect pathways to the brain through the olfactory

An ultrasonic diffuser. With this method, you add a few drops of oil to water, and switch the unit on. Almost instantly, it will release a cool jet of scented mist.

Sea buckthorn berries *(Hippophae rhamnoides)*. The healing qualities of the essential oil derived from the seeds and berries of this coastal and riverbank plant inspired the nickname "liquid gold" in Tibet, China, and Mongolia.

nerves. Here, they affect the glands that control emotional, neurological, and immunological functions. Essential oils are also absorbed in minute quantities through the skin and can be effective for certain skin conditions. When inhaled, they have a direct effect on the sinuses, throat, and lungs, making them an ally against respiratory ailments. Essential oils can also benefit the circulatory system by increasing the circulation-stimulating effects of massage.

One key aspect of aromatherapy is called synergy—the way a combination of essential oils possesses more healing power than any single oil has on its own. Below are some potent combinations.

STRESSBUSTER Mix together lemon, lavender, bergamot, peppermint, vetiver, and ylang-ylang.

MOOD ELEVATOR Blend chamomile, lavender, jasmine, neroli, and peppermint oils.

MEMORY BOOSTER Mix sage, ginger, rosemary, bergamot orange, and lemon balm oils.

ENERGY SURGE Use black pepper, clove, tea tree, cinnamon, cardamom, angelica, rosemary, and sage.

HEADACHE RELIEF Blend together eucalyptus, peppermint, sandalwood, and rosemary.

HEALING HELPER Mix lavender, calendula, rose hip, everlasting, and sea buckthorn.

SLEEPYHEAD Mix chamomile, lavender, jasmine, rose, bee balm, marjoram, and ylang-ylang.

IMMUNITY AID Blend together oregano, frankincense, lemon, cinnamon, and eucalyptus.

PAINPROOF Mix lavender, chamomile, clary sage, juniper, rosemary, and peppermint.

STOMACH SOOTHER Use lemon, orange, ginger, dill, fennel, chamomile, clary sage, and peppermint.

OPEN THE SEVEN CHAKRAS

Advocates of spiritual practices, such as meditation and yoga, believe that aromatherapy can open up blocked chakras, the centers in the body through which energy flows. Each of these seven "wheels" of energy also has its corresponding essential oils.

- **Root chakra:** centers on basic needs; it is stimulated by angelica, cedarwood, myrrh, frankincense, patchouli, and spikenard.
- **Sacral chakra:** influences creativity; it is activated by rose, orange, clary sage, patchouli, cardamom, and sandalwood.
- **Solar plexus chakra:** influences identity; it draws power from cloves, black pepper, cinnamon, geranium, ginger, grapefruit, peppermint, and rosemary.
- **Heart chakra:** focuses on giving and receiving love; it is enhanced by jasmine, lavender, orange, rose, and ylang-ylang.
- **Throat chakra:** centers on communication; it is stimulated by basil, bergamot, cypress, peppermint, and spearmint.
- **Third-eye chakra:** influences wisdom, intelligence, and dreams; it is associated with angelica, clary sage, frankincense, juniper, marjoram, rosemary, and vetiver.
- **Crown chakra:** promotes a deeper understanding of ourselves beyond the physical or material; it is influenced by cedarwood, jasmine, lavender, myrrh, neroli, rose, and spikenard.

There are a multitude of essential oils and blends that can be used for an aromatic or healing massage.

SKIN AND BODY BENEFITS

DON'T OVERLOOK TOPICAL APPLICATIONS LIKE MASSAGE AND SKIN CARE

In addition to inhaling essential oils for their healing qualities, you can apply them topically. You can massage them into your skin; warm them in your palms to increase intensity; or use them for facial care or skincare. By massaging or stroking these oils onto warm skin, their healing aromatics are released while they are being absorbed.

BODY MASSAGE

Essential oil massage provides a variety of benefits: it can treat stress, anxiety, headaches, insomnia, acute or chronic pain, arthritis, rheumatism, backaches, and joint and muscle injuries, as well as reduce inflammation, elevate immunity, and regulate male and female hormones. Massage is a part of natural childbirth and can be used as a relaxation aid while pregnant and during the delivery. Oil massage also increases circulation, which helps to reduce pain. It is recommended, along with hot baths containing essential oils, to ease discomfort after sports or

DID YOU KNOW?

• *Despite the many advances in technology, science has not been able to replicate the chemical constituents of essential oils. The components that nature combines in one plant can number in the hundreds or even the thousands, making them impossible to synthesize in the laboratory.*

workouts. And don't forget to massage your feet, with all their reflexology acupressure points that affect your internal organs.

Healthy Solutions

To prepare an essential oil rub, the suggested ratio for dilution is 15 drops of essential oil per ounce of carrier oil for a 2.5 percent solution. For children under 12, a .5 to 1 percent solution using 3 to 6 drops is safe. Bear in mind that it is not advisable to use these oils near the eyes, mouth, mucous membranes, or genital areas.

RESCUE REMEDY: *You can apply hot compresses augmented with essential oils to wounds, bruises, or injured joints and also on muscles or to the abdomen for periodic cramps. Place 10 drops of a single oil or a blend in 4 ounces of hot water. Dampen a cloth, and wrap it around the injury. Healing oils include lavender, sage, rosemary, and myrrh.*

RESCUE REMEDY: *Direct palm inhalation involves placing a few drops of a nonirritating essential oil in one palm, warming it between the hands, and then inhaling it deeply. This supplies quick exposure to the health-promoting properties of the oil, including emotional balance and respiratory relief.*

FACIAL CARE

When used as moisturizers or facial scrubs, essential oils can slow the effects of aging, speed the healing of skin outbreaks, reduce the appearance of acne scars, boost the skin's immunity, control sebum production, detoxify the complexion, increase circulation, improve and brighten skin tone, provide hydration when used with water, and soften and smooth the skin's surface.

Healthy Solutions

The proportions for blending facial treatments are typically 3 to 6 drops of oil per ounce for sensitive skin and 6 to 15 drops per ounce for normal skin.

RESCUE REMEDY: *Prepare a moisturizer by combining 1 ounce of a light carrier oil, like jojoba or argan, with 2 drops of two or three of the following oils: lavender, peppermint, chamomile, rose, rose geranium, and lemongrass. To treat acne, add a few drops of evening primrose, rosemary, or borage oil. To combat aging, add sea buckthorn or rose hip seed.*

If you prefer, you can buy essential oil blends crafted for specific needs, such as a calming mix of jasmine and vanilla.

MAKE IT YOURSELF
Blended Body Rubs

You can blend these massage oils for a variety of beneficial results. The following ingredients should be diluted in a tablespoon of carrier oil, and placed in a small, dark-colored glass jar with a lid. Mix oils thoroughly, pour into the jar, and store in the refrigerator. Shake well before use.

This massage oil is perfect after a long run or a strenuous workout at the gym.

- 4 drops cinnamon
- 2 drops ginger
- 3 drops chamomile

Overcome the stress of a busy day as muscles relax and tension fades.

- 6 drops orange
- 4 drops neroli
- 3 drops vanilla

Regain your energy with a citrus or minty pick-me-up. After blending, place in refrigerator for use as a cooling, refreshing skin tonic.

- 6 drops grapefruit
- 3 drops lime
- 4 drops thyme

Inspire a romantic mood with these exotic, aromatic blends that can be warmed slightly before gently smoothing over skin.

- 5 drops sandalwood
- 15 drops ylang-ylang
- 3 drops black pepper
- 2 drops ginger

RESCUE REMEDY: *Concoct a refreshing spritzer by combining a total of 15 drops of essential oils with 2 ounces of distilled water in a small spray bottle. Shake the mixture before using. You can blend aromatics like peppermint, lavender, rosemary, lemon, grapefruit, geranium, and ylang-ylang.*

RESCUE REMEDY: *Make an exfoliating scrub for face or body by combining 1½ cups of granulated sugar with of ¼ cup of carrier oil (olive, coconut, grape, or sweet almond) and 6 to 8 drops of lavender or lemon oil. Combine the oils, and then mix into the sugar. Transfer to a mason jar, and use to brighten your complexion and remove rough patches from feet and elbows.*

CHAPTER 8

NATURE'S POWER PANTRY

Introduction
POWER FOODS
THESE SMART DIETARY CHOICES OFFER OUTSTANDING HEALTH ADVANTAGES

Whether they are called power foods, superfoods, or real foods, certain fruits, vegetables, grains, and low-fat meats offer impressive amounts of vitamins and minerals, as well as systemic boosters and disease fighters like antioxidants and phytonutrients. The more researchers explore the health-building properties found in the produce and proteins we consume, the more benefits they uncover.

Keep It Sensible

As most of us realize, to achieve a healthy diet there are certain foods we need to avoid or limit in order to make the most of our daily caloric intake. The culprits include some supposedly "healthy" choices.

- Sugar is not only fattening and a leading cause of obesity, cardiovascular problems, and diabetes, it is also addictive.
- Transfats are extremely unhealthy chemically modified fats found in many processed foods.
- Artificial sweeteners may be calorie free, but in studies their use has been shown to result in subjects eating more and gaining weight.
- "Low-fat" foods are advertised as healthy, but they are highly processed and make up for lack of fat by adding sugar or artificial sweeteners.
- Highly processed foods are typically low in nutrients and high in additives and sodium.

There is often a conflict between the hot "new" diet plan and the "old" diet plan—carbs are bad one day and okay the next. Red meat is the enemy or white meat is the new broccoli. Rather than getting caught up in fad diets or the latest food craze, it makes more sense to establish sensible eating habits that work for your body and your metabolism.

- Meat is not necessarily harmful in small portions, but it should be in the form of poultry or lean cuts of grass-fed beef, lamb, or pork.
- Seafood and fatty fish, such as tuna or salmon, are healthy, filling, and rich in omega-3 fatty acids and other nutrients.
- Vegetables contain fiber and essential nutrients and should make up the bulk of our diets. Root vegetables like potatoes also contain fiber but are high in carbs.
- Fruits are delicious raw and rich in fiber and vitamin C. They do contain sugars, so reduce portions while dieting.
- Seeds and nuts, such as walnuts, almonds, sunflower seeds, and pumpkin seeds, contain many nutrients, but are also high in calories.
- Saturated fats, once vilified, raise levels of good cholesterol and are more stable for cooking.
- Full-fat dairy products contain healthy fats and calcium; milk from grass-fed cows also contains valuable vitamin K2.

Whether you are making dietary decisions that address a specific illness or ailment, need to control your weight, or simply choose to eat the right foods to maintain your health, in the following chapter you will learn about the value of the foods you already eat, discover new foods you might never have tried, and find recipes that allow you to combine these power foods with the herbs and spices you got to know in the previous chapters. *Bon appétit!*

(LEFT) **Nuts and seeds are healthy and delicious, but not low-calorie. Snack on them sparingly.**

(OPPOSITE) **Look for a farmers' market in your area that sells fresh, locally grown produce.**

Supermarket shelves are filled with cans and boxes of processed foods. If you must use them, learn to choose wisely.

BAN THE BOX

BYPASS PROCESSED FOODS AND REDISCOVER THE JOY OF COOKING

A century ago, packaged or processed foods were a rarity in most homes. Housewives prepared meals from scratch, using pantry staples like butter, milk, eggs, flour, sugar, chocolate, baking soda, and baking powder, as well as whole grains, fresh fruits and vegetables, and grass-fed meats or free-range poultry. Even though the preserving of foods in metal containers had been perfected more than a century earlier, many families could not afford these store-bought goods. It was during World War II that commercially processed foods came into their own. Today, most of a household's food budget is spent on packaged products—many of which are devoid of nutrients and filled with a multitude of additives.

Processed foods can include anything in a box, can, glass jar or bottle, paper package, or plastic bottle, tub, wrapper, or bag that has been altered in some way prior to consumption. They can contain one or more of the 3,000 additives that are regularly added to food in the United States—including flavorings, colorings, scents, and preservatives, as well as sugars, artificial sweeteners, and sodium. It's no wonder these foods are blamed for the rise of obesity in America, as well as an increase in type-2 diabetes and hypertension.

There are several tiers of processing that range from benign handling to serious tampering.

• Pre-made meals, like frozen dinners, are among the most heavily processed foods.

- Ready-to-eat foods like deli meats, crackers, and breakfast cereals are heavily processed.
- Foods that have ingredients added to augment their flavor or texture (sweeteners, colors, oils, preservatives) include jarred tomato sauce, salad dressings, yogurt, and cake mix.
- Minimally processed foods include bagged salad greens or cut vegetables or bagged roasted nuts, which have been processed for convenience.
- Some foods are processed to capture their peak flavor and to lock in nutrients. These include canned tomatoes and frozen veggies and fruits.

Outside the produce or dairy aisle, it's difficult to walk through a modern grocery store and find anything that is not processed. That does not mean you can't buy food in your local supermarket. You just have to shop wisely.

Healthy Solutions

A smart shopper must learn how to read the nutritional labels found on packaged foods. First, you need to compare the listed serving size with the amount you actually eat. The listed serving size for spaghetti is usually one cup; many people eat two cups, so right there you have a discrepancy—you will need to double all values. The calorie count lets you determine how the food will affect your weight. Total fats will list saturated fats separately; choose foods that are low in these fats. Total carbohydrates include sugar, starch and dietary fiber, which can all raise blood sugar levels. Dietary fiber is listed next; opt for foods that furnish at least three or four grams per serving. The sodium content is important for many people, including those with high blood pressure; try not to exceed 2,300 mg daily. The daily requirement column on the right lets you know the amounts the USDA recommends and is based on consuming 2,000 calories a day.

Even if you are experienced at shopping for nutritious meals, there are also several so-called healthy foods you need to reexamine. For instance, veggie chips are fried in trans fats, and pre-made smoothies are high in fat, sugar, and calories. Two of the biggest offenders are fruit yogurt and granola.

Fruit yogurt is a mixed blessing. Most brands of yogurt offer high-quality protein, calcium, active cultures of probiotics, B vitamins, and a cancer-fighting compound called conjugated linoleic acid (CLA), but many fruit varieties also contain dessert levels of sugar, artificial sweeteners, colors, and flavors, and additives. The sugar content alone is problematic. To maintain a healthy gut, you need to limit sugar intake, otherwise disease-causing microbes will flourish and crowd out beneficial flora. This end result far outweighs any probiotic benefits a heavily sweetened fruit yogurt offers.

PANTRY PICK: *Plain yogurt can be delicious if you mix in your own fresh fruit, dry-roasted nuts or seeds, and a dollop of honey.*

Granola has been touted for years as a natural, wholesome breakfast food, but it is loaded with sugar—often more than one type.

PANTRY PICK: *Make your own nutritious granola by combining 3 cups rolled oats, 1 cup puffed rice, ½ cup pumpkin seeds, ½ cup flaked coconut, and ½ teaspoon salt. Mix together ½ cup apple juice and ½ cup pineapple juice, and reduce over heat. Add ¼ cup honey. Coat the granola with the syrup, and spread over a cookie sheet. Bake for 45 minutes at 325 degrees, tossing halfway through. After cooling, stir in ½ cup dried cranberries or blueberries; store in an airtight container.*

Rather than buying heavily sweetened fruit yogurts, make your own healthy versions. For example, blend frozen or fresh strawberries with low-fat plain yogurt, and then layer the mixture with homemade granola and fresh berries.

WHERE TO SHOP?

HOW TO FIND THE FRESHEST, HEALTHIEST FOODS

The advent of the whole foods, slow foods, and farm-to-table movements in the last few decades are indicators that many consumers are anxious to choose healthier dietary options than processed or packaged foods. They may be seeking organic vegetables or grass-fed meats, free-range eggs or poultry, or raw milk, nuts, or honey, or locally grown products . . . or all of the above.

Healthy Solutions

Gone are the days when shopping for groceries simply meant heading to the nearest chain supermarket. These days, nutrition-conscious consumers can find healthy choices in many venues.

> ### DID YOU KNOW?
>
> • *To receive the USDA's CERTIFIED ORGANIC label, farms need to meet rigorous standards and pay for inspectors, so many small organic farmers now use CERTIFIED NATURALLY GROWN. This label indicates that they follow the USDA standards, but belong to a grassroots organization in which farmers audit one another to ensure sustainable practices.*

FARMERS' MARKETS Local farmers and artisanal bakers sell seasonal produce, free-range eggs, grass-fed meats, canned jams and relishes, homemade pasta, baked goods, and other healthy food options at relatively small, hometown markets. You can often find herbs to plants, handmade soaps, and other handicrafts. Weekends are the prime time to visit farmers' markets; most are held on Friday afternoons or on Saturday or Sunday mornings. Some large cities boast larger markets, like Seattle's Pike Place Market, that are open daily.

CHAIN SUPERMARKETS In response to the demand for healthy options, new supermarket chains have arisen—or existing chains have revamped—catering to nutrition-minded shoppers and natural foods advocates as well as those curious to try new foods. These chains offer a range of benefits.

- The Whole Foods chain, which celebrates the natural lifestyle, is considered the gold standard when it comes to healthy food options. It has an extensive range of fresh produce, ultra-fresh fish and seafood, prepared foods with comprehensive labels, bakery goods that contain no artificial ingredients, preservatives, or trans fats, and each of its stores specializes in local products.
- The Trader Joe's experience is very much like shopping in a specialty store, with healthy foods from around the world. This chain's own reasonably priced brands are also made without artificial colors or flavors, preservatives, or MSG.
- Safeway is a traditional supermarket chain that is now marketing organic brands as well as locally grown produce. The superior offerings of organic spices and packaged nuts have earned this franchise many converts.

OPEN
SWEET CORN
CUT FLOWERS
PEPPERS
BROCCOLI
ZUCCHINI
CUCUMBERS

If you live in the country or are just driving through, look for a roadside farm stand that offers the day's harvest.

Large chains have listened to consumers' desire for healthier options and now carry a wider range of produce, meats, and others foods, including organic vegetables.

- Hannaford is a small supermarket chain in the Northeast, but it challenges Whole Foods when it comes to certified-organic and locally grown products. It also features the Guiding Stars nutrition-rating system that makes picking out the healthiest options a snap.
- The Food Lion megachain, located in the Mid-Atlantic and Southeast, has its own natural foods brand, Nature's Place, and also follows the Guiding Stars program. The chain's boutique offshoot, Bloom, offers outstanding produce and nutritious recipes that can be printed on-site.
- Albertson's has more than 500 stores in the American West and offers its own brand of organic products, American Harvest, that on average costs 15 percent less than name brands. Its Healthy Eaters program offers kids tours of the stores with a registered dietitian.
- Other notable chains include Publix in the Southeast, which caters to the whole family, including pregnant moms and preschoolers; Harris Teeter in the Southeast, which offers more than 600 varieties of fruits and vegetables and shelf tags that point out nutritious choices; and SuperTarget, with its mini-marts that offer many natural food options and the trans fat–free Archer Brand of baked goods and snacks.

ASIAN MARKETS These are several national chains of Asian supermarkets that offer fresh produce and exotic spices and also a whole world of colorfully packaged processed foods—desserts, ramen, and seafood blends, for example. Check out these stores for reduced prices on produce, spices, fresh flowers, and hard-to-obtain sauces and condiments or noodle and rice varieties. Many neighborhoods also have small Asian or Indian groceries that carry similar stock. Depending on where you live, there might be stores in which Latino, Indian, Italian, Middle Eastern, Greek, Polish, French, or kosher items are offered.

SPECIALTY STORES These are the butcher shops, fish markets, and gourmet groceries that specialize in hard-to-find items, artisanal foods, or unique dishes made in small quantities with high-quality ingredients. If you are planning a special meal or event—and don't mind the higher price tags—specialty stores are where you will find fresh quail, Kobe beef, sea urchins, and Fair Trade coffees.

ONLINE OPTIONS You may want to shop locally for produce, but to flavor a meal, you may need to look farther afield. Exotic or hard-to-find ingredients (especially spices) are often readily available online.

A FRESH APPROACH

A number of recent "foodie" movements are shaking up the worldwide food industry.

- Whole foods are defined as plant foods that are unprocessed or unrefined, or processed or refined as little as possible—a "product of nature rather than industry."
- Slow foods was a grassroots movement founded in Italy in 1986 by Carlo Petrini; it offers an alternative to "fast foods" by promoting traditional cuisines and the farming of crops and livestock within the local ecosystem.
- The farm-to-table movement encourages restaurants and schools to serve local foods, ideally by buying products directly from local, family-owned farms, ranches, wineries, breweries, and bakeries.

MIGHTY MICRONUTRIENTS

DECODE THE VITAL VITAMINS AND CRITICAL MINERALS FOUND IN FOODS

A well-balanced diet, one rich in fruits, vegetables, and whole grains, should supply most of the vitamins, minerals, and nutrients the body needs, including disease-fighting antioxidants. Although many of these micronutrients can be taken as supplements, consuming them in fresh food is the most natural way.

VITAMINS

These are the organic compounds that we need in varying amounts to stay healthy.

- The vitamin A family—including beta-carotene—affects immunity, reproduction, and, especially, vision. A medium sweet potato offers 560 percent of the Daily Value (DV). Vitamin A is also found in beef liver, fish, milk, eggs, and carrots.
- The B-complex vitamins include thiamine (vitamin B1), which helps the body turn carbohydrates into energy and keeps the brain and nervous system running properly. Dried yeast contains 11 mg per 100-gram serving, pine nuts offer 1.2 mg, and soybeans have 1.1 mg. Riboflavin (vitamin B2) is an antioxidant that helps the body fight disease and produce red blood cells. Beef liver is the best source, with 3 mg per three-ounce serving. Niacin (vitamin B3) helps convert food into energy and

> **DID YOU KNOW?**
>
> *Humans have often linked the food they ate with how it affected their health—for instance, deducing that limes prevented scurvy—but vitamins and their benefits were not discovered until 1912, by Dr. Casimir Funk, who detected active properties in unpolished rice husks and called them vitamines—vital amines.*

aids the digestive system. Dried yeast and peanuts and beef and chicken liver are good sources. Vitamin B6 helps form hemoglobin, stabilize blood sugar, and create disease-fighting antibodies. One cup of canned chickpeas offers 55 percent of DV, but fish, beef liver, and poultry also provide it. Folate (vitamin B9) can prevent birth defects and help new tissues and proteins form. It is found in beef liver, dark leafy green vegetables, fruit, nuts, and dairy products. Vitamin B12 is vital for a healthy nervous system and the formation of DNA and red blood cells. Clams, beef liver, trout, salmon, and tuna are the best sources.

- Vitamin C is an important antioxidant necessary for protein metabolism and the synthesis of neurotransmitters. Oranges and sweet red peppers top the list, each offering more than 100 percent of DV. Other excellent sources are kiwi, kale, broccoli, strawberries, grapefruit, guava, brussels sprouts, and cantaloupe.
- Our bodies generate vitamin D when we are exposed to sunlight. This spurs calcium absorption and bone and cell growth. Swordfish, salmon, and mackerel are good sources, but cod liver oil is the best.
- Vitamin E is a powerful antioxidant that protects cells from harmful molecules known as free radicals and boosts healthy blood vessel function. Wheat germ oil is the top provider (20.3 mg per serving, or 100 percent of DV) followed by sunflower seeds and almonds.
- Vitamin K, also known as phylloquinone, is crucial to blood clotting. Green, leafy vegetables are the best source. Kale leads the pack with 1.1 mg per cup, followed by collard greens and spinach and turnip, mustard, and beet greens.

Roast or bake sweet potatoes for a mega dose of vitamin A.

Dark green leafy vegetables, like broccoli, spinach, and kale, have a lot to offer, including vitamin K and calcium.

MINERALS AND OTHER NUTRIENTS

This category includes those essential compounds our systems need in order to function well.

- Calcium is the most abundant mineral in the body. More than 99 percent is stored in—and helps fortify—teeth and bones, while the remainder goes toward blood vessel and muscle function and hormone secretion. Dairy products contain the highest amounts: plain low-fat yogurt offers 415 mg (42 percent of DV) per serving. Also seek out kale and Chinese cabbage, fortified fruit juices, and cereals.
- Proteins in the body use iron to transport oxygen and grow cells. The two forms of dietary iron are heme iron (found in animal sources like red meat, fish, and poultry) and nonheme iron (found in plants like lentils and beans). Chicken liver contains the most heme iron, with 11 mg per serving, or 61 percent of DV.
- Lycopene, a chemical pigment found in red and pink fruits and vegetables, has antioxidant properties; research studies suggest it may help guard against heart disease and several types of cancer. Tomato products—tomato sauces, pastes and purees—contain up to 75 mg of lycopene per cup. Watermelon supplies about 12 mg per wedge.
- Lysine, or l-lysine, is an amino acid that helps the body absorb calcium and form collagen for bones and connective tissue. It also helps

produce carnitine, a nutrient that regulates cholesterol levels. Protein-rich animal foods, especially red meat, are good sources, as are nuts and legumes.

- Magnesium is essential—the body uses it in more than 300 biochemical reactions—maintaining muscle and nerve function, keeping heart rhythm steady, and keeping bones strong. Unrefined wheat bran offers the highest amount per serving. Other good sources include almonds, cashews, and spinach.
- Potassium is an essential electrolyte needed to control the electrical activity of the heart. It also builds proteins and muscle. One medium baked sweet potato contains nearly 700 mg. Tomato paste, beet greens, and white potatoes are also good sources, as are red meat, chicken and fish.
- Selenium is a mineral with antioxidant properties and it plays a large role in preventing chronic diseases. It also helps regulate thyroid function. Too much selenium can be harmful, so stick with canned tuna (68 mg per 3 ounces, or 97 percent of DV).
- Zinc plays a role in immune function, and it's also important for the senses of taste and smell. Oysters contain more zinc per serving than any other food (74 mg per serving, or nearly 500 percent of DV), but zinc is more often consumed in red meat and poultry.

Oysters pack a lot of nutrition inside their shells. These zinc powerhouses are high in protein and are excellent sources of vitamins C and B12, iron, and selenium.

Strawberries, raspberries, cranberries, and blueberries

BERRIES

THESE SMALL FRUITS ARE PACKED WITH FLAVOR, NUTRIENTS, AND ANTIOXIDANTS

Many plants provide small, colorful, edible fruits that are known for their delicious flavors and their health benefits. Botanically, berries are pulpy seed-bearing fruits produced from the ovary of a single flower. This definition also includes grapes, tomatoes, cucumbers, bananas, and eggplant. Plants that do not fit this description include strawberries, raspberries, and blackberries, which are called aggregate fruits because they develop from the merging of several ovaries from a single flower.

Berries were a seasonal staple for hunter-gatherers because they did not need any preparation and could be eaten right off the bush. They could also be dried and stored for use during the winter. Commercial cultivation of berries is now a major global industry, although some berries, such as lingonberries and cloudberries, are still almost exclusively harvested in the wild.

Many berries contain phytonutrients, like cancer-fighting antioxidants, plus anti-inflammatories and neurogenetic compounds that make new neurons and boost brain function. Natural healers suggest eating several servings each week to keep the mind sharp and to combat disease and chronic health problems.

DID YOU KNOW?

• *Native Americans mixed dried cranberries with game meat and fat to make pemmican, a high-energy food. Blueberries, cherries, chokeberries, and currants were also used, but only for ceremonial or wedding pemmican. This food was adopted by European trappers and explorers and today remains part of Canadian cuisine.*

STRAWBERRY

These sweet, scarlet members of the Rosaceae (rose family) are so popular that twice as many strawberries are produced worldwide than all other berry crops combined. The strawberry plant is a low-growing perennial with small white flowers that propagates via runners.

The Romans considered these fruits medicinal, but they did not cultivate them. Woodland strawberries, *Fragaria vesca,* were first grown by the French in the 1300s, while the musky hautbois strawberry, *F. moschata,* was cultivated in the late 1500s. The Virginia strawberry later became popular in Europe and America. Today, the most common strawberry is *F. x ananassa,* an accidental cross between the Virginia strawberry and the Chilean variety, *F. chiloensis.* These luscious red berries are eaten fresh or used to make jams, juices, pies, and ice cream.

Health Benefits

Strawberries contain vitamins C and K, B-complex vitamins, fiber, potassium, manganese, iodine, folate, magnesium, copper, and omega-3 fatty acids, as well as powerful antioxidants that may prevent macular degeneration of the eyes.

RASPBERRY

These sweet, pebbled fruits, also part of the Rosaceae, are produced by numerous species in the genus *Rubus*. They have woody, often thorny stems and perennial roots that produce berries during the second season. The plants can be invasive, spreading with basal shoots called suckers. The white or pink flowers provide nectar for honeybees. An important commercial crop in temperate regions, raspberries are harvested when the fruit has turned a rich red, black, purple, or golden yellow, depending on the cultivar. The fruit is used to make jams, pie fillings, and flavorings, and the leaves are crushed to make herbal teas. The most important cultivars are the red raspberry hybrids derived from *R. idaeus* and *R. strigosus* and the black raspberry, *R. occidentalis,* with its distinctive flavor.

Health Benefits

Raspberries contain extremely high levels of fiber, plus vitamin C, manganese, and antioxidants, including anthocyanins.

CRANBERRY

The cranberry is a dwarf evergreen shrub in the heath family (Ericaceae). The American cranberry, *Vaccinium macrocarpon,* is cultivated in North America and Chile, while *V. oxycoccos* is grown in central and northern Europe. The berries are larger than the leaves and when ripe turn a bright red. Even though they are acidic in taste, they are used for baking, jams, sauces, and juices or dried for use in cereals and snacks. The sauce is a traditional accompaniment to holiday turkey dinners in both the United States and Great Britain. American crops are harvested by shallowly flooding the bogs where cranberries grow; the floating berries are then corralled by machines.

Health Benefits

Cranberries offer vitamin C, fiber, and manganese, as well as beneficial antioxidant compounds. Natural healers recommend cranberry juice to treat cystitis—its proanthocyanidins speed up healing by preventing bacteria from clinging to bladder walls.

BLUEBERRY

This native perennial shrub of North America, a member of the Ericaceae family, is now grown worldwide. The plants can vary greatly—leaves may be evergreen or deciduous, lanceolate or oval, and heights can range from four-inch wild species (lowbush) to cultivars more than a foot tall (highbush). The bell-shaped pink or white flowers mature into deep purple berries that are coated with powdery epicuticular wax, known as bloom. The most common cultivated species in the United States is *Vaccinium corymbosum,* the northern highbush, with Washington State the country's largest producer. Blueberries are used to make jams, jellies, pies, and muffins and are added to snack mixes and cereal.

Health Benefits

Blueberries contain only moderate levels of vitamins C and K, manganese, and dietary fiber, but they offer anthocyanins and other antioxidants, now being studied for their beneficial effects on human health.

PANTRY PICK: *Before a workout, toss a handful of blueberries into a green tea smoothie or eat a bowl of berries with your morning cup. A recent study revealed that blueberries consumed with green tea stimulates the body to burn fat long after exercise is completed.*

Whip up smoothies with your choice of berries and a juice, yogurt, milk, or green tea base and some shaved ice for an easy way to get the health benefits of these fruits.

GRAPES

THIS FRUIT OF THE VINE LENDS RICH, COMPLEX FLAVORS TO DESSERTS AND WINE

When the grape's many contributions to world cuisine are calculated, it is no wonder that this small round berry was once referred to as the "queen of fruits." Its part in the production of wine alone warrants a place in the culinary pantheon. But its roles as a succulent dessert fruit and the source of a popular jelly, an iron-rich juice, and the ubiquitous raisin, as well as its many healing qualities, need to be factored in as well.

Botanically, grapes are berries: the pulpy, seed-bearing fruit of a woody perennial vine, a robust twining plant in the genus *Vitis*. They grow in heavy, hanging clusters—one vine can produce as many as 50—which are harvested in bunches once the fruit ripens. The vines themselves can live for six decades or more. The tiny, greenish, clustering flowers and the fruit form on new shoots called canes. Domestic grapes are hermaphroditic, reproductive organs of both sexes on one plant, while wild grapes tend to be pollen-producing males or fruit-bearing females.

Grapes range in color from blackish purple to deep red to pale green. These colorful fruits make a healthy snack.

> ### DID YOU KNOW?
>
> • *Prior to the 1600s, grapes were used exclusively for the production of wine and for medicinal purposes. French King François I discovered that a certain Chasselas grape made a delicious dessert fruit, and his courtiers followed his example. Grapes soon became popular for baking and snacking.*

Grapes are among the oldest plants on earth—archaeologists have found the remains of wild grape varieties that date back 130 million years. They likely originated in the region of the Caspian Sea—they were first cultivated 8,000 years ago in Mesopotamia. Viticulture eventually reached ancient Greece, whose sailors carried grapes to southern France, while Roman legions spread them across the rest of Europe and the British Isles. Several grape species grow wild in the New World— and were a valued part of the Native American diet— but colonists did not consider them suitable for producing wine, and so imported their European vines, *Vitis vinifera*.

Today, there are more than 10,000 different varieties of grapes grown commercially all over the world. The top producers include France, Italy, the United States, Spain, China, Turkey, Argentina, Iran, Chile, South Africa, and Australia. The majority of grapes are used for making wine—only 10 percent of the crop is sold as table grapes and another 5 percent is dried to make raisins. Table grapes, most often *V. vinifera,* are used to make jelly, jam, juice, grape-seed extract, vinegar, and grape-seed oil. *V. labrusca,* which includes the Concord variety, is an American grape used to make wines and jellies. It is found in the eastern United States and Canada. Another East Coast grape is the wild *V. riparia,* which is sometime harvested for wine.

Health Benefits

In ancient civilizations, grapes were more valued for their medicinal contributions than as a food source. Early physicians like Hippocrates, Galen, and Celsus prescribed grapes for urinary woes and digestive issues. Traditional healers throughout the centuries

Red wine grapes ripening on the vine. Most grapes varieties are grown for wine production.

have used them to treat coughs, gout, enlarged liver or spleen, eye infections, cholera, and smallpox.

Current studies have shown that the consumption of grapes is associated with the prevention of cancer, high blood pressure, heart disease, and constipation. Grapes are also used as part of a diet to decrease obesity and improve overall well-being. Fresh grape juice benefits the urinary and digestive system; it cleanses the gut and counteracts acidity. Grapes are also being studied as a possible treatment for macular degeneration and cataracts. Researchers are discovering it is the chemical constituents of this versatile fruit that give it the powerful healing qualities that make nutritionists label it a "superfood."

- The skin of the red grapes used in wine production contain the polyphenol resveratrol, which has been linked with improved heart health. This compound has been effective in treating acne when taken with existing medications.

- Grapes offer potent antioxidants called polyphenols that can slow or actually prevent the onset of certain types of cancer, including lung, esophageal, pancreatic, prostate, and colon.
- The fruit's fiber and potassium reduce the risk of heart disease, especially when combined with a reduced intake of sodium.
- The flavonoid quercetin found in grapes provides anti-inflammatory benefits that may reduce the risk of atherosclerosis and protect the body from the damage caused by LDL cholesterol. Quercetin may also alleviate the symptoms of seasonal allergies.
- Grapes contain vitamins C and K; calcium, for building strong bones; and antibacterial, astringent tannic acid. Black grapes also contain significant amounts of iron.
- The high amounts of water contained in grapes and other pulpy fruits help maintain hydration, making bowel movements more regular.

APPLE AND PEAR

DELICIOUS AND NUTRITIOUS, THESE TWO FRUITS SHARE THE SAME EARLY ANCESTOR

Apples and pears are both members of the Rosaceae (rose family) and bear similar-looking white or pinkish flowers. Both species are popular additions to fruit salads and creamy side dishes like Waldorf salad, and they both make excellent tarts. Each contains small, hard pits, or seeds. Nutritionally, apples and pears provide disease-fighting antioxidants and the water-soluble fiber pectin, so it is not surprising to learn that these two fruits evolved from a common ancestor some time between 50 and 35 million years ago.

Yet these two fruits are not without their differences—an apple's interior is smooth in consistency, whereas a pear's flesh is slightly grainy. Pears are much more susceptible to bruising and softening as they ripen. Apples hold their firmness for a relatively long time, making them a perfect choice for winter storage.

APPLES

The fruit of the apple tree *(Malus pumila)* has long been hailed as a "miracle food." These days, it is often included in top 10 lists of healthy foods—in

Granny Smith, Red Delicious, and Gala apples

> **DID YOU KNOW?**
>
> • *In 2010, an Italian-led consortium of scientists sequenced the apple genome at Washington State University using Golden Delicious apples. They identified more than 57,000 genes, which is the highest number of any plant genome studied so far, and more than the human genome, which numbers around 30,000.*

fact, the apple was named first in *Medical News Today's* recent list.

Apple trees are deciduous and, depending on variety, range in height from 6 to 15 feet. The leaves are serrated, and the flowers draw many flying pollinators. The skin, coated with epicuticular wax, can be bright red, dark red, pink, green, yellow, or bicolored or tricolored. Flavors range from tartly acidic to sweet and fruity, while the pale flesh, or exocarp, is yellow-white or pinkish.

Apple trees originated in Central Asia, where their ancestor, *M. sieversii*, still grows wild today. Apples trees were cultivated—and selectively bred—for thousands of years throughout Asia and Europe and came to the Americas with early colonists in the 1600s. These Old World apples soon spread along trade routes—a tossed core could generate several trees—and were grown in settlements and on farms.

Today, there are more than 7,500 apple cultivars with a wide range of characteristics. Certain varieties are purposely engineered for eating fresh, others for baking or the making of cider. Worldwide production is currently somewhere around 100 million tons, with the chief exporter, China, responsible for nearly 50 percent of the total output.

Health Benefits

Apples are rich in antioxidants, flavonoids, and dietary fiber—phytonutrients that are being studied for their ability to reduce the risk of cancer, high blood pressure, diabetes, and cardiovascular disease. Some other possible advantages of regularly eating apples include protection against Parkinson's disease and gallstones, slowing the effects of aging on the brain, and neutralizing irritable bowel syndrome.

PEARS

With their sweet, mild flavor, pears make the perfect ending to a rich or heavy meal. The Greek poet Homer praised them as the "gifts of the gods," most likely for their soft, melting flesh and grassy aroma. This bottom-heavy fruit grows on trees or shrubs in the genus *Pyrus*. They possibly originated in Western China and were native to the coastal regions of the temperate Old World, including Western Europe, North Africa, and Asia. The fruit was introduced to the Americas by early colonists. The trees can reach heights of 33 to 56 feet and produce a variety of leaf types—long and glossy or silvery and hairy, broad or lance shaped. They are shapely trees with lush blossoms, making them popular with landscapers and town planners. Remains of pears found in prehistoric pile dwellings around Lake Zurich attest to their early use as a food source. The Romans first cultivated pears and ate them raw or cooked, like apples.

Today, there are more than 3,000 pear varieties: the three most popular are the European pear, or common pear *(P. communis),* which includes familiar cultivars like the Bartlett (also called Williams), the Bosc, and the Comice pears; the Chinese white pear *(P. x bretschneideri);* and the Nashi pear *(P. pyrifolia).*

Ripe red-tinged Bartletts. This classic bell-shaped pear variety, also known as the Williams pear, is prized for its fragrantly sweet taste and a smooth, buttery texture.

Health Benefits

In addition to being low in calories, pears are a good source of dietary fiber, making them helpful for digestive issues. They are rich in the antioxidants that scavenge free radicals and the flavonoid compounds beta-carotene, lutein, and zeaxanthin. Studies indicate pears may be useful in combating cancer and supporting the immune system. They are also a good source of heart-healthy potassium.

For a warming winter beverage, simmer pear nectar or juice with allspice, vanilla, cinnamon, and a touch of lemon.

MAKE IT YOURSELF
Apple and Pear Salad

To gain the health benefits from both apples and pears, prepare a crisp, green salad.

YOU WILL NEED:
- 1 tart apple
- 1 ripe pear
- ¼ cup blue cheese, crumbled
- 2 mashed garlic cloves
- 20 slivered almonds
- large bowl of romaine lettuce
- extra-virgin olive oil
- red wine vinegar
- lemon juice
- oregano

WHAT TO DO:
- Slice the apple and pear, and combine with the blue cheese, garlic, and almonds.
- Toss with the romaine lettuce.
- Lightly drizzle with oil and vinegar, and add a dash of oregano and lemon juice.

STONE FRUIT
THESE TENDER DESSERT FRUITS OFFER FLAVOR AND ANTIOXIDANTS

Stone fruits are drupes—fruits that contain a large "stone" that is sometimes called a pit. These shells are made of hardened endocarp and contain the plant's seeds. Stone fruits belong to the *Prunus* genus, which also includes almonds, lychee, and mangoes and are members of the Rosaceae family. The trees are prone to damage during cold weather, so most prefer warmer climates. And because they bloom in early spring, their flowers can also be damaged by spring frosts. Cherries and plums are probably the hardiest of the stone fruits, nectarines the most delicate—and they are also susceptible to a disease called brown rot.

These fruits are the colorful treats we look forward to all summer—when the baskets at the grocery store and farmers' market are usually bursting with them. Stone fruits, with the exception of cherries, should be ripened at room temperature, stem end down, and only refrigerated once they are fragrant and soft.

> ### DID YOU KNOW?
> * *How disappointing to bite into a fresh peach and discover the flesh is mealy and tasteless! Mealiness is caused by several factors—the peach was picked too early and placed in cold storage or picked ripe and stored at improper temperatures. Buying local peaches, when you can, will avoid the problem.*

They can be eaten raw, baked into pies and cakes, roasted, poached, mixed in salads and smoothies, canned, and made into jams, jellies, marmalades, chutneys, salsas, and even wines and liqueurs.

These drupes are among the healthiest fruits and are the perfect size for tucking into a lunch box or carrying to work for an afternoon break. Stone fruits are a good source of ascorbic acid, which helps the body form the protein collagen found in connective tissue, cartilage, muscles, and blood vessels, and potassium, which helps support nerve and muscle function. They also provide a number of powerful antioxidants, those scavengers of harmful free radicals. Finally, never peel stone fruit—their skin provides insoluble fiber that has heart-healthy effects and can prevent constipation.

NECTARINES

Who doesn't love a ripe nectarine (*P. persica* var. *nucipersica),* with its delicate, honeyed scent and sweet-tasting flesh? These stone fruit favorites are closely related to peaches, being similar in size and color but lacking the fuzzy skin. Like peaches, the flesh of nectarines can be yellow or white. In fact, peach seeds may sometimes grow into nectarine trees, and vice versa. Like peaches, they originated in China more than 2,000 years ago. They were cultivated by the early Persians, Greeks, and Romans—Pliny's *duracinus*, noted in A.D. 79, is believed to be the nectarine. They were grown in 17th-century Britain and were brought to the New World by the Spanish. Today, they are cultivated in many semitropical regions, with California the top U.S. exporter. Popular commercial varieties include the large clingstone Quetta, the medium crimson John Rivers, and freestone Gower.

A basket of rosy nectarines. Smooth-skinned nectarines share the large pits that define this group of fruit.

Health Benefits

Nectarines provide heart-healthy dietary fiber, iron, calcium, and phosphorus, as well as antioxidant vitamins A and C. The deep red hue of the fruit indicates the presence of the powerful antioxidant beta-carotene, which protects the body from cancer and other diseases. Vitamin C provides tissue-strengthening collagen, boosts the immune system, and helps heal skin damage. As a low-calorie food, nectarines are also popular with dieters.

PEACHES

These luscious reddish yellow fruits with their downy skin are consumed year round—canned, they are a lunch box favorite and raw, they are prized by dieters

Easy-to-make Peachy Almond Popsicles are nutty and creamy treats for a hot summer day.

for their low calories—only 37 in a medium peach—and high-impact flavor. The fruit's scientific name, *P. persica*, might indicate origins in Persia, modern-day Iran, but they more likely originated in China 3,000 years ago. The Chinese still consider the peach the tree of life, and the fruit represents immortality. Europeans cultivated them and brought them to the New World: the Spanish to South America, the French to Louisiana, and the English to Virginia and Massachusetts. There are two types of peaches—in freestone peaches, the fruit does not cling to the pit; in clingstone varieties it does.

Health Benefits

Peaches are high in dietary fiber and vitamins A, B, and C and also provide calcium, potassium, magnesium, iron, phosphorus, zinc, and copper. They are rich in antioxidant phenols, including the trace mineral selenium, which helps protect cells from damage. In Hungary, peaches are eaten to ease anxiety and are called the fruits of calmness.

> PANTRY PICK: *Two small peaches can offer the same amount of potassium as a medium banana. Blend them in a smoothie with almond milk, ice, honey, and a dash of cinnamon.*

MAKE IT YOURSELF
Peachy Almond Popsicles

You just need Popsicle molds to freeze up these healthy summer coolers.

YOU WILL NEED:
  3 medium peaches
  ½ cup low-fat yogurt
  1½ cups almond milk
  ¼ teaspoon pure almond extract

WHAT TO DO:
• Pit and dice the peaches
• Place all ingredients in a blender, and puree until smooth.
• Pour mixture into molds, and freeze until solid, about two to three hours.

APRICOTS

These small golden fruits with their slightly velvety skin offer firm flesh and a sweet, slightly musky flavor. They originated in China and made their way to Europe by way of Armenia—accounting for the Latin name *P. armeniaca*. Some trees were grown in Virginia around 1720, but their cultivation truly began in the Spanish missions of California, around 1792, where they are still widely grown today. The leading producers worldwide are Turkey, Italy, Russia, Spain, Greece, the United States, and France. Dried apricots are popular for cooking or snacking and are often treated with sulfur dioxide to preserve their pale color. The essential oil distilled from apricot pits is known as bitter almond oil.

Apricots

Mottled-red Dapple Dandy pluots. Pluots are genetically one-fourth apricot and three-fourths plum.

Health Benefits

Apricots are rich in pectin, a water-soluble fiber that accounts for their creamy texture and that can help control high cholesterol. They also contain many antioxidants and nutrients, including catechins (anti-inflammatories), proanthocyanidins, and quercetin. Cooking apricots makes their yellow-orange carotenoids more available to the body: beta-carotene converts to vitamin A, which helps to maintain eyesight as we age, while lutein protects the retina from damaging blue light. These carotenoids also preserves skin membranes and enhance immune function.

PANTRY PICK: *Stew apricots in honey and water with star anise and cloves and serve with low-fat frozen yogurt for a decadently healthy dessert.*

PLUMS

Plums are possibly one of the earliest fruits cultivated by humans—plum tree remains have been found around Neolithic-age settlements in areas where plums did not grow wild.

There are two main types: oval-shaped common European plums, *P. domestica,* which likely originated around the Caucasian Mountains some 2,000 years ago, and large, round Asian plums, *P. salicina* (known as the Japanese plum or Chinese plum) and *P. simonii* (called the apricot plum and Simon plum). These are usually eaten fresh, while the European varieties are dried or used for preserves. The fruit's peel is smooth with a waxy surface, and the succulent flesh, ranging in color from red to deep blue-black, is firm and juicy. Plums came to America around 1720 and the easy-to-grow trees rapidly took hold with farmers. Noted American botanist Luther Burbank promoted plums in his writing, and he experimented with developing many cultivars.

Healthy Benefits

Plums contain fiber and vitamins A, C, and K. The latter helps strengthen the skeletal system, and low levels of the vitamin have been linked with increased risk of osteoarthritis of the hands and knees. Many studies have been done on the fruit's antioxidants—a particular phenol found in plums has been shown to neutralize a dangerous toxin called superoxide anion radical.

PANTRY PICK: *A cup of sliced plums or apricots furnishes roughly one quarter of your daily requirement of vitamin C. For a perfect parfait breakfast, intersperse fruit slices with crumbles of homemade granola and spoonfuls of low-fat yogurt.*

KISSIN' COUSINS

A number of unusual hybrids have been created between tart, juicy plums and sweet, fleshy apricots. The fruit dubbed the pluot is a plum-apricot cross with more plum in its parentage. A pluot tastes like a plum, but without the bitter skin. Plumcots are similar to pluots, but are of equal parentage, with a wide array of varieties depending on the kinds of plums and apricots used. Apriums are plum-apricot hybrids, but with more apricot characteristics. They look and smell like apricots, but their flesh is juicier and firmer.

CHERRIES

Like plums, cherries come in two types—sweet cherries *(P. avium),* which are eaten as table fruits, and sour cherries *(P. cerasus),* which are used for cooking and canning. Sweet varieties include Bing, Ranier, and Sweetheart; sour cultivars include Morello and Montmorency. Both types originated in Europe and western Asia; they do not cross-pollinate. Cherries were a favorite dessert fruit in ancient China, Greece, and Rome, and their popularity has continued into modern times. Like other stone fruits, they traveled to America with early settlers, probably in the 1600s. Cherries do not ripen off the tree, so they must be picked ripe and eaten fairly quickly.

Health Benefits

Cherries are a good source of vitamin C and also contain vitamin A, calcium, potassium, and iron. They provide high levels of antioxidants, like anthocyanins and cyanidins, which fight diseases and help boost memory. The antioxidants, in tart cherries especially, can reduce the risk of high blood pressure, stroke, high cholesterol, gout, and diabetes. Cherries have a very low glycemic index—22—making them an ideal snack for weight watchers.

Bing cherries

PANTRY PICK: *Cherries contain high levels of melatonin, the sleep-regulating hormone, so snack on a handful before bedtime or try this Sleepyhead Tea. Mix 1 cup of brewed chamomile tea with ¼ cup of tart cherry juice, and add a drop of almond extract. Drink hot or chilled.*

Damson plums show the wax bloom that covers the blue-black or purple skin. These clingstone fruits have a green flesh with a rich, somewhat astringent flavor. They are often used to make fruit preserves or jam.

DRIED FRUIT
ARE THESE TRAIL MIX FAVORITES HEALTHY TREATS OR SUGARY THREATS?

Dried fruits are sold as health foods in many places, but their credentials may not be so stellar. Many fruits can be sun dried or dehydrated for long-term storage—raisins, or dried grapes, being one of the best-known examples. The practice of drying fruit dates back to at least to 4000 B.C. in Mesopotamia. Soldiers on the march, merchants in caravans crossing deserts, or shepherds in distant summer pastures all welcomed a nutritious, portable food that resisted spoilage. Today, dried fruits can still be found in many regional cuisines. Grapes are the most commonly dried fruit, followed by dates, plums, figs, apricots, peaches,

> **DID YOU KNOW?**
>
> • *In order to preserve the color of certain pale fruits—golden raisins, apples, peaches, and apricots—sulfur dioxide is added to block any browning agents. Although it is normally harmless, SO_2 can induce asthma in sensitive individuals if it is inhaled or ingested. Anyone at risk should take care.*

apples, and pears. These are sold as "natural" dried fruits, with nothing added. Some sour fruits, like dried cranberries, cherries, strawberries, and mangoes, are infused with sucrose syrup. A third option is the candied dried fruits—also called crystallized or glacé fruit—which includes pineapple, papaya, and kiwi.

RAISINS

More raisins are processed worldwide than any other dried fruit. Grape cultivation began in the Mediterranean region around 4000 B.C.; raisins were first created by burying grapes in sand. The Romans consumed raisins in vast quantities, even presenting them to victorious athletes, and they were also adopted into the cuisine of Morocco and Tunisia. Today, they are a baking staple in most kitchens.

Health Benefits

When water is removed from a fruit, its sweetness becomes concentrated, and, in many cases, its medicinal properties do as well. But sugar content also increases. Raisins provide vitamin C and are high in antioxidants, but they are also up to 72 percent sugars, by weight. Still, research indicates that snacking on raisins three times a day can help lower high blood pressure.

PRUNES

Prunes are renowned for their ability to regulate the bowel, but they are also a tasty snack food, with a sweet, chewy, sticky texture. More than 1,000 cultivars of plums are grown specifically for drying, most of them freestones. Prunes may be used for desserts and baking, or pureed and substituted for fat in cakes, quickbreads, or muffins. The process of drying plums to make prunes likely began several

Sticky black prunes, which are made from a vast selection of plum cultivars, are a tasty way to get dietary fiber.

thousand years ago around the Caspian Sea and spread as trade routes expanded. Today, California is the world's leading producer of prunes, using a variety of French plum called Agen.

HEALTH BENEFITS

Prunes provide soluble fiber, which helps to lower cholesterol and normalize blood sugar, as well as vitamins A, C, and K and copper and potassium. They contain several unique phytonutrients—the antioxidants neochlorogenic and chlorogenic acid. They also increase the body's absorption of iron.

DATES

Date palms *(Phoenix dactylifera)* were among the first trees domesticated in the Fertile Crescent, around 6,000 years ago. These trees were so fecund, producing up to 300 pounds of fruit a year, that dates became a food staple—and have remained so in many cultures. Whether eaten raw, hard-dried, or soft-dried, dates add flavor and texture to meat dishes, breads, and desserts.

Health Benefits

Dates were once used as a tonic against fatigue. They contain fiber (which boosts heart and colon health), vitamin B6 (which improves brain function),

Fresh and dried figs

and potassium, copper, manganese, and magnesium (which helps lower blood pressure). Dates also provide anti-inflammatory properties, and they can offer digestive relief.

FIGS

In some parts of the Middle East, figs *(Ficus carica)* once rivaled dates in popularity. Dried figs were often used as funerary offerings by the Egyptians and enjoyed at table by the Romans. They are still used in many regional cuisines and as a healthy snack fruit.

Health Benefits

Figs are high in fiber and provide vitamins A, B1, B2, B6, and K, omega-3 and omega-6 fatty acids, and magnesium, manganese, calcium, copper and potassium. Fig leaf tea can help lower high triglyceride levels.

CANDY CULTURE

Dating back to the 1300s, candied fruits, ginger root, and citrus peels—called comfits or sweetmeats—were repeatedly drenched in a sugar solution to protect them from spoilage. The Mesopotamians and Chinese had once used honey to preserve fruit, but it was the Arabs who raised candying to an art. As the Arab conquest spread to southern Europe, so did candying. Italian recipes of the 1500s incorporate sweet dried fruits, and they are still seen today in panettone, cassata, and cannoli filling. Although the candied fruits found bulk packaged in supermarkets provide the health benefits inherent in the fruit, any pluses are negated by the amount of sugar they contain.

Up Close
SYSTEMIC WARRIORS
POWERFUL DISEASE FIGHTERS CAN BE FOUND IN MANY EVERYDAY FOODS

A rainbow of produce. Color can often tell you what kind of benefits a fruit or vegetable offers, from the antioxidant and nutrient-packed greens to the carotenoid-rich yellows and oranges to the anti-inflammatory red, purple, and blues.

Our earliest ancestors valued plants as sources of sustenance, but they eventually had some idea that certain things they ate gave them a sense of vitality—and even made them feel better when they were ill. Today we know that a number of compounds help our bodies fight diseases and keep our immune systems strong. Fruits and vegetables, already rich in fiber, vitamins, and minerals, also contain beneficial phytonutrients.

Phytonutrients

Phytonutrients are inert chemicals found in plants that protect them and enable them to thrive. Some act to ward off insect attacks, others may protect a plant from UV radiation. When we consume plants, we gain the same health-promoting benefits: the antioxidants, anti-inflammatories, and organ-protecting properties. There are more than 10,000 recognized phytonutrients, and researchers estimate that there may be as many as 20,000. They are responsible for giving produce plants their varied colors and their nutritional properties. In fact, these powerful allies against disease are why health professionals advise eating 5 to 12 servings of fruits or vegetables each day. And the USDA proclaims that consuming a diet rich in phytonutrients can be an effective strategy for combating cancer and cardiovascular risks.

These compounds are especially concentrated in produce plants, but they are also found in herbs and spices, legumes, and nuts and seeds. Richly colored plants may be valuable sources of phytonutrients, but off-white plants like garlic and onions contain high amounts of sulfur-containing phytonutrients.

Phytonutrients allow cells to communicate and function at their highest levels, facilitating the proper sequence of enzymatic reactions. The resulting biochemical reactions lead to healthier tissues and organ systems, the detoxification of foreign substances, a bolstered immune system, and muscles that perform on demand. Different ones work in synergy—a reason supplements don't always have the same effect as the actual food source: supplements can't replicate all the key cofactors in the plant. Some of the phytonutrients found in our food include the following examples.

ANTIOXIDANTS Researchers believe that cancer occurs when oxygen-free radicals and reactive oxygen species trigger a series of mutational events—including damaging DNA in cells, cell membranes, and proteins. Antioxidants are highly beneficial compounds that bind to oxidation radicals, thus interrupting cell injury or even preventing it. A wide range of antioxidants occur in nature, many of them providing benefits to specific parts of the body.

- Fat-soluble alpha- and beta-carotenes promote eye and skin health and may combat lung and cervical cancers. They are found in orange and yellow plants such as carrots, cantaloupes, pumpkins, apricots, and winter squash.
- Orange-yellow produce contains cryptoxanthin, which may suppress cancer cell growth. It occurs in oranges, peaches, nectarines, and papayas.
- Antioxidant lycopene works to maintain prostate health and may have anticancer properties. It also promotes healthy, smooth skin and promotes bone health. Lycopene is found in yellow or pink produce like tomatoes, guava, and watermelon.
- Flavonoids have anti-inflammatory properties that are beneficial for heart health. They can be found in parsley, blueberries, black tea, citrus fruits, cocoa, and wine. Most prominent among the flavonoids are the anthocyanins, which have a long history in natural healing. They occur in red, purple, or blue plants, like strawberries, beets, eggplant, red and blue grapes, red cabbage, plums, red apples, and cherries and may be effective for protecting the liver, fostering heart health, lowering blood pressure, improving eyesight, and suppressing cancer.

- Lutein and zeaxanthin are important to eye health and the immune system. They are found in yellow-green produce like corn, green and yellow peppers, green peas, honeydew melons, kiwis, romaine lettuce, and spinach.
- Proanthocyanidins are beneficial for urinary tract health and are found in dark-colored produce like black chokeberries, blueberries, black currents, broccoli, and kale.
- Resveratrol is an anti-inflammatory that may protect the blood vessels in the heart and prevent blood clots. It is found in wine, grapes, berries, cocoa, and peanuts.

ADDITIONAL AIDS Other valuable phytonutrients include indigestible carbohydrates (nonstarch polysaccharides, or NSPs) like tannins, pectin, hemicellulose, and mucilage, also known as fiber; detoxifying agents like indoles; and alkaloids like caffeine and theobromine. Fiber is especially important: it adds bulk to foods, prevents the absorption of toxins, prevents constipation by decreasing gastrointestinal transit time, and protects colon mucous from cancers. It also prevents the reabsorption of bile salts and so lowers LDL-cholesterol levels in the blood.

Vitamin C–rich guava. Pink-fleshed fruits, like guava, can also promote prostate health.

WHAT ABOUT PHYTOSTEROLS?

Also known as plant sterols, these compounds dwell in the cell membranes of plants. Found in vegetables, fruits, nuts, seeds, and legumes, they have been part of our diet throughout human history. They are poorly absorbed in the gut and appear to block the absorption of cholesterol, helping to lower LDL-cholesterol levels. It is best to get them from whole plant foods; you should avoid phytosterol-enriched foods.

Sliced cantaloupe along with a canary melon and a honeydew melon. All three are varieties of muskmelon.

MELONS
THESE SUCCULENT FRUITS BRING THEIR BOUNTY TO SUMMER TABLES

Some of the world's tastiest fruits, are also, it turns out, some of its healthiest. Melons contain water for hydration, immunity-boosting vitamins, and valuable trace minerals. These members of the Curcubitaceae family are known for their sweet fleshy interiors and thick, protective rinds. Botanically, a melon is a form of berry, or pepo—a term used for the fruits of the gourd family with a many-seeded interior and hard exterior. They are annuals that grow on long trailing or climbing stems, producing large, coarse leaves, and white or yellowish flowers. Plants contain flowers of both sexes, with male flowers dominating the early growing season. Most melons prefer temperate to semitropical settings.

Melons likely originated in Africa and southwest Asia, arriving in Europe near the final days of the

DID YOU KNOW?

• *There is now a trend toward cultivating small, "personal-sized" watermelons, which are quicker to grow and easier to handle for shippers and shoppers. Fancifully named cultivars include Sugar Baby, Precious Petite, Orchid Sweet, Yellow Doll, Early Moonbeam, and the two-pound Little Baby Flower.*

Roman Empire. Recent archaeological discoveries indicate that they may have already been in Sardinia during the Bronze Age. They were also among the first plants to be cultivated, both in Europe and the New World. Certain Indian tribes in the Southwest began developing their own unique cultivars derived from melons brought to the Americas by the Spaniards. Many cultivars have been created commercially, especially from muskmelons. Below are some of the more popular melon varieties and the range of healthy properties they provide.

WATERMELON

What good is an outdoor party or summer picnic without berry-bright wedges of watermelon for dessert? These largest members of the melon clan originated in southern Africa, and there are indications that they were cultivated in ancient Egypt. A prime commercial crop today, watermelons (*Citrullus lanatus*) are bred in a number of sizes, to be disease resistant, and to produce soft, white seeds, making them virtually "seedless." Certain cultivars can go from seed to harvest in fewer than 100 days. Some favorite varieties include Jubilee, Black Diamond, and Georgia Rattlesnake.

Similar to pumpkins, the rinds of whole watermelons can be carved into fanciful designs or the melon can be partially hollowed out and used as a container for fruit salad or iced drinks. The rinds are delicious when pickled.

Health Benefits

Once thought of as simply a sugary, watery dessert fruit—like KoolAid in a rind—watermelons surprised researchers once they began exploring their

> ### MAKE IT YOURSELF
> ## *Watermelon Ginger Granita*
>
> Add the zing of ginger to frozen watermelon for a delicious and healthy summer treat.
>
> YOU WILL NEED:
> 6 cups watermelon, deseeded and cubed
> ¼ cup fresh lime juice
> ½ cup sugar or equivalent sugar substitute
> 1 lime, zested
> 1-inch piece ginger, cut into coin-sized pieces
> Grated ginger for garnish
>
> WHAT TO DO:
> • Place all ingredients in a blender, and pulse until well blended.
> • Pour the mixture into a shallow dish, and freeze for at least an hour.
> • When frozen, scrape with a fork, and spoon into glasses. Garnish with ginger, and serve.

nutritional benefits. For one thing, it turns out that of all fresh produce they are the top providers of the bright red carotenoid lycopene, a powerful antioxidant. Watermelons also provide vitamin A, important to eye health; vitamin B6, which aids immunity by producing antibodies and supporting white blood cells; vitamin C, which can slow the signs of aging; and potassium, which is useful for relieving muscle cramps.

MUSKMELON

This venerable melon (*Cucumis melo*) is the wellspring of many cultivated varieties, including the smooth-skinned honeydew, the ridged Crenshaw and casaba melons, and the netted cantaloupe, Persian, and Christmas melons. Muskmelons are native to Iran, Anatolia, and the Caucasus and were also found in India and Afghanistan. Muskmelon varieties will cross with others within their species, but not other members of the gourd family. You can eat flavorful muskmelons either fresh or dried.

Health Benefits

Muskmelons are rich in vitamins A, B9, and C, as well as minerals like potassium. They are also packed with fiber and beta-carotene.

Watermelon Ginger Granita is a delicious, healthy, and refreshing homemade Italian dessert for hot summer days.

Crenshaw and casaba melons

CANTALOUPE

These tannish melons with their rough, netted, or reticulated rinds reveal succulent orange flesh and a sweetness that rivals the flavor of peaches. The North American cantaloupe (C. melo var. cantalupo) is another cultivar of the muskmelon that originated in the swath of land that lay between India and Africa. Its name, which comes from the Italian city Cantalupo, a papal county seat near Rome, was bestowed on the melon after its introduction to Italy from Armenia. It became an American commercial crop in the late 1800s and is now the most popular melon in the country. The European cantaloupe appears quite different from its American cousin, with lightly ribbed, gray-green rind, but its flesh is equally as sweet.

Health Benefits

These melons are a good source of vitamins C and A, as well as the beneficial carotenoid beta-carotene. This antioxidant supports mucous membranes, eye health, and immunity. (Health note: Prior to shipping, some cantaloupes are washed in bleach to kill any surface mold or bacteria, like Salmonella. Still, it is wise to scrub a cantaloupe before slicing it to avoid contamination of the interior flesh.)

CASABA MELON

This is another cultivar of the muskmelon. Casaba melons (members of the Inodorus group of C. melo) are ovoid in shape, with a point at the stem end. When ripe, they have a tough yellow rind, which can have greenish markings, that is etched with furrows. The sweet flesh ranges from white to a pale creamy green and offers subtle hints of pear and cucumber. Most weigh in at about five pounds. They are part of the winter melon group, named not for their growing season, but for their hardiness and long shelf life. They were first introduced into the United States from Kasaba, Turkey, in the late 19th century.

They are usually eaten raw or in salads, Pureed, they work in both sweet and savory dishes, especially recipes that include curry, coconut milk, red chilies, and salty cheeses. Like cantaloupes, they should be washed before cutting—the deep grooves can hold dirt and contaminants.

Health Benefits

These melons are a good source of vitamins C and B6 and folate. Their mineral content includes choline, potassium, and magnesium.

CRENSHAW MELON

The Crenshaw is a cross between the casaba melon and the Persian melon. In natural food circles it is considered the "Cadillac of melons" for its succulent sweetness. The exterior is similar to the casaba—ovoid, ridged, and yellowish green, with a pointed end and waxy finish; the tender, slightly spicy flesh is a golden pink in color. When these melons are ripe, the seeds will rattle, the rounded end will become soft, and the aroma should be detectable. Crenshaws can be eaten raw, mixed into salads, or paired with cured meats, cheeses, almonds, lime, and mint.

A SURPRISE CURE

After Alexander Fleming's 1928 discovery that the mold Penicillin notatum inhibited staph germs, the search began for a prolific species of the mold for mass producing the antibiotic. In 1941, a moldy cantaloupe in a Peoria, Illinois, grocery was discovered to contain the highest-yielding strain of the mold, P. chrysogeum, boosting output of the life-saving medicine.

Health Benefits

Crenshaws are low in sodium and fat and contain no cholesterol. They are also an excellent source of vitamins A, B6, and C.

HONEYDEW MELON

These pale, smooth, yellow melons with their celadon green flesh are always welcome on a hot day. The honeydew (another cultivar of *C. melo* in the Inodorus group) is a muskmelon cultivar, part of a French group called White Antibes. It grows in semi-arid conditions and probably originated in Africa or in Persia. The Egyptians considered it a sacred food, and the Romans first spread it through Europe. Columbus carried the seeds with him to the Americas, and today it is found in markets throughout world. A ripe melon will have a noticeably sweet aroma. Unripe melons can be left at room temperature for several days.

Grilling melons caramelizes their natural sugars, releasing their sweetness while adding a tinge of smoky flavor.

PANTRY PICK: *For an unexpected take on these traditional summer fruits, try grilling watermelons, Crenshaws, cantaloupes, casabas, or honeydews. Slice the melons into thick chunks, and then lightly brush both sides with olive oil. Grill over high heat for about five minutes, until grill marks have formed and the flesh has slightly softened. Sprinkle with salt, if desired.*

Health Benefits

Honeydew melons contain high levels of vitamin C—one cup offers a hefty 34 percent of the daily recommended intake. They also provide vitamin B6, the co-enzyme that allows enzymes to activate chemical processes and which helps in the creation of the mood elevator seratonin; potassium, beneficial for the functioning of the heart and blood vessels; and both soluble and insoluble fiber, the former balancing blood sugar levels, the latter keeping food moving through the dietary tract.

PANTRY PICK: *Honeydew pairs especially well with Italian prosciutto and fresh mozzarella cheese for a refreshing midday meal. Slice the melon and the cheese, and wrap a pair of each with a strip of the meat, and then grate black pepper over the plate.*

A melon melange made with honeydew, cantaloupe, and watermelon. This classic dessert or palate cleanser calls for no more than a melon baller. Melons have such rich flavor, they are delicious straight from the rind.

Colorful citrus fruits, including, lemons, limes, oranges, and red and yellow grapefruits

CITRUS FRUIT

SWEET, TART, OR SOUR, THESE JUICY FRUITS OFFER IMPRESSIVE LEVELS OF VITAMIN C

Their sweetly tart pulpy flesh and dimpled rinds set apart citrus from other fruits. They come from flowering trees or shrubs in the *Citrus* genus, part of the Rutaceae family (rue or citrus family). They may have originated in Australia and New Guinea or in Southeast Asia, near northeast India and Burma. The substantial fruits we know today likely evolved over millions of years from small edible berries. Citrus plants were first domesticated in Asia—Alexander the Great brought bitter oranges to southern Europe from India, and lemons reached Italy during the Roman era. The orange trees of Florida, often thought to be native, are the offspring of trees planted by Spanish explorers. The majority of commercial citrus fruits are hybrids, created over the past thousand years from just three species—the mandarin orange *(Citrus reticulata)*, the pomelo *(C. grandis)*, and the citron *(C. medico)*.

The fruit of the citrus tree is a hesperidium, a specialized berry, either globular or elongated, with a leathery rind, or peel. The outer skin is a pericarp known as the flavedo, or zest. Next is the white,

> ### DID YOU KNOW?
>
> *· English sailors on long sea voyages once had little to eat beyond hard biscuits and salted meat. When they began to develop scurvy, a disease caused by a vitamin C deficiency, ships were stocked with limes, known to prevent the disease. As a result, British seaman came to be called limeys.*

spongelike albedo, or pith, and finally there is the endocarp. The fruit's segments, called liths, contain locules filled with juice vesicles, or pulp. Citrus fruits are rich in vitamin C, and organic produce offers even higher levels of the vitamin than commercial crops. Citrus fruits also contain bioactive compounds called flavanones that may reduce the risk of ischemic stroke in women.

Other popular citrus fruits include tangerines, tangelos, bergamot oranges, Israel citrons, bitter oranges—used for marmalades—blood oranges, Buddha's hands, citrons, clementines, desert limes, kaffir limes, finger limes, kumquats, mandarin oranges, Meyer lemons, and ugli fruit.

ORANGE

Citrus x *sinensis*, the common orange, is also called sweet orange. This is to distinguish it from the bitter orange (*C.* x *aurantium*), which is used to produce marmalade. The orange tree is a flowering evergreen that averages 30 feet in height, with oval, crenelated leaves and fragrant white blossoms—a favorite of bees and said to be an aphrodisiac. Sweet orange varieties include the Valencia and the navel orange, cousins include the bergamot orange *(C. bergamia)*, known for flavoring Earl Grey tea, and the blood orange, valued for its bright red pulp. Oranges are the most widely grown fruit trees globally, and account for more than 70 percent of the citrus crop. Brazil, China, and India are the top producers.

Health Benefits

Oranges contain more than 170 phytochemicals and 60 flavonoids and are the ascorbic acid champs—one medium orange supplies 130 percent of the daily vitamin C requirement. They also provide B vitamins, folate, calcium, copper, and potassium.

LEMON

The lemon *(C. limon)* is a small elliptical bright yellow fruit produced by a flowering evergreen tree. Its exact origin is unknown, but it may have developed in or near Assam, in northeast India, Burma, or China. Lemons were popular in ancient Egypt, Greece, and Rome and were used as ornamental trees in Islamic gardens. They were first cultivated in Europe in the mid 1400s and came to the Americas with Columbus. With their bright, tart taste they are used to flavor baked goods, salads, and beverages. They also make effective antiseptic cleansers.

Health Benefits

Lemons are rich in vitamin C, providing 64 percent of the Daily Value (DV) per four-ounce serving, as well as vitamins A and E, B-complex vitamins, calcium, copper, iron, magnesium, potassium, phosphorus, and zinc. They also provide healthful polyphenols, terpenes, and tannins.

LIME

Limes are small green citrus fruits, similar in size to lemons, but with a higher sugar and acid content. Wild limes were first cultivated in Southeast Asia and only transported to Europe and Africa around A.D. 1000. The most common limes in the United States are the Persian lime *(C. x latifolia)*, the key lime *(C. x aurentifolia)*, and the kaffir lime *(C. hystrix)*.

Health Benefits

Limes have high levels of vitamin C. A single lime supplies roughly 35 percent of DV, and it also contains beneficial phytonutrients, such as polyphenols and terpenes, as well as antioxidants, including flavonol glycosides.

GRAPEFRUIT

This large, round tropical fruit *(C. x paradisi)*, with its tart, slightly bitter flavor, originated on Barbados. It grew from an accidental cross between the sweet orange and the pomelo, both introduced from Asia in the 1600s. It was first called forbidden fruit; the common name refers to the way the fruit clusters on the tree, similar to grapes.

Health Benefits

With its combination of fiber, potassium, lycopene, vitamin C (64 percent of DV in a half of a medium-sized grapefruit), vitamin A (28 percent), and choline, this fruit promotes heart health. Some research has shown that eating grapefruit can lower blood lipids, such as triglycerides.

PANTRY PICK: *Combine grapefruit, tangerine, and orange segments in a heat-proof bowl and lightly sprinkle with honey. Place under a broiler until the fruit begins to caramelize. Garnish with mint, and enjoy this dish for breakfast or lunch or as a healthy snack.*

Broil your citrus favorites for a light, healthy side dish.

BANANA AND PLANTAIN

THESE FINGERLIKE FRUITS ARE RICH SOURCES OF NUTRIENTS

Exotic fruits of the tropics, bananas and plantains have fascinated explorers and botanists for centuries. And that was before scientists understood all their health benefits.

These soft, elongated, thick-skinned fruits are produced by plants in the *Musa* genus, especially *Musa acuminata.* Many are hybrids are the cross of *M. acuminata* and *M. balbisiana,* and what we know as green or cooking plantains are this hybrid (usually called *M.* x *paradisiaca).* They grow from underground corms in warm, moist, rainforest conditions. Reaching heights of up to 16 feet, bananas are the largest herbaceous flowering plants. They are tall and sturdy, often mistaken for trees with thick trunks. These are actually false stems, or pseudostems. The large leaves are made up of a stalk (or petiole) and a blade (or lamina). The base of the petiole forms a hollow sheath, and it is a collection of these sheaths that make up the supporting stem. When the plant matures, flower spikes begin to grow inside the pseudostems until they emerge at the top. Each stem produces a single spike, or inflorescence, also called the banana's "heart." The fruit develops from the heart in a large cluster made up of tiers, or hands, with up to 20 "fingers" to a tier. A cluster may contain from 3 to 20 tiers and weigh upward of 100 pounds.

Bananas are native to Indo-Malaya and Australia and were probably first domesticated in the Kuk Valley of New Guinea around 8,000 years ago.

Red bananas

DID YOU KNOW?

• *Bananas are radioactive and more so than any other fruit. This is due to their high levels of potassium— and the presence of an isotope, potassium-40, which is found in naturally occurring potassium. No worries, though: the amount of radioactivity is not cumulative and the principle radioactive component is excreted.*

They dispersed throughout the Asian tropics roughly 2,000 years later and probably reached Africa around 1100 B.C. In the 11th century, Arab traders carried the fruit to Southern Asia and the Middle East, and by the 1200s, the Japanese were using banana fibers for kimono textiles. During the 1500s, Portuguese traders established bananas in Brazil, and they eventually became a major plantation crop throughout South and Central America and the Caribbean.

It's hard to believe, but most bananas grown in the past were red and green, and many varieties required cooking. Then in 1836, Jamaican Jean François Poujot found a banana tree displaying unusual yellow fruit on his plantation. When he tasted the fruit, he realized it was naturally sweet and did not require cooking. These sweet bananas were soon being imported to New Orleans, Boston, and New York as a plated dessert, and they were the hit of the Philadelphia Centennial Exposition in 1876. The Cavendish banana, propagated in the greenhouses of William Cavendish, sixth duke of Devonshire, is another sweet cultivar and the most common variety sold today.

In the Western Hemisphere and Europe, the sweet varieties are referred to as bananas, and the starchier cultivars that require cooking are called plantains. In Southeast Asia and other tropical regions where many more types of bananas are grown—there are almost 1,000 varieties all told—both terms are used interchangeably. Plantains are still cooked or fried as a vegetable and can be used in a manner similar to potatoes. Today, they rank 10th among important staple crops that are used to feed world populations.

Health Benefits

Bananas are 75 percent water and 25 percent dry matter, and they offer the following advantages.

- Bananas are a notable source of potassium—9 percent of the Recommended Daily Intake is found in a medium banana. This mineral is key for controlling high blood pressure, lowering risk of heart disease, and maintaining kidney function.
- As a snack for those watching their weight, bananas are surprisingly filling, plus they contain only about 105 calories and little fat.
- This fruit also provides vitamin C and B6, manganese, magnesium, and folate. It contains the fiber pectin, which may moderate blood sugar levels after meals and help ease the digestive process.
- The antioxidants in bananas include dopamine and catechin, which both scavenge free radicals and help prevent cell damage that can lead to disease or cancer.
- Bananas are beneficial to athletes and workout fans—they can prevent the muscle cramps and soreness caused by sustained exercise.

Green plantains

Plantains also contain potassium, as well as vitamins A and C. They are a superior source of dietary fiber and offer energy-boosting carbohydrates.

PANTRY PICK: *The easiest way to take advantage of the many health benefits of bananas is to slice them on top of homemade granola or hot oatmeal. To use them in fruit salads, sprinkle them with lemon juice to avoid browning. Their creamy texture also makes a perfect base for smoothies. Try an antioxidant Banana-Blueberry Blast by blending a large banana with 1 cup fresh or frozen blueberries, 1 cup coconut water or almond milk, 2 tablespoons rolled oats, and two or three ice cubes.*

Banana-Blueberry Blast. This simple recipe combines the energy-boosting health benefits of bananas with antioxidant blueberries. Creamy bananas are a great way to add texture to just about any kind of smoothie you can concoct.

COCONUT AND POMEGRANATE

THESE TWO POWER FRUITS HAVE JUSTIFIABLY BEEN MAKING HEADLINES

Every once in a while a particular food tickles the public's fancy—witness the craze for a certain brand of gooey donut in the 1990s or fanciful cupcakes in the 2000s—but recently those superstar or trending foods have been of the healthy variety. And two of the most lauded lately are the coconut and the pomegranate. Both are native to India, but these two fruits have little else in common—except for their high levels of nutrients and their current availability in juice form in even the most unhip of grocery stories.

> ### DID YOU KNOW?
>
> • *Immature coconuts, called tender-nuts or jelly-nuts, are harvested for their coconut water, or milk, which is now immensely popular. Consumers need to watch out for brands that add flavorings or sugar, however; their "health drink" might then have nearly the same sugar content as a can of soda.*

COCONUT

Coconuts are extremely versatile—utilized for food, beverages, cooking oil, fuel, ropes, matting, cosmetics, and fragrances—and they have recently become the new darlings of natural food advocates. The coconut tree (*Cocos nucifera*) is a member of the Aracaceae, or palm family. Coconuts likely originated in India and Indonesia and were dispersed by floating on ocean currents. The palm reaches a height of 100 feet and produces long (12 to 20 feet) pinnate leaves called fronds. The inflorescences display flowers of both sexes, with the female dwarfing the male. These flowers produce three-pound, hard-shelled fruits—up to 75 annually—that are technically drupes, not nuts. The husk consists of the exocarp, the leathery skin; the mesocarp, a thick layer of fibrous pulp called coir, which has both traditional and commercial uses; and the endocarp, the hard brown shell. The fruit's name comes from the Spanish and Portuguese word *coco*, meaning "head" or "skull"—because the three indentations on the endocarp form a pattern resembling a face. The white, fibrous coconut meat that lines the shell has a naturally sweet, rich flavor. When dried, the flesh is called copra, and it remains a dietary staple for many cultures, as well as a cash crop that was once greatly sought after.

Health Benefits

Coconut meat is packed with nutrients: it contains 17 out of the 20 essential amino acids required for forming protein, especially threonine, which supports the production of collagen—necessary for building connective tissue. The fruit also provides dietary iron for muscle health and is a terrific source of fiber, which can help reduce abdominal fat and boost metabolism, creating a thermogenic effect that increases calorie burn. The meat actually contains more fiber per serving than bran or any other grain. Both the meat and the milk are high in folate, the B vitamin that supports red blood cells; potassium, which helps reduce high blood pressure and bloating; and calcium, the builder of bones. Another plus: the medium-chain fatty acids in a coconut's saturated fats are actually beneficial to humans.

PANTRY PICK: *Coconut is delicious raw. Shred some over your morning cereal, a fruit salad, or nutty snack mixes. Add a handful to a smoothie to increase its oomph, or blend ¼ cup into yogurt.*

Coconut drinks may be hogging the health spotlight these days, but the meat is also loaded with nutrients.

Start your day with a power breakfast of berry yogurt topped with pomegranates, raspberries, coconut, and granola.

POMEGRANATE

This slightly awkward fruit—with its inaccessible ruby-red seeds—was once relegated to the "oddities" section of the produce aisle, along with okra and plantain. But pomegranates are finally having their day, and it is a well-deserved turnabout.

The pomegranate *(Punica granatum),* which comes from a small deciduous shrub or a tallish tree, is a member of the Lythraceae (loosestrife family). The plant produces multiple spiny branches and bright red flowers, along with a berry sized between an orange and a grapefruit. This berry consists of a leathery exocarp, with rows of succulent, sweet-tart seeds packed like sardines within. (The secret to removing them is to score the pod in four equally spaced longitudes, then peel back the skin to reveal the fruit.)

The plant is native to—and continues to be cultivated in—the Mediterranean, Middle East, and northern India. Pomegranates arrived in China along the Silk Roads and via sea merchants. The venerable Spanish city of Granada was named for the pomegranate by the occupying Moors, and it was

the Spaniards who introduced the fruit to the New World in the 1500s. Today it is grown in many regions globally and remains under cultivation in California and Arizona. The late 20th century saw an increase in the fruit's market visibility in Europe and the United States, which possibly lead to the juice's current surge in popularity.

Health Benefits

Pomegranates have been medicinal plants since ancient times; health claims for the fruit include combating heart disease, high blood pressure, inflammation, and certain cancers. They are also considered to possess antiviral and antitumor properties. They are a good source of vitamins A, C, and E and folic acid, and they are loaded with antioxidants—including flavonoids (three times the number found in green tea). These may help prevent the oxidation of LDL, or bad cholesterol.

Pomegranate can be ingested as fresh seeds, or as a syrup, paste, nectar, or concentrate. Tea made from the peel can ease an upset stomach or diarrhea.

The now-familiar pineapple was once prized as a hothouse rarity. We now appreciate it for its many nutritional benefits.

TROPICAL FRUIT

THESE EXOTIC BEAUTIES ARE RICH IN VITAMINS AND ANTIOXIDANTS

To European explorers used to their familiar apples and pears—and perhaps an occasional orange—the colorful, succulent, sweet-tasting fruits of the tropics must have seemed otherworldly. Imagine biting into a juicy slice of pineapple for the first time, or sampling the complex flavors of mango and papaya or the melting texture of kiwi. These once-exotic fruits, long prized by their own cultures, are now available at most Western supermarkets, along with lesser-known varieties like lychee, ugli fruit, and dragon fruit.

DID YOU KNOW?

• *Durian* (Durio zibethinus), *a large Southeast Asian fruit with a spiky rind, has been described as the "stinkiest fruit on earth." When opened, it has a custardlike texture, but the fruit's stench is so foul that there are laws in several countries against bringing durian onto public transport or into hotels.*

PINEAPPLE

The pineapple (*Ananas comosus*) is the most commercially significant member of the Bromeliaceae family. The large, conical pineapple is actually a multiple fruit made up of coalesced berries. It grows upright from a stocky plant with sharp, leathery leaves, whirled around a single stem and displays spiky deep pink flowers. The plant originated between southern Brazil and Paraguay but soon spread across South America and Central America. The Maya and Aztecs both cultivated it, and Columbus called it the "pine of the

Indies." European aristocrats outdid each other building greenhouses to cultivate the rare fruit, and specimens were often set out only for display. This was when pineapples became the symbol of hospitality—you really honored a guest if you actually served one. When English nurseryman John Kidwell introduced pineapples to Hawaii, they begat a transformative industry on those small islands. Large-scale cultivation by Dole and Del Monte was underway by the early 1900s, and at one time Hawaii was synonymous with sunshine, surfing, volcanoes, and pineapples. Today, however, Costa Rica is the top exporter.

Pineapples are eaten raw, grilled, stir-fried, and baked and can be used in sweet or savory dishes. The are commercially dried, juiced, and used in preserves. In the Philippines, the tough leaves are used to produce the fabric piña and wallpaper.

Health Benefits

Pineapples are like wellness "bombs"—they provide high levels of antioxidants, such as vitamin C and beta-carotene, as well as vitamin B6, thiamine, folate, potassium, copper, manganese, calcium, magnesium, and fiber. This potent combination of nutrients can help lower the risk of macular degeneration of the eyes, reduce inflammation of joints, help to heal wounds, protect the body from infections, lower the risk of cognitive disorders like dementia, ease digestion, and reduce the risk of cancer, heart disease, and arthritis. The fruit's high fiber and water content makes it effective for preventing constipation. Even though the juice is acidic, there is some indication that it has an alkalizing effect in the stomach, which may benefit those with acid reflux disease

Pineapples also contain a group of enzymes called bromelain that are associated with the breakdown of complex proteins. (Thus the sore-mouth feeling some people get after eating the fruit.) It also makes pineapple juice excellent as a marinade and meat tenderizer. Bromelain may possess anti-inflammatory and anticancer properties and is used to reduce swelling of arthritic joints and aching muscles.

A smoothie bowl made with a nutritious blend of mango and kiwi topped with almonds, coconut, and chia seeds.

PANTRY PICK: *Make Tropical Pops by blending 3 cups chopped pineapple, ⅓ cup milk, and 3 tablespoons honey, and then freezing the mixture in Popsicle molds.*

MANGO

The mango seems to whisper of tropic isles and exotic vistas. It is a stone fruit, or drupe, produced by a number of tall, flowering trees in the Anacardiaceae family. These trees are native to South Asia, where most species grow wild, but after the common or Indian mango (*Mangifera indica*) was domesticated, cultivation spread to many tropical regions. India and China are the current top exporters.

There are now hundreds of mango cultivars—often several are grown together for better pollination. The top cultivar at the moment is Tommy Atkins, a seedling of Haden, which first fruited in Florida in the 1940s and was rejected by agricultural researchers.

Mangoes

In the end, its high productivity, disease resistance, shelf life, size, and appealing color won out.

Mangoes have a smooth peel, which can be yellow, orange, red, or green, depending on the cultivar, and soft, sweet flesh that has been compared to a ripe plum in taste. They are used in many cuisines, from Mexican salsa to Indian chutney, and are often eaten green. The mango is the national fruit of India, Pakistan, and the Philippines and the national tree of Bangladesh.

Health Benefits

Mangoes offer high levels of fiber, pectin, and vitamin C that all work to lower levels of LDL cholesterol. Its antioxidants can protect the body against a colon, breast, and prostate cancers and leukemia. Eating one cup of diced mango supplies 25 percent of the Daily Value of vitamin A, so necessary for eye health. The fruit also helps to retain the body's alkali reserves by supplying tartaric acid, malic acid, and citric acid.

PANTRY PICK: *To make a mango lassi, a popular South Asian beverage, combine 1 cup chopped ripe mango with 1 cup plain yogurt, ½ water, and 4 teaspoons honey. Blend, and top with a dash of ground cardamom. For a healthy breakfast or light summer meal, try a mango-kiwi smoothie bowl. Freeze 2 cups of chopped mango and 1 cup of chopped, skinned kiwi. Blend with 2 tablespoons honey and ⅔ cup ice. Top with shaved coconut, almonds, chia seeds, and kiwi and mango chunks.*

The ingredients for the classic Indian beverage called a mango lassi: mango, yogurt, honey, and cardamom

A seed-filled sliced papaya

PAPAYA

A member of the Caricaceae family, the papaya (*Carica papaya*) is native to the South American tropics. It has naturalized in Florida, the Caribbean, and several countries in Africa. This fruit is also known as pawpaw or papaw, and Columbus called it the "fruit of the angels." The tree is sparse, typically single stemmed, and grows from 15 to 33 feet in height. It bears large, deeply palmate leaves and graceful white or yellow flowers. These can be male, female, or hermaphroditic. Most commercially grown papayas fall into the latter category. The flowers, which have a sweet fruity fragrance, open at night and are pollinated by moths. The fruit is actually a large berry that ranges from 6 to 18 inches in length; its skin goes from green to orange while ripening.

Ripe papayas are typically peeled and eaten raw; the unripe fruit is cooked in curries and stews or added to salads—cooking is necessary because the unripe fruit has high levels of latex. Papayas are ready to eat when the skin softens to the consistency of a ripe avocado and turns orange or amber. The fruit is a popular ingredient in Thai and Indonesian cooking, and it ranks fourth in worldwide tropical fruit production, behind bananas, oranges, and mangoes. In the United States, dried, crystallized papaya in bulk packs is sold as a health food, but like all glacé fruits, it is high in sugar. Look for dried unsweetened brands.

Health Benefits

Papayas are high in water and fiber, promoting good bowel health. They are an outstanding source of vitamin C—157 percent of the recommended Daily Value—and also contain vitamin A, folate, and potassium. The antioxidants in papayas, including the carotenoid lycopene, are better absorbed than in any other fruit or vegetable. Research indicates that fermented papaya extract can reduce the oxidative damage to DNA that causes cancer and loss of cognitive function. The fruit also contains the enzyme papain, which aids the digestive process. It breaks down the tough protein chains found in muscle meat, making papaya an excellent meat tenderizer.

KIWI

Named for New Zealand's famous flightless bird, this small, brown fuzzy fruit with its luscious green flesh was once called Chinese gooseberry. The climbing, woody kiwi vine (*Actinidia deliciosa*), which produces an egg-sized berry with a unique flavor, is native to China, where the fruit was harvested in the wild. It was New Zealand that began the first commercial plantings in the early 20th century. Today, kiwi is a favorite addition to salads, fruit bowls, and smoothies.

Health Benefits

Kiwis are rich in vitamin K and also offer carotenoids like provitamin A beta-carotene and lutein, as well as omega-3 fatty acids. It is a star when it comes to vitamin C: one kiwi supplies 106 percent of the recommended Daily Value. Its dietary fiber is partly found in the edible skin, which is often discarded.

> PANTRY PICK: *Wow guests with this stunning—and healthy—dessert. Halve dragon fruits, chopping the flesh into bite-sized chunks. Fill the halved skins with chunks of mango, kiwi, starfruit, and papaya, and serve.*

OTHER EXOTICS

How many times have you walked past some odd-looking fruit at the supermarket aisle and wondered what it tasted like? Don't be intimidated—most of these exotics are tasty and nutritious.

DRAGON FRUIT Native to the Americas, dragon fruit, or pitahaya, grows on the *Hylocereus undatus* cactus known as the Honolulu Queen. The fruit's skin is bright red with green scales—hence the name. The flesh is sweet and can be sliced and eaten or peeled first. Dragon fruit is a good source of vitamin C, fiber, and iron and provides several types of antioxidants, including flavonoids. Try it with Greek yogurt.

An exotic fruit salad made with kiwi, papaya, starfruit, mango, and dragon fruit served in dragon fruit bowls

UGLI FRUIT A variety of tangelo, ugli fruit (*Citrus reticulata* × *C. paradisi*) was discovered growing wild in Jamaica. The name comes from the unsightly greenish orange rind, which is wrinkled and loose. The taste is sweet, tending toward the tangerine. It offers anti-inflammatory, anticarcinogenic, antiviral, and anti-allergic effects and high levels of vitamins C and A and fiber, as well as 4,000 polyphenols and 60 flavonoids.

LYCHEE Native to China, lychee (*Litchi chinensis*), is often served as a dessert fruit in Chinese restaurants. The fruit is borne by a tall, tropical evergreen tree, which is the only member of the genus in the Sapindaceae. The fruit has a bumpy red or orange peel with a sweet, pale fleshy interior. The fruit's perfumelike scent is often lost in canning. Lychee provides high levels of vitamin C and B vitamins, as well as potassium, thiamine, folate, and copper.

STARFRUIT (*Averrhoa carambola*) comes from a tree native to Southeast Asia and the South Pacific. It gets its name from its distinctive shape—usually five ridges running down its sides that when cut in cross-section resembles a star. The entire fruit is edible and is rich in antioxidants, potassium, and vitamin C.

LEGUMES

THESE BENEFICIAL PLANTS OFFER HIGH LEVELS OF FIBER, PROTEIN, AND ANTIOXIDANTS

These are plants that truly give back. Among the many benefits of legumes is their ability to return much-needed nitrogen to the soil. Technically, legumes are simple fruits, developing from a simple carpel, or pod, that opens along one or both sides. They are part of the pea or bean family (Leguminosae), which is the most numerous group of plants in the rain forests and dry forests of North America, South America, and Africa. Edible legumes probably originated in the Himalayan foothills of Afghanistan, but they are now cultivated all over the world.

Many legumes contain a mechanism for nitrogen production—symbiotic bacteria called *Rhizobia*, which are found in the nodules of their roots. *Rhizobia* supply vital nitrogen to the plants as they grow, and once their reproductive cycle is completed, that nitrogen returns to the earth as the plants decompose. Legumes typically grow as vines or form

> **DID YOU KNOW?**
>
> • *Farmers have learned to rotate crops to different fields each year so that the same crop is not grown over and over in one location. This is important for pest control and because it allows the planting of legumes, like alfalfa or clover, that will return nitrogen to depleted soil.*

bushes. Most feature a distinctive papilionaceous, or butterflylike, flower with five parts: an upper lobed standard, two wings, and two lower conjoined petals called the keel.

There are more than 11,000 species of legumes, and cultivated varieties are classified as forage, grain, blooms, pharmaceutical/industrial crops, fallow/green manure crops, and timber species. Grains that are grown for their dried seeds and used to feed humans and animals are also called pulses. These include beans, peas, soybeans, lentils, peanuts, and lupines.

Nutritionally, legumes offer high levels of protein, fiber, and dietary minerals. They are also a good source of resistant starch, which is broken down by bacteria in the large intestine, producing the short-chain fatty acids that are utilized by the intestinal cells for food energy. Vegetarian meals containing legumes are currently being studied for their potential to reduce or prevent metabolic syndrome, a cluster of conditions that can include obesity, high blood pressure, high triglycerides, and low HDL cholesterol. Research indicates that consuming one cup of pulses daily may reduce blood pressure and control cholesterol levels.

BEANS

Edible beans are divided into dry beans, which are represented by the genera *Phaseolus* and *Vigna* and dry broad beans, or fava beans, genus *Vicia*. Beans were a very early food source for humans—they were grown in Thailand at least 9,000 years ago, and in the Americas, cultivated remains have been found in a Peruvian cave dating back to 2000 B.C. The leading producers of dry beans today are Burma, India, and Brazil. Following are some edible legumes that should become part of your balanced diet.

The bloom of the scarlet runner bean, which is grown both as a food source and as an ornamental plant. *Phaseolus* blooms are noted for their attractive butterfly shape.

KIDNEY BEANS These substantial beans, a variety of the common bean *(P. vulgaris),* originated in Mexico but are found in many types of cuisine. They come in a range of colors, especially dark red, and are full of nutrients, but are toxic when raw.

PINTO BEANS These speckled beans are cousins of red kidney beans. They are Southwestern favorites and the hardy basis of chilies and refried beans. Like any bean that is purchased dried, they need to be soaked overnight in a large pot of water before using in recipes.

BLACK BEANS Another variety of the common bean *(P. vulgaris),* black beans are known for their creamy texture and are sold either canned or dried. They make an excellent salsa ingredient and go well with crunchy corn in burrito fillings and vegetarian soups.

NAVY BEANS Also known as also known as Boston beans, haricots, pearl haricot beans, and white pea beans, small white navy beans were so named because they were a staple for shipbound seamen. This variety of the common bean *(P. vulgaris)* is the source of canned pork and beans and can also be used in salads, stews, soups, and casseroles.

CHICKPEAS These pale amber beans, also called garbanzo beans *(Cicer arietinum),* are statistically the most consumed beans in the world. They are native to the Middle East, where they feature in many regional dishes. Chickpeas can be used in salads or soups, formed into balls called falafel and served fried inside pita or mixed with sesame paste (tahini), lemon juice, and garlic to make hummus, an increasingly popular dip.

LIMA BEANS Also known as butter beans, pale limas *(P. lunatus)* likely originated in Guatemala; they are sold fresh, frozen, or dried. They are impressively high in fiber—53 percent of the DV—and can boost colon health and reduce LDL cholesterol levels.

DRY BROAD BEANS Also known as fava beans, dry broad beans *(Vicia faba),* have been found in early human settlements and were first cultivated in the Middle East more than 8,000 years ago. They are eaten while young and tender and are popular in France, China, Latin America, and southern Asia.

BLACK-EYED PEAS This soul food staple is a subspecies of the cowpea *(Vigna unguiculata).* It was first introduced to American South as early as the 17th century. There are many varieties, ranging in size from small to large, They are pale with a distinctive eye (usually black). They contain calcium, protein, fiber, vitamin A, and other nutrients.

MAKE IT YOURSELF
New Age Three-Bean Salad

Both this twist on a three-bean salad and its herbal vinaigrette are bursting with nutrients and antioxidants.

YOU WILL NEED:
1 15-ounce can each of chickpeas, black beans, and red kidney beans, drained and rinsed
two stalks celery, chopped fine
½ onion, chopped fine
3 tablespoons olive oil
⅓ cup apple cider vinegar
2 tablespoons honey
1 sprig fresh rosemary, chopped
¼ teaspoon black pepper; salt to taste

WHAT TO DO:
• Mix together beans, celery, and onion.
• Whisk together the remaining ingredients, and drizzle over beans.
• Refrigerate for 12 hours before serving.

Also included with the beans, are the bush beans and pole beans. These types of runner beans are the unripened fruit and protective pods of various cultivars of the common bean *(P. vulgaris)*. They are better known as green beans or string beans, those limp canned beans that often get made into winter casseroles. Fresh green beans are a whole other experience—steam them for ultimate flavor and to preserve their color. Young green beans are also wonderful added to salads, for extra snap.

Green beans, also known as string beans

Health Benefits

Beans are power-packed with nutrients—high in fiber, protein, and antioxidants. They are also low in fat. When eaten daily, they can help prevent heart disease, regulate blood sugar levels, reduce the risk of birth defects, and help control weight. These highly versatile legumes are also easy to grow, even in a small garden. Pole beans, in particular, like to sprout up, rather than out.

Try a pesto variation made with tender pea shoots, spring onion, and walnuts early in spring when the pea plant's leaves are tender and flavorful—and full of antioxidants.

PEAS

The pea *(Pisum sativum)* is also known as the green pea, common pea, garden pea, or field pea. It is an annual that may be a low-growing plant or form climbing vines. The distinctive butterfly-shaped flowers—usually white to purple—mature into pods that contain small, round, seeds. Both immature pea seeds and the young pods of snow peas are eaten as vegetables. Archaeological evidence found in the Fertile Crescent suggests that humans have been cultivating these little vegetables since 8000 B.C., and early pea plants were found in the Mediterranean region that date back around 4,000 years. A species called field peas is used to produce the dried split peas used in soups, which were a staple of medieval cooking. Eating young fresh peas is a more modern culinary convention.

Health Benefits

Peas are rich in fiber, protein, vitamins A, B6, C, and K and phosphorus, magnesium, copper, iron, zinc, and lutein, but they can also be starchy. Although their peptides have less ability to banish free radicals than some other plants, they are able to chelate—remove—heavy metals or other toxins from the body.

PANTRY PICK: *For a fresh take on classic pesto, in early spring, pluck the leaves or shoots of the garden pea plant to replace the traditional basil. Coarsely chop about 4 ounces of the pea greens, and place in a blender or food processor with 1 clove garlic and 2 spring onion bulbs, ⅓ cup walnuts, ¼ cup extra virgin olive oil, ½ cup finely grated Parmesan, 3 tablespoons fresh lime juice, and a pinch of sea salt. Cover, and pulse until combined.*

Five types of lentils (from left to right): yellow, red, and brown. At top are black belugas and, at bottom, green lentils.

SOYBEANS

The soybean *(Glycine max)* is an edible legume that is native to East Asia. It is classified as an oilseed rather than a pulse. This low-lying green plant grows to about five feet in height and displays small white, pink, or purple self-fertile flowers that mature into hairy pods with two to four seeds. Soybeans can be black, blue, brown, yellow, or green in color. Edamame is a variety of soybean that is less oily and more tender than traditional soybeans; it is easy to grow and adds texture to hot or cold dishes. Soy meal is used as an inexpensive source of protein in animal feed and packaged foods, like dairy substitutes. The main soybean producers are the United States, Brazil, and Argentina.

Health Benefits

Soybeans are an excellent source of protein—they contain more protein per acre than any other crop—as well as calcium, iron, molybdenum, and copper. They also provide B vitamins, manganese, and phosphorus, along with omega-3 fatty acids, fiber, magnesium, and vitamin K. They can help boost metabolism, support bone and heart health, address digestive issues, improve circulation, and act as a general tonic. Soy is the source of soy milk, which is used to produce tofu. Unfortunately, as much as 90 percent of the current U.S. crop is genetically modified, meaning soybeans may present health and environmental risks.

LENTILS

These hardy, earthy legumes seem perfect in warming winter dishes, but they also make great additions to salads and summer recipes. The lentil *(Lens culinaris)* is a bushy annual plant that reaches 16 inches in height. The plants are native to the Near East, and their cultivation goes back to early human settlements from 9,500 to 13,000 years ago. The lens-shaped seeds can be red-orange, green, yellow, and black. Often eaten with rice, they are a dietary staple throughout India, Nepal, Pakistan, and Bangladesh. The top world producers are Canada, India, and Australia.

Health Benefits

Lentils are good sources of potassium, phosphorus, calcium zinc, niacin, and vitamins B6 and K. They also have the second-highest ratio of protein per calorie after soybeans. Their high levels of slowly digestible starch can make them valuable for those suffering from diabetes.

Up Close
THE TOFU QUESTION
IS VERSATILE, LOW-FAT BEAN CURD REALLY THE ANSWER TO A VEGAN'S PRAYER?

Blocks of tofu and tempeh. Both are made from soy, but tofu comes from soy milk and tempeh from soybeans.

Once the natural food movement—and the vegetarian and vegan lifestyle—had firmly caught on in the late 20th century, savvy consumers went looking for a product around which they could build healthy meals. They discovered a low-fat, meatless protein that was first made more than 2,000 years ago during the Chinese Han dynasty, a white, cheeselike substance that soaks up the flavors of anything it is cooked with—a food called tofu.

Tofu, or bean curd, is made from soy milk, which is processed from soybeans *(Glycine max)*, a legume in the pea family. The milk is coagulated using a chemical agent, creating curds that are then pressed into rectangular white cakes. These can be soft, firm, or extra firm in texture. The chemical coagulants used are salts, like calcium sulfate, calcium chloride, or magnesium chloride; acids; or enzymes. Salts result in a tender tofu that can be brittle, and acids produce a silken, almost gelatinous tofu. To achieve a firm or extra-firm tofu, the cakes are pressed through cheesecloth to remove excess moisture.

Tofu has long been a staple of Asian cuisine. The production method was introduced to Korea and Japan in the 8th century and possibly found its way to Vietnam in the 11th century. Benjamin Franklin even sampled tofu, writing of a "Chinese cheese" he'd eaten in London. The name comes from the

Japanese *tofu,* by way of the Chinese *tou-fu* or *doufu,* meaning "curdled bean." The spread of tofu through Asia coincided with the rise of Buddhism—with the religion's restrictions against eating meat, tofu, with its high protein content and meaty texture, became a welcome substitute.

The tofu sold in the United States is intentionally bland—a blank slate that a cook can embellish; Asian consumers prefer a more traditional beanlike taste. Tofu may be included in both sweet and savory dishes and can be eaten raw, stewed, fried, stir-fried, added to salads, or stuffed. When marinated like meat, it will absorb the flavors of herbs, spices, and sauces.

The Pros and Cons

In traditional Chinese medicine, tofu is considered to have cooling properties that can invigorate the spleen, restore *qi* (life force), and detoxify the body.

Sautéed Tofu Curry makes a hearty vegan main dish.

Nutritionally, it is low in calories and high in protein and iron. It contains all eight essential amino acids and impressive amounts of manganese, selenium, and phosphorus, as well as vitamin B1, copper, and zinc. Depending on the salts used for curdling, it can be a good source of either calcium or magnesium.

Tofu was embraced wholeheartedly by health-conscious Westerners, but some recent research has been unsettling. Soy, the basis of the soy milk used to create tofu, is one of the most commonly genetically modified foods in the world—up to 90 percent of the U.S. crop is GMO. These altered foods can kill the beneficial bacteria in the gut and cause liver and kidney problems. Soy also contains phytoestrogens, which can block normal production of estrogen and has been linked to breast cancer. It can also impact thyroid function, and it contains a number of antinutrients that may interfere with digestion, cause kidney stones and leaky gut syndrome, and block mineral absorption. It has also been linked with the development of cognitive problems. The solution is to limit intake of regular forms of tofu and concentrate on fermented tofu products like natto and tempeh, which do not cause the same negative effects.

MAKE IT YOURSELF
Sautéed Tofu Curry

Indian cooks incorporate tofu so skillfully, it's hard to believe they are not using meat. This vegetarian curry also features an array of beneficial herbs ands spices.

YOU WILL NEED:
2 tablespoons olive oil
1 tablespoon sesame oil
1 cake extra-firm tofu, cubed
½ small onion, chopped
⅓ teaspoon turmeric
¼ teaspoon chili powder
1 teaspoon each of coriander powder, cumin powder, and garam masala
1 clove garlic, minced
1 small tomato, chopped
1 sprig cilantro, chopped
1 tablespoon sesame seeds

WHAT TO DO:
• Heat oil in a nonstick fry pan, and sauté tofu until firm and slightly browned, about 20 minutes, and then set aside.
• Add onions to pan, and cook over medium heat until translucent; add garlic and spices, stir well, add tomato, and heat for about two minutes.
• Return tofu to pan, and heat until tofu is coated with the spice mixture.
• Top with cilantro, sesame, and lime juice.

A variety of crucifers: white cabbage, cauliflower, kohlrabi, brussels sprouts, Savoy cabbage, red cabbage, and broccoli

CRUCIFERS

THESE CRISP CABBAGE COUSINS ARE NUTRITIONAL POWERHOUSES

Cruciferous vegetables are so named because the flowers of these plants display four equal-sized petals—creating a crosslike or crucifix shape. This inspired the former family name, Cruciferae, but scientists recently agreed on the name Brassicaceae (mustard or cabbage family). These vegetables are also called "cole crops," as in cole slaw. This goes back to the Latin *caulis,* referring to the stalk of the cabbage plant.

There are also two scientific groupings within the family—*Brassica oleracea,* a species that includes broccoli, brussels sprouts, cabbage, cauliflower, collards, and kale; and *Brassica rapa,* the species that includes turnips and Chinese cabbage. Both species represent a major cross-section of healthy and incredibly flavorful produce.

DID YOU KNOW?

• *During the Middle Ages, when children wanted to celebrate All Soul's Eve, or Halloween, they carved faces into turnips and used them as lanterns as they roamed about wearing hideous masks—all in an attempt to scare off evil spirits. In Scotland, the carved turnips were called tumshie heads.*

Most crucifers possess a similarly stellar nutritional profile—among all vegetables, they offer the highest levels of vitamin A, vitamin C, folic acid, and fiber. Their vitamin K content has been studied intensively with regard to their anti-inflammatory and anticancer properties. Studies cite their impressive antioxidant potential to lower the risk for several types of cancer. They also offer a substantial amount of protein. Their omega-3 fat content is not as notable, but it is in the form of alpha-linolenic acid (ALA), which is the building block for other types of omega-3 in the body. These vegetables also contain more than 100 glucosinolates—phytonutrients that can lower the risk of certain cancers. To get the most of their many nutrients, eat cruciferous veggies raw and within a few days of being picked.

CABBAGE

Also known as headed cabbage, these leafy, densely layered annual vegetables comprise several cultivars of *Brassica oleracea*. They can be green, purple, or white in color and feature flat, curly, or crimped leaves—like those found in the Savoy cultivar. Cabbages were domesticated in Europe some time around 1000 B.C.—with selective breeding of the many varieties of wild *B. oleracea* occurring contemporaneously—and by the Middle Ages they were a garden staple. As they are today, cabbages were eaten raw, stewed, steamed, and pickled and fermented to make sauerkraut.

Health Benefits

Cabbage offers a rich source of vitamins C and K, plus moderate amounts of vitamin B6 and folate. Its phytochemicals may have an effect on several cancers, including colon cancer. Purple cabbage contains anthocyanins, which are also being researched for their anticarcinogenic properties.

BRUSSELS SPROUTS

Love them or hate them, there is no denying these small cabbagelike veggies have a powerful flavor. They are members of the Gemmifera group of *B. oleracea* and are cultivated for their edible flower buds. Likely first grown in Italy during the Roman Empire, they traveled to the New World with farmers in the 1800s. Modern chefs have adopted them as a "vegetable of the moment" and now roast, grill, or sauté them to accompany special dishes.

Health Benefits

Brussels sprouts contain impressive amounts of vitamin K and C and are a good source of fiber, vitamins A and B6, thiamine, folate, potassium, manganese, copper, calcium, and iron.

BROCCOLI AND CAULIFLOWER

A sturdy green vegetable, broccoli is part of the Italica cultivar group of the *B. oleracea* species. It displays large flower heads branching out from a thick, edible stalk. The plant began to be selectively cultivated round 600 B.C. in the Mediterranean region. A favorite of the Romans, it still plays a prominent part in Italian cuisine. It was brought to England from Belgium in the mid 1700s and came to America with early immigrants from southern Italy. Even though Thomas Jefferson cultivated the plant, broccoli did not become widely accepted in the United States until the 1920s.

Cauliflower is similar in appearance to broccoli, with its rounded head and thick stalk, but it is part of the Botrytis cultivar group. Unlike broccoli, with its edible flower buds, the edible portion consists of a white inflorescence meristem. Crossbreeding naturally occurring plants that hold more beta-carotene resulted in a vibrant array of cauliflower available in green (also known as broccoflower), purple, and orange varieties.

Cauliflower dates back to ancient Rome, where Pliny praised its flavor; 12th-century Arab writings indicate origins in Cyprus. It was introduced to France in the 1500s but only became popular in the 1600s, during the reign of Louis XIV. In 1822, the English brought it to India, and it was quickly assimilated into that country's vegetable-based cuisine.

Cauliflower cultivars are now bred in vibrant colors.

Health Benefits

Broccoli was in the vanguard of the healthy-eating revolution of the 1980s—and is still considered the crown jewel of nutritious vegetables. One cup of cooked broccoli contains the vitamin C of an orange and has only 44 calories. It also provides vitamins B1, B2, B3, and B6, calcium, iron, thiamine, riboflavin, niacin, and chromium. The darker blue-green or purplish florets contain more beta-carotene and vitamin C than the lighter-hued ones.

Cauliflower is high in vitamin C and offers moderate levels of B vitamins and vitamin K, manganese, phosphorus, potassium, and magnesium. It does contain several potent phytonutrients, but boiling can destroy up to 30 percent of their value. Opt for steaming, microwaving, or stir-frying. The colored varieties contain about 25 percent more vitamin A than the white.

KALE AND COLLARD GREENS

Also called leaf cabbage, kale recently took the natural health community by storm due to its extreme levels of vitamin K and powerful antioxidants. This sturdy, winter-hardy green or purple leaf vegetable goes back to ancient Greece, where it was both a food and a digestive medicine. By the Middle Ages, it was a cold-weather vegetable staple. There are several cultivars distinguished by their leaf type—curly, bumpy, plain, rape, or leaf and

Get the health benefits of crucifers by layering avocados, kale, and sliced radishes over nutty whole-grain toast.

spear. Kale's tender new leaves are mixed into salads, while older leaves can be used in stir-fries or soups.

Collard greens are similar to turnip greens and are native to the Mediterranean region. They have become part of American Southern cooking and are often steamed, which is the best way ensure their nutrients remain intact.

Health Benefits

Kale provides mega levels of vitamin K, as well as impressive amounts of protein, iron, and calcium. It contains antioxidants like beta-carotene, lutein, and retinol and is an excellent source of omega-3 fatty acids. Collard greens exceed the daily requirement for vitamins A and K and provide nearly 50 percent of vitamin C, as well as folate, calcium, iron, manganese, vitamin B6, magnesium, and riboflavin. They are also able to lower cholesterol levels.

PANTRY PICK: *To steam kale or collard greens, first swish them in water to remove any dirt. Add them to a steamer basket, and place inside a pot with boiling water that barely reaches the basket. Cook for 5 to 7 minutes. Greens should be wilted but still vibrant in color.*

RADISH

These crunchy, peppery root vegetables resemble small, red turnips. Radishes (*Raphanus sativa*) possibly originated in Southeast Asia, where wild forms still exist, and were first cultivated in Europe during pre-Roman times. Those early radishes were black, but displayed a number of sizes, shapes, and levels of heat. Radishes are typically eaten raw in salads or used as a garnish. They make excellent companion plants in the garden—their strong odor repels insect pests like aphids, cucumber beetles, tomato hornworms, and ants. Daikon, a large, mild Asian oilseed radish that is part of Japanese cuisine, has been making its way into Western kitchens.

Health benefits

Radishes contain high levels of vitamin C, as well as folate, fiber, riboflavin, potassium, copper, vitamin B6, magnesium, manganese, and calcium. They have antibacterial, antifungal, and detoxifying properties and can ease respiratory problems, help regulate blood pressure, and inhibit damage to red blood cells. They store best in a plastic bag with a damp paper towel at the bottom.

ARUGULA

This tangy, leafy lettuce lookalike *(Eruca sativa)* is called rocket in Europe. With the advent of the "salad culture" of the 1990s, when iceberg lettuce was supplanted by less-familiar leaf vegetables, arugula soon became a favorite. The plant originated in the Mediterranean, where the early Romans cultivated it as an herb—and an aphrodisiac, which later kept medieval monks from growing it.

Health Benefits

Low-calorie arugula is among the 10 most nutrient-dense foods. It provides beta carotene, lutein, and zeaxanthin for eye health, as well as vitamins K and C, folate, and iron. Its potassium, magnesium, and calcium promote cardiovascular health, and its flavonoids may hold a key to preventing cancer and diabetes.

> PANTRY PICK: *For a quick and nutritious summer meal, toss fresh arugula, quartered plum tomatoes, and broccoli florets with elbow pasta and a bit of olive oil.*

TURNIP, BOK CHOY, AND RUTABAGA

The turnip *(Brassica rapa* var. *rapa),* or white turnip, is a root vegetable cultivated in temperate climates that originated around 4,000 years ago in central and eastern Asia. Turnips are the swollen storage roots of the plant and located above the taproot. They are white below the soil and red above, where they receive sunlight. The leaves grow directly from the

Pasta with arugula, broccoli, and tomatoes

root's exposed "shoulders" and are eaten as turnip greens, similar in taste to their cousins collard greens.

A deep green, leafy Asian vegetable called bok choy or Chinese cabbage *(Brassica rapa chinensis)* is closely related to the turnip. Cooks around the world now use it in stir-fry dishes and soups.

The rutabaga *(Brassica napus* Napobrassica Group), also called a swede, originated as a cross between a cabbage and a turnip. The plant's hard, round root cooks into a pungent, fibrous vegetable that is a cold-weather favorite; both the root and leaves are used as livestock fodder.

Health Benefits

Turnips are high in vitamin C, and the greens are a good source of vitamins A, C, and K, folate, and calcium. Bok choy is a nutritional gold mine—it is rich in vitamin A, and its phytonutrients represent a full spectrum of more than 70 antioxidants. Rutabagas are high in vitamin C, as well as beta-carotene, potassium, and manganese, and they also supply fiber, vitamin B6, thiamine, magnesium, and phosphorus.

HOT STUFF

The cabbage family includes two very pungent root vegetables—wasabi *(Eutrema japonicum),* which produces a fiery condiment used with Japanese food, especially sushi, and the lusty horseradish root *(Armoracia rusticana),* which is ground into a creamy sauce that compliments many meat dishes. Horseradish is often used as a less expensive substitute in commercial wasabi products. Medicinally, horseradish can clear respiratory congestion, while wasabi offers anti-inflammatory relief for swollen joints.

UMBELLIFERS

THIS FAMILY OF HEALTHFUL VEGGIES IS KNOWN FOR ITS CLUSTERS OF FLOWERS

The Apiaceae family of aromatic flowering plants includes weeds like Queen Anne's lace and wild parsley, many cultivated herbs, and a number of vegetables—carrots, celery, and parsnips—as well as woody shrubs and small trees. Umbellifers prefer to grow during cool seasons rather than in the heat of summer. Every cultivated plant in this family acts as a beneficial garden companion—the clusters of small flowers, or umbels, that they form attract ladybugs, predatory flies, and parasitic wasps, which will prey on the pests of neighboring plants. Some umbellifer herbs also mask the scent of nearby plants from insect predators, making them more difficult to find. On the other hand, poisons extracted from plants in this family have been used as aids to suicide or to tip poisonous hunting arrows.

Rainbow carrots. Carrots are available in a variety of sizes, including baby, and colors like orange, yellow, and red.

> ### DID YOU KNOW?
>
> • *One noxious umbellifer, the giant hogweed (Heracleum mantegazzianum), was discovered by Victorian explorers in the Caucasus Mountains and carried back to Britain as a prize. They soon realized that its sap caused severe skin blisters when exposed to sunlight. This menace has now become invasive in the United States.*

CARROTS

The modern carrot (*Daucus carota sativus*) is the domesticated form of the wild carrot native to Europe and southwest Asia. There are two main types of this vegetable—eastern carrots that originated in Persia around the 10th century and western carrots that arose in Holland in the 1600s. Most school children would say that carrots are orange, but there exist heirloom cultivars in red, black, purple, white, and yellow, which cooks around the world are now rediscovering. Carrots are biennial plants, with the first year's sugars stored in the taproot to provide energy for the flowering of the second year's growth. Its name comes from the Greek *karoton*, from the Indus-European root *ker*, or "horn," based on its shape. Carrots were first cultivated for their edible seeds and greens. When a natural subspecies occurred with a more palatable root, it was selectively bred over time so that it became enlarged and tender and lost any woody qualities, resulting in the sweet-tasting carrot we know today. Carrots are currently one of the 10 most economically important crops in the world, with China the top producer.

Health Benefits

Carrots are supposedly beneficial to eye health due to the high levels of beta-carotene they contain—which is also responsible for their orange color. But unless someone has a vitamin A deficiency, eating carrots will not improve their eyesight or give them better night vision. This is a myth that was advanced by British Intelligence during World War II to explain why their pilots had such success during nighttime air battles. It was meant to cover the truth—new advances in Allied radar technology. Carrots also contain lutein, zeaxanthin, vitamin K, and vitamin B6.

PANTRY PICK: *Make an easy carrot slaw by grating 1 pound of carrots and ¼ of a cabbage head. Add ½ cup dried cranberries, and drizzle the mix with a citrus dressing of 3 tablespoons olive oil, 3 tablespoons orange juice, and 2 tablespoons honey.*

PARSNIP

This savory-sweet, cream-colored root vegetable *(Pastinaca sativa)* is a favorite in hearty dishes and soup stocks and as part of Sunday dinner in many parts of Britain. It is native to Eurasia and was probably prepared interchangeably with carrots by the Romans. Early Europeans used it to sweeten dishes before the advent of cane sugar. The parsnip traveled to North America with the French and British some time in the late 1700s, but it was supplanted as a starch by the advent of the potato in the mid-19th century. It is still somewhat undervalued there, even thought it can be baked, boiled, roasted, pureed, fried, or steamed. It can even be sliced thin and deep-fried to make chips.

Health Benefits

Traditional Chinese healers used parsnip roots as medicine—and no wonder. They contain powerful antioxidants that potentially have anticancer, anti-inflammatory, and antifungal properties. They also provide both soluble and insoluble fiber and can prevent constipation as well as lower LDL cholesterol levels. Parsnips are rich in vitamins and minerals, but most of these occur close to the root's surface; for best results, peel lightly or cook with the skins on.

CELERY

This marshland plant has been cultivated in the Mediterranean region since at least 800 B.C., when it was grown for medicinal purposes. Today, celery *(Apium graveolens)* is a popular vegetable with a long, fibrous stalk topped with curled leaves and a

Simmer carrots, celery, and parsnips with bay leaf and alliums, like shallots, spring and yellow onions, and chili peppers to make a rich vegetable stock.

slightly bitter flavor. There are two stalk varieties—green, or Pascal, the American favorite, and self-blanching, or yellow, popular in Europe and the rest of the world. Celeriac, a stubby variety, is grown in Europe for its edible root.

Health Benefits

Celery was once grown in the spring to make a cleansing tonic to counteract the winter diet of salted meat. This anti-inflammatory vegetable contains impressive levels of antioxidants and beneficial enzymes as well as folate, potassium, insoluble fiber, manganese, and pantothenic acid. It is a good source of vitamin A—in the form of carotenoids, vitamins C, B2, B6, and K, copper, calcium, magnesium and phosphorus. It is also a great diet aid—one stalk contains only 10 calories.

PANTRY PICK: *Umbellifers make a flavorful vegetable stock. Place coarsely chopped carrots, parsnips, celery, leeks, yellow and spring onions, and shallots in a large pot. Add a bay leaf (and a chili pepper, if desired), cover with water, and simmer on medium-high until the liquid is almost boiling. Turn to low heat, and cook for at least an hour. Strain the mixture, and pour into containers.*

Up Close

JUICING AND SMOOTHIES

LEARN TO EXTRACT THE LIQUID ESSENCE OF FRUITS AND VEGETABLES

A juice combo that include carrots, kale, ginger, orange, and lemon can help restore your energy.

Juicing is the process of extracting the juice from fruits, vegetables, and herbs. In theory, the result contains all the vitamins, minerals, and phytonutrients found in the original food source. Unfortunately, most of the pulp, or insoluble fiber, is left behind in the machine. Advocates for juicing maintain that it allows the body to absorb nutrients more easily without having to deal with fiber. They believe a regular diet of juices can reduce the risk of cancer, support the immune system, remove toxins from the body, help control weight, and ease digestion. For people who don't enjoy eating fresh fruits and vegetables, but know they need them for a balanced diet, juicing provides a tasty, palatable alternative. Plus, with so many types of produce to choose from, picky juicers can eventually come up with several combinations that please their palate and that also offer a sufficient range of nutrients.

There are three types of juicing machines with their own pros and cons. It's important to get a version you will use every day, so you should be aware of the different features and look into ease of use, ease of cleaning, how much room it takes up, how much juice it yields, and how much it costs. Masticating juicers chew the produce slowly, and offer a high yield that you can store for up to 72 hours. They tend to be compact, upright designs, but are pricey and difficult to clean. Centrifugal juicers use sharp blades to chop the produce and spin at high speeds to separate juice from pulp. There are low-cost models available, and they are easy to clean, making them good for beginners. The blade does not extract all the nutrients, however, and it is not effective at chopping greens and wheat grass. Twin-gear juicers crush the produce, opening cell walls and releasing a maximum of vitamins and minerals. The yield is high, they are quiet, and they can handle nuts, greens, herbs, and wheat grass. But they are expensive, heavy, and difficult to clean. If you do begin a juicing regimen with a centrifugal juicer, make only what you can drink at that time—the fresh juice is prone to developing bacteria. To make blends, you can juice individual items and combine them, or extract multiple ingredients at the same time.

The Blender Option

You can produce fresh juice by placing chopped-up produce in a blender or a bullet and liquefying it. This is called a smoothie, and you can augment it with almond milk or other liquids; with nuts and seeds; with protein supplements; or with probiotic powder.

Juice from a blender supplies you with the edible parts of the fruit or vegetable and its insoluble fiber. If you want something close to the full juicing experience, you can strain blender juices. Fruit-based juices contain a quantity of sugar and may provide unwanted calories. A ratio of 80 percent veg to 20 percent fruit will keep calories low.

Curative Combos

Below is a list of ailments or health requirements with the recommended ingredients you can combine in the juicer or blender to help manage them.

- Colds and flu: Carrot, pineapple, ginger, garlic
- Asthma: Carrot, spinach, apple, garlic, lemon
- Indigestion: Pineapple, carrot, spinach, lemon, peppermint, turmeric
- Skincare: Papaya, mango, lemon, ginger, cinnamon, rosemary
- Headache: Apple, cucumber, ginger, celery, kale
- Arthritis: Carrot, celery, pineapple, lemon, ginger, turmeric
- High blood pressure: Apple, beet, celery, cucumber, ginger
- Kidney support: Carrot, watermelon, cucumber, dandelion root, cilantro
- Constipation: Apple, carrot, cabbage
- Anxiety: Carrot, celery, pomegranate
- Depression: Carrot, apple, spinach, beet
- Stress relief: Banana, strawberry, pear

Strawberry, kiwi, blueberry, and peach smoothies

- Energy: Carrot, orange, lemon, kale, and ginger
- Fatigue fighter: Beet, green apple, spinach, chia, basil, cinnamon, goldenroot
- Anti-inflammatory: Coconut milk, mango, pineapple, peaches, curry
- Memory function: Pomegranate, beets, grapes
- Vitamin K booster: Seedless grapes, kale, parsley, avocado, ginger, lemon
- Hangover Helper: Beets, pears, spinach, pineapple, coconut water, ginger, tarragon

JUICING TIPS

Whether you're a juicing novice or an old hand, these tips will help you make the most of the experience.

- Wash produce thoroughly. Remove seeds, inedible skins, bitter peels, and large pits.
- Cut up produce just before juicing to avoid loss of nutrients.
- Change speeds from slow for soft fruits to fast for hard veggies.
- Drink juice as your first meal of the day.
- Swish juice in your mouth to let the digestive process begin with your saliva.
- Drinking raw kale, cabbage, or collard greens may suppress thyroid function.
- Granny Smith apples make a tastier base than carrots or beets in juicing recipes.
- Add lemon or lime juice to cleanse the digestive tract and stimulate the colon.

COMPOSITE VEGETABLES

THIS FAMILY INCLUDES THE UBIQUITOUS LETTUCE AND THE PRICKLY ARTICHOKE

The widespread Compositae, which is also known as the Asteraceae or the aster, daisy, or composite family, includes herbaceous flowers, herbs, and vegetables, as well as vines, shrubs, and trees. The name derives from the plants' flowers, which are a composite of many small individual florets that form a larger cluster, called a pseudoanthium. Lettuce is perhaps the best known vegetable in this family, but it also includes chicory, globe artichoke, and endive.

DID YOU KNOW?

• In ancient Egypt, lettuce was believed to symbolize sexual prowess in men and to promote romantic love and childbearing in women. The Greeks, however, associated it with male reproductive problems and served it at funerals. Wild lettuce has slightly narcotic properties, so the Anglo-Saxons called it sleepwort.

LETTUCE

This leaf vegetable (*Lactuca sativa*), a prime salad staple, was first cultivated by the ancient Egyptians. They developed it from a weedy plant, whose seeds were used to produce oil, into a succulent vegetable. The Greeks and Romans eagerly adopted it, and by A.D. 50, there were already a number of varieties, some with medicinal

Fresh butterhead. This delicate lettuce, with its ruffled outer leaves, lends a sweet buttery flavor to salads.

properties. Even more cultivars arose in Europe from the 1500s to the 1700s, many that are still grown today. Lettuce is a hardy annual plant that prefers cooler temperatures. If too warm, it bolts—produces flowers—and loses its tenderness. The three top types are leaf lettuce, used mainly for salads; head lettuce, like iceberg, which is popular in the United States; and cos lettuce, such as romaine, the long-leafed lettuce used in Caesar salads. Other cultivars include sweet, delicate butterhead (also known as bib or Boston lettuce) and summer crisp (also known as French crisp lettuce), which offers large, flavorful leaves.

Health Benefits

Lettuce may be the perfect diet food—low in calories and full of water for hydration—but its nutritional value depends on the cultivar. Although Iceberg lettuce is widely consumed in America, its health value is negligible. Romaine offers twice the protein, twice the calcium, three times the vitamin K, four times the iron, and eight times the vitamin C of Iceberg. It offers a whopping 17 times the vitamin A. Remember that the darker the lettuce–or most any vegetable—the higher the nutrient level. Pale Iceberg just doesn't cut it.

ARTICHOKE

The two vegetables called artichoke both fall into the composite group: the globe artichoke (*Cynara cardunculus* var. *scolymus*), a scaly, spiky plant bud with a tender heart, and the Jerusalem artichoke (*Helianthus tuberosus*), a slightly nutty root vegetable.

Globe artichokes are perennial thistles. First cultivated in the Mediterranean around 800 B.C., they were enjoyed by the Greeks and Romans. They fell out of favor soon after, but they were rediscovered in the 1500s. They are now part of Italian, Greek, and Middle Eastern cuisines. The plant grows from four to six feet in height and produces silvery, deeply lobed leaves. The edible parts of the bud consist of the plump lower portions of the bracts and the meaty base, or heart. The choke, or beard, is the silky mass of inedible immature florets above the base.

The Jerusalem artichoke, also known as sunchoke or sunroot, is a species of sunflower native to eastern North America. This perennial evergreen grows from four to nine feet in height, with rough, hairy leaves and yellow flowers. The edible roots or tubers resemble ginger, and can be pale brown, white, red, or purple. They are quite crisp when eaten raw and were a food source for Native Americans. They also impressed colonists, who sent specimens back to Europe. Ironically, the vegetable caught on there, while it languished in the United States. The plant is not technically an artichoke, nor is it from Jerusalem—Italian settlers called it *girasole,* or "sunflower," which may account for the name.

Health Benefits

Globe artichokes are nutrient rich—high in fiber, which can lower blood pressure and cholesterol levels, and in antioxidants, which can help prevent cancer and offer immune support. They are a top source of vitamins C and K, and also provide folate, magnesium, manganese, copper, potassium, and phosphorus. Jerusalem artichokes are also high in fiber, and contain vitamins A, C, and E, and antioxidant flavonoids, such as carotene.

CHICORY AND ENDIVE

A woody perennial, chicory *(Cichorium intybus)* is native to Europe and naturalized in the United States. It produces bright blue flowers and still grows wild in many areas. Its leaves are added to salads and the ground root can be used as a coffee substitute. A bitter, deep red, wide-leaf type of chicory, radicchio *(C. intybus* var. *foliosum)* is used to add pizzazz to salads. It is part of the traditional Italian pantry, and many varieties take their name from the regions where they

Globe artichokes. There are many cultivars with red or purple shading. No matter the color, artichokes are prized for the delicate flavor of the fleshy hearts.

originated. Belgian endive, or *witlof* in Dutch, is another slightly bitter variety; it forms a compact head and is grown out of sunlight to keep the smooth leaves a creamy white.

In the same genera is endive, a leafy vegetable that is native to Asia Minor. There are two main cultivar types: curly endive, like frisée *(C. endivia* var. *crispum);* and broad-leaf endive, like escarole *(C. endivia* var. *latifolia).*

Health Benefits

Chicory contains calcium, iron, carotene, thiamine, phosphorus, riboflavin, vitamin C, and niacin. Radicchio provides vitamins C and K, B-complex vitamins, copper, iron, manganese, and zinc. It can ease digestion, maintain metabolism, detoxify the colon, and encourage weight loss. It also offers powerful phytonutrients and carotenoids. Low-calorie endive is high in fiber, antioxidant vitamin A and beta-carotene, vitamin K, and B-complex vitamins like folic acid and niacin. Escarole supplies the minerals manganese, copper, iron, and potassium.

Belgian endive

SPINACH AND BEETS
THE MEMBERS OF THE BEETROOT FAMILY ARE HIGH-VALUE VEGETABLES

It is no wonder that leafy green spinach is renowned for its nutritional value—beyond Popeye, nutritionists tout its many benefits. But this leafy green vegetable is not alone in its clan. Spinach is part of the Amaranthaceae, also known as the beetroot family. Other members include sugar beets, beetroot, Swiss chard, quinoa, and amaranth.

SPINACH

This annual leaf vegetable grows to a foot in height; it displays variable-shaped leaves and small yellow-green flowers that produce hard, lumpy fruit clusters. Spinach *(Spinacia oleracea)* likely originated in ancient Persia and traveled to China by way of India. By the 12th century, it naturalized around the Mediterranean, and a century later it became popular in England because it grew in early spring, when few fresh plants were available. The English name comes from the 14th-century *espinache,* a word without known origin, possibly derived from Andalusian Arabic for "green hand." There are three basic types: savoy spinach, the variety most often found in supermarkets, is dark green with curly leaves. Flat-leaf or smooth-leaf spinach, which is easier to clean than Savoy, is often grown for canning, freezing, soups, baby foods, and processed foods. Semi-savoy has moderately crinkly leaves; it can be eaten fresh or processed. China is currently the spinach champ, responsible for more than 90 percent of the global crop.

Health Benefits

Spinach provides a notable amount of iron—a raw 3.5-ounce portion supplies 23 percent of the Daily Value (DV). The same amount of cooked spinach offers 3.57 mg of iron compared to only 2.9 mg for a 3.5-ounce beef hamburger. On the other hand, spinach also contains oxalates that inhibit the absorption of iron, with the result that much of the iron it provides is unusable. These oxalates can also affect the absorption of calcium. Still, spinach does offer a lot of nutritional value when eaten fresh, steamed, or quick-boiled—at least 20 percent of the DV of vitamins A, C, and K, magnesium, manganese, and folate. It's also a good source of riboflavin, B6, vitamin E, calcium, potassium, and dietary fiber. For optimum benefits, eat spinach within a day or two of purchasing; otherwise, it looses much of its nutritional value.

BEETS

The *Beta vulgaris* species includes a number of commercially significant cultivars that are classified into five groups: The Altissima Group, the sugar beet, represents a major commercial crop—these beets contain high concentrations of sucrose, which is extracted to produce table sugar. Spinach beet, or chard, is in the Cicla Group; this plant dates back to 2000 B.C., when it was used medicinally. The leaves can be cooked like spinach. Swiss chard, a leafy vegetable with substantial midribs, belongs to the Flavescens Group. Beetroot, also known as beet, table beet, garden beet, or red beet in the United States, is in the Conditiva Group. It is the nutritious

Fresh spinach leaves

A colorfully vibrant smoothie made from spinach, beets, apples, and almonds is packed with nutrients.

taproot portion of *B. vulgaris vulgaris.* The Crassa Group contains a fodder plant, the mangelwurzel, developed for its nutritious tubers.

The beet's wild ancestor was the sea beet, *B. vulgarism maritima.* It is still found throughout coastal Europe and in North Africa and western Asia. Today, cultivated beets are grown globally in temperate regions without severe frosts.

Health Benefits

Recent reports that beetroot can improve stamina and enhance athletic performance, control high blood pressure, and increase blood flow, have boosted its popularity. Beetroots are also a source of phytonutrient pigments called betalains. Two of these—betanin and vulgaxanthin—have antioxidant, anti-inflammatory and detoxifying properties. In lab tests, betanin has been shown to reduce tumor cell growth. All the *Beta vulgaris* cousins covered here provide vitamin C, potassium, manganese, and

folate. Sugar beets contain a protein called leghemoglobin that is nearly identical to human hemoglobin; it may one day provide a lifesaving blood substitute when blood donation supplies fall short of the demand.

PANTRY PICK: *Combine beets with spinach for an energizing antioxidant smoothie. Peel and chop 1 beet and 1 apple, and place in a blender. Add two large handfuls of spinach, about 4 almonds, 1 cup of apple juice, ½ cup almond milk, the juice of 1 lemon, and crushed ice, as needed. Blend until smooth.*

WASH CAREFULLY

Environmental studies have shown that spinach is one of a dozen produce plants most heavily contaminated by pesticides. Always wash spinach thoroughly before eating, even if it is the packaged variety.

The heirloom Maris Peer potato plant displays the distinctive flowers of the nightshade family: bell-shaped petals in shades of purple or white with deep yellow pendant stamens.

NIGHTSHADES

THESE OLD AND NEW WORLD VEGETABLES HAVE NOW BECOME PANTRY STAPLES

t's perplexing to consider that the Solanaceae, or nightshade family, which is responsible for so many of the vegetables we enjoy, is also the source of plants like belladonna and tobacco that contain poisonous alkaloids. The family is a significant and diverse one—featuring annual and perennial flowering plants in the form of flowers, vines, shrubs, and trees that produce important crops such as herbs, spices, and medicinal plants. It is also extremely ancient— the fossil of a tomatillo found in Argentina dates back 52 million years. The most commercially significant genus is *Solanum,* which includes tomatoes, potatoes, and eggplant. The genus *Capsicum* includes the chili pepper.

Nightshades are full of nutrients and other beneficial compounds, but they can also cause a number of health problems, including leaky gut syndrome, and can trigger immune reactions similar to those caused by gluten or dairy allergies. Acidic tomatoes, in particular, can bring on episodes of gastroesophageal reflux disease, or GERD.

POTATOES

Potatoes present a humble appearance—brownish, lumpy, dull. Yet they have, in their time, provided a source of sustenance to entire sectors of society. This starchy tuberous plant (*Solanum tuberosum*) originated in the Andes Mountains near southern Peru, where it was domesticated from 7,000 to 10,000 years ago. The Spanish carried the tuber to Europe in the latter half of the 16th century, and, after some resistance from suspicious farmers, it became a staple food of the laboring classes—to the point where the potato may have been responsible for the European population boom of the 19th century. Sadly, a mid-century potato blight destroyed crops and caused a famine among the poor in Ireland and Scotland; at least a million people died as a result, and a million more emigrated to North America.

Potato plants grow to about two feet in height and produce pink, white, red, purple, or blue flowers. The fruits look like green cherry tomatoes, but like all other parts of the plant, save the tubers, they are full of a toxic alkaloid, solanine. Selective breeding over thousands of years has resulted in more than 5,000 cultivated varieties in eight or nine species, including potatoes produced specifically to be baked, boiled, or fried. Currently, potatoes are the top vegetable crop in the world, with China and India the main producers.

Health Benefits

Even though potatoes are considered a starchy vegetable, a medium-size spud contains only 110 calories and supplies more potassium than a banana. They are a very good source of vitamin B6 and a good source of fiber, vitamin C, niacin, copper, manganese, phosphorous, and pantothenic acid. Potatoes also provide antioxidant protection in the form of carotenoids, flavonoids, and caffeic acid, as well as rare blood-pressure lowering compounds known as kukoamines.

> PANTRY PICK: *For a nutritious snack or light lunch, pop a russet or Idaho potato into a microwave for 7 to 10 minutes, and then garnish with low-fat sour cream and a sprinkling of diced green onions or dill weed. Or top with 1 tablespoon pesto and a chopped small plum tomato.*

TOMATOES

Few vegetables are as easy to grow in temperate regions and as satisfying to bite into, sun warmed and straight off the vine, as the tomato (*S. lycopersicum*).

Technically, the tomato is a fruit, as so many "vegetables" are, a berry consisting of an ovary with multiple seeds. The plant originated in Central and South America, and was cultivated by the Incas and the Aztecs from around A.D. 700. When the fruit was introduced to Europe in the 16th century, it was accepted in the southern regions, but farther north, especially in England, it was thought to be poisonous and grown only as an ornamental. In America, tomatoes became a kitchen staple around the time of the Civil War and have remained a favorite for salads, sauces, stews, and soups ever since, with hundreds of varieties to choose from. Tomatoes were also the first commercially available genetically modified food—as a variety called Flavr Savr—but no GMO tomatoes are currently marketed.

Health Benefits

Tomatoes furnish impressive amounts of vitamins A, C, and K, potassium, and manganese and significant amounts of fiber, vitamin B6, thiamine, and folate, as well as magnesium, phosphorus, and copper. Red tomatoes contain the antioxidant lycopene, but according to studies, the form of lycopene found in yellow tomatoes may actually be more easily absorbed. They also show evidence of the rare blood pressure–lowering compounds known as kukoamines that were recently found in potatoes. Fresh tomatoes have been linked to improved heart health by lowering cholesterol and triglycerides, and tomato extracts may keep platelets from clumping together.

Hillbilly tomatoes. This heirloom cultivar originated in West Virginia in the 1800s.

Turn your garden bounty of nightshade vegetables into impressive-looking, as well as delicious, ratatouille.

EGGPLANT

Also known as the aubergine in England and France, this glossy purple, ovoid vegetable (no surprise—also technically a fruit) was domesticated from a plant called the thorn or bitter apple *(S. incanum)* with two domestications likely occurring in East Asia and South Asia during prehistoric times. The eggplant *(S. melongena)* is a perennial in the tropics and a half-hardy annual in temperate regions. Its white flesh is solid and meaty, but turns quite tender when boiled, steamed, or stir-fried. Like its other nightshade cousins, its leaves and stems can be toxic. New cultivars have resulted in alterations in size and color—from tiny "egg" eggplants to skinny "finger" eggplants to large varieties of over two pounds and hues ranging from white to green or yellow to purple with white stripes. Oddly, in early Italian folklore, the vegetable was believed to bring on insanity, but that

didn't stop the Italians from including eggplant in a variety of regional dishes. It also figures strongly in Greek, Middle Eastern, Indian, and Asian cookery.

Health Benefits

Eggplant is high in fiber, but low in calories, and it has the ability to create a true feeling of fullness during a meal. It is a very good source of vitamin B1 and copper and a good source of manganese, vitamin B6, niacin, potassium, folate, and vitamin K. It also contains bioflavonoids that can help control high blood pressure, and the skin is rich in phytonutrients such as nasunin and chlorogenic acid that improve circulation and nourish the brain.

PANTRY PICK: *Use your garden harvest or farmers' market finds to create the classic Provençal ratatouille Puree 1 large tomato, and layer it on the bottom of a casserole dish with half an onion, finely chopped. Stir in 2 minced garlic cloves, ¼ teaspoon oregano, ¼ teaspoon crushed red pepper, 1 tablespoon olive oil, and salt and pepper to taste. Cut an eggplant, zucchini, red bell pepper, red onion, and 3 cherry tomatoes into very thin slices (easiest if you have an adjustable-blade slicer), and layer them over the tomato. Drizzle 1 tablespoon olive oil over the vegetables, and again season with salt and pepper. Crumble a few sprigs of thyme over it all, and then cover the dish with a piece of parchment paper cut to fit inside. Bake for approximately 45 to 55 minutes.*

CHILI PEPPER

These hot peppers (genus *Capsicum*) originated in Mexico and Central and South America, where they figured in the diet of the indigenous peoples for more than 7,500 years. Columbus brought chilies

PRECIOUS HEIRLOOMS

Within the past few decades, dedicated farmers and gardeners began seeking out the seeds of older varieties of fruits and vegetables—"heirloom" cultivars that had been handed down through families. These throwbacks often feature unusual colors or shapes and give modern diners a chance to savor a much wider range of flavors than the produce Big Agriculture dictates that we consume—which in many cases are the fruits and vegetables that have the most commercial potential: those that last the longest and travel the best. Look for fresh heirloom produce at farmers' markets or specialty stores, or order seeds online.

Several chili pepper varieties: a long green serrano, a lantern-shaped Scotch bonnet, a smooth green jalapeño, a chunky yellow habanero, and fingerlike cayennes

back to Spain in 1493 and wrote of their medicinal properties a year later. They received their common name because black pepper was so highly prized in Europe at that time that the appellation "pepper" was applied to any plant that provided heat—which chilies certainly did. Portuguese traders carried these peppers to Asia, where they were soon assimilated into Indian, Chinese, and Southeast Asian cuisine.

There are five domesticated species in this genus.

- *C. annuum* includes bell, wax, jalapeño, cayenne, and New Mexico chili peppers.
- *C. frutescens* includes oblong malaqueta, tabasco, and Thai peppers.
- *C. baccatum* includes South American aji peppers and the Peppadew, Lemon Drop, and Bishop's Crown cultivars.
- *C. pubescens* is the South American rocoto pepper (called the manzano pepper in Mexico).
- *C. chinense,* or bonnet peppers, features the fieriest examples, like naga, habanero, and Scotch bonnet. This species includes the top two record holders on the Scoville scale (which measures a pepper's heat): the Carolina Reaper and the Trinidad Moruga Scorpion.

Squat, rounded bell peppers are the variety most often used as a side dish or salad vegetable in the United States. They are called sweet peppers or simply peppers in the United Kingdom and Canada. This cultivar group of *C. annuum* produces peppers in hues of green, red, yellow, orange, chocolate brown, vanilla white, lavender, and purple. Due to a recessive gene, bell peppers are the only members

of the *Capsicum* genus that do not manufacture the heat-producing chemical capsaicin. (The Mexibelle hybrid of the bell does contain enough capsaicin to furnish a small amount of heat.)

Health Benefits

Peppers offer lots of nutritional bang for the buck and are also highly medicinal. They are low in calories, high in vitamins A and C, B-complex vitamins, potassium, copper, iron, and fiber, as well as antioxidant carotenoids. These nutrients are useful for fighting infection, reducing high LDL cholesterol levels, combating fatigue, improving cognitive function, keeping hair and skin healthy, preventing macular degeneration of the eyes, and regulating blood pressure. Chili peppers also contain capsaicin—when applied topically, it binds with pain receptors, creating a burning sensation that draws pain away from injured or swollen joints and muscles. Be aware that some hot chilies are capable of burning the fingers, lips, eyes, or mucous membranes. Chefs often coat their fingers in cooking oil before slicing them.

TOMATILLO

The piquant, green tomatillo *(Physalis philadelphica),* with its papery husk, is a lesser known nightshade vegetable. Native to Mexico, it has been used as a food source for millennia and is often incorporated into Mexican dishes for its sweet-sour flavor.

Health Benefits

Tomatillos are excellent sources of fiber, niacin, potassium, and manganese and also supply vitamin C and K, iron, magnesium, and phosphorus.

Tomatillos

An array of summer squash. Summer squash is harvested earlier and should be eaten raw or only lightly cooked.

SQUASH AND PUMPKIN

GOURD FAMILY VEGETABLES FURNISH NUTRITIONAL SUBSTANCE AND EARTHY FLAVORS

Nothing evokes the fall season like a meal that features squash like butternut and acorn or a front porch bedecked with carved pumpkins. And little says summer like a cool, refreshing cucumber salad made with sour cream and dill. In addition to these season-evoking vegetables, the Cucurbitaceae family, also known as the gourd or marrow family, includes luffas and melons. There are roughly 98 genera and 975 species in the family, which can be found in tropical and temperate climates. Their edible fruits are believed to be some of the earliest cultivated in both the Old World and the New. The majority of cucurbits are annual vines, but there

> ### DID YOU KNOW?
>
> • *The multicolored, oddly shaped inedible gourds that appear at harvest time or Halloween are members of two genera—Lagenaria and Curcubita. When they are dried, gourds become hollow and can be used as table or porch decorations or have entry holes drilled in them and hung outside as birdhouses.*

are also woody lianas, thorny shrubs, and even trees. Squash vegetables produce large white or yellow flowers with hairy stems that are bisexual, with male and female flowers occurring on the same plant or on different plants. The fruit is a modified type of berry called a pepo, hence the scientific name *Cucurbita pepo* that is applied to many plants in this family.

SQUASH

This New World vegetable traces its origins back more than 10,000 years to Mesoamerican settlements. Squash was one of the "three sisters" crops that Native Americans planted together for hundreds of years to maximize their land, a concept that they later shared with European settlers. Ideally, the corn stalks grew upright; the climbing beans used the corn for support and nourished the soil; and the squash spread out around the corn and beans, discouraging weeds. Squash is divided into two varieties: robust winter squash (which can be the species *C. pepo, C. maxima, C. mixta,* or *C. moschata)* and delicately flavored summer squash (nearly always a variety of *C. pepo).*

SUMMER SQUASH Sweetly flavorful summer squash is harvested when immature, while the skin is still thin. They can be eaten raw, sautéed, made into breads, and even baked and blended into smoothies. The edible yellow blossoms are delicious when battered and fried. This group includes the following varieties, most of which are *C. pepo* cultivars.

- Green and golden zucchini are the same cuke-shaped plant, only the yellow variety is slightly more tender. They have smooth, thin skin and can be eaten raw in salads or steamed. (Try making strips of both with a wide potato peeler for a fresh ribbon salad.)
- Round squash, also known as avocado squash or round zucchini, is a pale green globe with darker green mottling. It is dense, making it perfect for stuffing and roasting.
- Straightneck squash, or yellow summer squash, is similar to zucchini, but it tapers at the neck. There is also a crookneck summer squash that is very similar in taste.
- Zephyr is an attractive hybrid, gourd-shaped with a yellow top and a vibrant green bottom. These squash are thin-skinned and easy to cook, offering a winning flavor and texture.
- Pattypan squash looks like a small flying saucer with rippled edges; it tastes the same as round squash, but its novel appearance makes it popular with restaurants.

PANTRY PICK: *Mix any type of steamed summer squash with diced red and green peppers and a dash of paprika and lime juice to create the perfect side dish to serve with tacos or chili-marinated grilled steak.*

Health Benefits

Squash is an excellent source of vitamins A and C, and also provides B-complex vitamins, fiber—including pectin, anti-inflammatory omega-3 fatty acids, folate, magnesium, potassium, iron, and copper. Its antioxidants, which include vitamin C, superoxide dismutase, alpha-carotene, and beta-carotene, can help support the body's immune system to combat disease.

WINTER SQUASH These mature, thick-skinned vegetables are more nutritious than their summer cousins, but their vines tend to spread out and require more space. For small yards, try a bush or semibush cultivar. Winter squash can be prepared many ways, but they are not eaten raw. Squash seeds can be roasted for snacking or used as a source of oil. Some popular varieties are listed below.

- Buttercup squash *(C. maxima)* is round, green, and compact, with orange flesh that smells like cucumber but cooks up mild and a bit dry.
- Hubbard squashes *(C. maxima)* are sweet and delicious, with pumpkin notes. Blue hubbard is that culinary rarity—a truly blue food. It is a large tear-dropped-shaped squash, and its blue-gray skin tends to be covered with bumps. Hokkaido, or red kuri squash, looks like a small red-orange pumpkin with ridgeless skin.
- Turban squash *(C. maxima)* gets the award for showiest vegetable. This multicolor, mottled squash has an irregular shape, and often looks like elaborate headgear fit for a sultan. Its flavor is mild and nutty. These squash can be hollowed out and used as decorative soup tureens.

Turban squash

- Kabocha *(C. maxima)* is a large squash with a round and squat shape. The mottled dark green skin is often dense and bumpy. The flesh is smooth and sweet with a slightly nutty flavor.
- Spaghetti squash *(C. pepo pepo)* has a cylindrical shape and can range in color from cream to bright yellow. When cooked, its insides develop into thin strands resembling pasta that have a chewy texture and mild flavor.
- Acorn squash *(C. pepo var. turbinata),* named for its squat shape, is known for the subtle nutty flavor of its orange flesh. The rind is a dull deep green with small orange splotches. Acorns can be steamed, roasted, baked, sautéed, or microwaved.
- Butternut squash *(C. moschata)* is pear shaped, with a slim neck and bulbous base. The skin is a dull amber with rich yellow-orange, sweet-tasting flesh inside.

Autumn Soup served in Hokkaido squash shells. Pumpkins and hearty winter squashes, such butternut or acorn, are perfect for making warming autumnal soups.

MAKE IT YOURSELF
Autumn Soup

This recipe incorporates a variety of healthful ingredients, including herb, spices, and veggies.

YOU WILL NEED:
2¾ pounds sugar pumpkin (or butternut or acorn squash), chopped into 2-inch pieces
½ cup extra virgin olive oil
1 large sweet onion, chopped
1 large carrot, peeled and chopped
1 clove garlic, minced
5 cups low-sodium vegetable or chicken stock
¼ cup low-fat yogurt
½ teaspoon each nutmeg and cinnamon
salt and red pepper flakes
pumpkin seeds

WHAT TO DO:
- Combine pumpkin, onion, carrots, and garlic on a baking sheet. Add oil, sprinkle with salt, toss to coat, and then spread in a single layer. Roast until pumpkin is tender in a 450-degree oven, about 30 minutes. Let cool, then remove pumpkin skins.
- Add broth and pumpkin to saucepan, and then simmer for 20 minutes.
- Pour mixture into blender to halfway mark and pulse, then puree. Proceed in batches until all is blended, and then stir in spices.
- Stir in the yogurt, garnish with the pumpkin seeds, red pepper flakes, and serve.

PUMPKINS

Pumpkins *(C. pepo)* are cultivars of squash, but their flavor profile is often less sweet. In addition to their role as a vegetable—and favored pie filling—they are also used as landscape ornamentals during Halloween and Thanksgiving. Pumpkins likely originated in North America some time between 7000 and 5500 B.C.; unlike modern pumpkins, they were a crooked-necked variety that stored well. The rounded modern plant grows as a fibrous vine that produces both male and female blossoms. Home gardeners can aid pollination by brushing pollen from several male flowers onto the female flower— she's the one with the tiny gourd at the base. The mature fruit's ridged, orange or yellow shell is composed of smooth skin and dense flesh and contains a pulpy mass of seeds. Pumpkins are now grown all over the world as a food source, as animal feed, and for decoration.

Some of the more popular cultivars are listed here; you can order their seeds online.

- Pumpkin growers rejoice over new cultivars and some of the most precious are the mini pumpkins, including white Baby Boo, orange Jack Be Little, and mixed blends called Hooligan, Cooligan, and Bumpkin.

- Connecticut Field and Harvest Jack are two varieties commonly used for carved jack-o-lanterns at Halloween.
- Squat, relatively small sugar pumpkins like Sweet Sugar Pie have interiors packed with flesh and are bred for baking. When their pulp is properly drained of water, these pumpkins provide a delectable, custardy pie filling.
- Blue pumpkin seeds are available under the names Blue Max and Blue Doll, and French heirloom red-orange pumpkins as Cinderellas.
- Dill's Atlantic Giant is the variety you want if you yearn to grow mammoth pumpkins that weigh half a ton.

Cucumbers with leaves and flowers

Health Benefits

Pumpkin-flavoring is now a mainstay of autumn comestibles, featured in breads, donuts, ice creams, risottos, raviolis, and even beers and coffees. Yet there's a plus side to all that promotion—pumpkins are full of nutrients. One cup contains more than twice the recommended intake of antioxidant vitamin A, and they are a good source of fiber, vitamin C, riboflavin, potassium, copper, and manganese. Pumpkin seeds, also known as pepitas, contain a concentration of vitamins and minerals. Roasted, they made a tasty complement to salads or a nice addition to Greek yogurt, trail mix, or granola.

CUCUMBERS

The green, cylindrical cucumber *(Cucumis sativus)* is the fourth-most widely cultivated vegetable in the world—even though it is technically a fruit. Originating in India, cukes have been cultivated for more than 3,000 years. The Greeks and Romans helped spread them to other parts of Europe, and they made their way to the Americas in the 1500s. California and Florida supply the country during the warmer months, and Mexico steps in during the coldest part of winter. Worldwide, China is the chief exporter.

Cucumbers grow on trailing vines, usually on trellises or cages, and feature large leaves that shade the yellow flowers and then the maturing fruit. There are three types—slicing cucumbers, large and thick-skinned; smaller, thin-skinned pickling cukes; and long, narrow English cucumbers, often labeled burpless, that contain tiny seeds.

Health Benefits

Even thought cucumbers are 90 percent water, they still supply a range of nutrients: infection-busting vitamin C, anti-inflammatory vitamin K, energy-boosting vitamin B5, and the minerals manganese, potassium, and magnesium. They also contain powerful lignins that can contribute to reduced risk for a number of cancers.

RESCUE REMEDY: *To ease tired eyes and reduce swelling around your lower lids, simply place a slice of cucumber over each eye, lie back and relax, and let the astringent properties of the cuke leave you bright-eyed.*

SCRUB-A-DUB

Two species of the fibrous luffa—or loofah—fruit *(Luffa aegyptiaca* and *L. acutangula)* can be dried out once they are fully ripened and used as a kitchen cleaner or exfoliating bath sponge. The drying process removes everything except the network of xylem fibers. The luffa can be eaten as a vegetable when small and still green—it is common in Southeast Asian soups and stir-fries.

Up Close
VEGETARIAN LIFESTYLES
CHOOSE A MEAT-FREE DIET WITHOUT GIVING UP VITAL PROTEINS

Buddha bowls are healthy, gorgeous meals filled with a brilliant, colorful mix of grains, proteins, and veggies. This vibrant version features chickpeas, cucumbers, avocado, carrot, spinach, radish, microgreens, and sesame seeds.

Although avoiding meat in the diet may seem like a modern conceit, Egyptians from around 3200 B.C. abstained from eating animal flesh based on certain religious doctrines. Many notables in ancient Greece gave up meat as a way to avoid animal cruelty—they felt animal slaughter brutalized the human soul. Over the passing centuries various groups abstained from meat for health or moral reasons—for instance, Eastern religions like Buddhism, Hinduism, and Jainism prohibit the consumption of meat.

At the start of the 20th century, many people began investigating healthier food options like vegetarianism, and as the century progressed so did the public's awareness of the animal abuses inherent in factory farming. The counterculture movement of the 1960s contributed to the concept of preparing healthy meals without meat. The appearance of Mad Cow Disease in the 1990s and recent reports of commercial meat contaminated with *Listeria, E. coli,* and *Salmonella* bacteria have resulted in a marked decrease in meat consumption.

For most vegetarians, the aim is a healthier—and more humane—lifestyle, and there are several variations of this doctrine: lacto-ovo vegetarians eat eggs and dairy products; lactos eat only dairy; pescetarians avoid meat but consume seafood and fish; and vegans avoid animal products of any kind.

Smart Alternatives

A risk vegetarians face is a lack of the proteins found in meat and dairy. These building blocks of bodily health break down into the amino acids responsible for cell growth and repair. Proteins also take longer to digest, increasing the feeling of fullness during a meal. Below is a list of meat-free foods that provide excellent sources of protein.

QUINOA Although grains contain only a small amount of protein, quinoa, which is technically a seed, provides more than eight grams per cup. This includes all nine essential amino acids the body cannot produce on its own. This versatile "perfect protein" can be added to chilies, soups, and stews; used with honey and fruit as a hot breakfast cereal; and mixed into salads and vegetable dishes.

TOFU AND TEMPEH For centuries, tofu and tempeh have been trusted protein sources, offering 20 and 15 grams per half cup, respectively. Tempeh is especially healthy because it is fermented and provides digestive probiotics. Edamame is the soybean straight from the pod. Boiled, it contains 8.4 grams of protein per half cup and can be added to salads and pasta sauces. Nondairy milk made from soy is a good substitute for cow's milk, but it is high in calories: 100 per cup.

NUTS AND NUT BUTTERS Both nuts and nut butters supply healthy fats and proteins, making them a great fit for a plant-based diet. Nuts like cashews, pecans, and pistachios can also be high in calories, however, so opt for raw or dry roasted versions. Choose nut butters that have the fewest ingredients to avoid added sugars and oils.

White, black, and red quinoa

LEGUMES Most edible legumes are high in protein. Chickpeas contain 7.3 grams in just half a cup. They can be added to salads or blended with oil and herbs to make hummus. Peas and beans also contain high levels of protein—two cups of kidney beans offer 26 grams—plus their benefits remain in the canned varieties. Peas can be turned into a tasty pesto by blending them with pine nuts, mint, olive oil, and Parmesan cheese.

SEITAN This meat substitute, made with wheat gluten and seasoned with salts and spices, packs a walloping 36 grams of protein into a half cup.

SEEDS Many seeds are high in protein, with sunflower seeds topping the list at 7.3 grams per quarter cup. Chia seeds add both protein (4.7 grams in about two tablespoons) and fiber to dishes; they can be sprinkled over salads or mixed into smoothies—they plump up and develop a creamy texture. Hemp seeds provide 10 grams of protein per three tablespoons and can be added to smoothies and baked goods, as can sesame and poppy seeds.

THE WISDOM OF THE BUDDHA BOWL

Trending with vegans and other health-conscious eaters is the concept of the Buddha bowl. There is no one recipe for this nourishing—and colorful—array, but rather a simple formula of whole grains, plant proteins, and vegetables that supplies complete nutrition. Grains and starch form a base—try rice, barley, millet, quinoa, sweet potatoes, or corn. Add some protein in the form of tofu, tempeh, seitan, chickpeas, or beans, pile on your favorite fruits and veggies—both raw and cooked—and then sprinkle with nuts or seeds.

Alliums come in many forms, including round yellow, red, and pearl onions; teardrop shallots; and columnar scallions.

ALLIUMS

FEW PLANTS OFFER MORE TASTE AND SAVORY AROMA THAN THE ONION FAMILY

The *Allium* genus of flowering plants grows in temperate regions of the Northern Hemisphere. It includes hundreds of species, among them many edible vegetables. The genus is now a member of the Amaryllidaceae (amaryllis family), but for many years it was categorized as part of the Liliaceae (lily family). Alliums are characterized by having bulbs, some of which grow from rhizomes, and flowers that form umbels that bloom from the outer florets inward and grow on scapes, long hollow stems. Many alliums, such as garlic and shallots, can reproduce asexually through offsets—small, complete, daughter plants that form on the mother plant and are genetically identical clones.

AT A GLANCE

• *Mature onions have particularly large cells. This makes them ideal for examination under the microscope. Onions are often called into service in science or biology classes when students study cell structure and need to see actual examples.*

ONION FAMILY OPTIONS

A number of allium species have become popular staples in kitchens around the world.

ONIONS Also known as bulb onions or common onions, onions (*A. cepa*), are the most widely cultivated alliums. Their wild forebears no longer exist, and they are known only through cultivation, which began about 7,000 years ago in Asia. The ancient Egyptians revered the bulb as a symbol of eternal life, and Greek athletes ate them before the Olympic games. By the sixth century, healers were touting their medicinal benefits. Onions are extremely durable—they can be shipped long distances and stored for long periods. There are three colors: the traditional white onion is sweet; the robustly flavored yellow or brown onion is a good all-around variety; and the vibrant red onion is perfect for grilling. There are also mild, sweet cultivars, like the Vidalia, for people who suffer onion-related gastric distress. Onions can be toxic to dogs, cats, guinea pigs, and a number of other animals.

SCALLIONS Also called green onions, scallions (*A. cepa*) are young onions with small bulbs and a mild taste; they are used raw in salads, salsas, and Asian recipes or added to soups, noodle dishes, and curries.

SHALLOTS This variety of *A. cepa* looks like small, elongated onions and forms clusters of offsets. Shallots taste similar to onions but are less intense.

CHIVES Small perennials, chives (*A. schoenoprasum*) are the only alliums found in both the Old and New Worlds. The narrow, hollow leaves are typically snipped off above the base and used as herbs, lending zest to soups, potatoes, and fish dishes.

RAMPS These are seasonal, wild, woodland alliums of North America. Ramps (*A. tricoccum*) are harvested for their mildly piquant flavor, which is perfect for egg and potato dishes. The plants display wide, smooth, pale green leaves with hints of burgundy on the lower stems.

LEEKS Cultivars of the broadleaf wild leek (*A. ampeloprasum),* leeks date back to ancient Egypt. Rather than forming a bulb, they produce a long cylinder composed of large leaf sheaths; the edible portions lie between the white roots and the dark green tops. Chopped leeks add mild onion flavor to salads, soup stocks, and rice dishes.

GARLIC Renowned for its pungent aroma and dense, smoky sweet taste, garlic (*A. sativum*) is a segmented bulb that reproduces in offsets. It originated in Central and South Asia and is one of the world's oldest cultivated crops, used both as an herb and for its range of medicinal benefits.

PANTRY PICK: *Make a quick sofrito—a savory Latin sauce—by combining 4 mashed garlic cloves, 2 cups finely chopped onions, 2 tablespoons olive oil, ½ teaspoon rosemary, ¼ dried bay leaf, and 4 ounces of pureed tomatoes. Heat the oil and garlic over a medium flame, then add the onions, and sauté until brown. Add the tomato and herbs, salt to taste, and cook for 20 minutes.*

Health Benefits

For the most part, alliums provide similar health advantages. A wide range of sulfur compounds are what gives them many of their nutritional benefits, along with their intense flavor, strong smell, and tear-inducing properties. They can help provide protection of the heart, anti-cancer properties, lowered blood pressure, and reduced levels of LDL cholesterol and triglycerides.

Onions are 89 percent water and do not offer high amounts of nutrients, but they are low in calories and contain beneficial phytochemicals like phenolics, which scientists are now studying for their disease-fighting potential. Folk healers believe onions are "bacteria magnets" that can remove toxic substances from the body—one cold remedy calls for onions slices placed inside socks and worn overnight.

Garlic is a powerhouse of nutritional and medicinal benefits. It provides the sulfur-containing antioxidant compound allicin, which can reduce cholesterol levels and control high blood pressure and may have anticancer potential. Its antibiotic and antifungal properties, along with its selenium, quercetin, and vitamin C content, make garlic useful for combating colds, flu, and internal infections, treating wounds, and for general skincare. It is also a source of B-complex vitamins, iron, magnesium, manganese, phosphorus, potassium, sodium, and zinc.

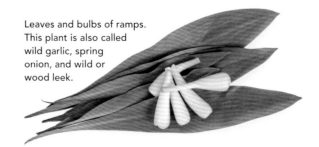

Leaves and bulbs of ramps. This plant is also called wild garlic, spring onion, and wild or wood leek.

MISCELLANEOUS VEGETABLES
MEET THESE VEGGIE FAVORITES THAT ARE UNIQUE IN THEIR FAMILIES

Crucifer, umbellifer, nightshade, and allium vegetables are all members of large families, but some well-known vegetables belong to smaller families or to those not necessarily known for producing edible plants.

ASPARAGUS

This perennial stalk vegetable originally grew wild, producing pencil-thin shoots in the vicinity of irrigation ditches and marshes. Years of selective breeding resulted in a more robust vegetable with a unique, slightly bitter flavor that chefs and diners adore. Native to much of Europe, northern Africa, and western Asia, these plants were once classified with onions in the lily family, but they now have their own family, Asparagaceae.

Most varieties are green, but those with some purple are said to be more tender and sweeter. There is also a delicate white variety that is grown underground. The Egyptians cultivated the plant for its taste and its diuretic properties more than 5,000

years ago, and, although ignored by Europeans until much later, asparagus continued to be favored by the Arabs. It traveled to the colonies with the Pilgrims, and was soon an established American crop. Today, California is the top U.S. producer. Asparagus should be eaten before the top of the spears open, or "fern out"; otherwise they turn woody. Also avoid overcooking—the stalks should retain a bit of crispness.

Health Benefits

Asparagus is an excellent source of vitamins A, K, B1, B2, C, and E, folate, copper, and selenium, and also provides fiber, manganese, phosphorus, potassium, choline, zinc, and iron. Natural healers believe asparagus can be helpful for treating fertility issues, PMS—especially bloating, depression, urinary tract infections, diabetes, cancer, and high cholesterol.

AVOCADO

This fruit of warm climates is part of the Laurelaceae family. The bay leaf, a popular herb, is part of this family, but in general it is not known for its edible species. Avocados *(Persea americana)* originated in what is now Mexico and may have existed for millions of years. The earliest remains found by archaeologists date back to 10,000 B.C. The name comes from the Nahuatl word *ahuacatl*, meaning "testicle," referring to the fruit's shape. Not surprisingly, it was considered an aphrodisiac.

The avocado fruit is technically a drupe, a large berry with a single seed. It is treated more like a vegetable by cooks, however, because its buttery flesh, however delicious, lacks sweetness. There are two commercial types—smooth green Florida avocados and smaller California, or Haas, avocados with pebbled skin that darkens as the fruit ripens.

Purple, white, and green asparagus

PANTRY PICK: *Serve diced avocado and steamed asparagus over romaine lettuce and crumbled hardboiled egg for an elegant luncheon dish. Drizzle each plate with a dressing of lemon juice, minced garlic, pepper flakes, and dry mustard, and then add olive oil and a touch of sea salt.*

Health Benefits

Green and black avocados are high in vitamin C and fiber but also high in carbohydrates and calories—one cup of the Florida variety has 276. Haas avocados are the far more common variety, and they contain more fat, but it is good fat that is heart healthy and beneficial to the skin. They are also best for making guacamole and stir-fries. Florida avocados are superior for slicing and dicing for use in salads and other cold dishes.

RHUBARB

This perennial plant poses another of those "Is it a fruit or a vegetable?" conundrums. Not quite a fruit, rhubarb *(Rheum rhabarbarum)* is a member of the Polygonaceae. This family includes the invasive plant knotweed, the herb sorrel, the grain buckwheat, and a fruit called sea grape, but rhubarb may be its only vegetable. It features large, crinkled, poisonous leaves and fleshy, reddish, edible stalks, or petioles, which are most often treated as a fruit.

Health Benefits

Rhubarb is rich in fiber C, K, and B-complex vitamins, calcium, potassium, manganese, and magnesium and provides antioxidant flavonoids like beta-carotene.

OKRA

Also known as gumbo, this flowering plant is part of the Malvaceae family. It is possibly native to South Asia, Ethiopia, or West Africa. The tall okra plant *(Abelmoschus esculentus)* flourishes in warm regions and produces lobed leaves, white or yellow flowers, and narrow, ridged fruit capsules of seven inches or so. This capsule's pentagonal cross-sections are filled with seeds that become very mucilaginous as they cook, creating a desirable "goo" that coats other ingredients in the pot. Okra is a key part of jambalaya, a Creole dish of New Orleans.

Fresh rhubarb. Chinese healers have used rhubarb for thousands of years, both as a cathartic and as a laxative.

Health Benefits

Low-calorie okra pods contain impressive amounts of fiber, vitamins A, C, and K, B-complex vitamins, and folates, plus essential minerals like calcium, iron, magnesium, and manganese, and valuable antioxidants. Research shows that it may also help diabetics manage their blood sugar levels.

SWEET POTATOES AND YAMS

Native to the American tropics, sweet potatoes *(Ipomoea batatas)* belong to Convolvulaceae. Of the 1,000 species in the family, including the morning glory, this is the only crop of commercial importance. The sweet potato plant is a perennial vine that produces hefty tubers, with tapered ends, thin skin, and orange or purple flesh that is sweet and moist.

Yams (genus *Dioscoreaceae)* are often confused with sweet potatoes. These cylindrical tubers are native to Asia and Africa and can be the size of a potato or grow to weigh 140 pounds. The rough, hairy skin varies from dark brown to pink and is easier to peel after cooking. The flesh may be white, yellow, pink, or purple; it can be starchy and dry.

Health Benefits

Raw sweet potatoes are rich in complex dietary fiber, carbohydrates, and beta-carotene and provide moderate amounts vitamins B5, B6, and manganese; baking results in higher amounts of vitamin C. Yams are considered the least perishable of the root vegetables; they supply potassium, vitamin B, manganese, thiamin, dietary fiber, and vitamin C.

Four kinds of edible mushrooms: meaty portobellos flanked by white buttons, oysters, and brown buttons

MUSHROOMS

EXPLORE THE TASTES AND TEXTURES OF THESE GIFTS FROM THE FOREST

Imagine the first person brave enough to taste a mushroom. After all, some edible varieties can be very daunting in appearance. Conversely, some innocent-looking varieties contain deadly poisons. Yet, over time, our Stone Age ancestors sorted out which forms of fungi they could safely eat and which ones they should pass by. Often this decision was abetted by local wildlife—if deer or squirrels nibbled it, humans reasoned, it must be fairly safe to consume.

Technically, edible mushrooms are the fleshy, umbrella-shaped fruiting bodies of certain macrofungi—those large enough to be seen by the naked eye. They can grow above- or belowground—the former sometimes appearing to spring up on lawns after a soaking rain. In reality, minute fruiting bodies, called the pin stage, can take several days to form, but enlarge swiftly with the absorption of water. Mushrooms can either be harvested in the wild or cultivated commercially. (Never eat a wild mushroom unless an expert has identified it.)

Historically, mushrooms intrigued the ancients both as a food source and as a medicine. The Egyptians associated them with immortality and served them only to royalty. Other civilizations used them in religious rituals or believed they imparted superhuman strength. In Europe, Louis XIV was possibly the first to

> **DID YOU KNOW?**
>
> • *The primary role of fungi is to decompose organic matter in a process called bioremediation, including petroleum products and pesticides built on a carbon structure. This means fungi have the potential to eradicate environmental pollutants and contaminants, providing they are not toxic to the fungi themselves.*

cultivate them, in caves near Paris. In the late 1800s, American gardeners tried their luck at growing them without success, but by the 1920s, they were an established crop. There are currently more than 20 species under cultivation, including the following examples.

• Button mushrooms (*Agaricus bisporus*) are the most popular variety in the United States. These white or brown mushrooms can be used raw in salads and cooked in soups, sauces, and meat and vegetable entrées. With a mild flavor, they add texture to dishes.

• Portobello mushrooms, also *A. bisporus,* are buttons that have grown up and out, spreading their caps. They are tasty, beefy giants that can serve as a replacement for meat, especially when grilled.

• Cremini mushrooms (*A. bisporus*) look like baby portobellos, but they are merely more mature buttons with deeper flavor.

• Porcini mushrooms (*Boletus edulis*) can be nearly as large as portobellos. They are meaty and golden, with a creamy, nutty flavor. Prized by Italian chefs, they are used in ravioli, pasta sauces, and vegetable soups. Dried porcinis should be soaked in hot water for at least 15 minutes before using.

- The chanterelle *(Cantharellus cibarius)* is a beautiful, golden, flower-shaped fungus that also provides floral, somewhat peppery, notes to dishes. It works on top of an entrée or with eggs. Because their moisture content is high, chanterelles should be dry sautéed, allowing them to release their own juices.
- Conical morels (genus *Morchella)* are sac fungi that have been described as withered honeycombs. They are not exactly attractive, but their rich taste and chewy texture makes them worth their higher cost.
- Delicate, white enoki mushrooms are cultivars of *Flammulina velutipes.* With their tiny caps and long stems, they may resemble bean sprouts, but they are full of flavor. A favorite of Asian cooks, they remain crisp in sauces and soups.
- Shitake mushrooms *(Lentinula edodes)* are often found in Chinese, Japanese, or Korean dishes that call for a substantial mushroom that supplies umami—a savory element.
- Hen of the woods *(Grifola frondosa),* also called the maitake—Japanese for "dancing mushroom" —grows in white and amber clusters at the base of trees (most often oaks), usually in late summer or early autumn. It adds rich, earthy flavors to dishes and can reach weights of 100 pounds.
- Wide-capped oyster mushrooms *(Pleurotus ostreatus)* may have an otherworldly appearance— did tiny aliens just descend onto your plate?— but they offer sweet flavor and a delicate consistency. Depending on the season, they may even provide a slight anise note to recipes. Because they are easily cultivated, oyster mushrooms are fairly inexpensive.

Hen of the woods sprouting from a log. Also called ram's head, sheep's head, and maitake, these mushrooms grow in clusters of whirling caps that resemble earthy florets.

Health Benefits

Mushrooms are low in calories and are cholesterol, fat, and gluten free. Most provide similar health benefits—they are high in protein, fiber, vitamin C, B-complex vitamins. They also contain certain antioxidants that are unique to mushrooms—such as the powerful ergothioneine (in 12 times the concentration found in wheat germ)—as well as polyphenols like carotenoids, flavonoids, and ascorbic acid. Hen of the woods mushrooms are prized in Asia as medicinal mushrooms, and recent research indicates that they can stimulate the immune system cells in cancer patients. They also have a hypoglycemic effect and may be effective in the management of diabetes.

THE DIVINE TRUFFLE

Among mushroom aficionados, there is only one Holy Grail: a black or white pebbled fungus that grows on the roots of certain trees and is sniffed out by trained dogs or pigs. Truffles (genera *Tuber* or *Terfizia)* are the fruiting body of a subterranean sac fungus; they may look like lumps of coal, but their rich, earthy taste is said to elevate any dish. Chefs refer to them as the "diamonds of the kitchen," and at $3,600 per pound for white truffles, they are the most expensive food on earth. They are also highly nutritious, providing protein, calcium, potassium, phosphorus, and magnesium, as well as vitamins K, D, B2, B3, and B5.

GRAINS

THESE SEEDS CONSTITUTE THE "BREAD OF LIFE" FOR MUCH OF THE WORLD

Grains, or cereals, are dry, hard seeds that are harvested and milled for human and animal consumption. Botanically, they are caryopses, fruits of the grass family, Poaceae (formerly Gramineae). Because they are more durable long term than other food staples, like fruits and tubers, many grains have become agriculturally industrialized, mechanically seeded and harvested on a massive scale, and stored in enormous grain silos as they await shipping to distant locations.

The use of grains by early humans goes back much further than scientists once believed. When archaeologists found plant starch granules deep in a cave in Mozambique, where they could not have grown, and tools with starch residue on them, they realized that our ancestors had begun processing wild grains at least 100,000 years ago.

Many weight-conscious people eliminate grain products like bread and cereal at the first sign of a few extra pounds. Meanwhile, the USDA advises eating six to eight ounces of grains daily, at least half of them whole grains. Whole grains not only contain fiber, they also provide a range of vitamins, minerals, and

beneficial phytochemicals. So unless a person suffers from celiac disease or some other form of gluten intolerance, grains should not be dismissed from the diet on a whim.

A GALLERY OF GRAINS

These are the major cereal grains that feed the planet.

CORN A native grain of North America , corn, or maize *(Zea mays),* quickly spread to much of the civilized world and is now the largest grain crop globally. It is used as a vegetable, to make flour, as livestock fodder, as biofuel (ethanol), and as a raw material in industry. Although it is a major food source, corn is not as nutritious as other cereals—its protein is of poor quality, and it lacks niacin. Its low-quality gluten cannot produce leavened bread, but corn flour is popular in Latin America for making masa, the dough used to create flat breads like tortillas.

OATS These grain seeds *(Avena sativa)* are used to feed both humans and livestock. Their wild ancestors grew in the Fertile Crescent of Mesopotamia, but domesticated oats are now found in most temperate regions. When rolled or steel-cut, they are an excellent source of protein, fiber, B vitamins, and several minerals, but especially manganese. Their acknowledged ability to lower blood cholesterol has made them a valued natural foods resource.

WHEAT Based on evidence in early human settlements, this staple grain (genus *Triticum*) dates back at least 8,000 years. Today, it is grown on more acreage than any land crop. It is a very good source of carbohydrates, and with a 13 percent protein content, it is the main source of vegetable protein for humans—although quality is low in terms of amino acids. Whole-grain wheat also provides fiber and

Steel-cut oatmeal with fresh blueberries, red raspberries, almonds, and muesli. Oatmeal has made a comeback as the go-to breakfast of the health conscious.

Humans have relied on grains for sustenance for hundreds of thousands of years. Cereal and seed grains, top row, from left: white rice, barley, brown rice, and millet; middle: buckwheat and black rice; bottom: wheat, corn, and oats

many nutrients. In a small portion of the population, wheat gluten triggers celiac disease and other gastric problems. Wheat is categorized by seasons, seed hardness, and color, including high-protein hard red winter and hard red spring and low-protein hard white and soft white, which are ideal for baking. Durham is an amber wheat that produces yellow semolina granules when milled.

BARLEY This versatile cereal grain *(Hordeum vulgare)* grows in temperate regions and is known for its nutty flavor and chewy texture. It was first cultivated in Eurasia around 10,000 years ago. In addition to its use in breads, salads, stews, and soups, it is also fermented for making beer and distilled beverages. It is high in maltose, a sugar used in Chinese cooking. In the wild, the mature barley seed spikelets break apart to disperse the seeds. Domesticated barley spikes do not shatter—the result of a genetic mutation—making the ears much easier to harvest. Barley is the fourth-most abundant grain globally, with dozens of cultivars. Health-wise, its dietary fiber feeds the bacteria in the digestive tract—and that broken-down fiber produces short-chain fatty acids called butyric acid, which can help combat colon cancer.

NOT-SO-GREAT GRAINS

Unfortunately, modern refining techniques frequently strip away the bran and germ from many grains, leaving behind a nutrient-depleted product. Whole grains, on the other hand, include all parts of the plant's kernel—the bran, germ, and endosperm—and in their original proportions. When shopping for whole-grain products, look for labels that list grain in the first three ingredients. And just because a loaf of bread is brown does not mean it's wholesome—many "wheat" breads are colored with molasses or brown sugar.

RYE This yellowish or grayish grass *(Secale cereale)* looks like a long, slender version of wheat. It still grows wild in Turkey, where it likely originated. There have been small findings of barley at sites in Asia Minor from the Neolithic period, but no others until 1800 to 1500 B.C. Rye has been cultivated widely in Europe since the Middle Ages—the rye belt now stretches from northern Germany and Poland across Ukraine and Belarus to central and northern Russia. It is also produced in North America, Argentina, Brazil, Chile, Australia, New Zealand, and northern China. Rye is used to make American rye whiskey in the United States. Canadian "rye" is often made with corn mash. Rye has the ability to improve the pollination abilities of wheat when there is cross-pollination between the two species. The fiber in rye is unusual: it binds with water molecules and creates a feeling of fullness. Rye also contains magnesium, phosphorus, and copper.

SPELT A staple in Europe from the Bronze Age to the Middle Ages, spelt *(Triticum spelta)* has a varied history—it is currently a relict crop in Central Europe and is only now being rediscovered by the natural foods community and organic farmers—mainly because it requires less fertilizer. It may be a subspecies of its close cousin common wheat *(T. aestivum)* through a complex hybridization process with Emmer wheat and the wild goat grass of the Near East. Spelt flour contains a moderate amount of gluten, making it suitable for baking. It has also been used to make beer, gin, and vodka. Nutritionally, it provides fiber, manganese, phosphorus, and niacin.

SORGHUM This is a genus of flowering grasses. One species, *Sorghum bicolor,* is grown for its grain, while other species are used for fodder, alcoholic beverages, and ethanol. The grain originated in Africa, but is now is found all over the world.

Whole-grain spelt loaf studded with sunflower seeds. Even after milling, spelt grains retain their bran and germ, which means it bakes into highly nutritious bread. Spelt's protein also results in a light loaf with a soft texture and nutty flavor.

S. bicolor is as a source of bread in some regions, but is primarily grown for its sweet syrup, which is similar to molasses. Nutritionally it provides impressive amounts of dietary fiber, plus niacin, riboflavin, thiamine, magnesium, iron, copper, calcium, phosphorus, and potassium. The bran contains a type of antioxidant not found in many foods, which can reduce the risk of certain cancers. For those with wheat or gluten sensitivity, it is an acceptable alternative. It is the fifth-most important grain crop in the world, with Nigeria, India, Mexico, and the United States the top producers.

MILLET Also called pearl millet *(Pennisetum glaucum),* this grain is not just for the birds, although it does feature heavily in packaged birdseed. Millet is an ancient grain that was grown in Africa and India since prehistoric times and is now enjoyed in many parts of the world outside the United States. It plumps up when cooked and is a gluten-free substitute for wheat. This heart-healthy grain contains fiber, iron, copper, phosphorus, manganese, and magnesium.

Pumpkin Millet Porridge with chewy raisins

MAKE IT YOURSELF
Pumpkin Millet Porridge

You can serve this silky millet porridge for breakfast or as an autumn dessert.

YOU WILL NEED:
⅔ cup dry millet
¾ cup rice milk
¾ cup water
1 cup pumpkin puree
1 cup canned coconut milk
1 teaspoon ground cinnamon
½ teaspoon ground ginger
¼ teaspoon ground nutmeg
1 tablespoon maple syrup

WHAT TO DO:
• In a saucepan, combine millet, rice milk, and water, and bring to a boil.
• Turn off the heat, and whisk in the pumpkin.
• Whisk in the remaining ingredients, and then pour the mixture into a greased two-quart casserole dish.
• Cover, and bake in a 350-degree oven until the millet has softened and absorbed most of the liquid. Let stand, and then serve.

SUGARCANE A tall, bamboo-like grass called sugarcane (genus *Saccharum),* part of the same family as cereal grains, is considered an agronomic crop, like corn or wheat. It is also the world's largest crop, by production quantity. The juice of the cane plant, which is popular in many tropical countries, is full of nutrients, and just one glass provides a natural burst of energy. It is also an alkaline—rich in calcium, potassium, and magnesium, which creates an internal environment that discourages diseases like cancer. Its sugar has a low glycemic index—it does not send blood glucose spiking, not even in diabetics. Sugarcane elevates protein levels in the body, and its antioxidants protect the liver from infections.

RICE The seed of a species of grass, rice *(Oryza sativa)* is the most commonly consumed staple for more than half the world's population, especially in Asia. It is normally an annual plant, but in the tropics it can produce a ratoon crop—where the upper plant is harvested, but the lower plant remains untouched—for up to 30 years. Rice is labor intensive to grow and harvest, and the seedlings do best in flooded fields, called paddies. Still, rice can be cultivated almost anywhere that there is ample water, even on terraced hillsides. Brown rice contains some nutrients—magnesium, phosphorus, and vitamin B5—and provides high levels of energy compared to others staples, while refined white rice offers no significant micronutrients, but equal amounts of energy.

Up Close
SMALL WONDERS
DISCOVER THE BENEFITS OF CRISP SPROUTS AND DELICATE MICROGREENS AT HOME

Healthy can be hearty. Top a spinach, avocado, tomato, and hummus sandwich with the homegrown sprouts of your choice.

t might have begun as part of the hippie counterculture movement or as a natural foods concept, but the idea of growing edible plants in the home appeals to many people. Herbs were probably one of the first foods to be used in a windowsill garden, but recently they have been joined by sprouts and even more recently by microgreens—plant seedlings—as an easy-to-grow sources of fresh produce.

Sprouts

Sprouts are the tender stems that emerge from germinated seeds, nuts, or grains. They are crisply delicious and can be used in sandwiches, salads, or stir-fry recipes. They are also inexpensive and typically take less than a week to grow. Some seeds that respond well to sprouting include alfalfa, broccoli, red clover, lentil, mung bean, pumpkin, sunflower, and chia. Most of these seeds can be bought at a health food store or ordered in bulk online. Make sure to specify organic sprouting seeds.

Sprouts may appear pale and wispy, but they actually provide the benefits of a plant in its most biologically concentrated form. For instance, a cup of broccoli sprouts contains 7.5 mg of vitamin E compared to 1.5 mg in a cup of raw or cooked broccoli. And because the body stops producing certain enzymes, and its ability to battle disease lessens as we age, sprouts can boost antioxidant vitamin C content and also raise the chlorophyll content, creating a hostile environment for bacteria. Broccoli sprouts contain from 10 to 100 times the glucoraphanin of mature vegetables. Glucoraphanin is an antioxidant that enzymes transform into two compounds—raphanin, an antibiotic, and sulforaphane, which has anticancer and antimicrobial properties. Most sprouts are excellent sources of fiber, manganese, riboflavin, and copper and also provide protein, thiamine, niacin, vitamin B6, iron, magnesium, phosphorus, and potassium.

PANTRY PICK: *For a satisfying veggie sandwich, layer baby spinach leaves, sliced avocado, fresh-picked cherry tomatoes, chickpea hummus, and sprouts or microgreens between slices of a nutty whole-grain bread.*

Microgreens

These diminutive greens have captured the imagination of the natural foods community—and many people outside it. Also called "vegetable confetti," microgreens are the seedlings of edible plants like herbs and vegetables. They differ from sprouts, which are eaten in their entirety, because

Snipping fresh sunflower microgreens. Grow microgreens in soil and sprouts in easy-to-make containers.

they are harvested with scissors after two to four weeks of growth. They also require both soil and sunlight to grow to the proper height for snipping. The most commonly used seeds are lettuce, kale, spinach, beet, radish, watercress, cilantro, basil, amaranth, cabbage, mustard, chia, sunflower, and buckwheat. Microgreens can be added to sandwiches, wraps, smoothies, and salads.

Like sprouts, microgreens are concentrated sources of nutrition and loaded with beneficial enzymes. Greens grown from cabbage, cilantro, or radish may contain up to 40 times the nutrients of the mature plants. These baby greens provide amino acids and high levels of antioxidants, which can promote heart health and fight disease. These plant-based foods also address issues like obesity and diabetes, support healthy skin, and can lengthen life expectancy.

SET UP A MINI GARDEN To prepare a soil base for your greens, you will need organic soil, a shallow tray, an optional grow light, and microgreen seeds,

- Add one inch of organic soil to a shallow tray or dish, then scatter seeds fairly thickly on top (no need for thinning—they won't grow that big).
- Cover seeds with a thin layer of soil, and mist the soil with filtered water. Place in a south-facing window with lots of sunlight.
- Mist soil three times a day. Greens should be ready to harvest in two to four weeks. Cut with small scissors just above the soil line.

MAKE IT YOURSELF
Sprouting Jar

You can purchase sprouting trays, but it's easy to make a sprouting jar from a canning jar with a piece of cheesecloth held in place over the top with an elastic band. Make sure the seeds you use are safe for sprouting (some, like kidney beans, can be dangerous) and take care to avoid bacterial growth. If the sprouts show any mold, throw them out, and start over.

YOU WILL NEED:
1 teaspoon seeds (such as alfalfa, broccoli, red clover, chia, lentil, mung bean, pumpkin, or sunflower)
1 cup filtered water
1-quart canning jar, sterilized

WHAT TO DO:
- Place a teaspoon of seeds in the jar, add filtered water, and cover with cheesecloth.
- Leave overnight or for 12 hours, then rinse the seeds in a fine strainer several times.
- Return seeds to jar, cover again with cheesecloth, and place upside down at an angle, on a dish rack or cake rack, to let excess water drain off. Rinse sprouts several times a day, and return to angled position.
- Harvest sprouts within three to seven days. They should form a tangle of thin pale threads and have green tips just forming. Rinse again, and then store in a covered container for four or five days.

PSEUDOCEREALS

THESE NOURISHING FRUITS AND SEEDS ARE TREATED SIMILARLY TO GRAINS

Pseudocereals are nongrass dicots that produce fruits and seeds and are used the same way as grains—ground into flour or cooked in liquid. Many of these species are of ancient lineage—at one time sustaining communities, then forgotten for centuries, and now being rediscovered by modern generations determined to eat well. Many of them contain higher-quality protein than traditional grains, and all are gluten-free.

DID YOU KNOW?

• *To augment their natural benefits, many pseudocereals are subject to processing treatments like germination, puffing, and fermentation, which can alter their nutritional qualities by reducing antinutrients like tannins or phytates that slow absorption, or by improving their digestibility and increasing the availability of nutrients.*

A PSEUDOCEREAL SAMPLER

Many of these "grains" are being studied anew for their culinary potential and for their health benefits, as well as for their ability to sustain communities in famine-prone regions.

BUCKWHEAT Common buckwheat (*Fagopyrum esculentum*) it is the seed of a fruit related to rhubarb. It makes a good substitute for people with grain sensitivities. Along with the antioxidant flavonoid rutin, which can lower LDL cholesterol, it contains magnesium, the mineral that lowers blood pressure. Buckwheat is sold as groats or flour and is used for pancakes and noodles. Bees love fragrant buckwheat flowers and make a dark, flavorful honey from them.

HANZA A little-known member of the Capparaceae, or caper family, hanza (*Boscia senegalensis*) originated in West Africa, and is now being considered for its potential to address hunger in the Sahel region—it can improve nutrition and food security, encourage rural development, and support sustainable land management. Also, the fruit matures at the start of the rainy season, when other crops are just being planted. The seeds are similar to chickpeas and can be used in soups, stews, and porridges.

CHIA A New World member of the mint family, chia (*Salvia hispanica*) is a nutritious seed, once prized by the Inca and Aztec cultures. Chia seeds are high in fiber, calcium, and phosphorus and provide both omega-3 and omega-6 fatty acids. They expand greatly when cooked and have a gel-like texture. Add them to health shakes and smoothies, bake them into muffins, or mix them with yogurt.

PANTRY PICK: *Chia pudding is a great base for a healthy dessert. In a mason jar, combine ⅔ cup chia seeds, 2 cups coconut, soy, hazelnut, cashew or almond milk, and ½ teaspoon vanilla extract (for added sweetness you can also add 1 tablespoon maple syrup or honey). Cover, and shake well, making sure the ingredients are well mixed Place in the fridge for a couple of hours or overnight. Top with your favorites fruits, nuts, and seeds.*

Chia pudding topped with strawberries, black and red raspberries, and blueberries

QUINOA An ancient food staple of the Andean cultures, quinoa *(Chenopodium quinoa)* is a member of the amaranth family. It comes in red, white, or black varieties and looks similar to couscous. It has become the darling of the health food crowd because it provides a complete protein, containing all essential amino acids. It is also high in fiber, B vitamins, potassium, calcium, and magnesium.

> PANTRY PICK: *Once you have learned to prep quinoa, you can use it in meat, vegetable, and fruit dishes—and also prepare its junior relative kañiwa. You will need 1 cup quinoa and ½ teaspoon kosher salt. First soak the quinoa in 2 cups of water for 15 minutes to dissolve the bitter coating. Drain, rinse, and add to a pot with 1½ cups water, and the kosher salt. Bring to a boil, cover, and simmer for 15 minutes. Fluff with a fork, and serve as a side dish, as a breakfast cereal with fruit, or use it instead of rice in ethnic dishes like chilies or curries.*

KAÑIWA A species of goosefoot, kañiwa *(Chenopodium pallidicaule)* is quinoa's much smaller cousin. It lacks the saponin coating of quinoa, making it easier to prepare. Otherwise, its cooking process and nutritional makeup are similar. When boiled, it is nuttier and crunchier than quinoa and not as fluffy.

AMARANTH Also known as love-lies-bleeding, red amaranth, and Prince-of-Wales-feather, amaranth (genus *Amaranthus)* is native to Peru and Mexico. Several species are raised for their seeds or "grain"—*A. caudatus, A. hypochondriacus,* and *A. cruentus.* Amaranth is being considered by world health groups as an inexpensive, easy-to-harvest crop that could benefit indigenous peoples in rural areas prone to famine. It is high in protein and iron, is a good source of vitamin C, and is easy to cook.

FLAXSEED A cool-weather crop, flaxseeds *(Linum usitatissimum)* are rich in protein. They are the top whole-food source for lignan, a phytonutrient associated with prolonged survival in cancer patients. They also contain omega-3 fatty acids, soluble fiber, and boron. Try adding them to salads and smoothies.

A quinoa Buddha bowl, topped with roasted eggplant, chickpeas, cherry tomatoes, fresh spinach, and hummus

SESAME AND POPPY These seeds are edible, nongrass dicots, similar to pseudocereals. Sesame seeds (genus *Sesamum)* are known for their pungent oil and for adding a nutty-tasting crunch to Asian dishes. They provide fiber, phytosterols, vitamin B6, folate, thiamine, calcium, magnesium, phosphorus, and tryptophan. The tiny seeds of the opium poppy *(Papavar somniferum)* have been harvested for thousands of years in the Middle East. They are used in baked goods and to make oil. They supply iron, copper, calcium, potassium, manganese, and zinc.

Health Benefits

Pseudocereals are currently garnering interest from nutritionists and food scientists over their bioactive components, including phytosterols, polyphenols, saponins, and essential minerals. They certainly offer a lot of bang for the buck in terms of health-building nutrients. They provide equal amounts of fiber to grains but contain higher levels of unsaturated fats, like lysine, and their starch granules are smaller and fewer in quantity. Amaranth and quinoa are both rich in arginine and histidine, essential nutrients for children and infants. All pseudocereals contain minute amounts of bitter-tasting saponins, which provide anti-inflammatory, antimicrobial, anticarginogenic, and cholesterol-lowering properties.

A sampling of nuts, including almonds, hazelnuts, walnuts, pistachios, and peanuts

NUTS

THESE TENDER MORSELS ABOUND WITH PROTEIN, MINERALS, AND ANTIOXIDANTS

Nuts, which conveniently fall from trees when mature and are feasted upon by many animals, were undoubtedly one of the earliest foods of our species. At an archaeological dig in Israel, researchers discovered startling evidence that nuts were a significant part of our primitive ancestors' diet more than 780,000 years ago. The remnants they found included almonds, prickly water lily, water chestnuts, and two varieties each of pistachios and acorns. There was also evidence of pitted stones at the site, tools used to crack open quantities of hard-shelled nuts. Similar stones have been found in North America and Europe and date from around 8,000 years ago. Native Americans placed a nut on their "pitting" stones and then used a larger rock, the "hammer" stone, to crack it open. The nuts they collected included beechnuts, hickory nuts, chestnuts, and walnuts. They were ground with a mortar and pestle to make flour and nut butter, and the shells were burned as fuel. If whole nuts were boiled in water, the fat was skimmed off and saved.

Nuts fall into four groups: drupes, such as almonds, walnuts, and pecans; enclosed seeds, like peanuts; naked seeds, such as a pine nuts; and true nuts, like hazelnuts or chestnuts. In a culinary sense, the nut category comprises any oily kernel inside a hard, inedible shell. In the kitchen, nuts are used for cooking, baking, salads, and smoothies; commercially they are found in baked goods, cereals, snack foods, and cooking oils and are used to manufacture scents, flavorings, industrial lubricants, and automotive fuel.

> ### DID YOU KNOW?
>
> *During the 20th century, pistachio nuts were dyed a deep red, which turned the fingers a telltale pink. One theory for this was that a Syrian importer wanted to distinguish his nuts from his competitors. The likely reason is that the beige shells become mottled and the dye evens them out.*

NUT FAVORITES

Get acquainted with some of the world's tastiest and most popular nuts.

- Almonds *(Prunus dulcis),* which are mentioned in the Bible, were one of the earliest nuts to be cultivated in the Middle East. Crusaders returning from the Holy Land introduced the nut to Europe in the form of marzipan, a confection made of almond paste.

- Chestnuts (genus *Castanea)* have been cultivated since at least 2000 B.C., and by the 19th century, these nuts were a staple food of the poor. Though their popularity has waxed and waned, they are still eaten roasted, as part of stuffings, and, soaked in wine or glazed in honey as a confection.

- The peanut *(Arachis hypogaea)*, a legume, is used more like a true nut. They are native to South America, where they have been used for more than 2,000 years. Spanish and Portuguese slave traders carried them to Africa, and African slaves introduced them to the North American colonies. They started as a food for the poor, but before long the entire world was clamoring for roasted, salted peanuts and peanut butter.
- Cashews *(Anacardium occidentale)* are native to Brazil, but since the 1500s have been grown in India and Africa. They are always packaged and sold hulled because a caustic oil exists between the fruit and shell.
- Walnuts *(Juglans regia)* are native to Iraq, where remains have been found dating to 50,000 B.C. They were the "food of the gods" according to the Greeks and Romans. Later, English ships carried them as trade items throughout the Mediterranean, leading to the name English walnuts.
- The pecan *(Carya illinoiensis)* is the only major nut of North America; pecan remains found at a Texas site go back to 6100 B.C. It later became a staple of Native American tribes and European settlers.
- Brazil nuts *(Bertholettia excelsa)* grow in the Amazon basin; they are large seeds arranged in a segmented pod.
- Pistachios *(Pistacia vera)* have been cultivated for thousands of years in West Asia and Asia Minor and remain part of many regional dishes, both savory and sweet.
- Pine nuts (genus *Pinus*) are the edible seeds of roughly 20 species of pine trees. They are popular in pestos, salads, and baking.
- Macadamia nuts (genus *Macadamia*) originated in Australia's Queensland rain forests. They were brought to Hawaii in the late 19th century and also flourished there.
- Hazelnuts (genus *Corylus*) go back at least to 2838 B.C., when a Chinese manuscript names them one of the "five sacred nourishments." These nuts, also known as filberts, flavor baked goods, liqueurs, and sweet sandwich spreads.

PANTRY PICK: *Making nutritious and flavorful nut butters is easy with a food processor or a bullet with a flat blade. Add 1½ cups of fresh or roasted walnuts, almonds, hazelnuts, pistachios, or cashews to the receptacle, and blend until creamy, cleaning the sides with a spatula, and adding water or honey until the consistency is correct. Store in a sealed container in the refrigerator.*

Health Benefits

Nuts are one of the healthiest foods on earth, providing impressive amounts of protein, very few carbs, and—in varying amounts—fiber, vitamin E, magnesium, phosphorus, copper, manganese, and selenium. The antioxidants they contain, including polyphenols, have a greater ability to scavenge free radicals than those found in fish. Walnuts and almonds, in particular, protect cell walls from oxidation. In weight-loss studies comparing nuts to olive oil, the participants eating nuts lost an average of two inches from their waists. Even though nuts tend to be high in calories, research indicates that the body does not absorb all of them. Nuts can also lower triglycerides in people with diabetes and obesity, and in one test, whole pecans reduced levels of LDL cholesterol in subjects two to eight hours after consumption—possibly due to their high levels of monounsaturated and polyunsaturated fats.

Homemade peanut and walnut butters

SEAFOOD

NET A NUTRITIONAL HAUL WITH THE BOUNTY OF OCEANS, LAKES, AND STREAMS

Residents of island nations or populations along seacoasts typically consume diets rich in fish and shellfish. Statistically, they also tend to have much lower rates of heart attack, cardiovascular disease, and stroke. Researchers eventually discovered the link—that the high levels of omega-3 fatty acids found in a fish-based diet were, among other benefits, capable of cleansing the arteries of the built-up cholesterol plaque that can precipitate cardiovascular events. This revelation placed seafood—fish and shellfish—high on the list of healthy dining options, especially for those seeking a protein-rich alternative to meat.

FISH MARKET OPTIONS

With the spotlight on fish in so much of the health news, even small supermarkets offer a wide range of saltwater and freshwater options, along with shellfish.

SALTWATER AND FRESHWATER FISH Commercial seafood includes freshwater fish, such as trout, catfish, and bass, and saltwater fish, like cod, herring, tuna, flounder, sole, and tilapia. Some species, such as salmon, are hatched in fresh water, go to sea as adults, and then return to fresh water to breed, or spawn. Smaller fish, like smelt, are often served whole; larger fish are filleted. Most fish can be baked, poached, steamed, or "cooked" in an acid like vinegar or lime juice to make ceviche. Only very fresh high-end fish, like ahi tuna, should be served raw as sushi. Among the healthiest choices are troll- or pole-caught albacore tuna from the United States or British Columbia, wild-caught salmon from Alaska, and farmed rainbow trout and Coho salmon. Pacific wild-caught sardines are an inexpensive and highly nutritious option—these tiny fish pack more omega-3 in a three-ounce serving than just about any other food, and they also contain plenty of vitamin D.

SHELLFISH For all their strange—even buglike—appearance, shellfish offer delectable flavors. There are three edible groups: crustaceans such as lobsters, crabs, and shrimp; mollusks, which include bivalves like clams, mussels, and oysters; gastropods, or sea snails, like conch and abalone; and cephalopods like octopus and squid; and echinoderms, such as sea urchins and sea cucumbers. Crustaceans are delicious eaten boiled or steamed, but are also prized flavor enhancers for soups, casseroles, and salads. Use the shells and carcasses with herbs and spices to create a rich fish stock that can be frozen. Bivalves can be shucked and eaten raw, steamed in broth, or baked. Octopus can be slow cooked, and squid can be sautéed—but avoid deep-fried calamari. Sea urchin roe is considered a delicacy.

For a healthy salad, toss watercress with salmon and avocado, and top with goji berries and pumpkin seeds.

PANTRY PICK: *Many cultures crave the flavor profile created by mixing fish with shellfish—from Spanish paella to French bouillabaisse and Italian cioppino to Vietnamese mi quang. Buy a pound each of shrimp and some form of white fish and a dozen clams or mussels, and then boil the fish in stock for an hour with fennel and saffron or your own spice blend, adding the shrimp and mollusks and tomatoes, potatoes, or other soup vegetables near the end.*

Health Benefits

All types of seafood provide similar benefits—they are low in saturated fats and cholesterol and high in protein and nutrients like B-complex vitamins. Salmon is especially rich in vitamin A, and the fatty skins of salmon and tuna contain high levels of vitamin D. They also provide phosphorus, selenium, and magnesium. Perhaps their most valuable nutritional constituent is their high levels of omega-3 fatty acids, those medicinal miracle workers. In addition to protecting the heart and brain, they can help prevent or treat depression, boost cognitive

Italian cioppino—one of the many ways the world enjoys a rich mix of seafood. Globally, seafood provides humans with more protein than cattle, sheep, or poultry.

function, and lower the risk of Alzheimer's in women, enhance fetal growth and development, maintain eye health, and keep skin glowing.

Large, coldwater fish like swordfish and shark are rich in omega-3 fatty acids, but they also contain disturbing levels of methylmercury. As top food chain predators, they suffer from a buildup of the toxic chemicals contained in smaller fish.

Many populations of wild fish have also been overharvested. Farm-raising fish such as salmon, catfish, and tilapia, called aquaculture, seemed like an ideal solution to both concerns. Unfortunately, the same problems plague the fish-farming industry as occur in the factory farming of livestock—pollution, overcrowding, disease, and inferior nutrition. Farmed fish are fed genetically modified corn and soy, as well as fishmeal that accumulates carcinogenic industrial chemicals like polychlorinated biphenyl (PCB) and dioxin. PCB concentrations can be eight times higher in farmed salmon than in wild salmon, and levels of omega-3 acids may be reduced by 50 percent.

Fresh rainbow smelts ready for poaching with lemon, thyme, rosemary, peppercorns, and coarse sea salt. These little nutrient-packed fish are also low in mercury.

GO FISH!

When shopping for whole fish, look for bright, bulging eyes, a firm skin, and a clean, briny smell. Gills should be pink or red and wet. Avoid any seafood that smells fishy or "off." Filleted fish should be moist and have no changes of color. Fresh mollusk shells should always be closed. And don't forget to ask your fishmonger for the catch of the day. With packaged fish, look for the Marine Stewardship Council's seal, indicating that the fish's entire production process was inspected and met sustainable standards.

Arugula and snow pea salad topped with grilled chicken. Keep meat and poultry portions small compared to greens.

LEAN MEATS

LEARN THE HEALTHIEST CUTS AND HOW TO PREPARE THEM

O f the five basic tastes—sweet, sour, bitter, salty, umami—perhaps most compelling to the human palette is umami—a savory unctuousness that is frequently supplied by meat. This craving might hark back to the days of Stone Age hunters, who sought out meat to survive, fatty meat in particular. Alas, we are no longer hunter-gatherers, and research has shown that diets heavy in fat can be detrimental to the heart and place individuals at risk for obesity, diabetes, high cholesterol, inflammatory diseases like arthritis, and cancer. Most commercial meat also contains hormones, antibiotics, and other drugs, which can cause cancer and lead to antibiotic-resistant bacteria.

MEAT OPTIONS

Advertisements often tout certain cuts of meat—including beef, pork, and lamb, along with poultry—as healthy alternatives to our favorite fatty cuts of beef or pork. Yet much of this spin is sponsored by

> **DID YOU KNOW?**
>
> • *The billion and a half cattle on ranches and in feedlots generate more harmful greenhouse gases than cars, planes, and other types of transportation put together. This factors in the related aspects of feeding, watering, and transporting them, plus their own methane emissions.*

livestock and poultry breeders, who, naturally, insist that their products are safe. Lean cuts may offer lower levels of fat, but they still contain some amount of saturated fats, drugs, and hormones. For those who choose to eat meat, moderation is the safest course. For instance, two to three ounces of cooked meat or skinless poultry equals one serving. Try to limit meat to three or four days a week and augment meals with fish, eggs, nuts, and seeds.

BEEF Lean beef cuts include flank steak, sirloin tip, eye of round, top round, tenderloin, top loin, rump roast, and extra-lean ground beef. Veal comes from young bovines, frequently surplus male dairy calves, and is inherently low in fat.

PORK Lean cuts of pork include center loin, tenderloin, and Canadian bacon. Cured pork items like American bacon, sausage, and ham, are not only high in fat but also contain added salt.

POULTRY Chickens, turkeys, and Cornish game hens all provide the leanest meat. Chickens can be purchased as entire birds or as breasts, thighs, drumsticks, or wings. Turkeys are sold as whole birds, and also packaged as breasts and drumsticks. For the best low-fat results, poultry should be baked, broiled, grilled, or stir-fried.

PANTRY PICKS: *To add a protein boost to a salad, toss arugula with snow pea pods, top with grilled chicken, and drizzle on a dressing made from 1 tablespoon soy sauce, 2 teaspoons sesame oil, 1½ tablespoons white vinegar, 1 tablespoon olive oil, and 1½ tablespoons honey.*

LAMB A lean, tender red meat, lamb comes from young domestic sheep. The tougher meat of older sheep is called mutton. Lamb is sold in racks, shoulders, chops, shanks, breasts, legs, and saddles.

PANTRY PICK: *For a small dinner party entrée, lightly baste lamb chops or lean pork chops with olive oil, and then sprinkle with fresh rosemary and garlic, a bit of pepper, and a pinch of salt, and then broil or grill them. Serve with a mesclun salad of mixed baby greens.*

When shopping for meat or poultry, these tips will help you make healthy decisions.

- Choose cuts of meat containing less than three grams of fat per ounce.
- Look for meat with a USDA "Select" or "Choice" grading rather than "Prime," which tends to be more fatty. When buying poultry, look for a USDA rating of Grade A or B.
- Prepare poultry with the skin and fat removed.
- Be aware that ground chicken and turkey can be as fatty as ground beef because the oilier dark meat is often included.
- Shop for organic, free-range, hormone-free, and grass-fed meats whenever possible.
- Buy meat at a local farmers' market or directly from the farm; that way you can ask about how the livestock is raised.

Here are a few guidelines for preparing meat or ordering it in a restaurant.

WILD GAME

Lean varieties of game animals include bison, venison, elk, squab, pheasant, and rabbit. Farm-raised ostrich and emu are also considered lean sources of protein.

- When following a recipe, replace a portion of the meat with beans, mushrooms, or tofu.
- Experiment with preparing unfamiliar lean cuts of meat; use low-calorie marinades and rubs to give them added flavor.
- When dining out, order meat that is prepared with dry-heat or moist-heat methods—baked, broiled, steamed, poached, or grilled.
- Eat only half the meat in your entrée, and bring the rest home for the next day.
- Avoid meat that has been breaded, battered, fried, or covered in creamy sauces or butter.

Health Benefits

Meat and poultry provide high levels of protein, B vitamins (especially B12), vitamin E, iron, zinc, and magnesium. Lean cuts do contain less saturated fat than other portions. Store-bought chop meat might have traces of bacteria picked up during the mass grinding process. To be safe, pick a cut of meat and have a store butcher grind it. Poultry meat also carries bacteria, especially *Salmonella,* that can cause food poisoning. It is vital to handle it with care and avoid cross-contamination—for instance, putting raw and cooked meats on the same tray. Poultry contains hormones and drugs as well, so shop for free-range and hormone-free chickens and turkeys if possible.

Lamb chops, ready for grilling with rosemary, garlic, and peppercorns

DAIRY DILEMMAS

MUST WE GIVE UP OUR CREAMY DAIRY DELIGHTS FOR PLANT-BASED SUBSTITUTES?

Dairy foods project an aura of good health: picturesque farms, green grass, and contented cows and clucking chickens come to mind— yet many milk products also contain saturated fats and traces of the hormones, drugs, and medicines given to cows. Controversy continues over whether the latter group constitutes a health hazard or not. Discord also arises over saturated fats, which are found in milk products and eggs. Some scientists—and the American Heart Association—still warn against these fats, while others insist that they are beneficial—lowering LDL, protecting the liver, enhancing immunity, and helping body tissues retain omega-3 fatty acids. For those concerned over the safety of dairy foods, there *are* alternatives available. In cases in which the alternatives have proved to be bland or unpalatable, as with egg substitutes, or ended up being a worse option, as happened with margarine, it is necessary to weigh the nutritional or "comfort" benefits of dairy foods against the possible heath risks of continuing to eat them regularly.

GOT MILK?—OR NOT

Many Americans grew up hearing the virtues of cow's milk repeatedly extolled in ads, but milk is not precisely the ideal food the dairy industry would have us believe. There are reports of milk heightening the risk of breast cancer in women or Parkinson's disease in men or causing headaches, acne, asthma, fatigue, and digestive issues. Cows also ingest

> **DID YOU KNOW?**
>
> • *In regions where milk consumption is heavy, such as Europe, people continue to produce the milk-digesting enzyme lactase into adulthood. In countries where cow's milk is less common, like Japan, children stop producing lactase as they grow out of infancy. In those places, lactose intolerance can afflict entire populations.*

contaminants like dioxin and melamine, which show up in their milk. There is also increasing awareness of humane issues within the dairy industry.

Milk is meant to supply nutrition to mammalian infants, and most babies produce far less lactase—the enzyme needed to digest lactose—when they are weaned. The cow's milk people drink throughout their lives is formulated specifically to nourish a calf. It's debatable whether humans require it at any age. As for those long-standing claims that the calcium content in milk builds strong bones, a Harvard study showed that a high intake of calcium, even from dairy products, is not associated with lowered risk for fractures or osteoporosis.

Still, bovine milk has been part of the human diet for at least 8,000 years. Dairy cows offered a portable "on-the-hoof" source of nutrition to nomadic peoples and those settling new lands.

Health Benefits

Make no mistake—milk *does* have nutritional value. It provides essential amino acids, plus the proteins whey and casein, which can preserve lean muscle mass and raise the metabolism during a weight-loss regimen. Along with calcium, it supplies potassium, phosphorus, vitamins A, B12, B2, and D, riboflavin, and niacin. Milk from grass-fed cows also offers high levels of omega-3 fatty acids compared to grain-fed cows.

A lineup of classic dairy products: butter, cream, yogurt, milk, eggs, and cottage cheese

Four of the many different types of nondairy milk alternatives: hazelnut, oat, coconut, and almond

PLANT-BASED ALTERNATIVES

Whether people are giving up milk for ideological or for health reasons, there are a range of substitutes that can stand on their own as sources of protein and disease-fighting properties, including soy, almond, cashew, hazelnut, rice, oat, and coconut milks.

Health Benefits

- Soy milk, once the leader of the nondairy pack, has been under fire lately—for one thing, its soybean sources are genetically modified, and for another, it contains phytic acid, which can inhibit the absorption of essential minerals. Yet soy milk is still the least processed of the dairy alternatives, and it's high in protein and low in saturated fats.
- Almond milk, a mixture of nuts and water, has been a favored drink since the Middle Ages. It is low in calories and contains high levels of vitamin E, manganese, selenium, magnesium, potassium, zinc, iron, and phosphorus. It also offers the highest levels of calcium of all nuts. On the down side, it lacks that protein punch, with only one gram per serving.
- Cashew milk, a recent entry in the category, has a subtle flavor and is a good source of fiber, copper, magnesium, and antioxidants. It is, like almond milk, low in protein. Pair it with quinoa or bean dishes.
- Hazelnut milk has a nuttier flavor than cashew or almond milks, which makes it a perfect coffee creamer. It is naturally gluten- and lactose-free, low in calories, containing no cholesterol or saturated fat. It also is a good source of vitamins B1, B2, and B6 and an excellent source antioxidant vitamin E.
- Rice milk has little nutritional value and is higher in sugars than its competitors, but it holds up under heat when used in baking.

- Oat milk, made by soaking oats in water, is naturally lactose free. This low-calorie alternative has a taste similar to cow's milk. Nutritionally, it contains phytochemicals, calcium, potassium, phosphorus, E, A, and B vitamins, and folic acid.
- Coconut milk—the kind sold in a carton in the dairy case, not the type that comes in a small can, which is thick and full of saturated fats—is naturally sweet, with a pleasing, creamy texture. It is loaded with easily digested medium-chain triglycerides, which help to fight fat, as well as potassium and fortified vitamins—as much as 50 percent of the daily recommended intake of B12 in some brands. Because coconut milk is relatively high in saturated fats, it is best used in smaller quantities: to top off coffee, tea, cocoa, or hot cereal or to add to smoothies made with other nondairy milks for a richer taste.

CHEESE PLEASE

Cheese may be the most popular food on the planet. Consider its complex flavors, its divine meltability, its power to transform mundane dishes into masterpieces. Ponder the endless varieties—many countries have a national cheese, and some have dozens of signature cheeses—and its multitude of applications, from appetizers to salads to entrées to desserts.

Cheese is made by acidifying milk with vinegar or bacteria and then adding the enzyme rennet, which causes the protein, whey, to coagulate into curds. Cheese can be produced from the milk of cows,

To calculate a healthy portion of cheese, think of dice. Four dice equal a one-ounce serving of popular hard cheeses like Swiss (110 calories) and cheddar (115 calories).

goats, sheep, or buffalo, each with its own character and flavor. The earliest cheeses were created more than 4,000 years ago, possibly by accident. Cheesemaking was an established art by the time of ancient Rome, and cheese eventually became a valued staple throughout the world.

Health Benefits

Even with its legions of fans, cheese has been vilified for its saturated fat and cholesterol content. Yet researchers trying to confirm that cheese caused heart disease and stroke found no "significant association" between the intake of full-fat dairy products like cheese and the risk of coronary heart disease or stroke. In fact, full-fat cheese actually lowered levels of LDL cholesterol. Below are some additional benefits.

- Research suggests that butyrate, a chemical in cheese, can boost metabolism and help aid with weight loss. It may also stimulate the bacteria in the gut to produce even more butyrate. The highest amounts of butyrate occur in Gruyère, blue, Gouda, Parmesan, and cheddar cheeses.
- Butyrate protects the colon against cancer by nourishing and strengthening its cells and reducing the inflammation that can damage them and make them a target for tumors. Butyrate-dense cheeses are also being studied to assess the chemical's ability to help the body use insulin more effectively.
- Gym-goers and athletes should know that the protein in cheese contains amino acids, which are the building blocks of muscles. Ricotta cheese is a particularly good source of whey protein.
- Cheese is an excellent source of calcium. One ounce of cheddar provides 216 mg and one ounce of Parmesan offers 336 mg—or roughly one-third of the daily requirement.

IS BUTTER REALLY BETTER?

For many decades, butter has been blamed for a number of serious health conditions, including obesity and heart disease. Now, however, it has again been reevaluated and is provisionally acceptable to eat. The saturated fats in butter led to it being banished, but a number of scientists challenge the belief that these fats are inherently harmful—they feel that saturated fats actually raise levels of good HDL cholesterol and change harmful small LDL cholesterol into large LDL cholesterol, which is benign. Vegetable oil or corn oil margarine was once the recommended replacement for butter, but their trans fats have been shown to cause cardiovascular disease, which butter may not. So don't flee from butter as you might once have done, but do remember to consume it in moderation.

Health Benefits

In addition to the fat-soluble vitamins like A and E, butter provides rare vitamin K2, which is involved in calcium metabolism and may help reduce the risk of heart attacks. Butter also contains short-chain and medium-chain fats that increase satiety and promote the burning of fat.

EGGS IN THE BALANCE

Eggs often seem to be on a nutritional seesaw—good for us, bad for us; good, bad, good. Recently, there appears to be another downswing. Once again the complaint is that eggs are loaded with dietary cholesterol. This happens to be true—one egg contains the equivalent of a fast food megaburger. And cholesterol can have an oxidative and inflammatory effect on LDL, which may then cause plaque buildup in the carotid arteries. But as many researchers point out, simply consuming extra cholesterol in the diet does not necessarily raise cholesterol levels in the blood. Studies show that 70 percent of those who eat eggs experience little or no increase. And for those it does affect, the increase

Spinach and mushroom egg white frittata. If you need to control your intake of dietary cholesterol, leave the yolks out when making egg dishes like frittatas and omelets.

amounts to a mild elevation. Yet there are other health issues to consider—tainted eggs are also a frequent source of *Salmonella* food poisoning.

Health Benefits

On the plus side, there is evidence that eating eggs can actually increase the good HDL cholesterol in the blood, lowering the risk for heart attack and stroke. They also provide omega-3 fatty acids. For those who might still be yolk phobic, egg whites contain more than half the protein in the egg but lower amounts of cholesterol and fat. Eggs also provide selenium, vitamins D, B2, B6, and B12, zinc, copper, iron, and rare choline. Eggs are certainly a safer source of protein than fish or dairy foods that may be contaminated with chemicals, mercury, or PCBs.

CHOLESTEROL DEFINED

The word *cholesterol* has become a red flag, a buzzword indicating a serious health threat. Yet cholesterol is simply a waxy substance produced by the liver—or ingested as dietary cholesterol—that circulates through the blood to build cells. Problems arise when a diet high in trans fat or saturated fats triggers the liver to produce excess cholesterol. Too much of the bad low-density lipoproteins (LDL) cholesterol or too little of the good high-density lipoproteins (HDL) cholesterol may cause plaque to build on the inner walls of the arteries that feed the heart and brain. This narrowing can raise the risk of heart attack or stroke.

Even with new competition on the market, olive oil still ranks high, both for its health benefits and its cooking properties.

COOKING OILS
FIND THE HEALTHIEST OPTION AMONG THE MANY CHOICES OF FATS

Cooking oils not only flavor the foods we prepare with them, they also offer their own varied nutrients. Cooks, once limited to high-calorie butter, lard, vegetable oil, or corn oil, now find supermarket shelves groaning with healthier—and sometimes far less familiar—options. To help you choose, here are some factors to consider. For instance, can the oil withstand high temperatures, or will it start to smoke? How much or how little flavor do you want the oil to contribute to your dish? What are the nutritional benefits of a certain oil, and what sort of fats does it contain?

Fatty and oily foods come with a vocabulary of confusing terms describing the chemical structure of their fats. Before sampling new kinds of cooking oil, it may help to acquaint yourself with their benefits— and their failings.

> ### DID YOU KNOW?
> • *Extra virgin olive oil is produced during the first cold-pressing of the fruit (it is not extracted from seeds using solvents like other oils are), making it an oleic must—a monounsaturated omega-9 fatty acid made from the olive fruit, seeds, and skin. It also contains over 200 micronutrients and macronutrients.*

Questionable fats include saturated fats, which are chemically stable, meaning that they do not normally become rancid and are solid or semisolid at room temperature. They can elevate levels of LDL cholesterol and are found in animal fats and tropical oils. Trans fats also increase LDL cholesterol production and suppress HDL levels. They occur in hydrogenated foods like margarine and vegetable shortening.

Beneficial fats include monounsaturated fats, which are less chemically stable; they are liquid at room temperature and do not become rancid. The most common variety is oleic acid, found in olive oil and oils made from pecans, almonds, cashews, peanuts, and avocados. Polyunsaturated fats are also beneficial, reducing cholesterol levels; they occur in corn, safflower, sunflower, and soybean oils. Omega-3 and omega-6 fatty acids are polyunsaturated fats. Essential fats are the beneficial fatty acids our bodies cannot make, the ones we must obtain from the foods we eat.

Health Benefits

The following plant-based oils have superior health attributes—and often superior taste—compared to standard vegetable oil.

- Olive oil is still the gold standard of oils, with its monounsaturated fats, like omega-3, that help lower cholesterol. It is also loaded with antioxidants and polyphenols that benefit the heart. Extra virgin olive oil is taken from the first pressing of olives, and it has a darker color and less acidity than regular olive oil.
- Coconut oil is trendy right now. It does contains saturated fats that may raise LDL cholesterol, but they also raise the good HDL. Its greatest asset is that it withstands high cooking temperatures.
- Rapeseed and canola oils withstand the high temperatures of frying and grilling and are good sources of omega-3, -6 and -9 fatty acids. With the lowest level of saturated fats, these mild-flavored oils are among the healthiest cooking oils. Canola was bred from rapeseed *(Brassica napus)* cultivars to be low in erucic acid.
- Sunflower oil is polyunsaturated and does not overpower other ingredients. It contains omega-6 fats and vitamin E. It can increase energy, promote cell regeneration, and ease arthritis pain.

Brassica napus is the source of rapeseed oil, and cultivars of this mustard family species produce canola oil.

Safflower oil

- Safflower oil contains omega-6 fatty acids, oleic, and linoleic acids that can help manage obesity, diabetes, and PMS and boost immune function.
- Corn oil, long a kitchen staple, has been the subject of countless health studies. Composed mainly of polyunsaturated fatty acids, it is low in saturated fat. There is some evidence that it can help lower LDL cholesterol when used in moderation. It also contains antioxidant vitamin E.
- Sesame oil can be used to augment other blander oils with its rich nutty flavor, especially in Asian dishes. It is rich in zinc, copper, and magnesium and can reduce inflammation and increase metabolism.
- Peanut, or groundnut, oil offers high levels of mono- and polyunsaturated fats and is a good source of antioxidant E, the "skincare" vitamin.
- Avocado oil is high in vitamin E and has a nutty flavor that makes it ideal for salad dressings. On the downside, it contains no omega-3 oils and is high in calories and expensive.
- Grapeseed oil comes from the seeds that are a by-product of winemaking. The oil does not contain many of the nutrients found in grapes, however, and it is extracted using chemicals that include the toxic solvent hexane. This oil is high in polyunsaturated fats and contains vitamin E.
- Soybean oil is high in fatty acids and is reported to help reduce the symptoms of Alzheimer's.
- Mustard oil provides a piquant flavor to dishes. It can be used with high temperatures and is known to aid digestion and stimulate circulation.
- Rice bran oil is fairly new to the marketplace. It is made from the outer layer (bran) of the rice grain and contains oryzanol, useful for controlling cholesterol. Rice bran oil offers mono- and polyunsaturated fats and has a high smoking point.

HONEY

DISCOVER THE HEALTH ADVANTAGES OF THE HONEYBEES' FAVORITE FOOD

Honey is the closest thing to a miracle food we have on the planet, full of nutrients and antibiotic and antioxidant properties. It also does not become rancid over thousands of years. And it is made by tiny insect alchemists that collect plant nectar inside their bodies, pass it from mouth to mouth, and then store it as honey in perfectly hexagonal wax chambers—that they build from wax that is secreted by their bodies. If someone made up a story about animals producing such a food in such a way, they would be scoffed at. But it is all true.

Honey is an enzymatically activated, partially fermented organic natural sugar, and in addition to its sweet taste, it has no additives, digests easily for most people, and has an unlimited shelf life. It can be used in a wide range of dishes and adapts to most low-heat cooking. High heat can alter its consistency.

DID YOU KNOW?

• *Honeybees are engineered by nature to fiercely protect the hive—and the life-giving honey stored within. But when a large hive swarms—meaning roughly half the workers leave the home hive with an older queen seeking new quarters, they are particularly docile because they no longer have honey to guard.*

Based on a rock painting in Valencia, Spain, that shows a human collecting honey from a tree hive, the harvesting of honey from wild bees dates back at least 8,000 years. Other evidence shows our ancestors knew to subdue a colony with smoke before extracting the honeycombs. Honey was eaten, bathed in, and used by Roman soldiers to heal wounds. Honey is mentioned in the Bible—Israel was the "land of milk and honey" and John the Baptist lived off locusts and honey—as well as in the Talmud, the Koran, and the ancient texts of Asia. By the early Middle Ages, European nobles were steeping honey in wine to make mead.

The Egyptians first kept bees domestically around 4000 B.C., in cylinders made of unbaked, hardened mud. Like today's commercial apiarists, these beekeepers often moved their hives to follow blossoming crops, traveling up and down the Nile. The Greeks called honey the "nectar of the gods" and created terra cotta hives. In other regions, hollow logs, wooden boxes, and woven straw domes called skeps, all featuring a small opening to allow the nectar gatherers to enter and depart, served as hives.

Inside the hive, the female workers chew the nectar (carbohydrates) gathered from flowers and store it in combs. They fan the nectar to reduce the water content by 20 percent, eventually turning it into honey, which will feed the colony during the colder months. The pollen (proteins) they collect on their legs and bodies becomes facto-fermented "bee bread," which sustains larvae and workers both.

Commercially, honey is sold in supermarkets and at farmers' markets and is used as a sweetener. Varieties include wildflower, orange blossom, alfalfa, borage, Manuka, and buckwheat. Beeswax is used to produce smokeless candles, cosmetics, furniture

Honeybee on borage. Monofloral honey is the result of a predominance of nectar collected from a single type of plant. Each will have its own flavor notes. Borage honey has a floral bouquet with a hint of lemon.

Bee products, including honeycomb, jarred honey, a beeswax candle, pollen, and propolis granules

polish, and adhesives and to make preformed foundations for hives. Bee bread is sometimes sold for its nutrients, and royal jelly is used as a health and cosmetic treatment. In addition to producing these commodities, bees pollinate one-third of the planet's crops and are invaluable to many forms of agriculture. Unfortunately, bees are beset by colony collapse disorder, widespread use of pesticides, and loss of foraging areas.

Health Benefits

Raw honey has been valued for its medicinal qualities for thousands of years. In Ayurvedic medicine, it is used to enhance the abilities of other natural preparations and to treat eye problems, impotence, UTIs, and bronchial asthma. Research concurs that honey provides a wealth of nutrients, including flavonoids that prevent and fight disease, especially some types of cancer. It is antibacterial (bees add an enzyme that makes hydrogen peroxide) and antifungal, which contributes to its long shelf life and gives it the potential to treat gastric ulcers, which are often caused by the bacteria *H. pylori*. It can also help maintain glycogen levels for sustained energy and improve recovery time for athletes. Honey can ease stubborn coughs, and its antibacterial properties and the drying effects of its sugars make it excellent for treating burns and wounds. Because some honeys have a low hypoglycemic index, they don't "jolt" blood glucose levels and can even help regulate blood sugar. It can be used to ease allergies, induce sleep, and improve skin quality. Honey also contains both pollen and propolis—a sticky substance used in hive construction—that offer their own benefits.

Honey should never be fed to infants under one year of age because it may contain *Clostridium botulinum* spores that can cause illness. The spores are not harmful to children or adults.

A ROYAL REMEDY

Royal jelly, which is secreted by worker bees to nourish larval and adult queen bees, offers powerful healing capabilities. It contains several potent antioxidants that can halt the oxidation of cells. It is also able to stimulate brain function, enhance calcium absorption, help prevent hardening of the arteries, and protect women from the environmental estrogens found in plastics and cosmetics. Its high levels of B-complex vitamins, choline, and zinc allow it to increase collagen production and rejuvenate the skin.

CHAPTER 9

NATURE'S HOME HELPERS

Introduction
HOME SAFE
REPLACE TOXIC CLEANERS IN YOUR HOME WITH NATURE-BASED PRODUCTS

A problem with modern housekeeping is that manufacturers have provided so many specialized cleaning products—all with different chemical formulas—that people who use four or five in the course of a day are exposed to much higher levels of toxins than if they used one all-purpose cleaner. And in many cases, much higher levels than the manufacturers intended.

Commercial cleaners also affect the health of the planet—once they are washed down the drain, some portion of their chemical constituents inevitably enter the environment—the soil, the air, the water supply, and plant and animal life.

- Volatile organic compounds, which are used as performance enhancers, can damage neurological function, and other chemicals can act as respiratory irritants, carcinogens, or reproductive toxins.
- Phosphates used in laundry and dishwasher detergents to disperse dirt and grease can cause depletion of oxygen in rivers and lakes, resulting in algae blooms and fish mortality.
- Phthalates, which distribute dyes and fragrances in cleaners, are suspected of causing harmful hormonal effects.

Equally upsetting, there are few regulations for the chemicals in cleaners and no labeling rules, so consumers may not even know what they are being exposed to. Furthermore, many companies choose the chemicals in their cleaning products for their effectiveness and have little or no idea of what kind of damage they might do. There

are more than 80,000 chemicals in common use, and, not surprisingly, many of them have had scant research done on their side effects.

Green cleaners, advertised as safer for humans and the environment, are quite pricey, Also, some that are advertised as "green" are anything but—one popular brand was found to contain petrochemical solvents. After 25 green cleaning products were tested, 25 percent emitted chemicals that were classified as toxic or hazardous. When possible, check online for the MSDS, the product's material safety data sheet, to make sure it lives up to its claims.

Chem-Free Cleaning

If all this makes cleaning your house sound like walking through a Superfund site without a hazmat suit, take heart. The natural health community and some concerned companies have revived many traditional cleaning agents, those used before the chemical industry invaded most aspects of our lives. You will discover natural cleaners that leave stainless steel spotless, detergents that are gentle and effective, spot treatments that obliterate stains, bug and mouse repellents that will keep your house and yard vermin free, and flea and tick treatments that, unlike some chemical brands, will not harm your pets.

Start researching options for replacing harsh or toxic cleaning products, bathroom cleansers, laundry and dish detergents, fabric softeners, insecticides, pesticides, and herbicides, and you will be on your way to creating a safe, natural home that poses no chemical threat to you, your children, or your pets.

(LEFT) **Add citrus essential oils, which are natural and mild disinfectants, to homemade cleaners and polishes.**

(OPPOSITE) **Stock up on versatile—and inexpensive—baking soda, which has multiple home-cleaning uses.**

CLEAN AND GREEN
KEEP YOUR HOME SPARKLING AND YOUR LAUNDRY FRESH WITH NATURAL CLEANERS

Centuries ago, people knew a thing or two about natural cleaners and detergents—mainly because they were the only sort they had access to. Today, consumers who want to limit the amount of chemicals they and their families are exposed to are choosing many of these same substances to clean their homes and do their laundry, substances that in many cases are already right in their pantries. These household helpers include white vinegar, baking soda, lemon juice, and hydrogen peroxide, along with liquid castile soap, washing soda—called sodium carbonate or sodium ash—and borax—a naturally occurring mineral made up of sodium, boron, oxygen, and water. With these ingredients—and a few spray bottles and microfiber cloths—there are few cleaning and freshening tasks you cannot accomplish

When attacking dust or grime in each section of the house, start at the highest point in the room and then work your way down. Use a static duster that requires no sprays.

> ### DID YOU KNOW?
>
> • *A number of essential oils not only add a fresh fragrance to your cleaning products, they also provide powerful antimicrobial benefits. Try adding several drops of lavender, eucalyptus, or lemongrass oil to your natural laundry detergent and surface cleaner. Or place sachets scented with these oils inside the vacuum cleaner.*

IN THE KITCHEN

Kitchen surfaces not only need to be cleaned, they also need disinfecting. You can do this without chemical sprays by using baking soda or vinegar.

- Baking soda makes a safe scrub on metal or porcelain surfaces.
- Cutting boards and prep tops can be cleaned with lemon juice.
- To deodorize a smelly garbage disposal, add vinegar to the water in an ice cube tray, freeze it, and run a few cubes through the appliance.
- To de-grime an oven, apply a thick paste of baking soda and water, and leave it on overnight. The grime should easily wipe away the next day.
- Clean window glass and other glass surfaces with a spritz of a 50-50 vinegar-and-water solution and a crumpled newspaper.
- To unclog a backed-up drain, pour a cup of baking soda into the trap, then slowly add a half cup of vinegar. Cover for 15 minutes—while it bubbles like a grade school volcano—and then pour a pot of boiling water down the drain.
- To clean tarnished silverware, boil two to three inches of water in a shallow pan with a teaspoon of baking soda and a sheet of aluminum foil. Submerge the silver, and let the water boil two to three minutes. Remove silverware, and wipe tarnish away with a soft cloth.

IN THE BATHROOM

Like kitchen surfaces, bathroom surfaces need to be disinfected, as well as cleaned. To disinfect a toilet bowl, spray on a 50-50 vinegar-and-water solution, allow it to sit for several minutes, and then sprinkle on baking soda. Scrub well with a brush. Clean the seat, handle, and tank with the same solution, and then dry with a soft cloth. Finish by using the solution to wipe down the shower stall, tub, sink, and mirror.

The big three of natural cleaning: vinegar, baking soda, and lemon. You can use these in all rooms of the house.

IN THE LIVING ROOM

These gathering spots see a lot of use, collecting the general detritus of daily life. Here you may need a beater-brush vacuum and a sturdy scrub brush.

- Carpets get heavy usage and often retain odors. To refresh them, liberally sprinkle with baking soda, wait 15 minutes, then vacuum up the granules.
- Make nontoxic furniture polish with beeswax, almond oil, and lemon or orange essential oil.
- Remove water rings on wooden surfaces by gently rubbing toothpaste or mayonnaise mixed with ashes over the spot.
- Wipe switch plates and doorknobs with hydrogen peroxide.
- Clean unplugged electronics and screens with a microfiber cloth dampened with plain water.
- Lemon essential oil can be used to remove stains from carpets (test a small spot first).
- To deodorize smelly shoes or a stinky pet bed, take the item outside, and swipe with a damp rag infused with eucalyptus, lemon, or tea tree oil.
- Buy or rent a steamer to clean and refresh upholstery and draperies.

IN THE BEDROOM

For general cleaning, use the same routine as you would for the living room.

- To freshen bedding and linens, add two tablespoons of baking soda to the wash cycle.
- Air out mattress pads and pillows in sunlight for a few hours to kill bacteria.
- To sweeten the air and induce sleep, create fabric sachets from dried flowers and scent them with calming essential oils like lavender or ylang-ylang.

IN THE LAUNDRY ROOM

There are many effective green laundry detergents—eliminating phosphates was an early goal of environmentalists. For completely natural laundry detergent, check out soap nuts, which are berries of the soap tree *(Sapindus mukorossi)*. The shells surround saponin, a gentle natural cleaner that gets released during the wash. You can also make your green laundry detergent with only a few ingredients.

Line-drying laundry saves money and conserves energy.

PANTRY PICK: *You will need one bar of natural, unscented soap, plus washing soda, and borax. In a large bowl, grate the soap into fine particles, and then add 1 cup washing soda and 1 cup borax. Store the mixture in a large lidded container. Use ¼ to ½ cup for a normal load of laundry. In the dryer, instead of a commercial fabric softener, use felted wool dryer balls to fluff clothing.*

If you have space, consider line-drying your wash outdoors. This not only imparts a fresh, clean scent, it can also help remove strong odors while whitening and disinfecting your linens and clothes.

MAKE IT YOURSELF
Universal Cleaner

This natural cleaner and disinfectant can be used in every room in the house. Dispense it from a glass spray bottle.

YOU WILL NEED:
1 teaspoon borax
1 teaspoon liquid castile soap
½ teaspoon washing soda
5 to 10 drops of a refreshing essential oil—
   orange or grapefruit work well.
2 cups warm water

WHAT TO DO:
- Combine all ingredients in a glass bottle, and add the warm water.
- Shake well to disperse.

VERSATILE SALTS

SCRUB YOUR WAY TO CLEANLINESS WITH THESE NATURAL, GENTLE ABRASIVES

Salt is one of the oldest substances known to humans, and it was used for thousands of years not only to season dishes—it actually brightens flavors—but also as a food preservative. Keeping foods fresh without refrigeration was one of the key factors that allowed early cultures to expand and civilizations to rise. Salted foods provided out-of-season produce during the colder months and sustenance during long journeys. That was why salt, which was quite difficult to come by, was held at such a premium by our ancestors. Today, however, salt is the most common and available nonmetal mineral on the planet, and this abundance has led to multiple uses, including that of a safe household cleaner.

> ### DID YOU KNOW?
>
> • *Epsom salts—magnesium sulfate—are also handy around the house. To make a natural fabric softener, combine a cup of Epsom salts with 10 drops of your favorite essential oil, and add a quarter cup to your laundry during the first wash cycle. Your clothes will end up naturally soft and freshly scented.*

Keep a jar of inexpensive table salt with your cleaning supplies.

Salt in the form of sodium chloride was probably first used as a cleaner during the Middle Ages. It is nontoxic and inexpensive, and it provides a gentle scouring agent, which makes it an excellent substitute for harsh chemical cleaners. All versions of sodium chloride—unrefined salts like sea salt and Himalayan salt, and refined table salt, Kosher salt, and iodized salt—make equally good cleaners.

IN THE KITCHEN AND BATH

Salt can be used alone, or added to other natural cleaners, like white vinegar or lemon, to boost their cleaning and deodorizing capabilities. To a make a basic scrubbing paste, combine water, salt, and baking soda (with an optional drop of "green" dish liquid) and use it to de-grime counters, enamel, porcelain, and appliances.

- A handful of salt will put out a grease fire—it smothers the flames and dissipates the heat.
- Scrub cast-iron skillets clean with a handful of salt and a paper towel.
- Remove coffee and tea stains from mugs by applying a scrub of salt and green dish liquid.
- Swipe the inside of the refrigerator with salt and sparkling soda water.
- Salt and hot water can refresh a smelly drain.
- A paste of salt and vegetable oil will remove water rings on furniture.
- A paste of equal parts salt, flour, and vinegar is great for cleaning tarnished copper or brass. Rub paste on, wait half an hour, then wipe off, and buff. This also works for removing rust.
- To clean a hazy glass coffee pot, combine salt and ice cubes, and swirl them around the inside. The salt cuts the residue, and the ice agitates the salt for a more thorough scrub.

- If your spill red wine on a tablecloth, quickly blot it, and then cover with a pile of salt, which will absorb much of the leftover wine. Soak the cloth in cold water for an hour before laundering.
- Use salt paste on bath fixtures and grimy grout.
- Extend the life of new toothbrushes by soaking them in saltwater before using them.

IN THE LAUNDRY ROOM

Bring your salt canister into the laundry room to combat stains and other laundry issues.

- To keep colors from bleeding, add from a half to a cup of salt to your laundry water.
- Putting about a half cup of salt in the final laundry rinse can prevent clothes from freezing if you dry them outdoors in winter.
- To remove perspiration stains, combine four tablespoons of salt with a quart of very hot water, and sponge the solution over the stains until they fade. Rinse thoroughly.
- Remove mildew or rust stains from fabric by moistening them with salt and lemon, and then placing the item in the sun to bleach.
- Remove blood stains from natural fibers by soaking the cloth in cold salted water, and then washing in soapy warm water. Boil after washing.
- To clean a sticky iron, run it hot over a paper sprinkled with salt.

AROUND THE HOUSE

You can turn to salt for a variety of indoor and outdoor home solutions.

- To keep ants at bay, sprinkle salt where they access your kitchen or bath—backsplashes, doorways, or windowsills. They dislike walking on salt.
- To keep fresh flowers from wilting, add a dash of salt (or sugar or aspirin) to their water. This also works for fresh Christmas trees.
- Put several inches of damp salt in the bottom of a vase of artificial flowers before arranging them. When the salt dries, it will hold them in places.
- Refresh dusty or grimy silk flowers by placing them in a paper bag with a quarter cup of salt and shaking them gently.

Just grab the salt shaker if you spill red wine on a tablecloth. The salt will keep it from setting.

- Salt paste can remove the mineral residue left behind in a glass vase or on the sides of fish tanks.
- Use a "spackle" made of two tablespoons salt and two tablespoons corn starch mixed with water to fill in hairline cracks or nail holes on Sheetrock or plaster walls.
- When flames flare up from dripping grease on the barbecue grill, throw salt on them. It will reduce the flames without cooling the coals.
- Douse lingering fireplace embers with salt to put them out for the night.
- To relieve the pain and swelling of a bee sting, immediately dampen the area with a salt paste.
- Treat mosquito bites or poison ivy with an itch-relieving soak in saltwater, or a poultice made of salt and olive oil.
- Keep natural wicker furniture looking great by scrubbing it with a stiff brush and salt water.
- Soak the bristles of a new straw broom in saltwater before using it to extend its life.
- To remove a greasy spot from the carpet, mix one part salt with four parts rubbing alcohol, and rub it vigorously over the spot.
- Soak candles in a strong salt solution for a few hours. When they dry, they will be nearly dripless.

PEST PATROL

USE NATURAL REPELLENTS TO RID YOUR HOME AND YARD OF INSECTS AND RODENTS

There is no shortage of pest treatments available at the home improvement store, from ant and roach sprays and mosquito and flea repellents to mouse and rat poison to weed and bug killers. What these products all have in common is that they contain chemicals that can be hazardous to your family's health. Fortunately, there are many natural solutions available that address these pesky problems.

DID YOU KNOW?

• *Neem oil, a natural insecticide, is extracted from the evergreen neem tree of India* (Azadirachta indica). *The tree's leaves, seeds, and seed oil contain a compound called azadirachtin, which repels both mosquitoes and bed bugs. The oil can also be used on garden plants to keep destructive pests away.*

INDOOR PESTS

The safest way to handle ants, roaches, moths, mice, and other home invaders is to take in the welcome mat.

- Leave mint teabags or crushed mint leaves or cloves near places where ants are most active. Or place cucumber slices near doors or windowsills—ants have an aversion to them.
- If you trace the ants back to their nest, leave a lime slice or a line of cayenne pepper, cinnamon, or coffee grounds at the entrance.

Cedar and lavender can help repel moths. You can also spray lavender oil and water on carpets where moths may have laid eggs.

- To make ant bait, mix a quart of water with a teaspoon of borax and a cup of sugar. Dip a cotton ball in the solution and leave it in a pierced paper cup where ants congregate. They will bring the bait back to the nest, where it will eventually kill the colony. (Keep bait away from pets and children.)
- Sprinkle diatomaceous earth where roaches congregate—the sharp edges of the tiny particles will cut their exoskeletons and kill them within a few days.
- Place sachets of catnip in cupboards and cabinets where roaches gather.
- Clothes moths that damage woolens will avoid cedar chips and fabric sachets filled with mint, rosemary, thyme, or lavender.
- Repel mice by placing 30 drops of peppermint oil on each of 10 or 15 cottons balls and setting them where mice roam—cabinets, baseboards, behind appliances. Mice dislike the sharp odor.
- Sprinkle cayenne pepper where you have seen mouse droppings, like storage boxes. It irritates their eyes and noses and sends them fleeing.
- Dryer sheets are effective for keeping mice out of enclosed spaces like pantries and food bins. Humane traps allow you to relocate mice away from your neighborhood.

PET PESTS

Pets carry fleas and ticks into the home, which may then hitch a ride on human hosts.

- Scatter diatomaceous earth under swing sets and in children's play areas to discourage ticks.
- Slice a lemon, pour boiling water over it, and let it soak overnight. Then sponge the liquid over your dog's coat to give fleas the brush-off. Do not use on cats.

- Make a pennyroyal herbal sachet for your dog. Cedar also works against fleas—look for cedar-filled sleep mats for your pets.
- Add brewer's yeast or apple cider vinegar to your pet's food to repel fleas from the inside out.
- A geranium oil sachet can be placed on your dog's collar to repel ticks. (Do not use this oil on cats.) If ticks do attach, remove them with tweezers, and make sure you get the head.

RESCUE REMEDY: To repel disease-bearing ticks, make a spray by combining 4 ounces each of witch hazel, apple cider vinegar, or vodka, and then add 30 drops of either bourbon, cedar, geranium, citronella, or lemon eucalyptus oil in a spray bottle. Add 4 ounces of distilled water, shake well, and spritz on skin and clothing. (Do not use on pets.)

OUTDOOR INSECT PESTS

Insect repellents can be especially hazardous because they are applied directly to the skin. DEET, the active ingredient in "deep woods" repellents, can cause rashes, swelling, itching, and eye irritation. Opt for natural versions.

- Clear your yard of any standing water in planter bases or buckets, where mosquitoes can breed.
- Essential oil of lemongrass, sage, and rosemary will repel mosquitoes. So will beeswax or soy citronella candles or citronella oil.
- Mix one part garlic juice to five parts water in a spray bottle. A few spritzes will keep insects away for hours.
- Plant marigolds beside your patio or deck. Bugs and flying insects avoid the scent.
- Hang wooden bat houses around your property to encourage these night fliers to roost. One bat can eat from 500 to 1,000 insects in one night.
- Purchase nontoxic pheromone mosquito traps.

GARDEN PESTS AND WEEDS

Protect your precious flowers and vegetables with organic sprays.

- To kill weeds growing on a patio or walkway, toss Epsom salts between the pavers or flagstones, and then spray with water.

Fill bamboo tiki torches with citronella oil to keep mosquitoes at bay during outdoor summertime evenings.

- Garlic spray discourages vegetable predators. Soak four cloves of garlic overnight in two teaspoons of mineral oil. Strain, and then add one pint of water.
- Natural insecticides include *Bacillus thuringiensis,* a bacterium that targets larvae, and pyrethrum, derived from chrysanthemums. There are also organic insecticide soaps and oils.
- Fend off hungry slugs by using diatomaceous earth around plants; surrounding them with copper strips; mulching them with seaweed; or recessing a can of beer into the soil—slugs will enter it, and drown.
- To prevent fungal growth on garden plants, combine two tablespoons tea tree oil with two cups of water, and spray plants with the mix every three to seven days.

RESCUE REMEDY: To make a pet- and family-safe weed killer, combine 2 quarts vinegar or lemon juice with ⅛ cup blue dish liquid (you can also add 1 cup Epsom salts). This solution will kill nearly every plant it hits, weed or not.

MORE INFO

LIFESTYLE REBOOT CHECKLIST
KEEP TRACK OF YOUR PROGRESS TOWARD NATURAL WELL-BEING

As you read through this book, discovering ways to safeguard your physical and mental health, improve your eating habits, and enhance other aspects of your life, occasionally refer to this chart to see if you have absorbed the key points from each chapter, checking off those you have mastered.

PART I: NATURE'S CURES

Chapter 1: Remedies for Common Physical Ailments

- ☐ Be aware that natural remedies have been used to treat disease and illness for many centuries.
- ☐ Reduce the effects of colds, flu, and respiratory ailments with expectorant herbs.
- ☐ Use anti-inflammatory herbs to combat the pain of arthritis and joint complaints.
- ☐ Ease stomach distress with soothing teas like chamomile and peppermint.
- ☐ Avoid foods and beverages that you know will trigger upper-GI discomfort.
- ☐ Make sure you are getting plenty of gut-healthy probiotics by eating yogurt, kefir, and other cultured or fermented foods.
- ☐ Keep your lower GI tract regular by consuming whole grains and produce that is high in fiber.
- ☐ Brush and floss your teeth at least twice a day.
- ☐ Always use a sunscreen of at least 15 SPF when outdoors, even on cloudy days.

Chapter 2: Soothe Emotional Stress

- ☐ Use teas and tisanes to ease anxiety or nervous energy.
- ☐ Consider yoga or tai chi to help relieve stress, and exercise regularly to release mood-enhancing endorphins.
- ☐ Set aside a small area in your home for yoga or meditation, and create a spa-like atmosphere in the bath to relieve daily stress.
- ☐ Loose weight safely by establishing sensible eating patterns, eating small, frequent, lean meals, and starting an exercise regimen.

- ☐ Reduce nicotine cravings by practicing yoga or meditation, drinking lots of water or grape juice, and taking ginger or ginseng supplements.
- ☐ Use herbs, supplements, relaxation techniques, and white noise machines to treat insomnia.

Chapter 3: Pregnancy and Infant Health

- ☐ Maintain a healthy diet during your pregnancy and take prenatal supplements.
- ☐ Choose a midwife to help you through all phases of pregnancy and delivery.
- ☐ Attend birthing classes with your partner, so that you will both know what to expect during childbirth.
- ☐ Consider a doula—a trained birthing aid— to assist with your comfort during delivery.
- ☐ Make your own additive-free baby foods from natural ingredients.
- ☐ Watch what you eat while breastfeeding—the taste of some foods may affect your baby.
- ☐ Look into acquiring a breast pump and storage bottles for milk so that others can feed your baby while you work or rest.

Chapter 4: Aging and Wellness

- ☐ Determine the health concerns you most need to address as you age.
- ☐ Discover the power foods and nutrients that can help promote a healthy heart and circulation and benefit the rest of your body.
- ☐ Learn to reduce cosmetic signs of aging through skincare and diet.
- ☐ Keep your brain sharp and your muscles toned by challenging yourself mentally and staying active physically.

PART II: NATURE'S PHARMACOPOEIA

Chapter 5: Medicinal Herbs

- ☐ Fresh herbs add earthy flavors and powerful phytonutrients to dishes.
- ☐ Healing herbs can be taken in foods, teas, smoothies, and supplements.
- ☐ Grow these alternative "medicines" on your windowsill or in your garden.
- ☐ Try maritime produce like seaweed and algae for major health benefits.

Chapter 6: Beneficial Spices

- ☐ Spices add sweet, savory, hot, or zesty flavors to dishes, as well as crucial micronutrients and healing properties.
- ☐ Use refined sugar and table salt sparingly, and seek out alternative seasoning like honey, stevia, black pepper, or garlic.
- ☐ Don't forget that dark chocolate is loaded with antioxidants (but also remember to indulge your cravings only sparingly).

Chapter 7: Essential Oils

- ☐ Discover the range of curative powers offered by these herbal and plant oils.
- ☐ Inhale, diffuse, or vaporize these oils to relieve respiratory and other complaints.
- ☐ Massage them into aching joints and muscles.
- ☐ Make your own essential oils using a carrier oil blended with one or more of your favorite healing and aromatic oils.

Chapter 8: Nature's Power Pantry

- ☐ Power foods hold the answer to many of your wellness needs, so increase your intake of healthy fruits, vegetables, legumes, whole grains, and seafood.
- ☐ Juicing is one way to maximize the nutrients found in fruits and vegetables.
- ☐ Try to eliminate processed and packaged foods from your diet.
- ☐ Nuts and seeds are high in nutrients, but might also be high in calories.
- ☐ Decrease your intake of refined grains, dairy, and fatty meats.

Chapter 9: Nature's Home Helpers

- ☐ Commercial cleaners contain a variety of chemicals, additives, and toxins that can be hazardous to the health of humans and pets.
- ☐ White vinegar, baking soda, and lemon have almost limitless uses in the home for cleaning and disinfecting.
- ☐ Table salt and Epsom salts are mild abrasives.
- ☐ Vinegar and an eco-friendly dish liquid make a powerful weed killer.
- ☐ Many herbs and natural substances are effective against flying insects, crawling home invaders, and pet parasites.

GLOSSARY

acid A chemical substance that neutralizes alkalis; typically, a corrosive, sour-tasting liquid.

adaptogen An herb that strengthens the body and the immune system.

alkaloid Any of numerous usually colorless, complex, and bitter organic bases (containing nitrogen and usually oxygen) that occur especially in seed plants. It is a basic organic compound with alkaline properties and generally has a marked physiological effect on the nervous and circulatory systems. It can act as an analgesic, local anesthetic, tranquilizer, vasoconstrictor, antispasmodic, and hallucinatory agent.

amino acid Any of a class of 20 molecules that are combined to form proteins in living organisms. The sequence of amino acids in a protein—and therefore protein function—is determined by the genetic code.

analgesic A medication used to relieve pain.

antiallergenic A substance that does not aggravate an allergy.

antifungal An agent that is destructive to fungi, suppressing their reproduction or growth.

anti-inflammatory An agent that reduces the heat, redness, and swelling of inflammation.

antimicrobial An agent that kills microorganisms or inhibits their growth.

antioxidant A chemical compound that protects against cell damage from oxygen-free radicals, molecules that are major causes of disease and aging. Antioxidants are found in many foods, including fruits and vegetables.

antiseptic A substance that discourages the growth of microorganisms.

antispasmodic A drug or substance that is used to relieve spasm of the involuntary muscles.

anthocyanin Any of a group of red-violet plant pigments.

astringent An agent that causes contraction or shrinkage of tissues; it is used to decrease secretions or control bleeding.

Ayurvedic medicine The ancient Indian system of sustaining health and fighting disease based on equilibrium with nature. *Ayurvedic* translates as "meaning of life."

biennial A plant whose life cycle extends over two growing seasons.

carotenoid A natural, fat-soluble pigment found in certain plants that provide the bright red, orange, or yellow coloration of many fruits and vegetables.

carpel The seed-bearing structure of a flower that is typically composed of an ovary, a style, and a stigma. The term *pistil* may refer to a carpel or group of carpels fused together.

collagen The main structural protein found in the skin and other connective tissues; an insoluble fibrous protein, it has both clinical and cosmetic uses.

cortisol A hormone, also known as hydrocortisone, involved in the regulation of metabolism in the cells; it also helps regulate stress within the body.

cultured A type of food that has been fermented—the process of breaking down a complex substance into simpler parts—using bacteria, fungi, or yeasts.

deciduous A plant that sheds its leaves annually.

decongestant A substance that shrinks the swollen membranes in the nose, making it easier to breathe.

diuretic A substance that increases the flow of urine from the body.

doula A woman or man who is trained to assist and provide comfort to a woman during childbirth.

drupe A fleshy fruit with a thin skin and a central stone with a seed inside.

enzyme A protein that accelerates chemical reactions.

essential oil A natural oil typically obtained from distillation and having the characteristic fragrance of the plant or other source from which it is extracted. *Also known as* volatile oil.

estrogen A group of hormones necessary for female sexual development and reproductive functioning.

expectorant A substance that stimulates removal of mucus from the lungs.

fiber A dietary material containing substances such as cellulose, lignan, and pectin, which are resistant to the action of digestive enzymes.

flavonoid A group of chemical compounds occurring in all vascular plants; they are found in many fruits, vegetables, teas, wines, nuts, seeds, and roots.

free radical A chemical that is highly reactive and can oxidize other molecules. When produced within cells, free radicals can react with membranes and genetic material to damage or destroy cells and tissues.

genus A level of classification in the plant kingdom below family; the first word of the two-name Latin binomial, which is always capitalized.

herbaceous A type of plant with little or no woody tissue, usually living a single season.

high-density lipoprotein (HDL) A lipoprotein that contains a small amount of cholesterol and carries cholesterol away from body cells and tissues to the liver for excretion from the body. Lower levels of HDL increase the risk of heart disease. The HDL component normally contains 20 to 30 percent of total cholesterol.

hormone A regulatory substance produced in an organism and transported in tissue fluids such as blood or sap to stimulate certain cells or tissues into action.

inflammation The immune system's response to tissue injury or harmful stimulation caused by physical or chemical substances. Release of inflammatory chemicals and increased blood flow to affected areas result in swelling, redness, and pain.

inflorescence Group or cluster forming the complete flowering head of a plant.

infused oil The result of an herb or plant part being soaked or macerated in oil and heated. The infused oil is then strained out.

infusion Tea made by steeping an herb in hot water.

insulin A hormone needed to convert sugar, starches, and other food into glucose (blood sugar); excessively high blood glucose levels can lead to diabetes.

inulin A complex sugar—a polysaccharide based on fructose—found in the roots of various plants; as a dietary fiber it can improve heart and gut health.

keratin A sulfur-containing fibrous protein that forms the main structural constituent of horny epidermal tissues such as hair, nails, hoofs, claws, horns, etc.

legume Any member of the Leguminosae that bears nodules on its roots that contain nitrogen-fixing bacteria. Includes peas, beans, and clovers.

low-density lipoprotein (LDL) The major cholesterol carrier in the blood. LDL transports cholesterol from the liver and intestines to various tissues. High levels of LDL are linked to coronary artery disease.

mucilage A gelatinous substance produced by some plants that is often used in herbal medicine as a soothing agent.

naturalization The process that occurs when a non-native plant escapes into the wild and survives.

naturopathy/ic A system of therapy that avoids drugs and surgery and emphasizes the use of natural remedies.

osteoporosis A medical condition in which the bones become brittle and fragile due to loss of tissue as a result of hormonal changes, or a deficiency of calcium or vitamin D.

pectin A polysaccharide extracted from the cell walls of plants, used in making jellies and jams.

pepo Any watery, fleshy fruit of the melon or cucumber type with numerous seeds and a firm rind.

pharmacopoeia A book containing an official list of medicinal drugs together with articles on their preparation, usually produced by legislative authority; or a stock or collection of medicinal drugs.

phenolic A large group of chemicals derived from phenol that contribute to the color, taste, flavor, and medicinal actions of many plants. In wine grapes, phenolics are found widely in the skin, stems, and seeds. *Also called* polyphenol.

phytochemical A chemical found naturally in plants that has metabolically active qualities.

phytoestrogen An estrogen-like compound occurring naturally in legumes and other plants; it can both mimic the effects of estrogen or act as an estrogen antagonist.

phytomedical Pertaining to medicine based on active ingredients within an herbal base, sometimes used to describe all plant-based medicines.

phytonutrient A substance found in many plants that is believed to be beneficial to human health and to help prevent certain diseases.

polyphenol *See* phenolic.

poultice A preparation of fresh, moistened, or crushed dried herbs, applied externally.

rhizome A somewhat elongated, usually horizontal, subterranean plant stem, often thickened by deposits of reserve food material, that produces shoots above and roots below; distinguished from a true root in having buds, nodes, and usually scalelike leaves.

saponin Any of several glycosides in plants that make a soapy lather if mixed with water.

sepal One of the separate, green parts that surround and protect the flower bud and extend from the base of a flower after it has opened.

stamen The pollen-bearing organ of a plant, consisting of the filament and the anther.

stigma The receptive tip of a carpel or several fused carpels in the female reproductive parts of a flower.

stolon Stems that grow at the soil surface level or just belowground that form adventitious roots at the nodes, and new plants from the buds; often called runners.

tannin A group of simple and complex phenol, polyphenol, and flavonoid compounds bound with starches. Aside from their astringent, mouth-puckering properties, these chemicals can help stanch bleeding from small wounds, slow uterine bleeding, reduce inflammation and swelling, dry out weepy mucous membranes, and relieve diarrhea.

teratogen An agent or factor that causes malformation of an embryo.

tincture A plant medicine prepared by soaking an herb in water and ethanol (never isopropyl alcohol); traditional herbal preparations are dispensed as alcohol-based liquid medicines.

tisane An herbal tea.

umbel An inflorescence that consists of a number of short flowers stalks, called pedicels, that spread from a common point; their appearance is similar to umbrella ribs.

volatile oil *See* essential oil.

ABOUT THE AUTHORS

Author NANCY J. HAJESKI writes adult and young adult nonfiction under her own name. Recent titles include *National Geographic Complete Guide to Herbs and Spices*, *National Geographic Birds, Bees, and Butterflies*, *Life-Size Birds*, *Ali: The Official Portrait of the Greatest of All Time*, and *The Beatles: Here, There and Everywhere*. Writing as Nancy Butler, she has produced 12 Signet Regencies, two of which won the RITA award from the Romance Writers of America. She has adapted the work of Jane Austen into graphic novels for Marvel Entertainment. Her *Pride and Prejudice* remained on the *New York Times* bestseller list for 13 weeks. Hajeski grows her own herbs and takes advantage of the free-range eggs and heirloom and organic produce at her local farmers' markets in the Catskill Mountains.

The author would like to thank National Geographic editor Susan Straight for all her helpful input and support during the production process and her team for their attention to detail. Many thanks to designer Lisa Purcell at Moseley Road and photographer Jonathan Conklin and his wife, Virginia, for contributing the photo on page 78 of their adorable daughter, Dylan.

TIERAONA LOW DOG, M.D., has long been an advocate for health care that is compassionate, effective, equitable, and environmentally conscious. She is the founding director of Medicine Lodge Ranch, a natural medicine school in Pecos, New Mexico. A leading expert in integrative medicine, particularly in the area of women's health, she is the author of many textbook chapters, peer-reviewed scientific articles, and books, including National Geographic's *Life Is Your Best Medicine*, *Healthy at Home*, and *Fortify Your Life*.

PHOTO CREDITS

Abbreviations
L = left; R = right; T = top; B = bottom
SS = Shutterstock

Front cover
StockFood/The Picture Pantry

Back cover
(T) Dionisvera/SS; (L to R) Marcin Jucha/SS;
PeopleImages/Getty Images; Yulia Furman/SS;
Hitdelight/SS

All border art by Lisla/Shutterstock.com; 2–3
Alexander Raths/SS; 4 Elena Schweitzer/SS; 5B marilyn
barbone/SS; 5T Valentyn Volkov/SS; 7 Lunov Mykola/
SS; 8 Phovoir/SS; 9 Polych/SS; 10 focal point/SS

PART I: NATURE'S CURES
12–13 Sunny Forest/SS

Chapter 1: Remedies for Common Physical Ailments
14 Stock-Asso/SS; 16 Snowbelle/SS; 17 Foxxy63/SS;
18 Yulia Furman/SS; 19 13Smile/SS; 20 Oxik/SS;
21 Em Arts/SS; 22 marekuliasz/SS; 23 LianeM/SS;
24 akepong srichaichana/SS; 25 D. Pimborough/SS;
26 kurhan/SS; 27 Lev Kropotov/SS; 28 natalia
bulatova/SS; 29 ZIGROUP-CREATIONS/SS; 30 Job
Narinnate/SS; 31 Ildi Papp/SS; 32 Ju1978/SS; 33
SMarina/SS; 34 Fortyforks/SS; 35L Tim UR/SS; 35R
Gayvoronskaya_Yana/SS; 36 LAURA_VN/SS; 37
Leighton Collins/SS; 38 George Rudy/SS; 39 F_
studio/SS; 40 alisafarov/SS; 41 kostrez/SS; 42
bbernard/SS; 43 mama_mia/SS; 44 Dennis W
Donohue/SS; 46 Africa Studio/SS; 47 Africa Studio/
SS; 48 Africa Studio/SS; 49 kazmulka/SS; 50 Vladimir
Mijailovic/SS; 51 JoyStudio/SS; 52 kazmulka/SS; 53
AlinaMD/SS; 54 Egyptian Studio/SS; 55 wasanajai/SS

Chapter 2: Soothe Emotional Stress
56 Zdenka Darula/SS; 58 LiliGraphie/SS; 59 JP
WALLET/SS; 60 Watchares Hansawek/SS; 61 Scisetti

Alfio/SS; 62 Elena Rostunova/SS; 63 beta7/SS; 64
JurateBuiviene/SS; 65 almaje/SS; 66 YuliaKotina/SS; 67
rawpixel.com/SS; 68 chrisdorney/SS; 69 kamui29/SS

Chapter 3: Pregnancy and Infant Health
70 YanLev/SS; 72 SUPIDA KHEMAWAN/SS; 73
Monkey Business Images/SS; 74 Juta/SS; 75 Iren_
Geo/SS; 76 Anneka/SS; 77 Pavel Ilyukhin/SS; 78
Jonathan Conklin Photography (courtesy of Virginia
and Jonathan Conklin); 79 Oksana Mizina/SS; 80
Alesya Selifanova/SS; 81 PHENPHAYOM/SS

Chapter 4: Aging and Wellness
82 Air Images/SS; 84 bonchan/SS; 85 Monkey Business
Images/SS; 86 Anna Kurzaeva/SS; 87 ThamKC/SS; 88
Luisa Puccini/SS; 89 Narong Jongsirikul/SS; 90 SaMBa/
SS; 91 Elena Veselova/SS; 92 Monkey Business Images/
SS; 93 kostrez/SS; 94 Nishihama/SS; 95 mama_mia/SS

PART II: NATURE'S PHARMACOPOEIA
96–97 Sebastian Duda/SS

Chapter 5: Medicinal Herbs
098 bernatets photo's/SS; 100 Dionisvera/SS; 101
JurateBuiviene/SS; 102 akepong srichaichana/SS;
103 Nikolay Litov/SS; 104 Mamsizz/SS; 105 Jiang
Zhongyan/SS; 106 Le Do/SS; 107 tab62/SS; 108
mama_mia/SS; 109 Oksana Mizina/SS; 110
Emilio100/SS; 111 Gulsina/SS; 112 ileana_bt/SS; 113
Oliver Hoffmann/SS; 114 spline_x/SS; 115 iva/SS;
116 dzmitry_2015/SS; 117 kanusommer/SS; 118
Unkas Photo/SS; 119 Scisetti Alfio/SS; 120
Crepesoles/SS; 121 Thanthima Lim/SS; 122 Jiang
Zhongyan/SS; 123 Dionisvera/SS; 124
Stevenrussellsmithphotos | Dreamstime; 125 ppl/SS;
126 Noppharat616/SS; 127 Maxal Tamor/SS; 128
Africa Studio/SS; 129 Ledo/SS; 130 Lunov Mykola/
SS; 131 Melinda Fawver/SS; 132 Elena Schweitzer/
SS; 133 Ostancov Vladislav/SS; 134 spline_x/SS; 135
Brzostowska/SS; 136 Margrit Kropp/SS; 137
wasanajai/SS; 138 Bjoern Wylezich/SS; 139

romantitov/SS; 140 Dani Vincek/SS; 141 Volosina/SS; 142 jopelka/SS; 143 Bozhena Melnyk/SS; 144 HandmadePictures/SS; 145 Balazs Kovacs Images/SS; 146 Maciej Olszewski/SS; 147 Belladonna / Deadly Nightshade *(Atropa belladonna)* by Otto Wilhelm Thomé, from *Flora von Deutschland, Österreich und der Schweiz*, 1885; 148 Emilio100/SS; 149 Elena Schweitzer/SS; 150 HandmadePictures/SS; 151 diy13/SS; 152 spline_x/SS; 153 Alonso Aguilar/SS; 154 unpict/SS; 155 ShutterOK/SS; 156 Nadalina/SS; 157 Bildagentur Zoonar GmbH/SS; 158 Andreja Donko/SS; 159 Nika Art/SS

Chapter 6: Beneficial Spices
160 Lukasz Janyst/SS; 162 Dimitar Sotirov/SS; 163 Nila Newsom/SS; 164 COLOA Studio/SS; 165 jeehyun/SS; 166 Blan-k/SS; 167 amphaiwan/SS; 168 Cindy Creighton/SS; 169 Rafa Irusta/SS; 170 AS Food studio/SS; 171 Elena Schweitzer/SS; 172 ThomsonD/SS; 173 Elena Schweitzer/SS; 174 Suratwadee Karkkainen/SS; 175 Africa Studio/SS; 176 Santhosh Varghese/SS; 177 marco mayer/SS; 178 Nattika/SS; 179 tarapong srichaiyos/SS; 180 Nailia Schwarz/SS; 181 Happy Zoe/SS; 182 Subbotina Anna/SS; 183 Kalcutta/SS

Chapter 7: Essential Oils
184 ddsign/SS; 186 Hortimages/SS; 187 wasanajai/SS; 188 Passakorn Umpornmaha/SS; 189T akepong srichaichana/SS; 189B Olyina/SS; 190 Botamochy/SS; 191 ANCH/SS; 192 Africa Studio/SS; 193 Volosina/SS; 194 Phil Date/SS; 195 Hitdelight/SS

Chapter 8: Nature's Power Pantry
196 JurateBuiviene/SS; 198 Elena Schweitzer/SS; 199 Jack Frog/SS; 200 Monkey Business Images/SS; 201 Africa Studio/SS; 202 A. L. Spangler/SS; 203 Sorbis/SS; 204 Hong Vo/SS; 205T Enlightened Media/SS; 205B bonchan/SS; 206 MaraZe/SS; 207 marcin jucha/SS; 208 Madlen/SS; 209 Andrew Hagen/SS; 210 topseller/SS; 211L Anna_Pustynnikova/SS; 211R JIANG HONGYAN/SS; 212 Sea Wave/SS; 213L MariaKovaleva/SS; 213R Anna Kucherova/SS; 214 Brent Hofacker/SS; 215T bergamont/SS; 216B Marian Weyo/SS; 216 SMarina/SS; 217 Valentina Razumova/SS; 218 denizya/SS; 219 mama_mia/SS; 220 margouillat photo/SS; 221 Alicia Christoffel/SS; 222 rj lerich/SS; 223L Brent Hofacker/SS; 223R AS Food studio/SS; 224 Elena Schweitzer/SS; 225 Foxys Forest Manufacture/SS; 226 Madlen/SS; 227T Anamaria Mejia/SS; 227B Anastasia Izofatova/SS; 228 vitals/SS; 229 JeniFoto/SS; 230 frank60/SS; 231T Katarzyna Hurova/SS; 231B Maks Narodenko/SS; 232L Cegli/SS; 232R Boonchuay1970/SS; 233 sarsmis/SS; 234 Miroslav Hlavko/SS; 235 Andrii Gorulko/SS; 236L zoryanchik/SS; 236T warat42/SS; 237 PI/SS; 238 Virginia Garcia/SS; 239 Elena Veselova/SS; 240 Valentyn Volkov/SS; 241 Gaus Nataliya/SS; 242 JeniFoto/SS; 243 Yulia Furman/SS; 244 Karissaa/SS; 245 JoannaTkaczuk/SS; 246 Syda Productions/SS; 247 5PH/SS; 248 Yulia von Eisenstein/SS; 249T Karissaa/SS; 249B geniuscook_com/SS; 250 Binh Thanh Bui/SS; 251 kuvona/SS; 252 Caron Badkin/SS; 253 South12th Photography/SS; 254 DarZel/SS; 255T JazzBoo/SS; 255B Binh Thanh Bui/SS; 256 Studio Barcelona/SS; 257 Sarah Marchant/SS; 258 zi3000/SS; 259 Madlen/SS; 260 zarzamora/SS; 261 id-art/SS; 262 ElenaGaak/SS; 263 julie deshaies/SS; 264 picturepartners/SS; 265 Nadezhda Nesterova/SS; 266 Robyn Mackenzie/SS; 267 puttography/SS; 268 Vladislav Noseek/SS; 269 Oksana_S/SS; 270 stevemart/SS; 271 Lepneva Irina/SS; 272 Nataliya Arzamasova/SS; 273 pada smith/SS; 274 Abramova Elena/SS; 275 Nataliya Arzamasova/SS; 276 Artem Samokhvalov/SS; 277 SMarina/SS; 278 DronG/SS; 279L ILEISH ANNA/SS; 279R Brent Hofacker/SS; 280 Alena Haurylik/SS; 281 Christian Jung/SS; 282 nevodka/SS; 283 Alexander Prokopenko/SS; 284 Max Lashcheuski/SS; 285 zoryanchik/SS; 286 DUSAN ZIDAR/SS; 287L Daniel Prudek/SS; 287R picturepartners/SS; 288 matteo sani/SS; 289 Bukhta Yurii/SS

Chapter 9: Nature's Home Helpers
290 JPC-PROD/SS; 292 Katia Vasileva/SS; 293 JPC-PROD/SS; 294 Brooke Becker/SS; 295 stefanolunardi/SS; 296 Andrii Gorulko/SS; 297 Lisa S./SS; 298 Irina Fischer/SS; 299 Ezume Images/SS

More Info
300–301 romantito/SS; 303 Valentina Razumova

INDEX

Boldface indicates main entry
with illustration.

Since 1888, the National Geographic Society has funded more than 13,000 research, exploration, and preservation projects around the world. National Geographic Partners distributes a portion of the funds it receives from your purchase to National Geographic Society to support programs including the conservation of animals and their habitats.

National Geographic Partners
1145 17th Street NW
Washington, DC 20036-4688 USA

Become a member of National Geographic
and activate your benefits today at natgeo.com/jointoday.

For information about special discounts for bulk purchases, please contact
National Geographic Books Special Sales: specialsales@natgeo.com

For rights or permissions inquiries, please contact
National Geographic Books Subsidiary Rights: bookrights@natgeo.com

ISBN: 978-1-4262-1892-7

Printed in China

18/RRDS/1

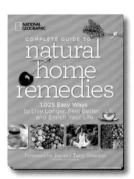
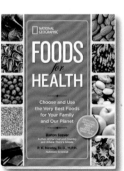